Praise for Marc J. Rosenstein's *Turning Points in Jewish History*

"The history of the Jewish people is remarkable but very difficult to teach. Here, impressively, Marc Rosenstein conveys the drama and complexity of Jewish history in a single accessible volume. Masterfully balancing the concerns of Jewish religious tradition with the insights of modern historical scholarship, *Turning Points in Jewish History* is an excellent tool for advanced study for adult and teen synagogue education as well as university courses."—RABBI ERIC H. YOFFIE, president emeritus of the Union for Reform Judaism

"Fantastic book! An extraordinarily accessible one-volume story of the Jewish people."—RON WOLFSON, Fingerhut Professor of Education at American Jewish University and author of *Relational Judaism: Using the Power of Relationships to Transform the Jewish Community*

"Rosenstein presents thirty pivotal moments in Jewish history with verve, insight, and pedagogical genius. This book evidences balance, deep knowledge, and a capacious view of the Jewish experience. The primary texts, time lines, and bibliographies are consistently well chosen; the side commentaries reliably guide the reader; and the texts for further discussion hit the sweet spot between canonical and provocative." —ALAN LEVENSON, Schusterman/Josey Chair of Jewish History at the University of Oklahoma and author of *Joseph: Portraits through the Ages*

"Master educator Marc Rosenstein makes each historical era just right for every reader. Interested in history? Here are well-crafted timelines and guides for deeper study. Interested in literature? Here are exciting original texts. Interested in philosophy? Here are significant Jewish ideas that have enriched Western civilization. Whether for a beginner or a teacher, I have never seen a better introduction to Jewish civilization, from 'In the beginning' until today."—NOAM ZION, senior fellow at the Shalom Hartman Institute, Jerusalem

"Marc Rosenstein's excellent book occupies a rare space in contemporary explorations of the Jewish past. It straddles history—the study of the past—and *toldot,* a Hebrew term referring to the unfolding of the generations. *Turning Points in Jewish History* empowers its readers to go beyond the false dichotomy of the academic and the empathetic. It helps link history with *toldot,* a reconstruction of what has been, a reflection on what is, and an inspiration toward what is yet to be."
—MICHAEL MARMUR, Jack, Joseph and Morton Mandel Provost of the Hebrew Union College–Jewish Institute of Religion

Turning Points in Jewish History

The Jewish Publication Society expresses its gratitude for the generosity of the following sponsor of this book:

Reynold F. Paris — In loving memory of my wife, Bette.

University of Nebraska Press

Lincoln

Turning Points in Jewish History

MARC J. ROSENSTEIN

The Jewish Publication Society
Philadelphia

∞

Library of Congress Cataloging-in-Publication Data
Names: Rosenstein, Marc, 1946– author.
Title: Turning points in Jewish history / Marc J. Rosenstein.
Description: Lincoln: University of Nebraska Press, [2018] |
"Published by the University of Nebraska Press as a Jewish
Publication Society book." | Includes bibliographical
references and index.
Identifiers: LCCN 2017052155
ISBN 9780827612631 (pbk.: alk. paper)
ISBN 9780827613836 (pdf)
Subjects: LCSH: Jews—History. | BISAC: history / Jewish.
Classification: LCC DS117 .r675 2018 | DDC 909/.04924—dc23
LC record available at https://lccn.loc.gov/2017052155

Set in MeropeBasic by Mikala R Kolander.

Dedicated to the memory of my parents,
Harry Rosenstein and Sylvia Jonisch Rosenstein
צבי הירש בן משה הלוי חלאטה, וסימה בת וולף ורבקה

Contents

Maps

Acknowledgments

It is my pleasure to thank a number of people who generously provided invaluable help in writing this book.

Rabbi Gregory Kotler and my colleagues at the Hebrew Union College–Jewish Institute of Religion (HUC-JIR)—Dr. Joel Duman, Dr. Joshua Holo, Rabbi Dr. Jan Katzew, Rabbi Naamah Kelman, Rabbi Dr. Michael Marmur, Dr. David Mendelsson, and Professors Dalia Marx and David Levine—all thoughtfully critiqued various chapters, in a number of cases saving me from embarrassing errors.

Batya Kaplan and the HUC-JIR library staff in Jerusalem were consistently, even enthusiastically, helpful in finding the texts I needed, when I needed them.

Rabbi Barry Schwartz of The Jewish Publication Society guided me through the process of conceptualizing and planning the book and then provided incisive criticisms of the manuscript.

I had always prided myself on being a man of few words, but then Joy Weinberg, my wise editor at JPS, cut me down to size, demanding concrete support for my airy generalizations and mercilessly slashing through nests of prepositional phrases to produce a coherent and readable whole.

Erin Greb, the cartographer, converted my crude sketches into clear and aesthetic maps.

I am grateful to the publishers who granted me permission to include text excerpts; they are acknowledged where these texts appear throughout the book. Special thanks are due to Erez Biton and Professor Avraham Shapira for personally permitting me to use excerpts from their works (in chapters 27 and 28 respectively).

The staff at University of Nebraska Press was helpful and gracious in responding constructively to the special challenges of formatting the book.

The opportunity to work with and learn from all of these people and the support and encouragement of my wife, Tami, combined to make this project both intellectually satisfying and great fun.

Introduction

Every person is an expression of a genome that has accumulated over millions of years. Each event along the way—each mutation, each pairing—has made its contribution to the particular set of characteristics of a given individual. This accumulation of genetic "experience," together with environmental factors and the choices made by the individual, determine a person's identity.

My own understanding of Judaism has always encompassed a similar sense of cumulative history. Each Jew represents an expression of the accumulated experience of the Jewish collective over the centuries. Each epiphany, each migration, each persecution, each innovation in the interpretation of the tradition becomes a link in the ongoing chain that defines any Jew at any moment in history.

In writing this book, I hope to share my own awe and enthusiasm with others, with as much transparency, objectivity, critical understanding, and sympathy as I can muster. I envision *Turning Points in Jewish History* as a tool for individual or group study of the sweep of the history of the Jewish people from its biblical beginnings until the early twenty-first century. I hope it will provide a window on the complex interaction of national identity, religious faith, individual choice, and environmental factors that have driven that history forward.

Of course, every event is a turning point of some kind, a factor in the algorithm that determines our identity. Trying to make sense of the virtually infinite set of turning points in any given history thus becomes an overwhelming challenge. Here, it seems to me that a comparison to biological evolution can be helpful. In trying to understand the infinite variation and complexity of life on earth, biologists look back at the evolutionary process and identify major innovations that led to changes in direction (e.g., photosynthesis, sexual reproduction, locomotion, extinction of the dinosaurs, upright posture, speech). In one sense, these "turning points" are artifacts, not actual events; they are products of our analysis and imagination that help us to make sense of what we observe. As such, of course, they are tentative, and periodically new evidence or new analyses cause scientists to change their understanding of the turns in the evolutionary path. Nevertheless, the process of identifying turning points and studying their impact allows us to organize a huge amount of information into a structure that makes sense to us.

Similarly, we can look back across Jewish history and identify certain formative transitions, when environmental factors, events, decisions, and discoveries combined to generate turning points whose impact was felt by all subsequent generations. Making a firm, objective identification of *the* turning points in Jewish history is a tricky business, and any attempt to do so is open to criticism and debate. On the other hand, the process itself has been, for me, fascinating and enlightening and indeed offers a way to make sense out of the rich, confusing accumulation of texts reflecting the experience of Jews through the centuries and around the world.

I have built this book around a selection of thirty turning points. In each case I have focused on a specific event, personality, or work that, while it may have been part of a longer-term, more complex process of change, expresses, even if only symbolically, a particular major transition. I hope that this attempt to distill Jewish history into a set of key transitions will help the reader, as it helped the author, get a clear view of "the big picture" and find thought-provoking connections between Jewish history and our current experience.

Why thirty? Why not ten—or three hundred for that matter? For one thing, I wanted the book to be of a reasonable length and touch on a variety of themes and episodes without being either too superficial or too encyclopedic. From this level of scope, I chose transitions that most Jewish historians would likely see as "major." For another, thirty lessons fits an academic year.

Our purpose is to understand how the Jews experienced, understood, and processed the events of history and how these events have influenced Jewish life, belief, thought, and practice. Therefore, the texts I have included are, for the most part, not the documents of historical archives—legal decrees, third-party descriptions, and so on—but rather Jewish responses to events: how Jewish thinkers and leaders—and sometimes ordinary participants—have recorded their understanding of important experiences.

No document can tell us more than what the author of the document thought—what he thought had happened, what he thought ought to happen or would happen, or perhaps only what he wanted others to think he thought, or even only what he himself thought he thought. None of this means anything until the historian has got [sic] to work on it and deciphered it. The facts, whether found in documents or not, have still to be processed by the historian before he can make any use of them: the use he makes of them is . . . the processing process.

—Edward Hallett Carr, *What Is History?* (New York: Vintage, 1967), p. 16

In some cases, the discussion focuses on the religious aspect of Judaism; in others, the emphasis is more on national elements. My underlying assumptions are as follows.

First, the Jewish people is both an ethno-cultural group (i.e., a nation) and a religion. While at different times in Jewish history one or the other dimension may have seemed to dominate, the overall history of the Jews is a complex interplay between these two dimensions of identity.

Second, while we often lack the data or the understanding to make clear-cut empirically based statements regarding cause and effect in history, events can be explained rationally, at least in principle. The causes and effects may be material or intellectual or spiritual, but they are potentially subject to rational analysis. It may well be that the overall arc of Jewish history reflects the workings of divine providence, but I do not believe it is fruitful to try to explain specific events by looking for evidence of local divine intervention. At the same time, it is important to acknowledge that throughout the ages, Jews often understood their historical experience as just such evidence. Understanding this understanding and its impact is one of the main themes of this book.

Each chapter is devoted to one turning point, and each follows a standard format that includes the following:

- A survey of the historical background
- A brief timeline to locate the moment chronologically and provide some context
- A primary text that offers insight into how the Jews understood their experience, with commentary

- An analysis of why this was indeed an important turning point and a survey of how the memory of the events has been preserved ("Legacy")
- A short "trigger text" chosen to stimulate discussion about the significance of the turning point
- A brief bibliography for further study

Suggested discussion questions for each chapter may be found by clicking on the Resources tab at https://jps.org/books/turning-points-in-jewish -history/.

While the book seeks to present a coherent story from Abraham to the present, and chapters refer to events that preceded them, each chapter can stand alone as a description and analysis of a particular transition. Thus, while the book is meant be read "straight through," I hope it will also be useful to those interested in learning solely about certain periods or events.

If you are using the book as the basis for a course, I suggest assigning the historical background and timeline for reading before the lesson. Then the lesson can be devoted to reading and unpacking the primary text—and to discussing the impact of the turning point. Both the trigger text and the online discussion questions can help enrich this discussion.

ON SACRED AND SECULAR TEXTS

The Bible is a religious book, describing God's interactions with the world in general and the Jewish nation in particular. Traditionally, the Bible is understood to be the word of God and thus timeless and true.

This book, on the other hand, is a secular history that considers religious belief as a central aspect of Jewish history that had great impact on events and on the Jews' understanding of those events. Therefore, the Bible will be viewed critically as a historical source, but with reverence as a religious text. I adopt the same approach with respect to other sacred texts, such as the Talmud.

The tension between viewing the Bible as the word of God and relating to it as a document written and compiled by humans is strongly evident when we try to use it as a historical source. Often, it is very difficult to reconcile the plain meaning of the text with the evidence of archaeology and of other texts; indeed, in many cases the "plain meaning" of the textual description is not even clear. The challenge of mapping biblical events onto "scientific" chronology has given rise to an extensive literature— polemic, religious, scientific, and apologetic. Addressing this challenge is beyond the scope of this book; thus, especially in the earlier biblical chapters, I have refrained from trying to give precise dates of biblical events.

If we see the Bible as the product of human authorship and/or editing, then it also follows that the writers/editors had a point of view, which naturally colored their descriptions of events. Indeed, sometimes it seems that editors may have been consciously attempting to build a text that gave voice to different and even opposing points of view. Trying to tease out these different strands can actually enhance our sense of the historicity of the Bible narrative, by explaining what otherwise might appear to be inconsistencies and internal contradictions.

> It is not that the biblical figures are unhistorical. I believe that we are standing at the beginning of a new era in biblical studies; whereas the past era did its utmost to prove that the Bible did not contain history, the coming era will succeed in demonstrating its historicity. By this I do not mean that the Bible depicts men and women and events as they are in actual history; rather do I mean that its descriptions and narratives are the organic, necessary, legitimate ways of giving an account of what existed and what happened. I have nothing against these narratives being called myths and sagas, so long as it is remembered that myths and sagas are essentially memories, actual memories, which are conveyed from person to person.
>
> —Martin Buber, *Mamre: Essays in Religion* (Melbourne: Melbourne University Press, 1946), p. 44

In the course of writing this book, I discovered that the challenge of navigating between myth and history is not limited to the biblical period. Even the most recent events can be viewed through different ideological and religious lenses, leading to very different perceptions of "historical truth." Thus, the study of history is actually not the study of "what happened," but the study of *our understanding* of what happened and its meaning to us.

I have tried to keep this subjectivity of our objectivity in mind in narrating the events surrounding the various turning points. It is beyond my knowledge—and often beyond anyone's knowledge—to be able to "nail down" all the "facts." Nonetheless, it is incumbent on all of us to examine carefully the stories that have been told about those facts, in order to glean the wisdom to help us know who we are and what we ought to do.

Additional Notes on Biblical Texts

The Hebrew Bible comprises thirty-nine books. The first five, covering the period from the Creation to the death of Moses, are referred to as the Torah, the Pentateuch, or the Five Books of Moses. The section called Prophets includes historical books covering the Jewish people's entry into the Promised Land under Joshua to the destruction of the First Temple, as well as books of poetic prophecies. The third section, Writings, comprises miscellaneous books including Psalms, Proverbs, the five scrolls, Job and Daniel, and historical accounts describing the return of Babylonian exiles under Persian rule.

In biblical texts, *Adonai* is translated as "Lord." The God of whom the Bible speaks had a name, based on the Hebrew consonants YHVH, but out of reverence, the tradition is not to call God by that familiar name; hence the English usage "Lord."

The Bible refers to the area roughly circumscribed by the Mediterranean, the mountains of Lebanon, the Jordan Valley, and the Red Sea as Canaan. Later, under the Romans, parts of this area were called Palestine, named for the Philistines who lived along the coast. In postbiblical Jewish literature, the name is *Eretz Yisra'el*, the Land of Israel. Since 1948, part of the region has been included in the State of Israel. These terms thus all overlap, and the boundaries of all of them are uncertain, vague, and/or controversial.

All biblical quotations are taken from The Jewish Publication Society translation. Unless otherwise noted, other Hebrew texts have been translated by the author.

Turning Points in Jewish History

1. Imagining the Beginning

THE CALL TO ABRAHAM, ~1500 BCE?

HISTORY

Myth and History

We begin, of course, with the beginning. But when, exactly, did it all begin?

Just as we ask of science at what point the primeval sun-cooked soup of organic compounds somehow configured itself to give rise to something we would later identify as "life," we ask of Judaism, can we identify a concrete event that marked the very first appearance of the Jewish religion and/or the Jewish nation on the stage of history?

And, similarly to the riddle of the origin of life, that moment is so far removed from our present experience, the best we can hope for is a tentative, somewhat speculative reconstruction.

Even defining what we are looking for as we seek to locate this moment is a challenge. The origin of the terms "Jewish" and "Judaism" is relatively late, based on the Kingdom of Judah (see chapter 6); indeed, even "Israel" refers to the name given to Jacob after his encounter with an angel (Genesis 32). The Patriarch Abraham is described as a "Hebrew" (Genesis 14:13), but given this term's usage in other contexts, it seems to refer not to a particular ethnic group, but to a social status (outsider, migrant). Moreover, one could argue that the birth of the *nation* was the Exodus from Egypt—or the entry into the land—and that the birth of the *religion* was the Revelation at Mount Sinai.

However, from the Torah onward through all the later layers of interpretation (in Christianity and Islam as well), we encounter a consistent claim that there is indeed one identifiable moment of origin of both the nation and the religion, the moment described in Genesis 12:1-2: "The Lord said to Abram, 'Go forth from your native land and from your father's house to the land that I will show you. I will make of you a great nation, and I will bless you.'"

The problem is, this claim is not really based on historical evidence. All we know is what is written in the Torah, and even that is characteristically telegraphic. The passage combines divine revelation ("The Lord said") with a personal act ("Go forth"), and assigns political significance to the act ("the land that I will show you . . . a great nation"). Who was Abram? How did the Lord speak to him? Why him? When and where did this happen? We do not have documentary or archaeological data that would enable us to answer any of the standard historical questions about this event.

Perhaps we need to admit that the story is not history, but myth—not in the sense of "not true," but rather in "expressing a truth that is not necessarily historical."

We do know that an underlying question is being addressed: How did it come to pass that one nation, early in its history, adopted a worldview that was substantively different from that of its environment and made this new view a core element of its identity, to be transmitted through the generations going forward? The answer, stated so laconically in the above verses, became central to the Jewish people's perception of its own history. And because the description is so spare, it gave rise to a great deal of creative interpretation throughout the generations.

Therefore, we can consider the call of Abraham[1] the initial turning point of Jewish history.

The Historical Context

In the second millennium BCE, from the Mediterranean coast eastward through Syria and down the Tigris and Euphrates valleys, there existed many independent city-states, organized in shifting alliances. Tribes from the northeast (the Caucasus and Persia) periodically invaded the area. At times, empires based in different Mesopotamian cities managed to consolidate their rule over large parts of the region. The city of Ur, mentioned as Abram's birthplace (Genesis 11:31), was the center of one Mesopotamian empire for part of this period. It is associated with Tel el Muqayyar in southeastern Iraq, where the remains of a large city have been excavated, off and on, for 150 years.

The strip of land between the Jordan and the Mediterranean (Canaan, the Land of Israel, Palestine) marked the westernmost edge of the Mes-

---

1. The Patriarch first enters the biblical narrative in Genesis 11:26 as "Abram." Later, in Genesis 17:5, God renames him "Abraham," explaining that this new name can be translated as "father of a multitude." The Bible and all later writers use "Abraham" from this point onward.

opotamian sphere of influence—coming up against the persistent eastward drive of Egypt.

A major ongoing and constantly developing controversy in modern biblical scholarship is how the Bible text relates to the archaeological findings from ancient Mesopotamia: Do these findings argue for—or against—the possibility that the Patriarchs and Matriarchs were actual historical figures whose adventures as recorded in the Bible correspond with the cultural reality of a specific time and place? This discussion is both complex and unresolved, but certainly some names and customs mentioned in Genesis have parallels in Mesopotamian sources from the second millennium BCE. For example, many such parallels appear in texts from Mari, a city in northern Syria, where thousands of documents from the early second millennium—up to the city's destruction in 1760 BCE—have been discovered.

The Religious Milieu

A great deal of art and literature from these ancient civilizations has been found and studied, so we know something of their worldview, social structures, and religious beliefs. Two distinctive features of ancient Mesopotamian religion are important to mention here.

First, a multiplicity of gods and spirits representing the features and forces of nature, engaged in an ongoing drama. Events in the natural and human world—storms and drought, famine and plenty, victory and defeat—reflect the playing out of this drama. The gods could be represented by physical images and propitiated by sacrifices.

Second, a cyclical, ahistorical understanding of time. No significance was ascribed to unique (non-recurring) historical events outside the cycles of day, month, year, and lifetime. People lived within the cycles of nature, which reflected recurrent events in the divine drama. For example, the seasonal dying and rebirth of vegetation was believed to be a manifestation of the annual dying and rebirth of the god Tammuz.

The "birth" of the Israelite religion represents the questioning of both these understandings. By the time the story had been written down in the Torah, it was clearly understood to imply that there is only one, supreme, unrepresentable god in the world and that this God's will and power could be seen in unique historical events affecting the lives of the Patriarchs and Matriarchs and their descendants.

Yet, the telegraphic nature of the account of Abraham's "call" in Genesis 12 ("Go forth from your native land and from your father's house to the land that I will show you. I will make of you a great nation, and I will bless you") leaves us without a clear understanding of just how this birth occurred. Was it the aha moment of the particular individual, Abraham? Was it an evolution across several generations? Was the call for the people to settle in a new land the product of a political power struggle, one group needing to differentiate itself from the establishment?

We cannot really reject these and other interpretations as infeasible, nor can we prove them. What we can say is that around the end of the second millennium BCE, a new worldview emerged out of the milieu of Mesopotamian pagan religion, a worldview based on the belief in a single, universal, omnipotent god and on the understanding that history is a record of this god's interactions with the world. The story of Abraham's call is an attempt to portray this innovation in a concrete, realistic way.

Timeline: 2350–~1200 BCE

Note: Dates are approximate. "Dominance" refers to cultural/political influence in the area of Canaan.

2350–2000	Dominance of the Akkadian Empire, based in Mesopotamia
2000–1900	Gutian invasion from Persia, political instability
2000	Beginnings of Mayan civilization in Mesoamerica
1900–1800	Dominance of the Ur dynasty, based in Mesopotamia; migration of Hurrians from Mitanni, northern Mesopotamia
1860	Beginning of Stonehenge construction
1800–1750	Dominance of Babylon: King Hammurabi
1800–1200	Range of dates that have been suggested for when Abraham might have lived
1720–1550	Dominance of the Hyksos (based in Nile Delta)
1700	First large-scale political organization in China: the Shang dynasty
1550–1295	Dominance of the Egyptian Eighteenth Dynasty
~1200	Transition from Bronze Age to Iron Age, with the spread of iron-working technology

PRIMARY TEXT

The first eleven chapters of Genesis describe the creation and history of the natural universe and human society, including the Flood story and the Tower of Babel. A genealogy of the generations from Noah brings us down to the birth of Abraham, whose immediate family is described in more detail than the previous generations, though we don't yet know why. At this point, the Torah makes the transition from the primeval history of the universe to zoom in on the particular history of the nation that would be called Israel.

Genesis 11:31–12:8

³¹Terah took his son Abram, his grandson Lot the son of Haran, and his daughter-in-law Sarai, the wife of his son Abram, and they set out together from Ur of the Chaldeans for the land of Canaan; but when they had come as far as Haran, they settled there. ³²The days of Terah came to 205 years; and Terah died in Haran.

Haran is on the way from Mesopotamia to Canaan, in present-day Syria. Note that Abram is actually just completing a journey begun by his father, the reason for which we are not told.

¹The Lord said to Abram, "Go forth from your native land and from your father's house to the land that I will show you.

²I will make of you a great nation,
And I will bless you;
I will make your name great,
And you shall be a blessing.
³I will bless those who bless you
And curse him that curses you;
And all the families of the earth
Shall bless themselves by you."

This god who speaks to Abram was known to him by name and worshiped by him through sacrifice at altars erected in different locations. Note that the Lord is simply the god that Abram worships and obeys; there is no implication that other gods don't exist. The commitment to monotheism imputed to Abram is

⁴Abram went forth as the Lord had commanded him, and Lot went with him. Abram was seventy-five years old when he left Haran. ⁵Abram took his wife Sarai and his brother's son Lot, and all the wealth that they had amassed, and the persons that they had acquired in Haran; and they set out for the land of Canaan. When they arrived in the land of Canaan, ⁶Abram passed through the land as far as the site of Shechem, at the terebinth of Moreh. The Canaanites were then in the land.

⁷The Lord appeared to Abram and said, "I will assign this land to your offspring." And he built an altar there to the Lord who had appeared to him. ⁸From there he moved on to the hill country east of Bethel and pitched his tent, with Bethel on the west and Ai on the east; and he built there an altar to the Lord and invoked the Lord by name.

part of the interpretive tradition; it is not stated in the text.

Note that specific geographical boundaries are not stated here.

The Bible continues its narrative of the Patriarchs and Matriarchs in the land of Canaan, with several sojourns back in Haran and in Egypt.

In the absence of other sources, readers of this text through the generations have used their own experience as an interpretive lens to try to understand "what really happened" when "the Lord said to Abram. . . ."

Within the Bible, Joshua's farewell speech to the people states what was apparently already the "official" historical understanding of Abram's role—and clarifies that his migration was seen as a rejection of the pagan gods of his homeland:

²Thus said the Lord, the God of Israel: In olden times, your forefathers—Terah, father of Abraham and father of Nahor—lived beyond the Euphrates and worshiped other gods. ³But I took your father Abraham from beyond the Euphrates and led him through the whole land of Canaan and multiplied his offspring. . . . ¹⁴Now therefore, revere the Lord and serve Him with undivided loyalty; put away the gods that your forefathers served beyond the Euphrates.

—Joshua 24:2–3,14

Later, the book of Jubilees, in the Apocrypha (about 200 BCE), takes a more micro view, imagining Abram's personal intellectual and spiritual experience as he observed the world and then, one night, suddenly saw it all differently and rebelled against the prevailing paradigm:

Abram was sitting on the night of Rosh Hashanah, studying the stars all night to learn the forecast for rain for the new year, sitting alone and observing. [Note: astrology was an important element of Mesopotamian religions.] And a word came into his heart, saying, "All the signs of the stars and the signs of the sun and the moon are in the hand of the Lord, so why am I studying them?" . . . And he prayed that night, saying, "God most high, You alone are God for me, You have created everything . . . and You have I chosen."

—Jubilees 12:16–18

Here God's call is an inner voice, a sudden insight that the established religion just doesn't make sense. The implication is that Abram has "discovered" monotheism: not just a particular god, but the only God. This story recurs in various versions in many later sources (including the Qur'an, 6:74 ff.); it was apparently convincing. Note too that Abram's prayer does not state that God has chosen him, but that he has chosen God! It seems that the call is a very human, personal experience. It is not a compulsion; this is Abram's decision.

One of the best-known (and loved) explications of the call is this account, found in various sources:

Terah was an idol-maker. Once he went out and left Abram to mind the store. A woman came in with a bowl of flour and told him to offer it to the idols. He took an ax and smashed all the idols except the largest one and put the ax in its hands. When his father came home and asked, "Who did this?" Abram answered, "I cannot tell a lie: a woman came in with a bowl of flour and told me to offer it to them. When I did, they began to argue, each claiming the right to eat first. Then the largest of them took up the ax and smashed them all." His father said, "Why are you mocking me? We know that they can't do this!" Abraham answered, "Let your ears hear what your mouth is saying!"

—*Bereshit Rabbah* 38:13

This midrash is a crude mockery of pagan faith. The pagans saw idols as representations of their gods but did not believe these representations had physical power—that they could swing an ax or eat a sacrifice. The midrash thus distorts pagan belief in order to ridicule it.

At the same time, it does attempt to answer what it meant for God to order Abram to leave his father's house. Perhaps Abram felt compelled to leave because he found the established religion spiritually or intellectually lacking.

Was the crucial moment when "the Lord said to Abram" a divine revelation, a human discovery, or somehow both? Because the biblical text is so brief and sparing of detail, over the past three millennia we have had plenty of opportunity to exercise our imaginations, fill in the gaps, flesh out the story. Perhaps most fascinating about this ongoing effort is the recurrent theme of seeking to understand one of the most significant developments in human history in terms of ordinary, everyday human experience.

LEGACY

Impact

It is frustrating that our first turning point, the big bang, the moment when Jewish history began, remains only vaguely knowable, outside the purview of the discipline of history. All we have to go on is one brief text whose authorship and date are subjects of controversy. Indeed, it may well be that the discovery of monotheism attributed to Abraham happened later and that he just happened to choose to worship the particular god that later became the subject of monotheistic belief.

Maybe this "turning point" was not a point in history at all. Perhaps the new worldview that rejected polytheism and saw evidence of God's presence and power in the accumulating experience of history as well as the cycles of nature was in fact a process lasting generations or centuries. By the same token, perhaps the "great nation" was actually an alliance of clans or tribes that adopted the Abraham story—and the monotheistic religion—as a unifying origin narrative and identifier. This evolutionary view is convincing to many.

However, whether we see the transition as an evolution or an epiphany, we are left with the same conclusion: sometime during the millennium between about 1700 and 700 BCE a new ethno-cultural entity—a new nation—came onto the stage of history, in the Land of Israel, bearing a revolutionary worldview.

Perhaps it is appropriate that the first turning point we are studying calls into question the very concept of "turning point." Often history is too complicated, and our knowledge too incomplete, to allow us to identify and assign a date to moments of significant transition. And yet there was a time when there was no Jewish nation and there were no believers in monotheism; and later there was a Jewish people, and monotheism began to compete in the marketplace of beliefs. If there was a "before" and an "after," then somehow there had to have been a moment or a generation or a century of transition. The story of that transition has been so powerful in Jewish thought and Western culture that its factual "truth" has become largely irrelevant. (We will encounter this same phenomenon in the next several chapters, as we examine turning points during the formative biblical period.)

We can say this: throughout its subsequent history, the Jewish people has been characterized by four distinctive features, all seen as having originated in the story of Abraham's call:

- They are a distinct nation, united with each other and differentiated from others by both kinship and belief.
- As a nation, they have a unique relationship with the god who is the God of all. They are committed to obeying God and to passing that commitment down to future generations.

- Time is historical, not cyclical. Abraham's experiences were unique and not recurring. His lessons had to be passed down to subsequent generations, who were to remember them, take them into account as they made their own decisions, and retell them to their own progeny.
- The people's connection to the Land of Israel is both part of their origin story and based on a divine commandment.

Memory

Abraham experienced a number of further encounters with God after the call described above. The accounts of these have all become central texts in Jewish thought—for example, the Jewish practice of circumcision (*brit milah*—the covenant of circumcision), attributed to God's command to Abraham in Genesis 17; Abraham's "bargaining" with God over the destruction of Sodom and Gomorrah (Genesis 18:16–23); and Abraham's binding of his son Isaac as an intended sacrifice (Genesis 22). Indeed, the account of Isaac's binding (*Akedat Yitzhak*) became part of the traditional daily liturgy as well as the Torah reading for Rosh Hashanah. This troubling story of absolute faith took on, like Abraham's "call" described above, mythical significance, giving concrete expression to the relationship between Abraham's descendants and God. Later, when Jews faced severe persecutions and even martyrdom in the Middle Ages (see chapter 14), this story resonated for them as they identified with Isaac, bound on the altar for sacrifice.

Both Christianity and Islam also view Abraham as the founder of monotheism—and thus as their own founder/progenitor. Judaism, Christianity, and Islam are therefore often referred to as the "Abrahamic religions." Abraham's key role in Christian and Muslim thought can be seen in these examples:

- Paul's epistles, in the New Testament, often refer to the belief that those who accept the Christian faith become spiritual descendants of Abraham; for example, Galatians 3:6–7: "⁶Thus Abraham 'put his trust in the Lord; He reckoned it to his merit' (Genesis 15:6). ⁷So you see that it is men of faith who are the sons of Abraham."
- Islam understands that the Arab nation is descended from Abraham through Ishmael (Genesis 16 and 21), so events from Abraham's life

story described in the Bible appear in the Qur'an as well (for example, the command to sacrifice a son, in Sura 37).

TEXT FOR DISCUSSION

Novelist Thomas Mann puts it acutely: Did God call Abraham or did Abraham call God—and what is the difference?

What had set him in motion was unrest of the spirit, a need of God, . . . irradiations of his personal experiences of God, which was a new kind altogether.

. . . In a way Abraham was God's father. He had perceived Him and thought Him into being. The mighty properties which he ascribed to Him were probably God's original possession. Abraham was not their creator. But was he not so after all, in a certain sense, when he recognized them, preached them, and by thinking made them real?

—Thomas Mann, *Joseph and His Brothers* (New York: Penguin, 1978), pp. 6, 285

FURTHER READING

Bloom, Harold, and David Rosenberg. *The Book of J.* New York: Grove Weidenfeld, 1990, pp. 193–99. Abram's call and its interpretation from a literary perspective.

Genesis 11:26–25:18. Abraham's life story.

Kugel, James. *How to Read the Bible.* New York: Free Press, 2007, pp. 89–106. A concise survey and synthesis of scholarship on the history of understanding Abraham's call and its historical context.

Millard, Alan R., and Donald J. Wiseman, eds. *Essays on the Patriarchal Narratives.* Winona Lake IN: Eisenbrauns, 1983. Essays summarizing, in depth, research on the Patriarchal narratives in Genesis in relation to our knowledge from archaeology and the study of ancient Near Eastern texts.

Pritchard, James B. *The Ancient Near East: An Anthology of Texts and Pictures.* Princeton: Princeton University Press, 2010. The classic collection of texts from the ancient Near East, originally published in 1950.

Speiser, Ephraim A. *Genesis.* The Anchor Bible. Garden City NY: Doubleday, 1964, pp. xliii–lii, 85–88. The Genesis narrative and Abram's call, examined in the context of ancient Mesopotamian culture.

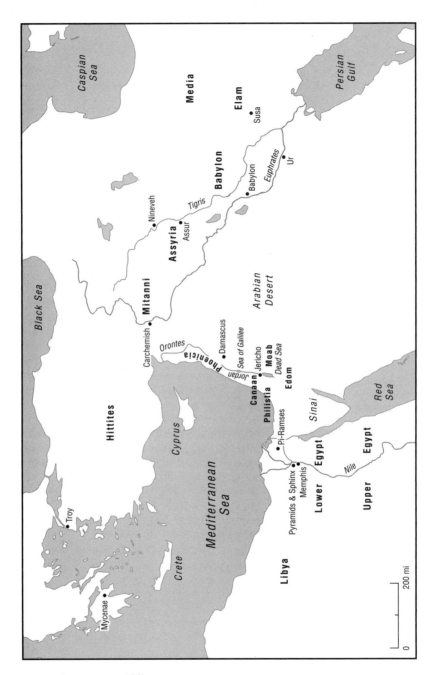

Map 1. The ancient Middle East, ca. 1200 BCE

2. Liberation from Slavery

THE EXODUS FROM EGYPT, ~1200 BCE?

HISTORY

Myth and History

After Abram hears God's call, the biblical narrative continues to focus on his further interactions with God, with his wife Sarai (later renamed Sarah), and with the inhabitants of Canaan (as well as those of Egypt, during his sojourn there on account of a drought in Canaan). The Bible then relays the adventures of Abram's descendants for the next three generations: Isaac (and Rebekah) and Ishmael, Jacob (and Leah and Rachel) and Esau, and Jacob's children. The book of Genesis ends with another drought-driven migration to Egypt, this time by Jacob and his whole clan.

The doubts and questions concerning the historical truth of Abram's call are equally relevant to the rest of Genesis. The various narratives shed light on the belief system of the Jewish nation, the relationships among its tribes, and the people's relationships with its neighbors, all the while resonating with the cultural and legal realia of the ancient Near Eastern environment. However, no textual or archaeological documentation proves the objective truth of these episodes or even the existence of the characters.

Thus, we can say with certainty that the story is true only in the mythical sense (as discussed in chapter 1). As such, it provides the basis for the history that came later.

While Genesis ends as a family saga, Exodus begins as an account of the vicissitudes of a nation operating on the stage of history. While uncertainties and controversies surround "what really happened" in both narratives, in Exodus the events are of a completely different order of magnitude. Therefore, the discourse changes. Whereas no archaeologist is digging for Jacob's pillow or Joseph's coat as described in Genesis, hundreds of books have been written addressing the actual historicity of specific events described in Exodus, seeking to determine everything from which Pharaoh was involved and where the Israelites labored as slaves to how the ten plagues might have occurred and what geological or meteorological phenomenon might explain the splitting of the sea.

With the move from a family saga that even feels mythical to concrete, large-scale events, the uncertainty regarding what "real" events stand behind the biblical narrative is even more unsettling. However, as with Abraham's call, we can say with surety that throughout Jewish history, the Exodus from Egypt has been understood as a key turning point, power-fully influencing all that came after.

The Biblical Narrative

According to Genesis, Abraham's great-grandson Joseph, on account of a family dispute, ends up a slave in Egypt and, by dint of his talents (and divine providence), rises to a high position in the government. He then exploits his status to help his family in a time of famine, bringing them from Canaan to live in Egypt. As generations pass, they prosper and multi-ply. A new Pharaoh perceives the Israelites as a threat and seeks to weaken them by forced labor and even infanticide. These events had been fore-told in a prophecy to Abraham (Genesis 15:13–14) and thus are seen by the Bible as a demonstration of divine providence in history.

Even from a secular perspective, however, the events described (perhaps excluding the miracles) are not implausible: During a sojourn in Egypt the Israelites grew from a small clan to a large nation, they were enslaved there, and with their liberation they made a sudden entrance onto the stage of history, "a nation like all the nations."

When exactly was the crucial moment in the transition? It is possible to argue for a number of points along the narrative: Moses's birth; Moses's choosing to take action for a suffering Israelite; Moses's call by God in the desert; the tenth plague and hasty exit; the parting of the sea . . . However there is a finality in the instant when the sea has closed over the Egyptian pursuers and the Israelites find themselves free and unthreatened, out of Egypt with no possibility of return, facing an unknown future. What a climactic moment!

Scholarly debate on the historicity of the Exodus continues to be lively. Strong opinions range from acceptance of the biblical account largely at face value to denial that any of the events described actually happened. The arguments are largely based on differing interpretations of archaeological findings (which themselves are often ambiguous) and on differing views of the authenticity of the Bible text. Here are some of the major points of discussion in this debate:

- Evidence of Semitic minorities in Egypt, both as prisoners of war and as immigrants in times of drought in the east
- Evidence of the use of foreign workers in Egypt, in particular in the building of the city of Rameses (see Exodus 1:11)
- The appearance of authentic Egyptian names in the biblical narrative (e.g., Moses, Pharaoh)
- Correlations between the Joseph and Moses stories in the Bible and episodes and customs known from Egyptian inscriptions
- The unlikelihood that a nation would invent an origin story that depicts themselves as slaves
- But on the other hand: failure to find evidence of destruction/conquest in the archaeology of the relevant period in Canaan
- Egyptian control of Canaan through the period generally associated with the beginnings of the Israelite nation
- Some evidence suggesting that the Exodus story may represent the experience of just one tribe, the Levites, who succeeded in imposing it as a uniting national narrative
- Controversy regarding the age and origin of the biblical text and whether it can be viewed as a historical document

Hovering over the debate are issues of politics and religion, for, as in many areas of the world, "proof" of the authenticity of a particular historical narrative can be used as ammunition in modern religious and national disputes (e.g., who was here first). We are left, as in the previous chapter, with a plausible event that to date we can neither prove nor disprove: a stirring saga of oppression and liberation, the "birth of a nation."

Regardless, the Exodus is so central to the Jewish religion and to Jewish national consciousness that we cannot discuss Jewish history without it.

Timeline: ~1600–1069 BCE

~1600–1100	Mycenaean civilization in Greece
1550–1295	Eighteenth Dynasty in Egypt

~1500	Rise of Phoenician civilization along the Lebanon/Canaan coast
~1300	Rise of Assyrian Empire in Mesopotamia
1295–1186	Nineteenth Dynasty in Egypt
~1250–1200	Period generally suggested for the Exodus
1209	The first mention of "Israel" in an extra-biblical text—in an inscription in the funerary temple of Pharaoh Merneptah, in Thebes, celebrating an Egyptian victory over rebellions by Israel and other nations
1186–1069	Twentieth Dynasty in Egypt

Summary of Bible Narrative

Order of major events between Abram's call by God and the events of the current chapter.

Genesis 12	Abram's call
Genesis 16	Birth of Ishmael
Genesis 21	Birth of Isaac
Genesis 24	Isaac's marriage to Rebekah
Genesis 25	Birth of Jacob and Esau
Genesis 28–30	Jacob's marriages and offspring—the twelve tribes
Genesis 37–47	Joseph in Egypt
Genesis 46–47	Migration of the whole clan to Egypt
Exodus 1	Enslavement and oppression
Exodus 2	Birth of Moses and his upbringing
Exodus 3–4	Moses's call by God
Exodus 5–10	Moses's negotiations with Pharaoh; the first nine plagues
Exodus 11–13	The tenth plague, the first Passover, the departure
Exodus 14–15	The crossing of the sea and destruction of the Egyptian army

The question of how to map the biblical sequence of events onto the historical chronology of the region is mired in controversy. However, the date of approximately 1200 BCE is generally associated with the appearance of an Israelite nation in Canaan.

Primary Text

From Moses's first approach to Pharaoh, demanding that the Israelites be allowed to leave Egypt, the confrontation escalates. God continues to support Moses's demands with increasingly devastating plagues. Pharaoh wavers—but then still holds firm. Even after the most horrific plague, the slaying of all first-born Egyptians, Pharaoh releases the Israelites but then reneges and sets off in pursuit of the fleeing slaves. In the dramatic ending, the sea splits, the Israelites are rescued, and Pharaoh and his army are vanquished.

Exodus 14:8–14,21–30

---

[8]As the Israelites were departing defiantly, [9]the Egyptians gave chase to them, and all the chariot horses of Pharaoh, his horsemen, and his warriors overtook them encamped by the sea, near Pi-hahiroth, before Baal-zephon.

[10]As Pharaoh drew near, the Israelites caught sight of the Egyptians advancing upon them. Greatly frightened, the Israelites cried out to the Lord. [11]And they said to Moses, "Was it for want of graves in Egypt that you brought us to die in the wilderness? What have you done to us, taking us out of Egypt? [12]Is this not the very thing we told you in Egypt, saying, 'Let us be, and we will serve the Egyptians, for it is better for us to serve the Egyptians than to die in the wilderness'?" [13]But Moses said to the peo-

The theme of the Israelites' misgivings about leaving Egypt recurs a number of times before and after this point. It seems a realistic depiction of a universal human experience.

ple, "Have no fear! Stand by, and witness the deliverance which the Lord will work for you today; for the Egyptians whom you see today you will never see again. ¹⁴The Lord will battle for you; you hold your peace!" . . .

²¹Then Moses held out his arm over the sea and the Lord drove back the sea with a strong east wind all that night, and turned the sea into dry ground. The waters were split, ²²and the Israelites went into the sea on dry ground, the waters forming a wall for them on their right and on their left. ²³The Egyptians came in pursuit after them into the sea, all of Pharaoh's horses, chariots, and horsemen. ²⁴At the morning watch, the Lord looked down upon the Egyptian army from a pillar of fire and cloud, and threw the Egyptian army into panic. ²⁵He locked the wheels of their chariots so that they moved forward with difficulty. And the Egyptians said, "Let us flee from the Israelites, for the Lord is fighting for them against Egypt."

²⁶Then the Lord said to Moses, "Hold out your arm over the sea, that the waters may come back upon the Egyptians and upon their chariots and upon their horsemen."

The Hebrew for the sea in question is *Yam-Suf*, "Sea of Reeds." It has been suggested that the route out of Egypt began in the wetlands of the Nile Delta, where getting through—or sinking—might be a function of knowing where to step or of transitory meteorological or hydrological phenomena.

Suddenly, for the first time, the Israelites are participants in a large-scale geopolitical event: not a local skirmish between tribes, or the nomadic migration of a clan, but a drama involving a mass migration and the defeat of the army of a major world power.

²⁷Moses held out his arm over
the sea, and at daybreak the sea
returned to its normal state, and
the Egyptians fled at its approach.
But the Lord hurled the Egyptians
into the sea. ²⁸The waters turned
back and covered the chariots and
the horsemen—Pharaoh's entire
army that followed them into the
sea; not one of them remained.
²⁹But the Israelites had marched
through the sea on dry ground, the
waters forming a wall for them on
their right and on their left.

³⁰Thus the Lord delivered Israel that day from the Egyptians. Israel saw the Egyptians dead on the shore of the sea. ³¹And when Israel saw the wondrous power which the Lord had wielded against the Egyptians, the people feared the Lord; they had faith in the Lord and His servant Moses.

God—and the Israelites—step onto the stage of world history together in this event. And the text indicates that the Israelites now understand God and God's role in their history differently. Their doubts and complaints are hushed . . . for a short time.

The next chapter of Exodus is the Song at the Sea, a hymn praising God for having miraculously rescued the Israelites. It imagines the impression these events made on other nations in the area:

¹⁴The peoples hear, they tremble;
Agony grips the dwellers of Philistia.
¹⁵Now are the clans of Edom dismayed;
The tribes of Moab—trembling grips them;
All the dwellers in Canaan are aghast.
¹⁶Terror and dread descent upon them;

Through the might of Your arm they are still as stone —
Till Your people cross over, O Lord,
Till Your people cross whom You have ransomed.

—Exodus 15:14–16

Perhaps the miracle at the sea was so significant not only because it impressed the Israelites, but also because it was seen as proof of God's universal, absolute power over all of history. This theme recurs later, for example in the run-up to Joshua's conquest of Jericho, when Rahab, the prostitute who is helping the Israelite spies, says:

9I know that the Lord has given the country to you, because dread of you has fallen upon us, and all the inhabitants of the land are quaking before you. 10For we have heard how the Lord dried up the waters of the Sea of Reeds for you when you left Egypt, and what you did to Sihon and Og, the two Amorite kings across the Jordan, whom you doomed. 11When we heard about it, we lost heart, and no man had any more spirit left because of you; for the Lord your God is the only God in heaven above and on earth below.

—Joshua 2:9–11

In effect, Abraham discovered the idea of one, invisible God and began a personal, spiritual journey of a growing relationship across generations. Then the experience of Abraham's descendants at the Sea of Reeds revealed that this God had the power and the will to move heaven and earth — and sea — for the sake of that relationship. At the sea, God "went public," demonstrating that strength for Israel and all the nations of the earth to see.

Moreover, the event depicts the people as being totally dependent on God. After all the uncertainty, the flip-flops of Pharaoh, the frustration with Moses's seemingly ineffective interventions — at the shore of the sea the people are *in extremis*: nowhere to turn, nothing to do but "stand by and witness the deliverance" (Exodus 14:13). And once the sea closes over the Egyptians and the people find themselves in the Sinai desert, this total dependence becomes a fact of everyday life. (As we will see in chapter 3, dependence also becomes a key element in the covenant that is to shape Jewish life throughout all future generations.)

LEGACY

Impact

With the symbolism of crossing the sea arose a biblical image of birth/ redemption that has been forever central to Jewish theology, liturgy, and national identity. In the midst of raging waters, a passage miraculously opens for the Israelites. Once they pass through it, the channel disappears behind them, cutting off—washing away—their connection to their past and leaving them in a new world of uncharted desert. Here we have the "birth of the nation."

Why is this transition so significant?

Suddenly, we are dealing with a great nation. Whether there were really several million (according to the Bible six hundred thousand men, plus women and children, left Egypt) or a much smaller number, that nation required laws and institutions for internal governance. And its interactions with other nations had to involve diplomacy and warfare.

The nation also had to transition from powerlessness (slavery) to power (self-rule). With that power came responsibility. By means of its behavior, the collective would determine its own national fate. This link between freedom and responsibility is the foundation upon which the covenant between God and the Israelite people, sealed at Mount Sinai, will stand (see chapter 3).

That said, the people's release from human domination did not grant them full emancipation. Rather, the Israelites exchanged one master, Pharaoh, for another, God. As God said to Pharaoh, "Let My people go that they may serve[2] Me in the wilderness" (Exodus 7:16). This concept of the kingship of God would become central in Jewish thought (we will encounter it again in chapter 5 in the debate over establishing an Israelite monarchy).

Note that in the previous chapter, Abraham was ordered to leave his home culture in Mesopotamia and migrate to Canaan; in the current chapter, the nation is ordered to leave Egypt and migrate to Canaan. The symmetry adds up to a rejection of the dominant cultures both to the east and west of Canaan.

Together these two turning points set the stage for defining a new nation that is rooted in both the east and the west but will sit perched between

---

2. JPS translation: "worship." The Hebrew root *'e-b-d* can be translated as "serve" or "worship."

them, developing its own unique worldview. And Canaan's location will play a significant geopolitical role throughout Jewish history—up to the present.

Memory

A central element of the traditional morning and evening Jewish liturgy is the recitation of the *Shema* (Hear!) proclamation, "Hear, O Israel! The Lord is our God, the Lord alone" (Deuteronomy 6:4). This statement and auxiliary verses are placed within a framework of three blessings that articulate the Jewish worldview:

1. Recognition of God as creator of the universe—the God of nature.
2. Recognition of God as the lawgiver for the Jewish people.
3. Recognition of God as the redeemer of the Jewish people for having rescued them at the Sea of Reeds (this blessing quotes the verse Exodus 15:11, *Mi khamokhah. . .*, "Who is like You, O Lord, among the mighty . . .").

When the Ten Commandments are recounted in Deuteronomy, the Sabbath is explicitly linked to the Exodus:

> [14]You shall not do any work—you, your son or your daughter, your male or female slave, your ox or your ass, or any of your cattle, or the stranger in your settlements, so that your male and female slave may rest as you do. [15]Remember that you were a slave in the land of Egypt and the Lord your God freed you from there with a mighty hand and an outstretched arm; therefore the Lord your God has commanded you to observe the Sabbath day.
> —Deuteronomy 5:14–15

The Exodus thus came to be seen as an archetype for the weekly liberation from labor as provided by the Sabbath. The memory of slavery became a kind of moral guidepost for later generations, as expressed in the recurring refrain (e.g., Exodus 22:20): "You shall not wrong a stranger or oppress him, for you were strangers in the land of Egypt."

The larger Exodus narrative (*yetziat Mitzrayim*), especially the preparations for the tenth plague and the hurried departure after it (Exodus 11–

13), is commemorated in one of the liturgical high points of the Jewish calendar, the holiday of Passover (Pesach).

In addition to its place in the core liturgy, remembrance of the rescue at the sea is mentioned repeatedly in the psalms (e.g., Psalms 78:13, 136:13–15), and the Song at the Sea (Exodus 15) is recited in the introductory section of the daily morning service. The Exodus story is by far the dominant historical reference within Jewish liturgy.

TEXT FOR DISCUSSION

The traditional Passover liturgy asserts that the Exodus was not just a one-time event, but eternally present.

What does it mean "to see oneself as though one had come forth from Egypt"?

> In every generation a person must see himself as though he had come forth from Egypt, as it is said (Exodus 13:8): "And you shall tell your son on that day, saying, 'This is because of what the Lord did for me in my Exodus from Egypt.'"
>
> —*Mishnah Pesachim* 10:5 (quoted in the Haggadah recited at the Passover seder meal)

FURTHER READING

Exodus, chapters 11–15. The drama of the Exodus fills these chapters.

Friedman, Richard. "The Exodus Is Not Fiction." *Reform Judaism* 42, no. 3 (Spring 2014), http://www.reformjudaism.org/exodus-not-fiction. An analysis suggesting that the Exodus was experienced by one tribe, the Levites, who later succeeded in imposing it as a unifying narrative for an assembly of tribes.

Ginzburg, Asher (Ahad Ha'am). "Moses." In *Selected Essays of Ahad Ha'am*, translated and edited by Leon Simon. Philadelphia: Jewish Publication Society, 1912. A classic discussion on the "historical truth" of Moses by a great Zionist thinker.

Halpern, Baruch. "The Exodus from Egypt, Myth or Reality?" In *The Rise of Ancient Israel*, by Hershel Shanks, William G. Dever, Baruch Halpern, and Peter K. McCarter Jr., pp. 86–117. Washington: Biblical Archaeological Society, 1992. A lecture summarizing the scholarly debate on the evidence for or against the historicity of the Exodus, especially in the archaeology of Canaan.

Hoffmeier, James. *Israel in Egypt*. New York: Oxford, 1997. A detailed review of scholarship on the question of the historicity of the Exodus tradition, leading to a positive conclusion.

Kugel, James. *How to Read the Bible*. New York: Free Press, 2007, pp. 198–232. A concise survey and synthesis of biblical and archaeological scholarship on the sojourn in Egypt and the Exodus.

Velikovsky, Immanuel. *Worlds in Collision*. Garden City: Doubleday, 1950. This attempt to posit a scientific basis for the miracles associated with the Exodus was overwhelmingly rejected by the scientific community, which did not stop it from being a massive best seller. It is one well-known example of the ongoing effort to "prove" the Exodus and the fascination this effort engenders.

3. The Covenant

HISTORY

Time and Place

Traditionally, the Exodus from Egypt and the Revelation at Mount Sinai are closely linked, and a case could be made for treating them together as one turning point. If the key innovation is the establishment of a covenant between the Israelite people and God, then the redemption and the Revelation are the two elements of this contract: God's "side" is taking the people out of Egyptian slavery; the people's "side" is obeying the laws proclaimed at Sinai. The time between the two events was just a few months (Exodus 19:1)—not very long in historical terms.

However, in real time, the participants did not know what was coming. The newly freed slaves, fearful for their future on their own in the desert, could not have anticipated that God would soon—and fundamentally—change the rules of the game and the nature of their identity.

For the Israelite nation, then, liberation was a significant turning point—and it would be superseded by a new stage (another turning point): at the foot of Mount Sinai, the laws came to the people. The institution of a formal, law-based covenant between God and the Israelite people determined the direction of all subsequent history.

Like the Exodus, the account of the Sinai encounter describes a mass event experienced by the entire Israelite people. Some commentators (among them the eleventh-century poet and philosopher Judah Halevi in *The Kuzari* 1:88–91) have argued that if a few million people were present and gave their descendants a consistent report on this principal event, it could not have been fabricated. However, *Raiders of the Lost Ark* notwithstanding, no archaeological evidence or any other documentation confirms the biblical description—and we are unlikely to find any.

Several mountains have been proposed as Mount Sinai. One unproven but popular pilgrimage/tourism site is Jebel Musa ("Mount Moses" in Arabic) in the southern Sinai Peninsula, where a Greek Orthodox monastery (St. Catherine) was built in the sixth century. Perhaps it is not an accident that this world-changing event is believed to have taken place in an uninhabited no-man's-land; unlike so many other holy places around the world, no wars have ever been fought over ownership of Mount Sinai.

The Revelation at Mount Sinai "fits" in the biblical chronology just after the Exodus, around 1200 BCE. However, text-critical and archaeological scholarship generally sees the body of biblical law as having developed (with the incorporation of several distinct strands) over a period as long as seven centuries, all the way to 600 or even 500 BCE.

Nonetheless, in Jewish collective memory this process is represented by a singular event following close behind the Exodus and constituting the second element of the covenant: the people's accepting the obligation to obey God's commandments, as the response to their miraculous redemption from slavery.

Covenant

Archaeologists have discovered numerous documents from the Middle East in the second millennium BCE describing covenants—contractual agreements confirmed by sacred rituals. These address tribal alliances, real estate, commercial transactions—and, most significant for us, the covenant between a ruler and a vassal, in which the ruler pledges his protection in return for the subordinate's obedience and support.

While similarities exist between the standard format of such treaties and the structure of Exodus 19 (and the ritual of Exodus 24), there is no scholarly consensus about this model's influence upon the ideology of covenant that became so central in Israelite belief.

It is clear that the concept had parallels, if not roots, in the region. But the Sinai covenant was exceptional: it was not a local contract between a human ruler and his allies or subjects, but between the god who was seen as king of the universe and one particular nation. (As we will see in chapter 5, this belief in God as king was to become problematic when the nation needed to organize itself into a kingdom with an earthly ruler.)

The Bible contains several other examples where the term "covenant" is used to describe a commitment between God and humans:

- With Noah: the rainbow as a sign of a commitment by God not to destroy the world again (Genesis 9:8–17).
- With Abraham: "the covenant of the pieces," a mysterious revelation in which God commits to a vision of the future for Abraham's progeny (Genesis 15).
- With Abraham: circumcision as a sign of Abraham's commitment to God, over the generations to come (Genesis 17:1–14).
- With Joshua: essentially a renewal or reaffirmation of the original national covenant at Sinai (Joshua 24).
- With David: a commitment by God to sustain David's dynasty as the rulers of Israel forever (Jeremiah 33:19–22; Psalm 89:20–37). (As we will see in chapters 7 and 11, a dissonance between this covenant and historical reality will have significant impact on Jewish life and thought far in the future.)

The Sinai covenant, however, had distinctive features: directness between God and the whole nation, clear reciprocity, an all-encompassing nature (its provisions touch on every aspect of the life of the nation), large-scale public visibility, and linkage to an earthshaking historical experience.

Timeline: Legal Codes, ~1900–~200 BCE

>1900	The Code of Eshnunna is composed: an early Babylonian code of criminal law and damages.
~1790	King Hammurabi of Babylonia promulgates a detailed legal code.
~1250–1200	God reveals the Torah at Mount Sinai (traditional date).
~622	The High Priest under King Josiah finds a "book of the law" in the Temple (2 Kings 22); many scholars date the assembly of the Torah's laws to this period.
~600	Draco composes the first Greek legal code, the Draconian constitution, in Athens.
~450	The Twelve Tables, the first codification of Roman law, is enacted.
~200	Qin dynasty governs China by means of a detailed legal code.

Biblical Chronology of the Exodus

Exodus 1	From the arrival of Jacob's clan in Egypt to enslavement and Pharaoh's attempt at infanticide.
Exodus 2	Birth, childhood, and youth of Moses.
Exodus 3–4	Moses's call by God.
Exodus 5–11	The first nine plagues.
Exodus 12–13	The tenth plague and the Passover, when God spares the first-born of the Israelites and the Israelites depart Egypt.
Exodus 14–15	The miracle at the sea.
Exodus 16–17	The first stages of life in the desert: issues of food, water, war.
Exodus 18	Moses's Midianite father-in-law Jethro helps him organize a system of governance.
Exodus 19–20	At Mount Sinai, God proclaims the Ten Commandments, amid smoke and thunder, at the beginning of the third month, Sivan (i.e., a month and a half after the Exodus).
Exodus 21–23	A compendium of laws, primarily moral, is transmitted from God through Moses.
Exodus 24	A ceremony affirms the covenant, after which Moses is commanded to ascend the mountain to receive God's laws in writing; he spends forty days and nights there.
Exodus 25–31	A compendium of laws, primarily regarding ritual, is transmitted from God to Moses during his sojourn on the mountain.
Exodus 32–34	Despairing of Moses's return, the people and Aaron make and worship the Golden Calf; Moses smashes the tablets in anger, and returns to the mountain for another forty days to receive the Law again.
Exodus 35 to Numbers 10	The people remain encamped at Sinai for almost a year, learning and applying the laws relating to the portable sanctuary and the priestly ritual.
Numbers 10	The nation sets out from Sinai toward the Promised Land in the second year after the Exodus, on the twentieth of the second month (Iyar).

Numbers 11   Just three days after the people set out from Sinai,
                    there is another crisis of food and faith; the location
                    gets the name Kibroth-hattaavah (graves of craving).
Numbers 12   The Israelites march to Hazeroth and then to the wil-
                    derness of Paran.
Numbers 13–14   Moses sends scouts to check out the land of Canaan;
                    after forty days they return, but their mixed report cre-
                    ates panic. God then decrees that instead of immediately
                    entering the land, the people must spend forty years in
                    the desert, so that the generation of the Exodus will die
                    off before the entrance into the Promised Land.

PRIMARY TEXT

It can be difficult to follow the Sinai event in the Bible, as the text inter-
sperses its different narrative stages with passages detailing the laws. It
seems that the Revelation had several phases:

1. The initial public revelation, in which God spoke directly to the people, proclaiming the Ten Commandments
2. The formal ritual in which the people affirmed the covenant
3. Moses's forty-day sojourn on the mountain, where he received the
   remainder of the Law to relay to the people
4. The Golden Calf episode, wherein Moses smashed the tablets of the
   Law and re-ascended the mountain to receive the Law again
5. The subsequent year of encampment at the base of Mount Sinai,
   during which Moses taught the people the Law he had received

---

Exodus 24:3–18

---

[3]Moses went and repeated to the people all the commands of the Lord and all the rules; and all the people answered with one voice, saying, "All the things that the Lord has commanded we will do!"

The context of this verse is unclear. Just which commands did Moses repeat and then write down? The Ten Commandments? The contents of chapters 21–23? How and when did he receive these commandments, if

⁴Moses then wrote down all the commands of the Lord.

Early in the morning, he set up an altar at the foot of the mountain, with twelve pillars for the twelve tribes of Israel. ⁵He designated some young men among the Israelites, and they offered burnt offerings and sacrificed bulls as offerings of well-being to the Lord. ⁶Moses took one part of the blood and put it in basins, and the other part of the blood he dashed against the altar. ⁷Then he took the record of the covenant and read it aloud to the people. And they said, "All that the Lord has spoken we will faithfully do!" ⁸Moses took the blood and dashed it on the people and said, "This is the blood of the covenant that the Lord now makes with you concerning all these commands."

⁹Then Moses and Aaron, Nadab and Abihu, and seventy elders of Israel ascended; ¹⁰and they saw the God of Israel: under His feet there was the likeness of a pavement of sapphire, like the very sky for purity. ¹¹Yet He did not raise His hand against the leaders of the Israelites; they beheld God, and they ate and drank.

he had not yet gone up the mountain to receive God's dictation?

One major modern school of interpretation (the documentary hypothesis) argues that the Torah is an edited compilation of several separate documents representing different traditions and that inconsistencies and puzzles like this are a function of the editing process. For our purposes, what is important is that at some point during the process of the Revelation of the Law, a formal covenant was enacted, involving a public affirmation of commitment by the people, "sealed" in blood.

Immediately after the impressive ceremony of affirmation by the people, God puts a "signature" to the covenant by several miraculous experiences:

a) Moses and Aaron and Aaron's two sons, and seventy elders are allowed to "see" God (!) and survive.

b) Moses and Joshua are summoned to ascend the mountain, which is cov-

¹²The Lord said to Moses, "Come up to Me on the mountain and wait there, and I will give you the stone tablets with the teachings and commandments which I have inscribed to instruct them." ¹³So Moses and his attendant Joshua arose, and Moses ascended the mountain of God. ¹⁴To the elders he had said, "Wait here for us until we return to you. You have Aaron and Hur with you; let anyone who has a legal matter approach them."

¹⁵When Moses had ascended the mountain, the cloud covered the mountain. ¹⁶The Presence of the Lord abode on Mount Sinai, and the cloud hid it for six days. On the seventh day He called to Moses from the midst of the cloud. ¹⁷Now the Presence of the Lord appeared in the sight of the Israelites as a consuming fire on the top of the mountain. ¹⁸Moses went inside the cloud and ascended the mountain; and Moses remained on the mountain forty days and forty nights.

ered by a cloud, and after six days Moses is invited to enter the cloud.

c) During Moses's stay on the mountain, the people below see a "consuming fire" on the mountaintop.

The great twentieth-century Jewish philosopher Martin Buber elucidated what made the Sinai covenant so incomparable:

Only in the Sinai covenant is a holy action performed which institutes sacramentally a reciprocity between the One above and the one below. . . .

> A people can . . . be partner of such an act only if it already has the power
> to act and to operate as a unity. . . . Only . . . [after the experience of the
> Exodus] . . . it is able . . . to become partner to an act of covenant which
> can be consummated between a God and a people—not purely reli-
> gious, but only a religio-political, a theo-political, act.
> —Martin Buber, *Kingship of God*, pp. 123, 125–26

In other words, the covenant at Sinai was unique not only in being "between
a God and a people," but also in entangling politics and religion: the nation's
relationship to God would influence or even determine collective behavior
in every sphere, from criminal justice (Exodus 21:12–18) to torts (21:28–36)
and social welfare (22:20–26); from foreign relations (34:10–16) to family
law (Leviticus 18); and ritual (Exodus 29).

The belief in the literal truth of the description of the Revelation at Sinai
has been a central pillar of Jewish belief and identity from the time the
Torah was written until the rise of modern skepticism. At the same time,
questions about what was actually spoken and what was heard, what was
revelation and what was interpretation, have been part of every generation's response to the biblical description.

What later became the mainstream ideology of Judaism posited that the
Revelation at Sinai included not only the entire Torah (the Pentateuch),
but the entire body of oral interpretation that developed afterward—
and continues to develop. The midrash *Shemot Rabbah* (about eleventh
century) states, "And not only did the prophets receive their prophecy
at Mount Sinai, but all the scholars who arise in every generation—each
one of them receives his knowledge from Mount Sinai" (28:4). The Mishnah (~200 CE), Tractate *Avot* (1:1), states, "Moses received the Torah on
Sinai, and handed it down to Joshua; Joshua to the elders; the elders to
the prophets, and the prophets handed it down to the Men of the Great
Assembly . . . [and on to succeeding generations of rabbis]."

While the idea that both the Pentateuch as a book and the corpus of
interpretation known as the Oral Torah were presented, complete, to Moses
at Sinai is open to question, these passages from the Mishnah and midrash
seem to suggest a process of "handing down," of constant teaching and
interpretation. If so, then the Sinai event represented the beginning of an

ongoing process, anchored in, guided by, and inspired by that moment, but developing across the generations in response to new realities.

This process has created two genres of traditional literature: *halakhah* (the way), the body of law, applicable in each generation, based on the explication and expansion of the Torah laws; and *aggadah* (the telling), the literature of explanation and speculation—stories, theories, and interpretations that seek to understand the moral and theological meanings of the laws and of the Torah text in general. Both *halakhah* and *aggadah* would first be anthologized in the Roman period (see chapter 12).

Over the centuries, the ongoing process of interpretation and application produced a whole library full of codes, anthologies, and commentaries that continues to grow to this day—constituting the mechanism by which every Jew in every generation may be said to be "standing at Sinai."

LEGACY
Impact

Before the Sinai experience, the Bible doesn't really describe the moral content of Israelite identity. There are a few references to moral values, such as Abraham's famous challenge to God prior to the destruction of Sodom and Gomorrah ("Shall not the Judge of all the earth deal justly?" [Genesis 18:25]); yet there are also examples of problematic behavior (e.g., Jacob's cheating Esau in Genesis 27; Simeon and Levi's violent revenge on the Shechemites in Genesis 34; the near-murder of Joseph by his brothers in Genesis 38). The Bible suggests that the Patriarchs and Matriarchs held some kind of personal faith in God, but it does not specify particular values and behaviors required by this belief, except for the practice of circumcision (Genesis 17).

From the biblical text, then, it seems that early Israelite identity was primarily clan identity. For example, note the emphasis on finding spouses within the extended family, first for Isaac (Genesis 24) and then for Jacob (Genesis 28–29). After the Exodus, a *national* identity was forged out of this formative historical experience. And then, the Revelation at Mount Sinai was the origin of what we now identify as the Jewish *religion*—a religion based on a body of law, of commanded behaviors, covering every aspect of life, from ritual, criminal, tort, and family law to societal and economic norms. For all succeeding generations, being an Israelite (or later, a Jew) meant living in a social, religious, and moral framework determined by divine commandment and living with the knowledge that the nation's political and economic fortunes were conditioned upon obeying those commandments.

Thus, several ideas rooted in the Sinai experience shaped subsequent Jewish history:

- The belief that the Jewish people's degree of obedience to the commandments directly affected the historical vicissitudes of the nation. For example, defeat in battle did not mean that God was weaker than the god of the enemy, but rather that the Israelites were deserving of punishment for their disobedience; God was using the enemy as a means of chastisement.
- The Jewish religion was based on norms of behavior, not on professions of belief. While theological discussions were important and the law would be dry and empty without the faith standing behind it, still the Torah, including all its subsequent interpretations, was mainly concerned with the moral actions of the people.

The process of studying and clarifying what exactly the covenant between Israel and God requires of the people has been *the* central pillar of Jewish thought and scholarship ever since Sinai. Because the covenant is seen as the foundation-stone of both religious and national existence, understanding its particular terms is a crucial — and ongoing — challenge. And because there has rarely been consensus on its interpretation, robust and sometimes strident debates have arisen among scholars, communities, and ideological streams throughout the ages.

Memory

The Bible (Leviticus 23:15–21) describes a harvest festival seven weeks after Passover called Shavuot (weeks); because of the timing, later tradition associated this day with the Sinai Revelation, and Shavuot came to be called "the holiday of the giving of the Torah" (Chag Matan Torah).

Exodus 25–27 describes an elaborate procedure for preserving the Sinai experience by means of a perpetual institutional reenactment. The Israelites are commanded to build a *Mishkan* (a portable sanctuary), with a special cabinet (the Ark of the Covenant) at its center, to hold the two tablets received at Mount Sinai—this structure constituting the point of contact wherein God would continue revelations to Moses (Exodus 25:22). This function of symbolic Sinai later passed from the *Mishkan* to the Temple in Jerusalem—and from there to the study house and the synagogue (with its Ark holding the Torah scrolls).

Until the Middle Ages, certain communities recited the Ten Commandments as part of the daily liturgy, but this practice was discontinued because it gave support to claims that all the other commandments were less significant. Meanwhile, while the second commandment tended to limit Jewish religious representational art, representations of ritual objects were commonly used to decorate synagogues. Among these, the motif of the two tablets of the covenant (*shenei luchot habrit*) was (and remains) very popular.

TEXT FOR DISCUSSION

Abraham Heschel, a leading twentieth-century Jewish thinker, addresses the question of what happened at Sinai. What do you believe he meant by "to have suddenly been endowed with the power of seeing the whole world struck with an overwhelming awe of God . . . a perpetual event"?

Indeed, there is no perception that may not be suspected of being a delusion. But there are perceptions which are so staggering as to render meaningless the raising of such a suspicion. A cosmic fear enveloped all those who stood at Sinai, a moment more staggering than the heart could feel. The earth reacted more violently than the human heart: "The people trembled . . . the mountain trembled greatly" (Exodus 19:17f). Was that perception an illusion? *What* we see may be an illusion; *that* we see can never be questioned. The thunder and lightning at Sinai may have been merely an impression; but to have suddenly been endowed with the power of seeing the whole world struck with an overwhelming awe of God was a new sort of perception. . . .

Thus the word of God entered the world of man; not an "ought to," an idea suspended between being and non-being, a shadow of the will, a concession of the mind, but a perpetual event, a demand of God more real than a mountain, more powerful than all thunders.

—Abraham Joshua Heschel, *God in Search of Man* (New York: Harper & Row, 1955), pp. 196–97

FURTHER READING

The biblical passages devoted to law are Exodus 20–23, the book of Leviticus, and Deuteronomy 12–26.

Buber, Martin. *Kingship of God*. Translated by Richard Schiemann. New York: Harper and Row, 1967, pp. 121–35. Buber's understanding of the uniqueness of the Sinai covenant, based on literary and cultural-historical scholarship. Very dense.

Davidson, Robert. "Covenant Ideology in Ancient Israel." In *The World of Ancient Israel*, edited by Ronald E. Clements. Cambridge: Cambridge University Press, 1995, pp. 323–47. A review of the scholarly literature on the various covenants appearing in the Bible (e.g., Noah, Abraham, Sinai, David) and the cultural context.

Kugel, James. *How to Read the Bible*. New York: Free Press, 2007, pp. 233–79. A concise survey and synthesis of biblical and archaeological scholarship on the concept of covenant and the legal content of it.

4. Entering the Promised Land

CROSSING THE JORDAN, ~1200 BCE?

HISTORY

Forty Years in the Desert

According to the biblical account, the two turning points of the Exodus from Egypt and the covenant at Sinai were to have been followed immediately by a third: the entry into the land of Canaan, where the people would conquer and expel or destroy the current inhabitants, settle the land according to God's plan, and establish institutions and a way of life implementing the Torah laws.

But this plan was derailed. As Numbers 13–14 describes, Moses sent scouts to check out the land prior to conquest, and their discouraging prognosis on the difficulty of that conquest stirred a rebellion. As a result, God decreed that the nation would not enter the land immediately, but spend one year in the desert for each of the forty days the scouts had spent on their mission. The generation of slaves was to die out—they would not enter the Promised Land. Nor would Moses.

While the biblical text makes it clear that the forty years' wandering was a punishment, later interpretation often found positive value in it. There is a logic to allowing for turnovers of leadership—leaders of revolutions are not necessarily the best builders of institutions.

Interestingly, the Bible offers little detail about life during the wandering. The text describes the *Mishkan* (portable sanctuary) and the priestly cult and cites specific episodes of rebellion, but it does not tell us how the people lived. Many of the laws are prefaced by the phrase "When you enter the land" (e.g., Leviticus 23:10, 25:2; Numbers 15:2), suggesting they were not applicable in the desert. Indeed, as we learn from one text (which follows), even the Passover sacrifice was suspended during the forty years. Thus, while the covenant at Sinai gave meaning to the Exodus, the process was still incomplete: the covenant could not be fully realized without the entry into the land and into history, with the requirement of joint action, social organization, and economic self-sustenance.

37

What Really Happened?

The book of Joshua's description of the conquest of Canaan seems straight-forward. Except for reporting the signing of a peace treaty with the Gibeon-ites (Joshua 9), chapters 6–12 record a concise chronology of victory after victory, summarized in 11:23: "Thus Joshua conquered the whole country, just as the Lord had promised Moses; and Joshua assigned it to Israel to share according to their tribal divisions. And the land had rest from war."

The book of Judges, however, suggests that the Joshua account might not have been complete. Chapter 1 contains a catalog of towns and regions that remained unconquered at the time of Joshua's death and descriptions of continuing local battles. And in recent decades, battles have continued — among archaeologists.

The archaeological debate takes place on both the micro and the macro levels. For a micro example, consider Jericho, Joshua's most famous con-quest. Jericho has been located and excavated. Massive destruction has been found there; however, research indicates it took place much earlier than would be consistent with its place in the biblical narrative — the city had already been a ruin for centuries before the presumed date of Josh-ua's conquest, around 1200 BCE.

On the macro level, inconsistencies in the dates of the destruction — and the later founding — of settlements have led some archaeologists to com-pletely discount the truth of the conquest. Thus, several theories compete:

a) Military conquest as per the Bible.
b) A gradual infiltration of a new population that ultimately united as Israel.
c) No migration at all, but an internal social and/or religious revolu-tion among the Canaanite inhabitants, through which they adopted a new political organization and religion. This hypothesis gains cre-dence from the finding that Canaan had been under Egyptian rule until around 1200 BCE. Liberation from Egypt, in other words, might have been a local event.
d) Some combination of these.

Determining what really happened in Canaan has major implications regarding the historicity of previous events. If Israel arose from among rebels in Canaan and not from outsiders, then the Exodus, Sinai, and the desert wandering might all be an origin myth created later, with no basis in actual events. Many people find this possibility distressing.

Perhaps some day new methods or discoveries will provide a clearer picture of the historical truth. Meanwhile, rather than be drawn into the attempt to set a clear boundary between myth and early history, we can focus on the "bottom line": at one point in time there was no nation of Israel—and then, at a later point, there was such a nation, living in the land of Canaan, with a collective memory of the following:

- Liberation from Egyptian slavery
- Commitment to a divinely revealed body of law
- Formative generation-long mass migration, followed by a divinely guided and assisted conquest of the Promised Land

And so, subsequent generations saw the transition to settled life in the land of Israel as a key turning point in the life of the nation, confirming the covenantal linkage among God, nation, and land.

The Period of the Judges

The book of Judges may be understood in at least two ways.

First, after Joshua's conquest, there ensued a period of something between anarchy and a loose confederation of tribes, with no centralized government. Various tribes, headed by charismatic leaders, formed temporary alliances, in response to specific threats. Occasionally, the tribes even went to war against each other. The author of Judges seems to have disapproved of this situation, as evidenced by the recurrent refrain (which also concludes the book) "In those days there was no king in Israel; everyone did as he pleased."

Second, in keeping with the rejection of the full-conquest-by-outsiders model, Judges tells the "real" story: seminomadic tribes from outside Canaan (perhaps even some who had previously been enslaved in Egypt!) infiltrated the area, battling and/or joining tribes already living there in various temporary alliances, and haltingly moving toward some kind of political union with a common religion and culture (see chapter 5).

In any case, there seems to have been a period of about two hundred years prior to the first monarchy (generally dated ~1020 BCE) when the

Israelite nation was engaged in some combination of conquest, migration, settlement, uprising, and identity creation, leading to the effort to form a centralized monarchy.

Biblical Chronology of the Wandering and Conquest

Numbers 13–14	The scouts Moses sent return with a discouraging report, generating a panicked rebellion among the people; God decrees that the people must now spend forty years in the desert, arriving in Canaan only when the generation born in Egypt will have died off.
Numbers 27:12–23	God instructs Moses to view Canaan from afar and to appoint Joshua as his successor.
Numbers 33	A summary of the Israelites' desert route, station by station.
Deuteronomy	This book is presented as Moses's farewell, comprising a review of history, a summation of laws, and a moral charge to the people as the forty years of desert wandering draw to a close.
Deuteronomy 34	Moses dies.
Joshua 3–4	Joshua parts the waters of the Jordan, and the Israelites cross into Canaan.
Joshua 5	The males born over the forty years in the desert are circumcised; the manna ceases; the people begin to eat from the produce of the land.
Joshua 6–7	The Israelites conquer Jericho.
Joshua 8:1–29	The Israelites conquer Ai.
Joshua 8:30–35	A ceremony of recommitment to the Torah is held at Mount Ebal.
Joshua 9	The Gibeonites trick Joshua into signing a peace treaty.
Joshua 10–12	A detailed account of the Israelite conquest of the entire country.
Joshua 24:29–30	Joshua dies; no successor is mentioned.
Judges 1:19–34	A listing of cities and tribes in Canaan that the Israelites were unable to destroy.

Judges 3:5	"The Israelites settled among the Canaanites, Hittites, Amorites, Perizzites, Hivites, and Jebusites."

The Book of Judges (~1200–1000 BCE)

Chapter 1	The state of the conquest after Joshua's death.
2	Ideological overture—the pattern to be repeated in the ensuing account: the people worship other gods, so God punishes them through enemies; then God takes pity on them and provides a leader who helps them overcome the enemy, for the time being.
3:8–11	King Cushan-rishathaim of Aram oppresses the Israelites; Othniel the Kenizzite liberates them.
3:11–30	King Eglon of Moab oppresses the Israelites; Ehud ben Gera liberates them.
3:31	Shamgar ben Anath leads a struggle against the Philistines.
4–5	Deborah "the prophetess" and Barak ben Abinoam, a general, lead the people to victory against Jabin, king of Canaan.
6–8	Midian oppresses the Israelites; Gideon ben Joash leads them to victory.
9	One of Gideon's sons tries to establish himself as king; he holds on to power for only three years.
10	Tola ben Puah and Jair the Gileadite lead Israel in succession.
11–12	The Ammonites oppress the Israelites; Jephthah the Gileadite leads them to victory.
12:8–13	Ibzan of Bethlehem, Elon the Zebulunite, and Abdon ben Hillel the Pirathonite lead Israel in succession.
13–16	Samson leads the struggle against the Philistines.
17–21	Accounts of internecine fighting among the tribes.

PRIMARY TEXT

The book of Joshua picks up just where the plan had been diverted forty years earlier. Arriving at the Jordan, Joshua sends spies into the land to prepare for the conquest. This time, the scouts' report is encouraging (Joshua 2:24: "all the inhabitants of the land are quaking before us"). Before beginning the conquest, the people celebrate Passover for the first time since Egypt—and for the first time in the land.

Joshua 5:1–12

[1]When all the kings of the Amorites on the western side of the Jordan, and all the kings of the Canaanites near the Sea, heard how the Lord had dried up the waters of the Jordan for the sake of the Israelites until they crossed over, they lost heart, and no spirit was left in them because of the Israelites.

Joshua's splitting the waters of the Jordan served not only to prove to the Israelites that he was Moses's worthy successor, but also to put the "fear of God" into the other nations, as had the miracle at the sea.

[2]At that time the Lord said to Joshua, "Make flint knives and proceed with a second circumcision of the Israelites." [3]So Joshua had flint knives made, and the Israelites were circumcised at Gibeath-haaraloth.

The fact that circumcision, the most fundamental symbol of covenant, was not practiced during the forty years elicits the question, just what *was* practiced? Or maybe this passage refers to a mass conversion ceremony—implying that not all of those called Israel in the land had been part of the desert experience.

[4]This is the reason why Joshua had the circumcision performed: All the people who had come out of Egypt, all the males of military age, had died during the desert wanderings after leaving Egypt. [5]Now, whereas all the people who came out of Egypt had been circumcised, none of the people born after the exodus, during the desert

wanderings, had been circumcised.
⁶For the Israelites had traveled in
the wilderness forty years, until the
entire nation—the men of military
age who had left Egypt—had perished; because they had not obeyed
the Lord, and the Lord had sworn
never to let them see the land that
the Lord had sworn to their fathers
to assign to us, a land flowing with
milk and honey. ⁷But He had raised
up their sons in their stead; and it
was these that Joshua circumcised,
for they were uncircumcised, not
having been circumcised on the
way. ⁸After the circumcising of the
whole nation was completed, they
remained where they were, in the
camp, until they recovered.

⁹And the Lord said to Joshua,
"Today I have rolled away from
you the disgrace of Egypt." So that
place was called Gilgal, as it still is.

¹⁰Encamped at Gilgal, in the
steppes of Jericho, the Israelites
offered the Passover sacrifice on
the fourteenth day of the month,
toward evening.

¹¹On the day after the Passover
offering, on that very day, they
ate of the produce of the country, unleavened bread and parched
grain. ¹²On that same day, when

Similarly, perhaps this first observance of the Passover commanded
forty years earlier in Egypt can be
seen as an initiation into the Jewish
nation, a taking on of its previous
"turning points" by those who had
not experienced them.

Gilgal comes from the Hebrew root
"to roll."

This first Passover in the land marked
the formal end of the desert existence—no more manna, no more
moratorium on making a living or
on fulfilling all the Torah's laws, but
rather full responsibility for defense,

they ate of the produce of the land, the manna ceased. The Israelites got no more manna; that year they ate of the yield of the land of Canaan.

governance, social justice, and sustenance.

Note that the Israelites first consumed the grain of Canaan only after offering the Passover sacrifice, exactly as commanded in Leviticus 23:10–11,14:

> [10]When you enter the land that I am giving to you and you reap its harvest, you shall bring the first sheaf of your harvest to the priest. [11]He shall elevate the sheaf before the Lord for acceptance in your behalf . . . [14]Until that very day, until you have brought the offering of your God, you shall eat no bread or parched grain or fresh ears.

It is of course unclear how the Israelites could have offered a sacrifice from the new harvest and then been sustained by the produce when they had not yet begun the conquest of the land.

Moreover, the Torah ascribes two different meanings to Passover:

1. The commemoration of the miracle of the tenth plague, which "passed over" the households of the Israelites (Exodus 12)
2. A harvest festival, celebrating the new grain crop (Leviticus 23:4–21)

Both meanings find expression, respectively, in the first two Passovers—the one in Egypt that begins the desert wandering, and the one observed at its conclusion, upon entering Canaan.

Structural details such as these lend support to the argument that the Torah consists of a blending of several different strands of tradition into one text. Could it not be, for example, that Passover was indeed a harvest festival commonly observed by a number of tribes living in Canaan and then took on a uniting historical-national meaning as well, perhaps based on some of these tribes' historical memories?

In any case, the people's entry into the land appears to have engendered three major changes in the life of the nation:

- A shift from God's supplying the people with manna—always right on time and in just the right quantity—to the people's taking on full responsibility for their physical survival. From this point on, living in the land meant living *from* the land, by hard work. (There is an interesting parallel between Adam and Eve's expulsion from Eden and the Israelites' crossing from the desert into Canaan. In the desert, as in Eden, there was no need to work for a living. Outside of Eden, and within Canaan, bread was earned by the sweat of one's brow.)
- The transition from a nomadic existence to a settled life in the Land of Israel. While the people's connection to the land had been established with Abraham's migration there, the "taking possession" under Joshua transpires at an entirely unprecedented scale. From this point onward, the Land of Israel is understood and experienced as the national homeland and a key element of Israelite identity.
- The implementation of the full covenant: "When you enter the land" had finally come to describe reality. The people were now expected to order their lives according to the full code of covenant law.

The entry into Canaan can also be seen as the termination of the mythical period. A nation living in its land, building institutions, and experiencing tumult (wars, droughts, earthquakes, and internal political transitions) enters into the purview of historical research. It leaves stone structures, written documents, and references in the documents of neighboring peoples. If the Exodus represented the creation story of the nation, then crossing the Jordan represents the emergence of that nation from the realm of myth into the realm of history.

LEGACY
Impact

For over a millennium from this point on, Jewish history will primarily be the history of a nation in its land. The events and documents of this history concern borders and foreign policy, governance and social policy, and the relationship between religion and politics.

The entry into the land also begins a thousand-year struggle between two forces: those committed to upholding the obligations of covenant and those drawn to the vision of "normalcy."

For most "normal" nations, home, as Robert Frost wrote, is "something you somehow haven't to deserve." People are naturally, unconditionally, rooted in their homelands. By contrast, as the biblical account relates, God redeemed the people Israel from slavery and brought them to this land specifically in order to implement God's law there in everyday life.

Therefore, Israel doesn't get a "free pass" after finally putting down roots in this land. If the Israelites fail to uphold their part in the covenant—fail to live by the law—then they will lose possession of the land. At times (as we will see), the people will try to forget their unique covenantal relationship to their land and behave as though they bear no responsibility for their continued possession of it.

In essence, the first four turning points in Jewish history coalesce in making the conditionality of possessing the land a key element in Israelite ideology. And even beyond the millennium of life in the Land of Israel, through centuries living scattered in faraway diasporas, the centrality of the land and the covenantal relationship to it will continue as a central motif in Jewish liturgy and thought.

Memory

In Exodus 6:6-8, God promises the slaves, "I will free you . . . and deliver you . . . and take you . . . and bring you into the land." The escape from Egypt and the entrance into Canaan were thereby seen as one continuous action (and the forty-year interlude viewed as an unfortunate deviation from the plan). Perhaps that is why there is no liturgical or ritual commemoration of the Jordan crossing or the conquest. The liberation celebrated on Passover "covers" the entire process. The biblical text tells us that, in effect, Passover celebrations bracketed the people's full journey, from their desert wanderings (the Passover of the Exodus) through their entry into the land of Canaan.

Note that the cycle of the Jewish year is anchored in three pilgrimage festivals, Passover, Shavuot, and Sukkot, when the Israelites were commanded to bring offerings to a central shrine, first at Shiloh and later in Jerusalem (see Leviticus 23:4-22,39-44; Deuteronomy 16:16). While assigned historical meanings (Passover commemorating the Exodus; Shavuot, the Revelation at Sinai; and Sukkot, the desert wandering), all three seem originally to have been harvest festivals, rooted in the agrarian life of the inhabitants of the land—and hence rooted in the land itself.

This geographical rootedness helps to explain why exile from the land (see chapter 7) was so traumatic and why the longing for return to the land became institutionalized in the Jewish religion.

TEXT FOR DISCUSSION

Rabbi Abraham Isaac Kook (1865–1935), the first Ashkenazic chief rabbi of Palestine, emphasized the mystic connection of people and land. What are the geopolitical implications of his view? What alternative views might be suggested?

> Eretz Israel is not something apart from the soul of the Jewish people; it is no mere national possession, serving as a means of unifying our people and buttressing its material, or even its spiritual survival. Eretz Israel is part of the very essence of our nationhood; it is bound organically to its very life and inner being. Human reason, even at its most sublime, cannot begin to understand the unique holiness of Eretz Israel; it cannot stir the depths of love for the land that are dormant within our people.
>
> —Rabbi Abraham Isaac Kook, *Orot* 1, in English translation in Arthur Hertzberg, *The Zionist Idea* (Philadelphia: Jewish Publication Society, 1959), p. 419

FURTHER READING

Kugel, James. *How to Read the Bible.* New York: Free Press, 2007, pp. 365–416. A concise survey and synthesis of biblical and archaeological scholarship on the problematics of the conquest.

McNutt, Paula. *Reconstructing the Society of Ancient Israel.* Louisville: Westminster, 1999, pp. 33–63. Review of scholarship and comparison of models for understanding the origin of the Israelite nation in its land.

Shanks, Hershel, William G. Dever, Baruch Halpern, and Peter K. McCarter Jr. *The Rise of Ancient Israel.* Washington: Biblical Archaeological Society, 1992, pp. 1–85. A symposium of archaeologists, leading proponents of the various models of Israelite origins.

5. Establishing a State

"GIVE US A KING!" ~1000 BCE

HISTORY

"Like All Other Nations": From Judges to Kings

Here is a major question regarding the conquest/settlement/uprising of Israel in Canaan (discussed in the previous chapter): at what point did the individual tribes' identities become secondary to a common Israelite identity?

The Torah speaks of one nation, although it does hint of division and dissension between tribes, as in Numbers 13–14, when only the scouts representing the tribes of Judah and Ephraim give a positive report about the Land of Israel (also see Numbers 16). The all-important conquest, for example, was ostensibly carried out by a united people and its army, according to the book of Joshua.

But in the book of Judges, we encounter a different reality: seemingly independent tribes unite in temporary alliances against common foes — and occasionally even go to war against each other. A revealing example is the battle between two tribes, the Ephraimites and the Manassites from the region of Gilead. In Judges 12, Gileadite sentinels identify Ephraimite infiltrators by their inability to pronounce the letter *shin* — evidence that the tribes spoke different Hebrew dialects.

Indeed, the twelve "judges" described in the book seem in most cases to be merely the leaders of such local alliances, chosen for their military prowess and/or leadership skills. And after the victory they disappear from history. One exception, which offers insight into the people's ambivalence regarding lack of a united government, is the story of Gideon, who leads the tribes of Manasseh, Asher, Zebulun, and Naphtali to victory over the Midianites. As he prepares to return to civilian life, the people approach him with the proposal that his leadership be institutionalized — that he rule over them as king (Judges 8:22–23). Gideon refuses, arguing that the only king of Israel is God, and therefore there is no need of a human king. Later, Abimelech, one of Gideon's sons, tries, brutally, to install himself as king and manages to hold on to power for three years, though apparently only over the city of Shechem (Judges 9).

From a historical perspective, there are several possible interpretations of the Gideon episode, among them:

a) There existed a widespread belief that God was the king of Israel and thus a human king was irrelevant. Therefore the disunited status quo was ideal.
b) Local tribal leaders were unwilling to relinquish their sovereignty in favor of a national government.
c) There was no felt need for a permanent state with all the attendant costs, such as taxation, military conscription, and the loss of individual freedoms and local sovereignty in the face of a centralized bureaucracy.
d) This story originated later, when the Israelite monarchy already existed; it came to express criticism of the reality of monarchic rule.

The people's opposition to a monarchy, both before and after its establishment, would not have been surprising. The creation of a central government, by definition, constituted a threat to the tribes' sovereignty, raised the prospect of new obligations such as taxes and conscription, and seemed to undermine the belief in God as the one and only king.

But established it ultimately was—with the anointment of King Saul, around 1020 BCE, so apparently the benefits outweighed the costs. The likely impetus for the change was the rise of a new and powerful enemy, the Philistines.

The creation of a unified state began a new phase in Israel's development. It lasted for only a century, 1020–920 BCE, through the reigns of Saul, David, and Solomon. Nevertheless it came to be seen as the ideal against which, in retrospect, the Jews would compare the reality of being ruled by outsiders in all subsequent generations. While opposition to a united monarchy had been natural before its establishment and during its existence, once the monarchy was lost, it just as naturally became the object of nostalgic longing—for the "good old days."

The Philistines

The seafaring Philistines had settled along the coast from Jaffa down to Gaza, establishing five cities: Ashdod, Ashkelon, Ekron, Gat, and Gaza. Already at the time of the Exodus they were a factor to be reckoned with: God did not direct the Israelites northward along the coast from Egypt, the most direct route, to avoid the tribes' having to battle the Philistines there (Exodus 13:17). The Bible suggests the Philistines had exclusive ironworking technology, which gave them significant advantage in war against the Israelites (and presumably other Canaanite nations) (1 Samuel 13:19–22).

According to the book of Judges, the Philistines rule over Israel for forty years (13:1). Samson, of the tribe of Dan, becomes the first Israelite leader to contend with them. The colorful account of his adventures (Judges 13–16), in particular his romantic involvement with Philistine women, indicates that along with the enmity between the nations, there is also close contact.

Militarily, Samson succeeds in inflicting damage on the Philistines — for example, the biblical text (Judges 15:14–15) informs us that he singlehandedly kills a thousand of them — but they remain a powerful enemy; in 1 Samuel 4 they actually capture the Ark of the Covenant and hold it hostage for seven months. God intervenes with a plague (1 Samuel 6) and they return the Ark, but they remain a thorn in Israel's side for decades, with border areas changing hands and the ongoing threat of invasion (1 Samuel 7).

Unable to overcome the Philistines as a loose confederation, the elders of Israel assemble and ask the judge Samuel to appoint a king for them, "that we may be like all the other nations: Let our king rule over us and go out at our head and fight our battles" (1 Samuel 8:1–20, reproduced in this chapter). Economic reasons might have also encouraged the move to a centralized government, which could secure the roads and standardize measures and money, thus facilitating trade among the tribes.

In addition, a period of disorder and weakness in Egypt may have spurred the Philistines' rise — and this same power vacuum may have encouraged Israel's emergence as an independent state as well.

Saul and David

According to the biblical account, only one leader in the book of Judges — Abimelech — attempts to establish a dynasty. Samuel, who can be seen as the last of the judges (1 Samuel 1–7), tries to arrange for his sons to succeed him, but they are not worthy. The text (8:4–5) attributes the people's desire for a monarchy to this failure of succession. Given the geopolitical unrest, there may have been a felt need for a strong central government with an established means of continuity (dynastic succession) to replace the unstable and unpredictable status quo of charismatic leaders.

Acceding to the elders' demand, Samuel anoints the first king, Saul, from the smallest tribe, Benjamin. The text relays three different stories as to how Saul is selected: in 1 Samuel 9:1–10:16 he is out searching for some stray donkeys when he providentially encounters Samuel, who anoints him king; in 1 Samuel 10:17–27 Samuel chooses him in a public lottery; and in 1 Samuel 11 he is swept away by patriotic zeal to summon all the tribes to rebel against an Ammonite provocation. Perhaps all three events happened in succession; perhaps they represent the editing together of different traditions.

In any case, Saul seems to function well in the role of military chief. He manages to unite the people against their enemies by dint of his size (1 Samuel 10:23), his military prowess, and the fact that he was formally anointed and supported by Samuel. Under his rule, the Israelites rout the Amalekites and keep the Philistines at bay (but never decisively defeat them). The Bible doesn't tell us how the monarchy worked, what institutions were established, or what Saul did as king other than battle Amalekites and Philistines.

The text of 1 Samuel 16 through 2 Samuel 5 dramatically recounts the ongoing power struggle between Saul and a younger leader, David, from the tribe of Judah. As with Saul, there is more than one account of David's initial rise (1 Samuel 16 and 17), but in both stories, Saul perceives him as a threat early on, and years of cat-and-mouse games involving violence and treachery ensue.

After Saul's death, one of his sons, Ish-bosheth, is installed on the throne. He apparently rules over all the tribes except for Judah (2 Samuel 2:8–11), which remains loyal to David. Ish-bosheth's reign lasts only two years; ultimately, David succeeds in consolidating rule over all of the tribes and in ruling for forty years.

David seems to be effective militarily (keeping the Philistines mostly at bay and expanding the borders of the kingdom) and economically (enriching the kingdom through trade and spoils). He conquers Jerusalem and makes it his capital (2 Samuel 5), naming it "City of David." He presides over a hierarchic bureaucracy (8:15–18), brings the Ark into his capital (6:12–19), and has several royal wives, a golden crown, and a palace.

He also contends with tribal rebellions (e.g., 2 Samuel 20) and several dynastic struggles within his family (e.g., 2 Samuel 14–19), all of which eventually lead to his son Solomon succeeding him on the throne.

Like his father, Solomon reigns for forty years. The Bible tells us he expands the empire by conquest and alliances and builds up Jerusalem — including a royal palace and an impressive temple for the official cult (the sacrificial service of the priests, as described in the Torah). In the centuries to come, whenever the Jews refer to their glorious past, they are imagining Solomon's reign.

Alas, when Solomon dies, the centrifugal forces he and David successfully overcame for eighty years are too much for the governing abilities of his heir Rehoboam (1 Kings 12). According to the text, the kingdom falls apart, splitting into the Kingdom of Israel (ten tribes) and the Kingdom of Judah.

Archaeologists continue to debate the historical accuracy of these biblical stories. There is no extra-biblical evidence relating to Saul (the Bible itself does not specify the length of his reign), and the earliest references to the Davidic dynasty date from a later period — victory inscriptions by Aramean and Moabite kings who defeated Israelite kings in the ninth to eighth centuries BCE, found respectively at Tel Dan in northern Israel and at Dibon in Jordan.

In any case, the biblical account is itself impressive in its psychological and political realism. When we read it, sometimes it is hard to imagine it not happening.

Whether these events unfolded as described in the Bible, or at all, the glory days of the empire of David and Solomon endured in the collective memory of the Jewish people as utopia — a glorious picture of what their national life could be if they could only "renew their days as of old" (Lamentations 5:21).

Timeline: 1115–~920 BCE

1115   Tiglath-Pileser I establishes the second Assyrian Empire in Mesopotamia and begins a period of expansion and development.

1100	The Mycenean civilization in Greece declines.
1090	The Egyptian central government declines in strength under the Twenty-First Dynasty.
~1020	Saul is anointed as king.
~1000	David is anointed as king of Judah in Hebron.
~993	David is acclaimed as king of all Israel.
943	Ashur-dan II establishes the Neo-Assyrian Empire, to dominate the region for three centuries.
~940	David dies; Solomon is anointed as king.
~920	Solomon dies; the kingdom is divided into Israel (ten northern tribes) and Judah.

PRIMARY TEXT

In Moses's farewell speech, he says, "If, after you have entered the land . . . you decide, 'I will set a king over me, as do all the nations about me,' you shall be free to set a king over yourself." He then goes on to warn against such royal excesses as "many wives," "many horses," and "silver and gold to excess" (Deuteronomy 17:14–17). Later, after Saul is anointed, we encounter the following: "Saul also went home to Gibeah, accompanied by upstanding men whose hearts God had touched. But some scoundrels said, 'How can this fellow save us?' So they scorned him and brought him no gift" (1 Samuel 10:26–27). Thus, it seems the tension over monarchy was ongoing, both before and after a king was anointed.

This account of the people's conversation with Samuel, regarding their demand of a king, echoes and amplifies the warnings in Deuteronomy 17.

---

1 Samuel 8:1–20

---

¹When Samuel grew old, he appointed his sons judges over Israel. ²The name of his first-born son was Joel, and his second son's name was Abijah; they sat as judges in Beersheba. ³But his sons did not follow in his ways; they were bent on gain, they accepted bribes, and they subverted justice.

Interestingly, Samuel himself, committed as he seems to be to charismatic leadership (and opposed to monarchy) tries and fails to bequeath his position to his sons.

⁴All the elders of Israel assembled and came to Samuel at Ramah, ⁵and they said to him, "You have grown old, and your sons have not followed your ways. Therefore appoint a king for us, to govern us like all other nations." ⁶Samuel was displeased that they said "Give us a king to govern us." Samuel prayed to the Lord, ⁷and the Lord replied to Samuel, "Heed the demand of the people in everything they say to you. For it is not you that they have rejected; it is Me they have rejected as their king. ⁸Like everything else they have done ever since I brought them out of Egypt to this day—forsaking Me and worshiping other gods—so they are doing to you. ⁹Heed their demand; but warn them solemnly, and tell them about the practices of any king who will rule over them."

¹⁰Samuel reported all the words of the Lord to the people, who were asking him for a king. ¹¹He said, "This will be the practice of the king who will rule over you: He will take your sons and appoint them as his charioteers and horsemen, and they will serve as outrunners for his chariots. ¹²He will appoint them as his chiefs of thousands and of fifties; or they will have to plow his fields, reap his harvest, and make

The Talmud and later commentators wonder if the implication of the passage quoted from Deuteronomy is that God commanded establishing a state (a monarchy)—or if God was making a concession to the people's weakness. Here too: if God is really opposed to the people's demand, why does God give in?

Is the establishment of a state an ideal—or just the lesser of two evils, an unfortunate geopolitical necessity?

This description was written by someone who knew what he or she was talking about; see 1 Kings 4:7, 5:27–30, 9:18–22, 10:18–11:5. Indeed, most historians of the text believe that both the Deuteronomy passage and this one were written after Solomon's reign.

his weapons and the equipment
for his chariots. [13]He will take your
daughters as perfumers, cooks,
and bakers. [14]He will seize your
choice fields, vineyards, and olive
groves, and give them to his courtiers. [15]He will take a tenth part of
your grain and vintage and give it
to his eunuchs and courtiers. [16]He
will take your male and female
slaves, your choice young men,
and your asses, and put them to
work for him. [17]He will take a tenth
part of your flocks, and you shall
become his slaves. [18]The day will
come when you cry out because
of the king whom you yourselves
have chosen; and the Lord will not
answer you on that day."

[19]But the people would not listen
to Samuel's warning. "No," they
said, "We must have a king over us,
[20]that we may be like all the other
nations. Let our king rule over us
and go out at our head and fight
our battles."

Whether or not this exchange took place as reported, it expresses the
significant tension between those favoring a strong central government
and those seeking to preserve local and/or regional autonomy. This fric-
tion would persist in the political reality of the Israelite nation for a long
time, kept alive by the competing pressures of different ideological strands,
economic interests, hunger for power, manifestations of identity, and
danger from outside.

If we take the biblical narrative at its face value, we might imagine that once the people had conquered Canaan and settled into their tribal inheritances, they were happy to live in some kind of loose confederation, with ad hoc alliances led by charismatic chieftains (warlords?) as necessary. The Torah covenant could be kept in such a framework—a unified nation-state was not required. Only when confronted by an outside threat from an advanced and unified enemy did the tribes reluctantly agree to exchange their ideology of local autonomy under God's kingship for reduced sovereignty under a human king. Alternatively, we can accept the view that the Israelite nation arose from the coalescence of disparate local tribes and perhaps immigrant groups into a nation with a shared identity in a defined boundary. If so, then the biblical story of establishing the monarchy can be seen as reflecting this nation-building process.

One way or the other, unity did not come easily, nor did it last. Samuel's cynicism in listing the costs of a monarchy ("[The king] will take your sons . . . as his charioteers and horsemen . . . ; he will take your daughters as perfumers, cooks, and bakers. He will seize your choice fields . . . and give them to his courtiers" [1 Samuel 8:11]) is understandable when we read the accounts of failed monarchies both before and after Saul's anointment (Abimelech in Judges 9; Rehoboam in 1 Kings 12).

It is striking that in three thousand years of history, the Israelites lived as a united, independent nation in the Land of Israel for barely one hundred years—and even during that time they weren't really so united, wracked by years of civil war as David fought to replace Saul as king and then by internal rebellions during David's kingship.

Nonetheless, according to 2 Samuel 7:16, God promises David, "Your house and your kingship shall ever be secure before you; your throne shall be established forever"—and this promise (whether actually spoken by the prophet Nathan on God's behalf or produced by David's public relations apparatus) becomes a guiding principle in the nation's understanding of its own history ever after. David's dynasty had ruled by divine right and was never to be unseated. And if, somehow, no state was being ruled by a member of that dynasty, it was a temporary situation—a moment of divine punishment that would pass.

And so, the ideal of a united monarchy progressed from a reluctant concession to become a pillar of Jewish identity and belief.

LEGACY

Impact

Each developmental transition discussed to date—Abraham's call, the Exodus, the covenant, the land (and now the state)—left an indelible imprint on Israelite belief and identity that endures in Jewish thought and practice today. The establishment of a monarchy produced these significant developments:

- Prophecy: The tension between the need for a united polity (under a human king) and the resistance to a central authority (and belief that only God is king) became institutionalized in the phenomenon of prophecy (see chapter 6). This usually found expression in confrontations between kings and prophets—individuals who called the kings (or the body politic) to account, in God's name, when their actions conflicted with the demands of the covenant. The prophet Nathan, for example, holds a moral mirror up to David, reproving him for his adulterous affair with Bathsheba (2 Samuel 11–12). Ideally, of course, the Israelite king would rule according to the Torah (Deuteronomy 17:18–20); in reality, prophets were needed to press for the fulfillment of that ideal.
- Jerusalem as center: David conquered Jerusalem—a town strategically located to unite Judah with the northern tribes—and established it as the capital of the united kingdom. Solomon proceeded to build the Temple there, cementing the linkage between state and cult. Thus, Jerusalem rapidly took on the status not only of the center of the kingdom, but also *axis mundi*, the center of the world (where "God's name dwells"—1 Kings 8:29). Investing Jerusalem with this new meaning had a powerful impact on Jewish thought and liturgy throughout the ages.
- Utopia: For three thousand years since the reign of the Israelite kings, the Jewish people preserved an idyllic memory of a nation living in peace and prosperity in the land God promised them, ruled by a wise and devout king, and maintaining a healthy relationship with God by obeying Torah law and participating in the Temple ritual. The ideology that connects the covenant with this memory of

ideal existence has very likely been central to the survival of the Jewish people: If God established a covenant with Israel linking obedience to God's laws with national sovereignty in the land, then exile is not a function of military weakness (or God's impotence), but rather the consequence of disobedience. Thus, what is done can be undone. The people can aspire to regain God's favor and consequentially restore the lost utopia of land, state, and religion.

Memory

The word "messiah," *mashiach* in Hebrew, means "anointed one." Saul and then David and Solomon were not crowned; they were anointed with sacred oil. The united monarchy collapsed upon Solomon's death, and the Babylonians dethroned the last Davidic king of Judah in 586 BCE (see chapter 7) — but God had promised that David's dynasty would rule forever. Thus, the nation has awaited the fulfillment of that promise — the anointment of a scion of that dynasty in a restored kingdom — ever since.

In effect, the day Samuel poured a flask of oil on Saul's head (1 Samuel 10:1), he set in motion a belief in the Messiah, which has persisted as a powerful force in Jewish — and world — history.

There are many liturgical expressions of messianic expectation in Jewish liturgy. For one, this prayer appears in the traditional daily liturgy: "Hurry and restore the 'sprout' of David Your servant, and renew his glory through Your redemption."

The accounting of David's life also continues, varnished somewhat, in the memory of the people. The biblical account is remarkably three-dimensional, portraying David's Machiavellian machinations and personal moral foibles as well as his triumphs. Later generations tended to read the complexity out of the story, preferring to see David — like the period of his rule — as a model of perfection. The tradition that David (the musician — see 1 Samuel 16:14–23) authored the book of Psalms seems to have been an important factor in the "purification" of his memory.

TEXT FOR DISCUSSION

In this passage, the novelist Jerome Charyn takes the biblical account of Saul at face value. Yet, the Bible's unflattering description of Saul was likely written — or at least edited — by David's people. How, then, are we

to relate to biblical texts? How much do the history and presumed authorship of the text matter?

> [Saul] lacks David's sense of politics and song. Saul is a primitive: there
> is almost nothing he experiences in I Samuel that isn't related to fear —
> fear of Samuel, fear of David, fear of God, fear of Goliath and the Phi-
> listines, fear of his servants, fear of his son Jonathan. When he fails
> to destroy the Amalekites, and still spares their king and their cattle,
> Samuel rebukes him and says: "Though you are little in your own eyes,
> are you not the head of the tribes of Israel?" (15:17). Saul *is* little in his
> own eyes, because he never wanted to become king. What could that
> first king have been to the tribes of Israel? Half man, half god, prophet,
> warrior, and magician, a substitute for Jehovah Himself. Saul was much
> too simple and solitary a man to play at being a god. David can kill Goli-
> ath, talk to God, and mourn the dead Saul with an eloquence that bor-
> ders on the magical. . . . And Saul has nothing but his rages, his fears,
> and his own silence.
>
> — Jerome Charyn, "I Samuel," in *Congregation: Contemporary Writers
> Read the Jewish Bible*, ed. D. Rosenberg (New York: Harcourt Brace
> Jovanovich, 1987), p. 102

FURTHER READING

Buber, Martin. *Kingship of God*. Translated by Richard Schiemann. New York:
Harper and Row, 1967, pp. 59–65. A discussion of the historicity and theological implications of the Gideon story.

1 Samuel 9–31: Saul; 1 Samuel 16–2 Samuel 5: Saul and David; 2 Samuel 5–1
Kings 2: David's rule; 1 Kings 2–1 Kings 11: Solomon's rule.

Kugel, James. *How to Read the Bible*. New York: Free Press, 2007. Pp. 409–16: a
summary of scholarship on the transition from judges to a king; pp. 444–57:
the rise and fall of Saul.

Walzer, Michael. *In God's Shadow: Politics in the Hebrew Bible*. New Haven: Yale
University Press, 2012, pp. 50–71. A noted political scientist analyzes the origin and nature of the Israelite monarchy.

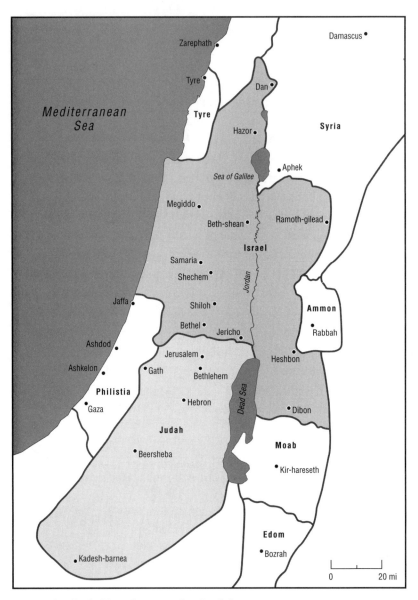

Map 2. The divided kingdom: Israel and Judah, ca. 900 BCE

6. The Fall of Israel

EXILE OF THE TEN TRIBES, 722 BCE

HISTORY

Division and Fall

David and Solomon succeeded in building an empire with all the accoutrements, including a royal palace, a centralized religious cult, a bureaucracy—and an ideology of a divinely ordained dynasty. However, whether because the tribes' unity was never very deep or because Solomon overreached in his grandiose projects of conquest and construction—or both—the empire did not last. Already in Solomon's lifetime, Jeroboam, an officer in the labor brigades from the tribe of Ephraim, sought to rebel (1 Kings 11:26–40); failing, he fled to Egypt (which hints at foreign involvement in his rebellion). The way the Bible tells it, because Solomon's heir Rehoboam lacked his father's political wisdom (12:1–12), around 920 BCE Jeroboam returned to the Kingdom of Israel and led the secession of the ten northern tribes.

Jeroboam established an alternative capital and an alternative cult, with its priesthood and calendar of festivals (1 Kings 12:25–33). For the next two hundred years, Israel (the ten tribes) and Judah were independent kingdoms—sometimes allies, sometimes enemies (e.g., 1 Kings 15:6,16–22; 2 Kings 14).

Since the Kingdom of Israel was destroyed well before the Kingdom of Judah, the biblical account we have represents the Judahites' version of events, in which the Israelite secession is cast in a negative light. According to this account, nine out of nineteen kings of Israel over two centuries ascended to the throne by means of a coup, and no dynasty lasted more than about fifty years. In contrast, in the same period Judah was ruled by twelve kings, all descendants of David, except for a five-year interlude in the mid-800s, when the queen mother tried to institute a different dynasty.

Counting the tribes can be confusing. Jacob had twelve sons (Genesis 35:22–26): Reuben, Simeon, Levi, Judah, Issachar, Zebulun, Joseph, Benjamin, Dan, Naphtali, Gad, and Asher (and a daughter, Dinah). But Joseph's posterity comprised two tribes, as his sons Ephraim and Manasseh each became a tribe. Thus, there were actually thirteen tribes. However, Levi's descendants, designated for cult service, were not assigned land but lived dispersed among the other tribes' lands, so there were only twelve tribal territories.

Then Simeon's territory was subsumed in Judah's in the south, and when the kingdom divided, Benjamin (whose land was adjacent to Judah's) stayed with Judah. Thus, the "ten tribes" of the north comprised Reuben, Issachar, Zebulun, Dan, Naphtali, Gad, Asher, Ephraim, Manasseh, and that portion of Levi that lived in their territories.

Over the years, the two kingdoms were constantly dealing with the shifting balance of power among Egypt and Mesopotamia and their local vassal states. Apparently Hoshea, the last king of Israel, calculated poorly in seeking Egyptian support against Assyria (see "Primary Text" below); the Assyrians proceeded to destroy the Northern Kingdom. Interestingly, Judah was also on the verge of destruction by Assyria when a plague miraculously struck the besieging army; they withdrew, leaving the Southern Kingdom intact (2 Kings 18–19).

The "Lost Tribes"

The biblical description of the Assyrian exile matches other sources that refer to the Neo-Assyrian Empire's policy of preventing rebellion by exiling elites and/or particular cities. Thus the report of a significant exile from the Northern Kingdom, eastward toward Mesopotamia, is credible. It is also likely that the Assyrians settled other migrants in the territory of Israel, and these mixed with the Israelites (and other Canaanites) who had stayed in place.

What remained of the northern tribes is not clear. On the one hand, the account in 2 Kings 17 (later in this chapter) indicates that a total population replacement took place. On the other hand, 2 Chronicles 30 describes King Hezekiah's sending an invitation to all the Israelites—in all twelve tribes—to come up to Jerusalem to celebrate Passover; and Hezekiah ruled in Judah *after* the Assyrian conquest of Israel.

In any case, the biblical account in 2 Kings has given rise to a rich tradition of legend and speculation regarding the whereabouts of the Israelites exiled by Assyria. Medieval travelers claimed to have visited their land. In 1654 a Dutch Jew, Manasseh ben Israel, tried to convince Oliver

Cromwell that the lost tribes were the native population of South America. If so, then the only place left without Jews would be England (which had expelled its Jews in 1290), and if Cromwell would re-admit them, messianic prophecies could be fulfilled. It didn't work.

Kings, Priests, and Prophets

Priestly leadership, described in detail in the Torah (especially in the book of Leviticus), was hereditary and responsible for the sacrificial cult as well as for interpreting the law of the covenant. Kings were a later phenomenon, seen as a utilitarian compromise that became, under David, a divinely ordained hereditary dynasty. This dual leadership structure, fully established under David and Solomon, continued to function in the Kingdom of Judah until its destruction in 586 BCE (see chapter 7).

This model became inscribed in the nation's collective memory as the ideal of national existence. Theoretically, at least, both the priests and the kings were committed to the covenant; their role was to teach, enforce, and enable national life according to Torah law, in order to sustain God's favor upon the nation, ensuring peace and prosperity.

However, human nature being what it is, both of these bureaucracies tended to yield to the temptation to see themselves as self-sufficient, forgetting or downplaying the conditionality of the covenant. Kings naturally relied on military power and diplomatic wiles (and marriages); priests believed in the magical power of their rituals.

Therefore, a third type of leadership came to play a vital role in the life of the nation: the prophets. According to the biblical accounts, the early prophets were independent, charismatic preachers and miracle workers who often risked their lives to speak the truth of the covenant to the power of priests and kings. The first example we encounter is Nathan, who represented the voice of the covenant in David's court (e.g., 2 Samuel 11–12). Later, 1 Kings 17 through 2 Kings 13 records the exploits and teachings of two major prophets from the north, Elijah and Elisha, described as men of action who intervened in political struggles and worked miracles. Perhaps the most famous of these episodes is Elijah's contest with 450 pagan prophets, when God sends miraculous fire to consume Elijah's sacrifice (1 Kings 18).

Most scholars see the careers of Nathan, Elijah, and Elisha as an earlier stage in the development of prophecy, preceding the model of the "literary prophet" that yielded the powerful poems preserved in the fifteen prophetic books from Isaiah to Malachi. Literary prophets such as Amos and Hosea (not to be confused with King Hoshea, to be discussed), who lived in the late decades of the Northern Kingdom (under Jeroboam II), railed against the Israelites' adoption of pagan rituals alongside their own. They exhorted the people that such a weakening of their commitment to the covenant's moral laws would surely lead to punishment in the form of defeat and destruction.

Timeline: The Northern Kingdom, Israel, 922–722 BCE

922–901	Jeroboam (by revolt); 1 Kings 11:26–14:20
901–900	Nadab (by succession); 1 Kings 14:20, 15:25–31
900–877	Baasha (by revolt); 1 Kings 15:27–16:6
~1100–850	Period when Homer lived
877–876	Elah (by succession); 1 Kings 16:6–14
876 (1 week)	Zimri (by revolt); 1 Kings 16:8–20
876–869	Omri (by revolt); 1 Kings 16:15–28
876	Division: Omri versus Tibni; 1 Kings 16:21–22
869–850	Ahab (by succession from Omri); 1 Kings 16:28–22:40
850–849	Ahaziah (by succession); 1 Kings 22:52–2 Kings 1:18
849–842	Jehoram (by succession); 2 Kings 3:1–27, 8:25–9:26
842–815	Jehu (by revolt); 2 Kings 9:1–10:36
815–801	Jehoahaz (by succession); 2 Kings 13:1–9
801–786	Joash (by succession); 2 Kings 13:9–14:16
786–746	Jeroboam II (by succession); 2 Kings 14:11–29
746	Zechariah (by succession); 2 Kings 15:8–12
745 (1 month)	Shallum (by revolt); 2 Kings 15:10–15
745–738	Menahem (by revolt); 2 Kings 15:14–22
738–737	Pekahiah (by succession); 2 Kings 15:23–26
737–732	Pekah (by revolt); 2 Kings 15:27–31
732–722	Hoshea (by revolt); 2 Kings 17:1–6
722	Assyrian conquest, exile; 2 Kings 17:4–6

Scholars differ on dating the various kings, by up to a ten-year margin of error; the date of the 722 BCE defeat, however, is accepted by all.

PRIMARY TEXT

In straightforward prose narrative, the books of Samuel describe the transition from the judges to the monarchy, from Saul to David, and David's rule. The books of Kings cover the end of David's life through the destruction of both Israel and Judah. After Israel's secession the narrative alternates between the two kingdoms, chronicling king by king in parallel. The books of Chronicles present a parallel account from David through the destruction of Judah, mostly ignoring the Northern Kingdom.

Across these six books, various redundancies and inconsistencies are evident, Elijah's miracles (among others) are open to question, and archaeologists cannot verify every person and event. However, echoes of the biblical account have been found in the texts of other nations, such as Assyrian inscriptions referencing Israelite kings and a Moabite inscription on the Mesha Stele (ninth century BCE; found in Jordan) that details relations between the Moabites and Israel. Therefore, most scholars treat the biblical narrative, at least in its broad outline, as a "real" historical framework.

---

2 Kings 17:1–8,13–14,21–24

---

¹In the twelfth year of King Ahaz of Judah, Hoshea son of Elah became king over Israel in Samaria—for nine years. ²He did what was displeasing to the Lord, though not as much as the kings of Israel who preceded him. ³King Shalmaneser marched against him, and Hoshea became his vassal and paid him tribute. ⁴But the king of Assyria caught Hoshea in an act of treachery: he had sent envoys to King So of Egypt, and he had not paid the tribute to the king of Assyria, as in previous years. And the king of Assyria arrested him and put him in prison. ⁵Then the king of Assyria

Shalmaneser V ruled 727–722 BCE. A decade earlier, under the previous Israelite king, Pekah, Shalmaneser's predecessor Tiglath-Pileser III had invaded Israel and carried out a first wave of deportation from the northern part of the kingdom (2 Kings 15:29).

marched against the whole land;
he came to Samaria and besieged
it for three years. ⁶In the ninth
year of Hoshea, the king of Assyria
captured Samaria. He deported
the Israelites to Assyria and settled them in Halah, at the [River]
Habor, at the River Gozan, and in
the towns of Media.

These destinations were in northern
Syria and Iraq, eastward into Iran.

⁷This happened because the Israelites sinned against the Lord their
God who had freed them from the
land of Egypt, from the hand of
Pharaoh king of Egypt. They worshiped other gods ⁸and followed
the customs of the nations which
the Lord had dispossessed before
the Israelites and the customs
which the kings of Israel had
practiced. . . .

See discussion of the nation's sins,
which follows.

¹³The Lord warned Israel and
Judah by every prophet [and]
every seer, saying, "Turn back from
your wicked ways, and observe
My commandments and My laws,
according to all the Teaching that I
commanded your fathers and that I
transmitted to you through My servants the prophets." ¹⁴But they did
not obey; they stiffened their necks,
like their fathers who did not have
faith in the Lord their God. . . .

[21]For Israel broke away from the House of David, and they made Jeroboam son of Nebat king. Jeroboam caused Israel to stray from the Lord and to commit great sin, [22]and the Israelites persisted in all the sins which Jeroboam had committed; they did not depart from them. [23]In the end, the Lord removed Israel from His presence, as He had warned them through all His servants the prophets. So the Israelites were deported from their land to Assyria, as is still the case.

[24]The king of Assyria brought [people] from Babylon, Cuthah, Avva, Hamath, and Sepharvaim, and he settled them in the towns of Samaria in place of the Israelites; they took possession of Samaria and dwelt in its towns.

Central Iraq, along the Euphrates Valley. See discussion (Memory) regarding the Cutheans and the Samaritans.

The books of Kings, in particular, are imbued with the covenant ideology that connects the nation's fortunes to its behavior; defeats only occur when they are deserved as punishment. However, the nature of the misbehavior is often somewhat vague. This text describes four different sets of sins that led to the destruction:

1. The king "displeased the Lord," though less so than his predecessors (verse 2).
2. Idolatry as well as following Canaanite customs and "the customs which the kings of Israel had practiced" (verses 7–8).
3. Ignoring God's laws and lack of faith (verse 14).
4. Seceding from the House of David (verse 21).

Was the sin the common custom of cementing alliances by building a temple to the ally's god? Was it a general culture of ignoring the social and moral commandments? Alternatively was it laxness in ritual? Or syncretistic practices combining Torah law and pagan customs? Sometimes it seems that the problem is on the grassroots level of general culture, and sometimes it seems the violation is on the diplomatic, national-symbolic level. The prophets Hosea and Amos suggest that injustice, lack of faith, and idolatrous practices all represent abandonment of the covenant:

Hosea 4:1-2: [1]For the Lord has a case / Against the inhabitants of this land, / Because there is no honesty and no goodness / And no obedience to God in the land. / [2][False] swearing, dishonesty, and murder, / And theft and adultery are rife; / Crime follows upon crime!

Hosea 7:10-11: [10]Though Israel's pride has been humbled / Before his very eyes, / They have not turned back / To their God the Lord; / They have not sought Him / In spite of everything. / [11]Instead, Ephraim has acted / Like a silly dove with no mind: / They have appealed to Egypt! / They have gone to Assyria!

Hosea 8:4: They have made kings, / But not with My sanction; / They have made officers, / But not of My choice. Of their silver and gold / They have made themselves images, / To their own undoing.

Amos 2:6-8: [6]They have sold for silver / Those whose cause was just, / And the needy for a pair of sandals. [7][Ah,] you who trample the heads of the poor / Into the dust of the ground, / And make the humble walk a twisted course! / Father and son go to the same girl, / And thereby profane My holy name. / [8]They recline by every altar / On garments taken in pledge, / And drink in the House of their God / Wine bought with the fines they have imposed.

Throughout all of the prophets' writings, themes of idolatrous worship (both popular and official) and of common immorality and injustice appear side by side. The implication is that idolatry leads to abandonment of belief in the covenant, which leads to abandonment of the law, which leads to general moral and social collapse—which leads to physical destruction at the hands of enemies.

LEGACY

Impact

The destruction of the Kingdom of Israel represents the first catastrophe in Israelite/Jewish history: ten tribes disappear without a trace. Later (see chapter 7) a parallel disaster will befall the remaining tribe of Judah, but the outcome will be different: Judahite identity will be maintained for centuries, both in the land and in exile. We do not know what accounts for the stark difference in consequences between the Israelite and Judahite tribes after conquest, but two factors have been suggested: the weakness of Israelite national identity, including its lack of robust institutions to maintain it in trying times; and the Assyrians' particular effectiveness in dispersing and suppressing conquered cultures, among them the Israelite kingdom.

Since the prophets (not only Amos and Hosea, but also those who were active in Judah after the fall of Israel) saw the disaster as a clear verification of covenant ideology, it likely served to strengthen their case for the covenant's validity. Belief in the covenant would therefore have provided a basis for the Judahites' expectation of return and restoration—including the restoration of all twelve tribes. Thus, the prophetic interpretation of the fall of Israel would become an important support for the covenantal understanding of history, and hence a source of hope for generations of exiles.

Jews are called "Jews" because, according to the biblical narrative, they are all descended from the surviving Kingdom of Judah. In Hebrew "Judah" is *Yehudah*; members of this tribe are *Yehudim*, which, anglicized, becomes "Jews."

In fact, "Israel" was a more inclusive term, as it referred to Jacob, patriarch of all the tribes. However, from the time of Jeroboam's rebellion, within the Bible, Israel came to signify the ten rebelling tribes (1 Kings 12:16–17): "[16] 'We have no portion in David, / No share in Jesse's son! / To your tents, O Israel! / Now look to your own House, O David.' So the Israelites returned to their homes. [17]But Rehoboam continued to reign over the Israelites who lived in the towns of Judah."

The theme of exile (*galut*) recurs throughout the Bible: Adam and Eve, Cain, Joseph, forty years of desert wandering. Being sent or kept away from home is one of the most traumatic human experiences. With the fall of Israel, this existential threat becomes historical reality on a national scale. Exile enters the people's consciousness as a vivid historical memory and remains central to Jewish experience and consciousness for all generations to come.

Memory

The prevailing sense of loss and the longing to restore and reunify the northern tribes became common themes among later prophets and, through them, entered the traditional liturgy (e.g., the haftarah [prophetic reading] for the second day of Rosh Hashanah, from Jeremiah 31; and for the eighth day of Passover, from Isaiah 11).

The existence of the lost tribes beyond the Sambatyon River (a mythical river that ceases flowing on Shabbat) was a popular legend in the Middle Ages. Through the years, various attempts have been made to "find" these tribes—in the Americas, in Africa, in Asia. The search continues even in our own day.

Today, the most likely claimants to the heritage of the northern tribes are the approximately eight hundred Samaritans (*Shomronim*, based on their roots in Samaria—Shomron) who live in two communities: one near Nablus/Shechem in Samaria, the West Bank north of Jerusalem, and one in Holon, near Tel Aviv. It seems the Samaritans are bearers of a tradition extending back to the Cutheans, one of the groups the Assyrians imported from Mesopotamia. They inhabited the north, stayed in place after 722 BCE, and continued to practice a diverging version of the religion of Judah that would later become Judaism. Apparently the Rabbis of the Talmud came to view the Cutheans' descendants as "sort of" Jews. These descendants shared some texts and practices with Rabbinic Judaism, such as reading and revering the Torah and the book of Joshua, but did not accept the later books or the Rabbinic interpretation, the Oral Law. Today, the Samaritans maintain these beliefs and practices. They also view Mount Gerizim, near Nablus/Shechem, as their holy mountain (not Jerusalem!) and (in what has become an exotic tourist attraction) perform the Passover sacrifice according to the biblical description. They are considered Jews by Israeli law, but not by *halakhah*.

In the New Testament, Luke 10:25–37, Jesus tells a story of a Samaritan who demonstrates morally superior behavior in comparison to that of a priest and a Levite; hence the "good Samaritan." The Rabbis viewed Samaritans as Jewishly inferior, and so Jesus upended the common assumption regarding the moral hierarchy.

TEXT FOR DISCUSSION

Ezekiel, one of the three major literary prophets, lived through the destruction of the Kingdom of Judah (see chapter 7); most of his prophecies were written while living in exile in Babylonia. Consider: was his vision of the reunification and restoration of the united kingdom a real political expectation or a poetic, utopian image to preserve hope and motivate repentance?

[21]Thus said the Lord God: I am going to take the Israelite people from among the nations they have gone to, and gather them from every quarter, and bring them to their own land. [22]I will make them a single nation in the land, on the hills of Israel, and one king shall be king of them all. Never again shall they be two nations, and never again shall they be divided into two kingdoms. [23]Nor shall they ever again defile themselves by their fetishes and their abhorrent things, and by their other transgressions. I will save them in all their settlements where they sinned, and I will cleanse them. Then they shall be My people, and I will be their God. [24]My servant David shall be king over them; there shall be one shepherd for all of them. They shall follow My rules and faithfully obey My laws.

—Ezekiel 37:21–24

FURTHER READING

Halkin, Hillel. *Across the Sabbath River: In Search of a Lost Tribe of Israel.* Boston: Houghton Mifflin, 2002. An account of one man's travels, in our time, to seek the truth behind the legend of the lost tribes.

Heschel, Abraham Joshua. *The Prophets.* New York: Harper and Row, 1962, pp. 27–60. A classical study of biblical prophecy by a major twentieth-century religious thinker; these pages comprise his chapters on Amos and Hosea.

Hosea and Amos (biblical books, first of the Minor Prophets). A critical view of the Kingdom of Israel, written a few decades before its destruction.

Lau, Benjamin. *Jeremiah: The Fate of a Prophet*. Jerusalem: Koren, 2013, pp. 17–32. An analysis of the relations between Israel and Judah a century after the Assyrian conquest.

Van De Mieroop, Marc. *A History of the Ancient Near East*. Malden MA: Blackwell, 2006, pp. 216–52. A compact account of the rise and fall of the Assyrian Empire.

Walzer, Michael. *In God's Shadow: Politics in the Hebrew Bible*. New Haven: Yale University Press, 2012, pp. 89–108. A look at the prophets from the perspective of their messages on international relations.

7. The Babylonian Exile

THE DESTRUCTION OF THE FIRST TEMPLE, 586 BCE

HISTORY

The Assyrian Threat Comes and Goes

When the Northern Kingdom, Israel, rebelled against Assyria in 722 BCE (see chapter 6), King Ahaz of Judah had chosen a different course: he allied his kingdom with the Assyrians and emerged mostly unscathed. It took seventeen more years, until 705 BCE, for Judah to rebel against the ruling power; Ahaz's son King Hezekiah, supported by Egypt, joined forces with other small kingdoms in the region and rebelled against Assyrian domination.

The Assyrian king, Sennacherib, stamped out Judah's first rebellion, wrought widespread destruction throughout the country, and made the Judahites pay for their disloyalty. The treasures Hezekiah was forced to send to Sennacherib as punishment are described in 2 Kings 18:14–16.

However, for unknown reasons, Sennacherib then suddenly ended his campaign without conquering Jerusalem (2 Kings 18:13–19:37; Isaiah 36–7) and returned home.

This surprising sparing of Jerusalem took on an important role in the people's collective memory—and may have influenced their decision to revolt the next time rebellion was on the public agenda, a century later.

Hezekiah's son Manasseh, who ruled for fifty-two years, seems to have maintained loyal subservience to Assyria, as the Bible describes widespread idolatry during his reign. Nevertheless, his reign represented a continuation of the Davidic dynasty.

In 627 BCE, Ashurbanipal, king of Assyria, died, unleashing instability and disorder in the kingdom, which culminated in the rise of a new kingdom, the Chaldean or Neo-Babylonian Empire. At the same time, Egypt was gaining strength.

It is not surprising that in this geopolitical reality, Judah was thinking once again of rebellion. The power vacuum was already enabling Judah to assert its cultural/religious independence internally. The king of Judah at the time, Manasseh's grandson Josiah, took the initiative to reassert the Torah's authority, by shutting down local idolatrous shrines, refurbishing the Temple, and renewing neglected practices such as the Passover sacrifice (see 2 Kings 22–23).

Rebellion against Babylonia

Alas, the vacuum did not last. In 605 BCE, the newly ascendant Babylonian power defeated Egypt and destroyed a number of Philistine cities that had been allied with Egypt.

Observing these events, Judah's leaders were divided over the proper course of action.

The ruling families asserted the then dominant view: Babylonia's power would not last and in any case would not prevail against Judah, as the experience with the Assyrians just a century earlier (i.e., Sennacherib's miraculous departure in 705 BCE) had proved. Indeed, Babylonia's weakness was evident: after all, Egypt had defeated Babylonia in 600 BCE.

Like all vassal states, Judah had to pay an annual tribute to the ruling empire as a sign of subservience. Stopping payment would be an act of rebellion. If Judah were to cut off tribute payments and prepare for military resistance, the ruling families insisted, the people could count on God's support of their rebellion. Moreover, God might even view their continuing to pay tribute as doubting divine power and surrendering the nation's distinct sovereignty and identity.

The prophet Jeremiah articulated the opposing view. Rebellion was hopeless, he argued, because the current reality was already an expression of God's plan: Babylonian rule was a punishment for the Jewish people's sins of syncretism and social injustice. The people's proper course of action was to accept Babylonian rule while continuing King Josiah's reform and purification initiatives — for, after all, God's support would remain conditional on Judah's obedience to Torah law.

Covenant and Politics

The stakes in this debate were high and the risks not symmetrical. If the status quo continued, the people's relationship with God could be maintained through the sacrificial worship at the Jerusalem Temple — and a Davidic king would occupy the throne — but Judah would remain a vassal state, paying oppressive tribute. If, on the other hand, Judah were to rebel and fail, the Temple and its cult might well be destroyed and the Davidic dynasty discontinued, a catastrophe of cosmic dimensions.

Thus, the public debate "to rebel or not to rebel" was much deeper than a disagreement about policy and strategy. Fundamentally it was a conflict born of religious perspective, rooted in opposing understandings of God's role in history.

In 598 BCE, siding with those who insisted that the nation could rely on divine providence (probably in the form of Egyptian support) to defeat Babylonia, King Jehoiakim withheld the regular tribute payment to Babylonia.

In response, the Babylonians invaded Judah.

King Jehoiakim died just then. His eighteen-year-old son Jehoiachin succeeded him just in time to surrender and to be taken prisoner in Babylonia, along with his court and thousands of the military and economic elite. His uncle Zedekiah was placed on the throne as regent.

Zedekiah attempted to play the role of vassal to Babylonia while conspiring with Egypt to rebel. Unamused, the Babylonians invaded once again and in 587 BCE laid siege to Jerusalem. The city held out until the summer of 586 BCE, when the walls were breached and the Temple was destroyed. Zedekiah's sons were killed before his eyes; he was blinded and carried off in chains.

Because the conflict was so deep-rooted, an expression of the people's beliefs about God's role in history, its violent resolution had far-reaching ramifications in terms of personal faith, group identity, and political organization. In order to survive this catastrophic discontinuity, Judaism would have to reinvent itself.

Timeline: 722–586 BCE

722 The Assyrians destroy the Kingdom of Israel; the ten tribes are exiled/dissolved.

728 Hezekiah accedes to the throne of Judah (2 Kings 18).

714 Hezekiah's rebellion against Assyria is quashed (2 Kings 18).

705 Sennacherib besieges Jerusalem but suddenly and inexplicably lifts the siege and departs (2 Kings 19).

697 Manasseh succeeds his father Hezekiah as king and does "that which was displeasing to the Lord" (2 Kings 21).

642   Amon succeeds his father Manasseh as king and continues his pol-
      icies (2 Kings 21).

640   Josiah succeeds his father Amon as king; he does "what was pleas-
      ing to the Lord and he followed all the ways of his ancestor David"
      (2 Kings 22).

624   Josiah begins the repair and remodeling of the Temple, in the course
      of which a scroll is found. Its contents (unknown to us) engender a
      national project of soul-searching, suppression of idolatry, a pub-
      lic ceremony of renewal of the covenant, and a restoration of Pass-
      over observance. Many scholars believe that the scroll "found" in the
      Temple was the biblical book of Deuteronomy, which may have been
      composed for the occasion (2 Kings 22–23).

609   Josiah is killed in battle (against Egypt); his son Jehoahaz succeeds
      him but reigns for only three months; the Pharaoh deposes and
      imprisons him, placing his brother Jehoiakim on the throne (2
      Kings 23:28–37).

597   Jehoiakim dies. His successor, his son Jehoiachin, is deposed
      and exiled by the Babylonians, who place another son of Josiah,
      Zedekiah, on the throne (2 Kings 24).

588   Zedekiah rebels against Babylonia; Jerusalem is besieged (2 Kings 25).

586   The walls are breached; the king is captured, blinded, and exiled;
      the Temple is burned. The Babylonians appoint a local Jewish
      governor, Gedaliah, who is soon assassinated by remnants of the
      Judean royal family (2 Kings 25).

PRIMARY TEXT

Born in the village of Anatoth, just north of Jerusalem, in the 640s BCE, the
prophet Jeremiah was deeply involved in the historic events from King Josiah's reforms through the destruction of Jerusalem and the Temple. His book
of prophecies, personal confessions, and firsthand depictions of these tur-
bulent years conveys, multi-dimensionally, both the events and the spirit
of the times. According to Rabbinic tradition, Jeremiah also authored the
biblical Scroll of Lamentations, expressing the people's grief and heart-
break after the Temple's destruction.

Here, Jeremiah describes one of his dramatic confrontations with those
who favored rebellion against Babylonia:

Royal Family Tree of Judah, Seventh to Sixth Centuries BCE

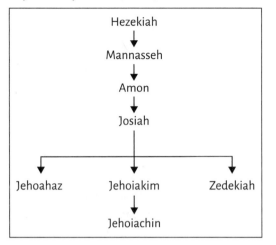

Jeremiah 26:1–24

---

¹At the beginning of the reign of King Jehoiakim son of Josiah of Judah, this word came from the Lord:

Under Jehoiakim, the first acts of rebellion take place.

²"Thus said the Lord: Stand in the court of the House of the Lord and speak to [the men of] all the towns of Judah, who are coming to worship in the house of the Lord, all the words which I command you to speak to them. Do not omit anything. ³Perhaps they will listen and turn back, each from his evil way, that I may renounce the punishment I am planning to bring upon them for their wicked acts.

Note: a theatrical protest—Jeremiah stands in the Temple court and prophesies its destruction.

⁴"Say to them: Thus said the Lord: If you do not obey Me, abiding by

the Teaching that I have set before you, ⁵heeding the words of My servants the prophets, whom I have been sending to you persistently— but you have not heeded— ⁶then I will make this House like Shiloh, and I will make this city a curse for all the nations of the earth."

Shiloh was the capital city before David established Jerusalem. It was in the territory of Ephraim—part of the Northern Kingdom destroyed in 722 BCE.

⁷The priests and prophets and all the people heard Jeremiah speaking these words in the House of the Lord. ⁸And when Jeremiah finished speaking all that the Lord had commanded him to speak to all the people, the priests and the prophets and all the people seized him, shouting, "You shall die! ⁹How dare you prophesy in the name of the Lord that this House shall become like Shiloh and this city made desolate, without inhabitants?" And all the people crowded about Jeremiah in the House of the Lord.

Note: the priests and prophets see Jeremiah's prophecy as blasphemy, and "the people" join the attack.

¹⁰When the officials of Judah heard about this, they went up from the king's palace to the House of the Lord and held a session at the entrance of the New Gate of the House of the Lord. ¹¹The priests and the prophets said to the officials and to all the people, "This man deserves the death penalty, for he has prophesied

Members of the aristocracy hold a public hearing at the Temple gate, at which the priests and prophets present their accusations—and Jeremiah argues in his own defense.

against this city, as you yourselves have heard!"

¹²Jeremiah said to the officials and to all the people, "It was the Lord who sent me to prophesy against this House and this city all the words you heard. ¹³Therefore mend your ways and your acts, and heed the Lord your God, that the Lord may renounce the punishment He has decreed for you. ¹⁴As for me, I am in your hands; do to me what seems good and right to you. ¹⁵But know that if you put me to death, you and this city and its inhabitants will be guilty of shedding the blood of an innocent man. For in truth the Lord has sent me to you, to speak all these words to you."

Note: "the people" have now changed sides.

¹⁶Then the officials and all the people said to the priests and the prophets, "This man does not deserve the death penalty, for he spoke to us in the name of the Lord our God."

¹⁷And some of the elders of the land stepped forward and said to the entire assembly of the people, ¹⁸"Micah the Morashtite, who prophesied in the days of King Hezekiah of Judah, said to all the people of Judah, 'Thus said the Lord of Hosts:
  Zion shall be plowed as a field,

And now a new argument is brought in Jeremiah's defense—that, a century earlier, a similar debate had

Jerusalem shall become heaps of ruins

And the Temple Mount a shrine in the woods.'

¹⁹"Did Hezekiah king of Judah, and all Judah, put him to death? Did he not rather fear the Lord and implore the Lord, so that the Lord renounced the punishment He had decreed against them? We are about to do great injury to ourselves!" . . .

²⁴However, Ahikam son of Shaphan protected Jeremiah, so that he was not handed over to the people for execution.

taken place, and the response of Hezekiah (a respected king) was not to punish the prophet, but to take his words to heart.

In any event, tensions apparently remain high and Jeremiah's life in danger, so he is rescued by friends.

Interestingly, this public political debate takes place in the Temple court. Jeremiah sets up his soapbox in the main place of assembly, where his message is most likely to be heard by the masses—and be most irritating to the leadership. From this "transcript" it is clear that Jeremiah was not alone in espousing his views. Rather, it seems that two parties were vying for the support of the masses:

The priestly establishment based its position regarding rebellion on the ideology that God's promise to David was unconditional and eternal: "Your house and your kingship shall ever be secure before you; your throne shall be established forever" (2 Samuel 7:16); therefore, the nation could count on God's protection. The Temple with its sacrifices was the lifeline protecting Israel and the Davidic kingdom from all evil, forever. God's presence dwelt in the Temple, which served as the contact point between Israel and God. To doubt this was blasphemy.

Jeremiah (like the prophets Isaiah, Amos, and Hosea before him) represented what has come to be called the Deuteronomic tradition. The book of Deuteronomy frequently reiterates the belief that God's favor to Israel — protecting the people against natural disasters and human enemies — is wholly a function of God's covenantal relationship with the people. Consequently, if the people failed to heed the Torah's commandments, collective punishment — drought, plague, conquest by enemies, exile from the land — would ensue. In this instance, the nation could only count on God's protection against Babylonian conquest if the people strictly adhered to the Torah and zealously rejected idolatry and injustice.

The establishment position had a supreme disadvantage. It saw the Temple's destruction as unthinkable — implying the failure of God, and undermining the whole system of belief. The Deuteronomic position, on the other hand, accommodated the possible destruction of the Temple — especially in view of the Northern Kingdom's experience. To Jeremiah and his cohorts, the loss of the Temple would lead not so much to a crisis of faith as to a crisis of conscience: What had we done to deserve this? What would we have to do now to undo it?

This polemic continued for a decade, in a number of colorful episodes narrated in the book of Jeremiah: a public confrontation between Jeremiah and another prophet, Hananiah, who takes the establishment position (Jeremiah 27–28); the king's demonstrative burning of a scroll of Jeremiah's prophecies (Jeremiah 36); and Jeremiah's being placed in the stocks (Jeremiah 20) and thrown into a dungeon (Jeremiah 37).

In the end, of course, Judah rebelled — and Babylonia crushed the rebellion. Davidic sovereignty, it turned out, was not eternal, and neither was God's house.

However, unlike the experience of the Northern Kingdom, the Judahites would not disappear. Both those exiled to Babylonia and those remaining in the land would succeed in regrouping, creating new institutions, and maintaining an identity (see chapter 8).

For those who, with Jeremiah, held to the covenant view of historical events, this outcome was deeply sad — but understandable, and offered hope for a future restoration, when God's punishment — and the people's repentance — would run their course. For the priestly establishment, however, this was the end.

LEGACY

Impact

Among the long-term effects of the destruction of the First Temple and the First Commonwealth are the following:

a) From this point on, the Jewish people came to understand its history through the covenant view / Deuteronomic lens. Once the unthinkable had happened—the Temple had fallen and the sacrificial cult been disrupted—the previously dominant priestly ideology became untenable. Henceforth, events were seen as acts in the ongoing drama of God's attempts to get Israel to hold up its side of the covenant. It was not always easy to live with this view, and there were attempts, over the centuries, to understand history differently. However, this remained the mainstream view.

b) A decentralized form of religious practice, of communication with God, had to be devised, in the absence of a Temple (and in view of the wide dispersion of the people). Though (as we will see in chapter 8), the Temple was actually rebuilt within the lifetime of some exiles, the very possibility of religious life without the Temple was established during this interim. Hence, while the Temple cult remained the ideal model of the relationship between God and the Jewish people, the foundation was laid for a replacement for the Temple: the synagogue (see chapter 12).

c) Living in exile became a constant in Jewish life from this point on. Significant Jewish communities were established outside the Land of Israel. While the Babylonians left much of the population and their local institutions in place, thousands—especially leadership elites— were forced into exile in Babylonia. Allowed to settle there and maintain a communal life, these exiles became the pioneers of a populous, prosperous, and culturally rich Jewish community. After the middle of the first millennium CE, Babylonia would eclipse the Land of Israel (despite the latter's ideological/religious hold) as the center of Jewish life. Even after the rise of European and North African centers beginning around 1000 CE, Babylonia remained an important community into the twentieth century (as Iraq).

d) Belief in a messiah who would restore the people to their rightful place began to develop. The logical conclusion of the covenant view of history was that restoration was to be expected; for example, Jeremiah (chapter 29) prophesied after the destruction: "⁴To the whole community which I exiled from Jerusalem to Babylon: ⁵Build houses and live in them, plant gardens and eat their fruit. . . . ⁷And seek the welfare of the city to which I have exiled you. . . . ¹⁰For thus said the Lord: When Babylon's seventy years are over, I will take note of you, and I will fulfill to you my promise of favor—to bring you back to this place."

At the time, the Jewish people perceived their new situation—the sudden loss of sovereignty and of the sacrificial cult that maintained their connection to God—as temporary. Deuteronomy and all the prophetic elaborations on it had emphasized that God would punish—but would also forgive. Affliction and exile were to teach the people a lesson, to bring them back to the covenant. Moreover, God had promised to David that his dynasty would rule forever (2 Samuel 7:16; also see chapter 5 in this volume). Therefore, the long-term prognosis was optimistic. The loss of sovereignty was an aberration that would pass when a new Davidic king would be anointed (*mashiach*, messiah). But when?

Once a few generations had gone by without the realization of this promise, the people's yearning for the messiah became institutionalized in the liturgy. Such prayer became a great source of strength and perseverance, a powerful sublimation of mourning for the lost utopia into hope for its restoration. However, time and again over the centuries, this sustaining hope led to misinterpretations of historical reality. Impatient (often desperately so) with the continuing exile, the people periodically put their faith in messianic pretenders, only to be disappointed each time (see chapters 11, 18, and 28).

Thus, much of what we know today as Judaism originated with the destruction of the Temple in 586 BCE:

· The centrality of the belief in the covenant as the engine of history
· The synagogue-based community
· Life in the Diaspora
· Belief in a messiah

Memory

Unlike the Assyrian exiles, after experiencing catastrophe the Judahites exiled to Babylonia succeeded in shoring up and maintaining a group identity through the generations. Over time they developed beliefs and practices to remember their experience and to keep the hope for restoration alive; for example:

- The fast of the Ninth of Av, commemorating the destruction of the Temple; and three minor fast days to remember events surrounding that disaster: the Tenth of Tevet, the Seventeenth of Tammuz, and the Third of Tishrei. For traditional Jews, the Ninth of Av is the only major full fast day in the calendar besides Yom Kippur. The period of three weeks from the Seventeenth of Tammuz until the Ninth of Av is a time of semi-mourning, which intensifies during the first nine days of Av, when, for example, meat is not eaten.
- Customs explained as signs of mourning for the destruction: for example, breaking a glass at weddings; always leaving a small section of the house unpainted.
- The inclusion of prayers for the restoration in the daily liturgy and in holiday observances, such as singing "Next year in Jerusalem" at the end of the Passover seder.
- A large literature of mourning and consolation, such as Isaiah 40, the biblical book of Lamentations, and Psalm 137: "By the rivers of Babylon, / There we sat, / Sat and wept, / As we thought of Zion."

TEXT FOR DISCUSSION

Simon Dubnow, a prominent twentieth-century historian (who perished in the Holocaust), seems to suggest that the exile was somehow part of Israel's mission rather than a punishment. What would the prophet Jeremiah say? Has history confirmed Dubnow's statement?

The providence of history . . . seemed to say: "Now you may go forth. Your character has been sufficiently tempered; you can bear the bitterest of hardships. You are equipped with an inexhaustible store of energy, and you can live for centuries, yea, for thousands of years, under conditions that would prove the bane of other nations in less than a single century. State, territory, army, the external attributes of national power, are for you superfluous luxury. Go out into the world to prove that a people can continue to live without these attributes."

—Simon Dubnow, *Nationalism and History* (Philadelphia: Jewish Publication Society, 1958), p. 262

FURTHER READING

Bright, John. *Jeremiah*. The Anchor Bible. Garden City NY: Doubleday, 1965, introduction and historical background. An overview of the history leading up to and through the destruction, based on biblical and non-biblical sources.

Heschel, Abraham Joshua. *The Prophets*. New York: Harper and Row, 1962, pp. 103–39. Heschel's study of Jeremiah.

Jeremiah, chapters 39-43. A description of Jewish life immediately after the destruction.

Lau, Benjamin. *Jeremiah: The Fate of a Prophet*. Jerusalem: Koren, 2013. A study of Jeremiah's prophetic career in historical context.

2 Kings, chapters 18-25.

Walzer, Michael. *In God's Shadow*. New Haven: Yale University Press, 2012, pp. 109-25. A discussion of how the nation understood and adapted to life in exile.

8. The Second Temple

HISTORY

Life Goes On

The Judean exiles' experience was quite different from that of the ten tribes.

For one thing, the Babylonians did not engage in large-scale exchanges of population, but only in removal of elites, to maintain control. Thus, while the destruction and exile had severe economic, political, and spiritual consequences, life continued in Judah. No foreign populations were imported, and most people were left on their land.

Moreover, the Babylonians did not seek to destroy the exiles' identity, but instead allowed them to settle together and maintain a community. Indeed, the exiled, deposed King Jehoiachin was ultimately released to house arrest and treated with the honor due a vassal king. Meanwhile, some Judeans were able to depart to the west and join existing Jewish settlements in Egypt.

Thus, the events of 586 BCE were traumatic, but they were not terminal. The nation was bruised but not erased.

In the aftermath of the destruction, the nation of Judah was able to regroup and rethink and reorganize—and thereby to survive as a nation with a distinct faith and a cultural identity. And they succeeded in doing this both in the Land of Israel and in their places of exile. The prophets, who had warned them before the catastrophe to obey God's laws in order to avoid punishment, now exhorted them not to lose hope, but to return to the law so that God would restore their land and Temple and sovereignty.

The major prophet of the exile was Ezekiel, who joined the first wave to Babylonia in 597 BCE and apparently lived out his life there. Besides prophecies of reproof, explaining and reminding the people why they were exiled, he also exhorted the exiles to reform, to believe, and not to lose faith, for a grand future awaited them (Ezekiel 37:21–23):

²¹I am going to take the Israelite people from among the nations they have gone to, and gather them from every quarter, and bring them to their own land. ²²I will make them a single nation in the land, on the hills of Israel, and one king shall be king of them all. Never again shall they be two nations, and never again shall they be divided into two kingdoms. ²³Nor shall they ever again defile themselves by their fetishes and their abhorrent things, and by their other transgressions.

And indeed, the destruction of the Temple did not end Jewish history.

Return and Rebuilding the Temple

Another upheaval in Mesopotamia, occurring just half a century after the destruction, seemed to give credence to the prophets' words. Cyrus the Great established the Achaemenid Empire, based in Persia, which swallowed Babylonia and expanded well beyond it—westward all the way to Libya. In 539 BCE the Land of Israel became part of this empire. As a matter of policy, the Persians ruled through alliances with local leadership and thus allowed a degree of autonomy among conquered peoples. Cyrus permitted the Jews who had been exiled to Babylonia to return to their land, to rebuild their Temple, and to reestablish their cult (but not, of course, their monarchy!).

This turned out not to be so simple, for several reasons:

- The Jews who had remained in Judah were poor and disorganized— not materially or spiritually ready for a historic restoration effort.
- The other peoples living in the land were not enthusiastic about the Jews' reestablishing any autonomous institutions.
- Life in Babylonia/Persia was good, and so most of the exiles' interest in returning was only theoretical.

The Persian period in the Land of Israel is notably lacking in textual evidence; our only sources are the biblical books dealing with these centuries, the prophets Haggai and Zechariah and the historical narratives of Ezra and Nehemiah. These accounts seem to telescope together events spread over at least a century, making the chronology hard to follow. The picture that emerges from a careful reading is this:

- *Shivat Tziyyon* (return to Zion) happened in some form during the first Persian century, from 539 to about 400 BCE.
- It took more than twenty years from Cyrus's decree for the Jews to build and dedicate a Temple in Jerusalem.
- In the course of this period, the cult was restored, and the Jews in Judah established some kind of local autonomy. Subsequent generations viewed this transition as a fulfillment of prophecy and as a new beginning—the opening of a distinctive era of history, the Second Temple period.

Ezra and Nehemiah

The prophetic books of Haggai and Zechariah are the only biblical texts that may date to the initial years of the return. Both claim to have been spoken/written during the early years of King Darius (~520 BCE). However, neither of them imparts much historical detail.

The main sources for events of this period are the books of Ezra and Nehemiah. Nehemiah was the cupbearer (server of wine) to King Artaxerxes of Persia (Nehemiah 1:10), which tells us something about the status of Jews in Persia at the time. If, as is generally thought, this reference is to Artaxerxes I, then Nehemiah's activity began around 445 BCE—almost a century after the initial return. His book describes his return to Jerusalem, with the king's support, and his efforts to rebuild and fortify the city and restore self-reliance, security—and Torah law. In Nehemiah 8 he refers to "Ezra the priest and scribe," who taught the law publicly and helped to restore ritual observance and endogamy.

In the book of Ezra, Ezra describes his delegation, by the same king, to return to Jerusalem and assist in rebuilding Jewish life there (Ezra 7). The first six chapters summarize the earlier history of the return, a century before Ezra's own lifetime: Cyrus's original decree and the initial response to the permission to return, which included construction of a basic structure for sacrificial worship, under the governor Zerubbabel and the priest Jeshua. The local populace (Samaritans and others) opposed the construction and lobbied the king to end it. The work appears to have stopped until

King Darius ascended the throne and reaffirmed Cyrus's original decree. And so, a Temple was built over the years 520–515 BCE.

The dedication ceremony is described in Ezra 6. Between the end of Ezra 6 and the beginning of Ezra 7 nearly a century elapses, and then the narrative of Ezra joins that of Nehemiah, describing their efforts on behalf of the Jews in the Land of Israel in the second half of the fifth century BCE.

At this juncture the historical account in the Bible ends — and no other sources describe the life of the nation in its land for the next two centuries.

Timeline: 597–332 BCE

597	The first wave of exiles leave for Babylonia, with King Jehoiachin (Jeremiah 52:28; 2 Kings 24).
586	Jerusalem is destroyed, generating a second wave of exile (Jeremiah 52:29; 2 Kings 25).
582	A rebellion against Gedaliah, who had been appointed governor by the Babylonians and who was assassinated by members of the Davidic royal family, leads to a third wave of exile (Jeremiah 40–41, 52:30).
582?	Some Judeans flee to Egypt, apparently joining others who had already settled there (Jeremiah 43–44).
562	King Jehoiachin is released from prison in Babylonia but kept in exile (Jeremiah 52:31–34).
551	Confucius is born.
539	Cyrus the Mede conquers Babylonia, the beginning of the Persian Empire in the region. Jews are allowed to return to their land (Ezra 1).
~538?	Returnees to Jerusalem begin rebuilding the Temple and offer sacrifices on the altar (Ezra 3).
~538?	Local resistance leads to cessation of the work on the Temple (Ezra 4).
522	Darius becomes emperor.
520	Work on the Temple resumes (Ezra 6).
515	The Temple is dedicated (Ezra 6:14–22).
~500–400	A Jewish community flourishes on Elephantine, an island in the Nile.

~445	Nehemiah, a Jewish officer in the court of the Persian king Artaxerxes, is permitted to go to Jerusalem as governor, to organize and fortify the city (Nehemiah 1–2).
428?	Ezra the priest is allowed to go to Jerusalem to lead a renewal of Jewish life, that is, the covenant (Ezra 7–10; Nehemiah 8).
384	Aristotle is born, in Greece.
332	Alexander of Macedon (Alexander the Great) conquers the Persian Empire, including the Land of Israel.

PRIMARY TEXT

There are several possibilities for the "turning point" marking the beginning of the Second Temple period: King Cyrus's decree; the laying of the Temple's foundation; the completion and dedication of the Temple; the renewal and rededication to the Torah under Ezra and Nehemiah. The description of the initial return and the excitement surrounding the renewal of sacrifices (in Ezra 1–3) is dramatic and informative and so seems an appropriate marker of beginning a new era.

Ezra 1:1–7, 2:64–65, 3:1–7,10–13

---

¹·¹In the first year of King Cyrus of Persia, when the word of the Lord spoken by Jeremiah was fulfilled, the Lord roused the spirit of King Cyrus of Persia to issue a proclamation throughout his realm by word of mouth and in writing as follows:

Jeremiah 29:10: "For thus said the Lord: When Babylon's seventy years are over, I will take note of you, and I will fulfill to you My promise of favor—to bring you back to this place."

²"Thus said King Cyrus of Persia: The Lord God of Heaven has given me all the kingdoms of the earth and has charged me with building Him a house in Jerusalem, which is in Judah. ³Anyone of you of all His people—may his God be with him,

Note: Cyrus by no means hints at any political independence or autonomy.

and let him go up to Jerusalem that is in Judah and build the House of the Lord God of Israel, the God that is in Jerusalem; [4]and all who stay behind, wherever he may be living, let the people of his place assist him with silver, gold, goods, and livestock, besides the freewill offering to the House of God that is in Jerusalem."

Note that it is taken for granted that not all will return and that those who stay behind will support the Temple project with material donations. No one seems surprised or concerned that the return was not universal.

[5]So the chiefs of the clans of Judah and Benjamin, and the priests and Levites, all whose spirit had been roused by God, got ready to go up to build the House of the Lord that is in Jerusalem. [6]All their neighbors supported them with silver vessels, with gold, with goods, with livestock, and with precious objects, besides what had been given as a freewill offering. [7]King Cyrus of Persia released the vessels of the Lord's house which Nebuchadnezzar had taken away from Jerusalem and had put in the house of his god. . . .

[There follows an inventory of the returned treasure, and a listing of the returnees.]

Interestingly, some of the returnees are listed by family/clan, while others are listed by the name of the town in Judah to which they were returning.

[2:64]"The sum of the entire community was 42,360, [65]not counting their male and female servants,

There is a wide range of estimates regarding how many Judeans were exiled and how many remained. We

those being 7,337; they also had 200 male and female singers. . . .

³:¹When the seventh month arrived—the Israelites being settled in their towns—the entire people assembled as one man in Jerusalem. ²Then Jeshua son of Jozadak and his brother priests, and Zerubbabel son of Shealtiel and his brothers set to and built the altar of the God of Israel to offer burnt offerings upon it as is written in the Teaching of Moses, the man of God. ³They set up the altar on its site because they were in fear of the peoples of the land, and they offered burnt offerings on it to the Lord, burnt offerings each morning and evening. ⁴Then they celebrated the festival of Tabernacles as is written, with its daily burnt offerings in the proper quantities, on each day as is prescribed for it, ⁵followed by the regular burnt offering and the offerings for the new moons and for all the sacred fixed times of the Lord, and whatever freewill offerings were made to the Lord. ⁶From the first day of the seventh month they began to make burnt offerings to the Lord, though the foundation of the Temple of the Lord had not been laid. ⁷They paid the hewers and craftsmen with money, and the Sidonians and Tyrians with food, drink, and oil

don't know how accurate Ezra's numbers are; the assumption, in any case, is that the returnees were a minority of the exilic community.

The seventh month is Tishrei; the first day is Rosh Hashanah.

Tabernacles = Sukkot.

At first, to avoid trouble with the locals (which indeed, came later) the returnees just set up an altar, so they could restore the cult without making too many waves. But then they moved forward.

to bring cedarwood from Lebanon by sea to Joppa, in accord with the authorization granted them by King Cyrus of Persia. . . .

Tyre and Sidon are on the coast of Lebanon.

[10]When the builders had laid the foundations of the Temple of the Lord, priests in their vestments with trumpets, and Levites sons of Asaph with cymbals were stationed to give praise to the Lord, as King David of Israel had ordained. [11]They sang songs extolling and praising the Lord, "For He is good, His steadfast love for Israel is eternal." All the people raised a great shout extolling the Lord because the foundation of the House of the Lord had been laid. [12]Many of the priests and Levites and the chiefs of the clans, the old men who had seen the first house, wept loudly at the sight of the founding of this house. Many others shouted joyously at the top of their voices. [13]The people could not distinguish the shouts of joy from the people's weeping, for the people raised a great shout, the sound of which could be heard from afar.

See Psalms 106:1, 136:1.

Generally when we speak of the Second Temple, we have in mind an image of the glorious edifice of Herod, from the Roman period, at the beginning of the Common Era. However, this text makes clear that the gap between the destruction of the First Temple and the beginning of the work on the Second Temple was less than a lifetime. The old men celebrating the laying of the foundation of the new Temple remembered the previous one and wept and rejoiced simultaneously. The First Temple stood for around 360 years; the Second Temple, in its various versions, lasted for nearly 600, until the Roman destruction of 70 CE (see chapter 10).

Some traditions see Zerubbabel, the governor of Judah under Persia who initiated the rebuilding, as a descendant of King Jehoiachin (a.k.a. Jeconiah; see 1 Chronicles 3:17–19). If so, then he was a scion of the Davidic dynasty, and it would have been possible for the people to see the full restoration as close at hand.

The prophecy of Haggai suggests, however, that the returnees were not so eager to rebuild the Temple. He tries to prod them to action (Haggai 1:2–4,10): "²Thus said the Lord of Hosts: These people say, 'The time has not yet come for rebuilding the House of the Lord.' ³And the word of the Lord through the prophet Haggai continued: ⁴Is it a time for you to dwell in your paneled houses, while this House is lying in ruins? . . . ¹⁰That is why the skies above you have withheld moisture and the earth has withheld its yield."

This glimpse of the returnees' priorities around 520 BCE, as well as Nehemiah's campaign for Sabbath observance a century later (Nehemiah 13:15–22), suggest that even after the trauma of the destruction and the exile, the nation persisted in the fickleness of its commitment to the covenant.

LEGACY

Impact

Perhaps the main long-term effect of the return to Zion was something that did not happen: the majority of the exiles in Persia, who had left Judah less than half a century earlier, did not return when the opportunity presented itself. Despite their expressions of mourning and sense of loss following the destruction and exile, in reality the Jewish people had rather quickly made a kind of peace with life in diaspora. The longing for restoration did not translate into a rush to actualize it; already at this early date, life in exile had become an acceptable alternative.

So, while the moment of exile in 586 BCE was the point at which all that came before was lost, the moment when the option of return and restoration was rejected can be seen as a new beginning. Jewish life in the Land of Israel would wax and wane over the next twenty-five hundred years, but never again would it be the whole story. The Babylonian community — and others—may have lived with an ideology of temporariness ("Tomorrow the Messiah will come and we'll all go back"), but their existence in the lands of their dispersion was permanent.

A corollary component of Jewish existence originating with the return to Zion was the sometimes comfortable and sometimes fraught relationship between the Jews of Israel and those of the Diaspora. Whether the center in Israel was weak or strong, it always held a geographical-historical-theological claim on the support and loyalty of diaspora Jewry. Just how strong a claim, and whether that claim extended to authority in interpretation of the law and in spiritual matters became a constant tension in Jewish life.

The Persian king's appointment of Ezra (see Ezra 7:12–26) and Nehemiah to serve as Jewish community leaders became an important precedent. Throughout the Middle Ages, diaspora Jewish communities were largely self-governing, with a dual authority structure: rabbis, who achieved their authority through knowledge of the Torah; and lay leaders (*parnasim*), usually wealthy individuals whose wealth (and power) made them of interest to the non-Jewish rulers of the land. In many cases, from Ezra and Nehemiah onward, the lay leaders' position of authority was rooted in the formal or informal support of the gentile king.

Memory

In our day, Jews do not commemorate the return to Zion liturgically or ceremonially. Nor do the books of Ezra and Nehemiah have a formal place in the liturgy or synagogue. Rather, the best-known remnant of the Persian period in later Jewish life is the holiday of Purim, which is based on the book of Esther. The book describes a rivalry between two courtiers of a Persian king, Haman and Mordecai the Jew. To eliminate Mordecai, Haman receives permission to have all the Jews in the kingdom killed. But Mordecai succeeds in placing his beautiful niece Esther in the royal harem. As queen she brings the matter to the king's attention and the tables are turned: the Jews are saved, and Haman and his supporters are destroyed. Despite its happy ending, the story highlights the moral emptiness of Persian culture (lots of alcohol!)—and the precariousness of Jewish life in exile. This biblical book may have served as an oblique criticism of those who were too comfortable to return to Israel when they could.

The custom of formal, regular, public reading of the Torah, with translation or explication, is traditionally credited to Ezra (Nehemiah 8:1–12). In the Torah itself, the only reference to public reading is in Deuteronomy 31:10–13, where Moses orders a public reading to be held every seven years. While Ezra's reading seems to be a one-time affair, later tradition views that event as setting the precedent for the custom of reading the Torah in public on the Sabbath, Monday, and Thursday, as well as for the practice of accompanying the reading with translation and commentary. This seems to constitute recognition of the need for explication and interpretation—in order to keep the Torah text alive and relevant for the community as the generations pass. Thus, the period of Ezra is remembered as the point at which Torah interpretation was established as a central practice and value in Jewish life.

Uncertainty and controversy surround the process and dating of the Bible's development and canonization. However, there is general scholarly consensus that the Torah—the Pentateuch, or Five Books, as we know it—achieved its final form by the time that Ezra staged his public reading, late in the fifth century BCE.

TEXT FOR DISCUSSION

Israeli Bible scholar Yehezkel Kaufman suggests that the return under King Cyrus was driven by "the longing for cultic holiness." If so, had the majority of exiles who chose not to return lost faith? Had they found a satisfactory alternative to the Temple cult? Were they satisfied with vicarious return through the committed minority?

> The prophet foretold a return to Zion which would be grand and miraculous, a cosmic event. But the actual return in the days of Zerubbabel, Ezra, and Nehemiah was a shabby affair, by grace of the heathen monarch and his officials. . . . The return to Zion was a product of the spirit of repentance which animated the nation, of the longing for cultic holiness. . . . Repentance had nurtured the wish to live according to God's will and the commandments of His law, which would be possible only in the land of Israel. The hope of complete political liberation was surely part of these aspirations. The piteous return to Zion was thought of merely as preliminary to the redemption. . . . But the move-

ment continued even when the dream of immediate political rebirth failed. It was nourished by the spirit of repentance and the yearning for cultic sanctity.

—Yehezkel Kaufman, *The Babylonian Captivity and Deutero-Isaiah* (New York: Union of American Hebrew Congregations, 1970), pp. 59–60

FURTHER READING

The books of Haggai and Zechariah, which date themselves to the period of Darius, just as the effort to rebuild the Temple was getting under way.

The books of Ezra and Nehemiah.

The book of Esther, which purports to describe Jewish life in Persia.

Myers, Jacob. *Ezra and Nehemiah*. The Anchor Bible. Garden City NY: Doubleday, 1964, pp. xix–xxxvii, lii–lxii. A concise overview of the history of the period and Ezra's and Nehemiah's accomplishments.

Walzer, Michael. *In God's Shadow: Politics in the Hebrew Bible*. New Haven: Yale University Press, 2012, pp. 109–25. A discussion of the Jewish adaptation to powerlessness as the key feature of exile.

9. Confronting the Challenge of Hellenism

THE HASMONEAN REVOLT, 167 BCE

HISTORY

Hellenism Comes to the Region

After centuries of being caught between the empires of Egypt and Meso-potamia/Persia, Alexander of Macedon's conquest of the whole region in 332 BCE brought the Jewish nation and the Land of Israel into a new cultural orbit, leading to significant innovations in Jewish thought and life.

Actually, what we now call Hellenization had begun in the previous century; even under Persian rule, the influence of Greek technology and culture was strongly felt along the eastern Mediterranean coast and farther east (as we know from the dominance of Greek goods in archaeological sites starting in the 400s BCE onward). Moreover, when Alexander Macedon ("Alexander the Great") established his capital in Persia and took a Persian wife, he saw himself as heir to both Greek and Middle Eastern civilizations and his role to unite them in his new empire. Hellenism was thus not simply the imposition of classical Greek culture in conquered territories, but a kind of fusion with local traditions.

Thus, while Alexander's conquest did not provoke cultural upheaval, it significantly changed the cultural landscape, and thereby ushered in a new era:

- Thousands of immigrants from Greece and southwestern Asia Minor—Greek soldiers, traders, and bureaucrats—brought with them governmental and educational institutions, religious beliefs, and material culture (e.g., dress, arts, architecture)
- Whereas Alexander expressed the desire to blend Greek and Middle Eastern culture, these Greek settlers largely viewed their own civilization as superior and accordingly gave preference in matters of trade and administration to locals who adopted Greek cultural mores.
- "Greek cities" (*polis*), established by Alexander and his successors, emerged in the conquered territories. Governed by an Athens-like

constitution and dominated by Greek immigrants, the polis featured institutions such as the *gymnasium* (for education and athletics) and temples (for worshiping the Greek gods). Acco (Ptolemais) and Gaza were early examples; later, Jerusalem too was granted polis status. A polis had jurisdiction over the rural territory around it, so its influence went beyond its walls.

- Greek became the language of public life, even though local languages continued to be used.

The infiltration of Hellenistic language, institutions, material culture, and beliefs was much more organized, assertive, and all-encompassing than had ever been the case with the various foreign cultural influences decried by the biblical prophets. And the world dominance of Hellenism, magnified by the sophistication and impressive accomplishments of its technology, governance, and educational institutions, increased the Jewish people's temptation to take it seriously.[3]

The Geopolitical Context

The arrival of Hellenism, however, did not diminish the ongoing power struggle between Egypt and Mesopotamia. Alexander's empire disintegrated upon his death, and after several decades of war, the situation stabilized into three kingdoms, each ruled by one of his generals or their successors: Ptolemy in Egypt, Seleucus in Syria, and Antigonus in Macedon.

This division did not bring peace. The Ptolemaic and Seleucid dynasties constantly struggled for dominance—and, of course, the Land of Israel remained a key battleground between them. However, since both powers were now part of the Hellenistic sphere of influence, a change in rule did not mean a radical change in culture.

Contemporary texts suggest that there were two hierarchies of leadership in Judea during this period: the hereditary high priesthood supplemented by its attendant bureaucracy—which the ruling powers recognized

3. While this chapter focuses on the political and religious vicissitudes of the Jews living in the Land of Israel during the Hellenistic period, that is not the whole story. Diaspora communities established by that time were also affected by this cultural wave. The best-known example is Alexandria, in Egypt, where a Jewish community arose around the time of Alexander's conquests and became wealthy and independent, developing its own unique synthesis of Judaism and Hellenism. The philosopher Philo (first century CE) was a "product" of this synthesis.

as the "official" leadership — and oligarchs who had amassed wealth and power as landowners, merchants, and tax collection contractors for the king. While the priesthood was committed to the Temple cult and Torah law, the oligarchs tended to embrace Hellenistic culture (not surprisingly, given the Hellenistic rulers' favor of locals who adopted their culture).

The Judeans' public life was punctuated by power struggles between these two sources of authority as well as by internal struggles within each. Various factions would ally themselves with either the Ptolemaic or the Seleucid kingdom, betting on the success of their particular patron.

Around 171 BCE, after a false rumor spread that the Seleucid king Antiochus IV had died while fighting in Egypt, the pro-Egyptian Judean faction in Jerusalem rose up against the Seleucid-backed High Priest Menelaus, attempting to replace him with their own candidate. Antiochus invaded, violently curbed the uprising, and restored order. Attempting to "pacify" Jerusalem, he established a military garrison in the city. Meanwhile, for unknown reasons, he instituted new policies that seemed aimed not just at repressing the rebellion, but at suppressing the Jewish religion itself: converting the Temple into a pagan shrine, plundering the Temple treasury, and prohibiting essential Jewish practices such as circumcision, the Sabbath, and the dietary laws.

These persecutions were not only inconsistent with Hellenistic ideology; they escalated a local power struggle into a war of liberation.

The Hasmonean Revolt

We don't know the backstory of Mattathias, a member of a priestly family from the town of Modi'in who is credited with initiating the uprising against Antiochus's provocative measures in 167 BCE. Our two main sources for the period, the books of 1 and 2 Maccabees, suggest that the people's revolt was essentially a struggle to reinstate the Temple religion and lift the bans on Jewish practice. As the text relates, "A Jew went up before the eyes of all of them to offer sacrifice as the king commanded, upon the altar of Modi'in. And Mattathias saw him, and was filled with zeal, and his heart was stirred, and he was very properly roused to anger" (1 Maccabees 2:23–24). This makes sense, since before Antiochus compromised the Temple's sanctity, more than two centuries had passed during which other conquering regimes (the Persians and Hellenists) largely respected that sanctity. On the other hand, reducing the ensuing war to an uprising of oppressed pious Jews against oppressing Seleucid Hellenists is almost certainly an oversimplification. While the religious struggle was real, it was also a "cover" for the various factions—priests and oligarchs, Ptolemies and Seleucids, and now Romans—as they continued jockeying for power.

Moreover, since the books of Maccabees were written when Mattathias's descendants were ruling the land, their depictions of the Maccabees as heroes of the struggle for religious and national independence shouldn't surprise us.

In later accounts, Mattathias is said to be descended from one Hasmonai, so many sources refer to the family as Hasmoneans. In 1 Maccabees 2:1–5, each of Mattathias's five sons is listed with a nickname. Judah's is "Maccabee." Since he assumed leadership after Mattathias's death, his name stuck, and the dynasty has since been referred to by both names, Hasmonean and Maccabee.

The Hasmoneans continued fighting intermittently from 167 BCE until 160/159 BCE, when the Seleucids, distracted by more serious rebellions elsewhere, allowed Jonathan (the fourth of Mattathias's five sons) to obtain, from a contender to the Seleucid throne, appointment as High Priest. Thus, the Hasmonean dynasty took over the high priesthood, becoming, nominally, the rulers of Judea.

Jonathan and his brother Simon, who succeeded him, managed to expand the territory under Judean rule to the coast and into Samaria. After another brief interlude of direct Seleucid rule, Simon's son John Hyrcanus and great-grandson Alexander Yannai continued to expand the empire, which ultimately included the coastal plain, the Golan Heights, and the whole east bank of the Jordan. Finally, in 67 BCE, civil war broke out between two Hasmonean factions, each led by one of two brothers—Aristobulus II and Hyrcanus II—who claimed authority. Both parties sought out Rome's support. General Pompey accepted Hyrcanus's invitation, marching into Jerusalem—and putting an end to the Hasmonean century.

Looking closely at the few texts we have about the Hasmonean revolt and rule, it appears that the revolt not only included battles against Seleucid forces, but also internal fighting among various factions within Judah. Moreover, while the rebels fought against the pagan desecration of the Temple and the ban on Jewish practices, they did not reject Hellenistic culture or practices or even foreign rule; indeed, they occasionally formed alliances with foreign powers, including the Seleucids. It is important to remember, too, that the Hasmoneans were priests—not descendants of David. Hence, the assumption of the title "king" by their later generations was highly controversial.

Timeline: 332–63 BCE

332	Alexander the Great conquers the region from Persia.
~301	Following Alexander's death in 323 BCE, his empire is divided into three kingdoms: Egypt and Syria/Palestine under Ptolemy, Mesopotamia and the east under Antiochus son of Seleucus, and Greece and Macedon under Antigonus. Palestine continues to be disputed in a series of wars between Ptolemy's and Seleucus's successors.
~250	Work begins in Alexandria on the Septuagint, the Greek translation of the Hebrew books that later became the Bible—as well as of some texts that weren't accepted into the biblical canon, collectively known as the Apocrypha. This will make the Bible accessible to Jews who don't know Hebrew and to gentiles and will serve as the basis for many translations into other languages.
200	As Egypt weakens, Seleucid rulers based in Antioch (Syria) conquer Palestine. Initially, Seleucid policy grants protection to the Jews and their religious institutions.
175	Antiochus IV Epiphanes returns from Roman exile to become king of the Seleucid empire. He appoints Jason as High Priest; under his rule Jerusalem is proclaimed a polis.
172	Menelaus bribes Antiochus to appoint him High Priest in Jason's place.
170–168	Antiochus invades Egypt twice; Roman intervention ultimately forces him to withdraw.
168–167	Meanwhile, a rumor that Antiochus has died encourages the pro-Egyptian faction of the Jews in Jerusalem to attempt to take over the city. Antiochus, very much alive and angry, returns from Egypt and brutally occupies Jerusalem. He sta-

tions a permanent garrison, bans key Jewish practices, plunders the Temple treasury, and converts the Temple into a pagan shrine.

166–164   A family of priests, the Hasmoneans (Maccabees), based in Modi'in, seventeen miles west of Jerusalem, leads an uprising against Seleucid rule and its local representatives and supporters. After a few years of guerilla warfare, Antiochus V, occupied with more serious challenges in the east, agrees to their terms, and the Temple is purified and rededicated. But hostilities continue on and off.

161   Judah the Hasmonean succeeds in establishing himself as king; he signs a treaty of alliance with Rome.

160   Seeing this expression of independence as unacceptable, the Selecucids invade and overwhelm the rebels. Judah is killed. The country returns to direct Seleucid rule.

152   Internal strife in the Seleucid Empire enables Judah's brother Jonathan to rise to power as High Priest in Jerusalem.

143   Jonathan is murdered. Another brother, Simon, succeeds him and continues his policies, playing rival Seleucid factions against one other to stay in power.

140   Simon exploits internal conflict in the Seleucid Empire to extract a commitment to Judean independence.

135   Simon dies; his son John Hyrcanus succeeds him.

134   Having consolidated his power, the Seleucid king Antiochus VII besieges Jerusalem, forces John Hyrcanus to capitulate, and restores direct Seleucid rule.

128   Renewed disorder in the empire allows John Hyrcanus to reassert independence.

104–78   Aristobulus succeeds his father John Hyrcanus but dies after a year, to be replaced by his son. Alexander Yannai rules as king and expands the kingdom, conquering the coast from Egypt to Lebanon, much of the Negev desert, and Transjordan.

76–67   Alexander's widow Salome (Shlomzion Alexandra) rules.

67–63   Salome's two sons Aristobulus and Hyrcanus vie for control. The power struggle between the factions loyal to each brother becomes a civil war.

63   Both brothers appeal to the Roman general Pompey for support. Marching from Damascus, Pompey sides with Hyrcanus, who opens the gates of Jerusalem for him. The Romans conquer the city.

Hasmonean Ruling Family Tree

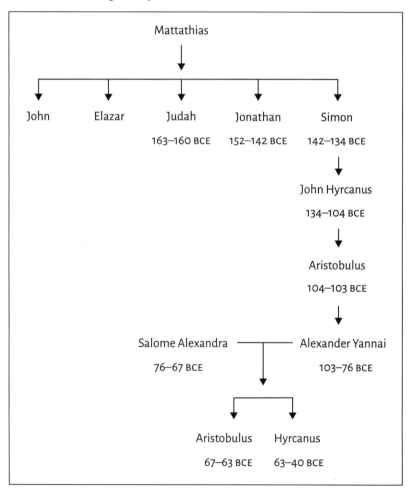

Note: Dates refer to years in power as ruler of Judea.

PRIMARY TEXT

Until the Bible was canonized in the first century CE, there were in circulation many more than the thirty-nine books of history, prophecy, and religious poetry that were ultimately included in the Hebrew canon. Some of
these were accepted in some versions of the Christian canon. The criteria
for canonization are not always clear; attempting to define them has kept
scholars busy for two millennia.

A subset of these books that appeared in the Greek translation of the
Bible (Septuagint)—1 and 2 Maccabees, Tobit, Judith, Ben Sira, and Susanna,
among them—collectively became known as the Apocrypha ("hidden" in
Greek). In most cases, since these books were not included in the Hebrew
canon, their Hebrew originals were not copied, became lost, and were
mostly unknown to the Jews until the modern period. These books were
preserved and passed down in Greek. The modern Hebrew term for them
is *sefarim chitzonim* (outside books).

The book of 1 Maccabees is thought to have been written originally in
Hebrew, in a style imitating the historical narratives of the Bible (e.g., Samuel, Kings), not long after the events it describes. It covers the story of the
Hasmoneans, from the provocations of Antiochus IV through the reign
of Simon (134 BCE). The book of 2 Maccabees is an abbreviation of a longer Greek work that focuses solely on the period of revolt (174–160 BCE).

---

1 Maccabees 2:15–41

---

[15]Then the king's officers who were forcing the people to give up their religion came to the town of Modin, to make them offer sacrifice. [16]And many Israelites went to them, and Mattathias and his sons gathered together. [17]Then the king's messengers answered and said to Mattathias, "You are a leading man, great and distinguished in this town, surrounded with sons and brothers; [18]now be

Today Modi'in is a modern city situated between Tel Aviv and Jerusalem.

Uncertainty remains as to what Antiochus actually did to suppress Judaism, as well as to the extent to which the revolt was a holy war as opposed to a rejection of foreign domination.

the first to come forward and carry out the king's command as all the heathen and the men of Judah and those who are left in Jerusalem have done, and you and your sons will be counted among the Friends of the king, and you and your sons will be distinguished with presents of silver and gold and many royal commissions."

[19]Then Mattathias answered and said in a loud voice, "If all the heathens in the king's dominions listen to him and forsake each of them the religion of his forefathers, and choose to follow his commands instead, [20]yet I and my sons and my brothers will live in accordance with the agreement of our forefathers. [21]God forbid that we should abandon the Law and the ordinances. [22]We will not listen to the message of the king, or depart from our religion to the right hand or to the left."

[23]As he ceased to utter these words, a Jew went up before the eyes of all of them to offer sacrifice as the king commanded, upon the altar of Modin. [24]And Mattathias saw him, and was filled with zeal, and his heart was stirred, and he was very properly roused to anger, and he ran up and slaughtered him

Note that the first casualty of the revolt is a Jew killed by another Jew. This hints at the fact that the conflict was not only a struggle against the Greek overlords, but also an internal matter.

upon the altar. ²⁵At the same time he killed the king's officer who was trying to compel them to sacrifice, and he tore down the altar. . . .

²⁷Then Mattathias cried out in a loud voice in the town and said, "Let everybody who is zealous for the Law and stands by the agreement come out after me." ²⁸And he and his sons fled to the mountains and left all they possessed in the town.

This appeal echoes Moses's words in the episode of the Golden Calf, "Whoever is for the Lord, follow me!" (Exodus 32:26).

²⁹Then many seekers for uprightness and justice went down into the wilderness to settle, ³⁰with their sons and their wives and their cattle, because their hardships had become so severe. . . . ³²And [the king's agents] pursued them in force and overtook them and pitched their camp against them and prepared to attack them on the Sabbath day. ³³And they said to them, "Enough! Come out and do as the king commands and you will live."

The rebels learn that in order to fight *against* the Greeks, they have to fight *like* the Greeks (i.e., on Saturday). In other words, even those who were most uncompromising in their rejection of the foreign culture would have to compromise their principles to preserve the faith.

³⁴And they said, "We will not come out nor do as the king commands, and break the Sabbath." ³⁵Then they hastened to attack them. ³⁶And they made no response to them; they did not throw a stone at them nor block up their hiding places. . . . ³⁸ . . . And they died . . . to the number of a thousand people. . . .

⁴¹On that day [Mattathias and his friends] reached this decision: "If anyone attacks us on the Sabbath day, let us fight against him and not all die. . . ."

Note that martyrdom—dying for one's belief—is not found in the Bible; this too might be a Hellenistic concept (cf. Socrates)!

Translation from Edgar J. Goodspeed, *The Apocrypha—An American Translation* (New York: Random House, 1959), pp. 379–81

Even though this text may describe mythical events, and even though it was lost to the Jews for hundreds of years, the picture it presents reflects how the nation remembered the Hasmonean revolt through the centuries. Allusions to the revolt found their way into later midrashic literature and into the liturgy. The story became one of a twofold struggle:

- Pious Jews, zealous for the purity of their faith, fighting their fellow Jews who had adopted Hellenistic culture with its pagan religion.
- An oppressed nation rising up against a cruel foreign conqueror.

Indeed, both elements were present, but there were others that the collective memory preferred to forget:

- Internal power struggles among priestly and oligarchic aristocracies.
- Even the most extreme rejectionists of Hellenism could not avoid absorbing its influences (such as fighting their enemies on the Sabbath).

LEGACY

Impact

The complex and ambivalent encounter between the Jewish nation and Hellenistic culture that reached a sort of climax in the Hasmonean century can be seen as foreshadowing the encounter between Judaism and Western culture for all the centuries to come. There were instances of extreme assimilation (e.g., young men who had themselves uncircumcised so as not to be embarrassed at athletic competitions) and radical rejectionism (as expressed in stories like that of Eleazar, who we learn in 2 Maccabees 6 preferred martyrdom to even giving the impression of eating pork).

However, between these poles there was a subtle, long-term accommodation—an ongoing process of trying to sort out which aspects of Hellenistic culture to accept and which to reject. Judaism and the Jews did not disappear into Hellenistic culture, but neither did they remain uninfluenced: Hebrew absorbed dozens of Greek loan-words; concepts from Greek philosophy and religion challenged and influenced Jewish thought (e.g., the belief in life after death); and indeed, the establishment of the holiday of Hanukkah as a victory commemoration (not commanded in the Torah) can be seen as a manifestation of Hellenistic influence.

The struggle for religious autonomy also became entangled with national identity and the aspiration for political sovereignty—an entanglement that continued during the Roman period (see chapter 10).

The Hasmoneans' campaigns of conquest also exacerbated the already fraught relationship between the Jewish and gentile populations in the region. The Jews had always lived side by side with other nations and religions in the Land of Israel (see chapters 5, 6, and 8) who did not share the vision of a divinely ordained Jewish hegemony in the land and hence often fought to undermine it. The Hasmonean rulers were guided by this vision of hegemony as well—and had the power to enforce it, even to the point of forcibly converting conquered nations to Judaism (e.g., the Edomites in the south).

Internally, the Hasmonean period saw the emergence of a variegated mosaic of approaches to interpreting the Torah covenant for application in the people's contemporary reality. What we know of this early development is gleaned from some limited references in the Apocrypha and from memories preserved in Rabbinic literature from at least three centuries later. The earliest explicit description appears in the writings of the late first-century CE historian Josephus Flavius. He identified three "parties" as having played significant roles in this process over the preceding two centuries (though it seems likely that each "party" comprised various subdivisions defined by ideological fine points and familial and political loyalties):

- Pharisees (Perushim: "those set apart," or perhaps, "interpreters")
  who claimed the right to interpret and adapt the Torah according to

various oral traditions and analytical methods; they also believed in reward/punishment in a future life.

- Sadducees (*Tzedukim*: descendants of Tzadok the priest [?]) who insisted on the literal meaning of the Torah without any human interpretive authority and who denied the immortality of the soul. They were members of wealthy priestly families.
- Essenes (*Isi'im*: etymology unclear), ascetics who lived apart in closed communities in order to preserve their standards of piety and purity.

Ultimately, the Pharisaic approach became dominant, and the Rabbinic leaders who emerged after the revolts against Rome (see chapters 10–12) saw themselves as the "heirs of the Pharisees," authorized to establish the "correct" interpretation of the covenantal demands—what came to be called *halakhah* (the way).

Meanwhile, other approaches beyond these three flourished during the Hasmonean period, including apocalyptic literature, which sought to understand the messianic meaning of historical events (the one example that entered the Hebrew canon is the book of Daniel); and Wisdom Literature, an ancient Middle Eastern genre with a fatalistic tone that appears in the Bible in Proverbs, Job, and Ecclesiastes; for example, Ecclesiastes 3:1: "A season is set for everything, a time for every experience under heaven."

Memory

The only major Jewish holiday not mentioned in the Bible is Hanukkah (= dedication), which celebrates the Temple's rededication after the Maccabees' first victory in 164 BCE. As described in 2 Maccabees 10, the first Hanukkah was a delayed celebration of the fall Sukkot festival; the Jews had missed the holiday because of the Temple's profanation, so as soon as it was purified they held a "make-up" Sukkot in December.[4] Subsequently the Maccabean leadership decreed that the holiday be observed annually as a victory celebration. Later, tensions developed between the Pharisees and the Hasmonean rulers; since the Hasmoneans were priests and not descended from David, the Pharisees perceived them as usurpers

---

4. Solomon (1 Kings 8) had dedicated the Temple—and Zerubbabel (Ezra 3) the reconstructed altar—during Sukkot.

of the Davidic throne (which might help explain why the books of Maccabees didn't make it into the Bible). The Pharisees then offered other rationales for the obligation to observe Hanukkah —the best known, from the Talmud (*Shabbat* 21b), being that it celebrated the miracle of a one-day supply of consecrated oil that kept burning in the Temple's "eternal lamp" for eight days.

In the past century, Hanukkah has taken on increased importance grounded in modern re-readings of the Hasmonean story. In the Zionist movement and then in the State of Israel, it has become a celebration of nationalism and military valor. In North America, it signifies the quest for religious freedom (and serves as the Jewish seasonal equivalent to Christmas).

TEXT FOR DISCUSSION

Traditionally, the Hasmoneans were seen as heroes, and the "Hellenizers" as assimilationists, betrayers of the covenant. However, in more modern times some Jewish leaders—among them Max Nordau, a close associate of Theodor Herzl in the Zionist movement—told the story differently. Could it be that the dichotomy is indeed not so simple?

> Let us take up our oldest traditions. Let us once more become deep-chested, sturdy, sharp-eyed men. . . . For no other people will gymnastics fulfill a more educational purpose than for us Jews. It shall straighten us in body and in character. . . . Our new muscle Jews have not yet regained the heroism of our forefathers who in large numbers eagerly entered the sports arenas in order to take part in competition and to pit themselves against the highly trained Hellenistic athletes.
>
> —Max Nordau (1849–1923), from a speech at the Second Zionist Congress, 1898, translation in P. Mendes-Flohr and J. Reinharz, eds., *The Jew in the Modern World: A Documentary History* (New York: Oxford University Press, 1980), pp. 547–48

FURTHER READING

Bickerman, Elias. *From Ezra to the Last of the Maccabees*. New York: Schocken Books, 1962. The classic modern study of this period; brief and accessible.

Cohen, Shaye. *From the Maccabees to the Mishnah*. Philadelphia: Westminster, 1987. A survey of the developing beliefs and institutions of Judaism during the Second Temple and early Rabbinic periods.

1 and 2 Maccabees in the Apocrypha.

Hayes, John, and Sara Mandell. *The Jewish People in Classical Antiquity*. Louisville KY: Westminster John Knox Press, 1998. Chapters 1 and 2 present a clear and detailed account of the Hasmonean century, with attention to the larger geopolitical context.

Hengel, Martin. *Jews, Greeks, and Barbarians*. Translated by John Bowden. London: SCM Press, 1980, pp. 49–126. A careful attempt to describe the meaning and impact of Hellenization.

Josephus Flavius. *Wars of the Jews*, book 2, chap. 8; *Antiquities of the Jews*, book 13, chaps. 10, 16; book 18, chap. 1. Josephus's descriptions of the Pharisees, Sadducees, and Essenes.

10. Roman Rule

HISTORY

Roman Rule

For over a century, calm largely prevailed in Roman-ruled Judea. Rome granted a degree of autonomy. The Temple cult functioned. There were no serious rebellions (only a few minor episodes). And, in some periods, Jewish kings—Herod, his son Archelaus, and his grandson Agrippa—ruled all or part of Judea. Indeed, Herod's long rule (37–4 BCE) was marked by territorial expansion, prosperity, and massive construction. Herod restored to Judea much of the area previously conquered by Alexander Yannai—from Gaza in the southwest to the Golan in the northeast—and added extensive territory beyond the Golan to the east. Efficient trade in this large kingdom (Herod built the important seaport of Caesarea) led to prosperity. Moreover, Herod rebuilt the Temple in Jerusalem on a grandiose scale. The "Temple Mount" we know today is an artificial platform he built by raising and extending the natural hill. Contemporaries of Herod's Temple described it as one of the "wonders of the world."

Nevertheless, the bottom line remained: Judea was not independent. Even the Jewish kings governed at the behest of the Roman emperor.

Still, national independence was not a widespread aspiration. Certain factions chafed at the situation and occasionally attempted the unsuccessful rebellion, but equilibrium was more or less maintained—that is, until the 50s and 60s CE, when a succession of procurators (Roman governors) ruled with such incompetence and greed that popular unrest took root and spread.

Finally, in 66 CE, the resistance boiled over into an organized military campaign. The Romans were forced to bring in reinforcements. In the course of two years, the Romans succeeded in suppressing the revolt in the Golan, Galilee, and coastal regions, leaving Jerusalem and environs in rebel hands. This stalemate lasted almost two years (apparently due to the

Romans' distraction by political upheaval at home). Finally, in the spring of 70 CE, the Roman general Titus set out to crush the rebellion by conquering Jerusalem. After a siege lasting four months, the Roman forces breached the walls, massacred the city's inhabitants, and destroyed the Temple.

The capital's fall and the Temple's destruction in 70 CE marked the end of an era, but not exactly the end of the war. It took the Romans until 73 CE to mop up nests of resistance in several desert strongholds, the last of which was Masada.

In the aftermath, the Romans elevated Judea to the status of a full province. This meant that the governors were of senatorial rank—aristocrats more likely to be competent and honest than the petty and often venal bureaucrats who had ruled before the revolt. The Romans also left the Tenth Legion (about five thousand men) garrisoned in Jerusalem, to maintain control.

Jewish Factions

As we saw in the revolts against Babylonian and later Seleucid rule, so too in the Roman period there was no consensus among the Jews as to how to deal with the ruling power. A number of factors came into play, and it is difficult if not impossible to tease them apart:

- Class conflict, and the conflicting interests of oligarchic families, Roman bureaucrats, peasants, and city-dwellers
- Roman imperial interests and local aspirations for national independence
- The struggle for power among various elites: priests, Hasmoneans, oligarchs
- The Romans' perceived interference in the Temple cult (e.g., Caligula's decree to install his statue in the Temple)

Josephus's three "parties" (Pharisees, Sadducees, and Essenes; see chapter 9) continued their importance through this period. In addition, other factions joined the conversation:

- Zealots: Groups who at various times rejected any compromise or acquiescence and tried to push—or force—their fellow Jews toward violent rebellion against Rome.

- The Qumran community (Essenes?—there is some controversy over this identification): Apparently a number of ascetic communities rejected the entire religious-political "marketplace" in order to devote themselves to lives of purification and contemplation—and preparation for the apocalypse. The best known of these was at Qumran, near the northwestern shore of the Dead Sea, where a trove of ancient scrolls (the Dead Sea Scrolls) was found in the 1940s and is still being deciphered.
- Christians: Before Christianity evolved into a distinct religion, competing with Judaism for converts among the pagans, a faction of the Jews believed that Jesus of Nazareth (who was executed by the Roman authorities in the early 30s CE) was the Messiah destined to lead the restoration of Judean independence under a Davidic king.
- Perhaps the silent majority: Those who simply tried to get along and get by—to maintain Jewish faith and national identity while accepting and enjoying the benefits of Roman rule. Josephus (see below) might be seen as an example of this accommodationist approach.

Except for the Zealots, there doesn't seem to have been a clear correspondence between the factions and positions regarding rebellion or compromise. But when the dust settled, the people's defeat and the destruction of the Temple led to the disappearance of the Sadducees (since the priesthood had become irrelevant) and the Zealots. Over the next few centuries, those who assumed the "mainstream" leadership of Judaism saw themselves as continuing the heritage of the Pharisees. The Christians ultimately split off, becoming an independent religion.

Consequences

The war was brutal and costly. Thousands of Judeans were killed in battles, sieges, massacres, and executions; thousands more were sold into slavery. (It was common Roman practice to sell war captives as slaves; slave labor was important in the Roman economy.) Many towns were destroyed, orchards uprooted, fields and silos burned or plundered. And, of course, Herod's beautiful Temple complex was torn down.

Nevertheless, it seems that within a generation, the land and its inhabitants had largely recovered. Towns were rebuilt, and the scars in the landscape healed. Most of the population remained in place and returned to their former routines. Many of those taken slaves were redeemed.

It is important to note that while telling the story of the Second Temple's destruction, Jews commonly speak of "destruction and exile," but in reality there was no forced mass exile after the Great Revolt. Whereas some Jews who found their way to the far reaches of the Roman Empire over the coming centuries arrived as slaves, most were economic migrants seeking a better life, especially after the Bar Kokhba revolt (see chapter 11).

In the short and long term, the main impact of the defeat was the loss of both the Temple and its cult—and consequently the need to develop an alternative spiritual center. This need led to significant, permanent changes in Jewish belief and practice.

Timeline: 63 BCE–73 CE

63 BCE	In the civil war between the Hasmonean brothers Hyrcanus and Aristobulus, Pompey intervenes on behalf of Hyrcanus, destroying the walls of both the Temple and the city, punishing the losing party, taking control over Hasmonean cities, and appointing Hyrcanus as High Priest and "ethnarch" (ruler—but not king).
63–40 BCE	Aristobulus and sons' continued efforts to regain control cause intermittent civil war throughout the period—and lead Rome to aggressively intervene in local government (e.g., destroying fortifications, dividing the area into sub-provinces, abrogating the High Priest's civil authority).
47 BCE	Julius Caesar wins in his struggle against Pompey, visits Judea, and affirms Hyrcanus's office as both High Priest and ethnarch. A degree of autonomy is restored; the Temple walls are rebuilt. At the same time, Caesar appoints as procurator (governor) Antipater, an oligarch from Idumea (Edom, south of Judea, which John Hyrcanus had annexed to Judea; see chapter 9).
44 BCE	Caesar is assassinated. Chaos ensues in the Roman government.
40 BCE	The Parthians (successors to the Persian Empire) conquer the region from Rome. Antipater's son, Herod,

escapes to Rome, where Mark Antony names him king of Judea. Herod returns as a Roman ally, raises an army, and embarks on a campaign to expel the Parthians and consolidate his own rule.

37 BCE   This is the year generally given as the beginning of Herod's rule. Antony eliminates Antigonus, the last Hasmonean pretender. Still, Herod, who is neither a priest nor a descendant of David, must contend with strong local opposition, which he puts down violently over the next seven years.

4 BCE   Herod dies. After crushing outbreaks of mob violence, his son Archelaus becomes ruler of Judea (including Samaria, Idumea, and the central coast).

6 CE   Emperor Augustus, founder of the Roman Empire, accuses Archelaus of having abused his power and deposes him. Augustus makes Judea and Samaria a minor province of the empire, ruled by procurators sent from Rome.

40 CE   Emperor Caligula attempts to have his statue installed in the Temple. Unrest ensues. His efforts ultimately fail.

44–66 CE   A succession of seven procurators, most apparently characterized by incompetence, greed, and/or cruelty, contend with a rising tide of popular discontent and escalating violent resistance.

66 CE   War breaks out. Along with military confrontations with Roman troops, violence breaks out between Jewish and pagan communities as well as between the radical rebels and the more moderate leadership of both the priests and the Pharisees.

70 CE   Titus besieges Jerusalem for four months. The city falls. The Temple is destroyed.

73 CE   The last outpost of the rebels, Masada in the Judean Desert, falls.

PRIMARY TEXT

The most complete account of we have of the Roman period in Judea, by far, is the Jewish historian Josephus Flavius (see "Memory" below). Internal Jewish writings from this period contain scattered descriptions of particular events that read as polemic exaggerations or simply folktales. But even if these are not scientific, they remain important for understanding how the Jews perceived and interpreted their experiences.

One of the best-known episodes of the time is chronicled in the Babylonian Talmud and parallel sources. This means that the text was compiled in the fifth century CE, about four hundred years after the events described. As with biblical texts encountered in previous chapters, we cannot prove that the events actually occurred as recounted here. But this story truthfully articulates how the Jews have always understood the revolt and its impact.

Babylonian Talmud, *Gittin* 56a–b

The *biryonim* were then [in the city]. The Rabbis said to them, "Let us go and make peace with [the Romans]," but they wouldn't let them, saying, "Let us go and fight them."

The Rabbis said to them, "You cannot succeed." So [the *biryonim*] arose and burned the supplies of wheat and barley, and there was a famine.

Abba Sikra, the head of the *biryonim* in Jerusalem, was the nephew of Rabbi Yochanan ben Zakkai, who invited him to meet in secret. When he came, [the rabbi] said to him, "How long will you continue thus—until you have killed everyone by starvation?"

He answered, "What can I do? If I say anything to them they will kill me!"

Here the Rabbis are set against the Zealots, called *biryonim* = "violent ones." The moderates seem to be opposed based on political realism; they think the uprising is hopeless and hence counterproductive. The Zealots turn on the moderates to undermine their authority and push the people to desperation.

The struggle between radicals and moderates echoes that in Jeremiah's time (see chapter 7). This secret meeting recalls the encounter between prophet and king described in Jeremiah 38:14–27.

Not surprisingly, there are family ties between leaders of opposing fac-

"[The rabbi] said, "Give me a plan to escape, maybe I can still save something."

He answered, "Pretend to be sick, so that everyone will come to visit you, and put something foul-smelling near you, so that they will say you have died. Let your students—but no one else—carry your coffin. . . ."

He did so, and Rabbi Eliezer carried him on one side, and Rabbi Yehoshua on the other. When they got to the gate, [the rebel sentries] wanted to stab him [to verify his death], but they said to them, "[The Romans] will say, 'They stabbed their rabbi!'" Then they wanted to give him a shove, but they said, "They will say, 'They shoved their rabbi!'" So they opened the gate for him and he escaped.

When he came to [Vespasian], he said, "Peace to you O King, peace to you O King!"

He answered, "You deserve death twice: Once because I am not the king and you addressed me as king! And again, because if I am king, why did you wait until now to come to me?"

tions. These lead to a creative "solution" to the internal conflict.

Even in times of siege, burial took place outside the city walls.

Emperor Nero sent the Roman general Vespasian to quell the revolt. When Nero died, a chaotic period in Rome ended with Vespasian being proclaimed emperor in absentia. He left for Rome and left the conclusion of the war in Judea to his son Titus.

He said, "You say you are not king,
but you must be a king, because
if you were not a king Jerusalem
would not be delivered into your
hand [as we know from biblical
verses]. . . . And regarding your
question, 'If I am king why hav-
en't you come to me until now?' the
biryonim wouldn't let me."

. . . At that moment a messenger
came to him from Rome, and said,
"Arise, for the emperor has died,
and the leaders of Rome have chosen you as head."

. . . [Vespasian] said, "I must go
now, and another will take my
place. But ask of me what I can give
you."

He said, "Give me Yavneh and its
wise men."

Yavneh was (is) a town near the
coast, west of Jerusalem (between
Jaffa and Ashkelon). It was a mixed
city (Jewish/pagan) and may have
been a site where the Romans
interned Jews who surrendered to
them; if so, then our story may be a
later attempt to put a positive spin on
this reality.

This story conveys the major transition in the life of the nation after
the fall of Jerusalem: the development of a long-term "replacement" for
the Temple and its cult. Recognizing that the revolt is both unstoppable
and doomed, Rabbi Yochanan and his colleagues prepare for the day after.

While the escape, and the conversation with Vespasian, may well not be
factual, the development of a new center where Pharisaic scholars began
adapting Judaism to its new circumstances does seem to reflect historical
reality. The Sanhedrin, the central legislative/judicial body that had con-

vened in the Temple complex, now moved to Yavneh, where it continued to function, though only with respect to matters not in the purview of Roman law. (Among the significant matters within its authority was control of the calendar—declaring the date of the new moon, setting leap years).

Rabbi Yochanan ben Zakkai, who lived approximately 30–90 CE, appears in Rabbinic literature as a key transition figure: the teacher of a generation of disciples who dominated the process of developing the Oral Law in the wake of the Temple's destruction. After the Zealots disappeared (it actually took a few generations—see chapter 11), those who advocated for—and institutionalized—limited autonomy, while accommodating to Roman rule, came to dominate the Jewish nation.

Note that by the time this account was written down in the Talmud, Rabbi Yochanan's disciples[5] had consolidated their leadership of the communities in both the Land of Israel and Babylonia—a process that took several centuries. Our story skips over the process, projecting fifth-century reality back onto first-century events and personalities.

LEGACY

Impact

The destruction of the First Temple by Babylonia had been a major turning point in Jewish history, creating both the need to function without the Temple cult and a model of life in exile (see chapter 7). Having learned that exile and destruction were real and not just theoretical possibilities, the nation was forced to develop institutions for living in this new reality (e.g., prayer in place of sacrifice, synagogue in place of Temple). Fifty years later, however, the sacrifices had been restored in Jerusalem.

Looking back from 70 CE, sacrificial worship in the Temple had continued for a thousand years—from Solomon to Titus—with only a brief interruption under Babylonia. On the one hand, the destruction of the Second Temple was deeply traumatic, a spiritual crisis; on the other hand, the possibility of such a destruction—and tools for surviving it—were already part of the nation's collective memory. Thus, the nation was able to build on the initial responses from the previous catastrophe (e.g., diaspora

5. Various terms are used to denote this leadership group: in Hebrew, *Rabbanim* (masters), *Chachamim* (wise ones), *Chazal* (acronym for "wise ones of blessed memory"); in English, Rabbis or sages.

institutions, synagogues, prayer, faith in a messiah), creating new institutions to sustain Jewish life both in the Land of Israel and in the Diaspora.

- The sacrificial service in the Temple was replaced with the institution of personal and communal prayer in the synagogue—a local community-based sanctuary that could exist in Israel or abroad and was controlled by local lay leaders and scholars, not priests. The transition was far from instantaneous; it would take a couple of centuries for the synagogue to become established as the long-term replacement for the Temple. In some cases, the role of prayer as a replacement for sacrifice was explicit; for example, the schedule of formal prayer services followed (and continues to follow) the structure of the daily and holiday Temple sacrifices. In other cases, the synagogue liturgy served to preserve the memory of the Temple service, through recitation of the rules for and descriptions of the Temple ritual.
- Over the next few centuries, the nation transitioned from national sovereignty (under the Hasmoneans) or partial autonomy (under Rome) to the local community as the unit of political, religious, and social organization. A new kind of leadership emerged in the absence of priestly and royal hierarchies: the Rabbis, who continued the Pharisaic methods and traditions for interpreting and applying the laws of the Torah to the ever-changing circumstances of life. Their teachings came to be referred to as the Oral Law—as distinguished from the Written Law, the original text of the Torah.
- If the synagogue was the "portable Temple," then this accumulating body of Oral Law (also referred to as the *halakhah*, "the way") was the portable homeland—an all-encompassing system of norms for personal and communal behavior, effective everywhere, rooting every aspect of life in the Torah.
- Despite these adaptations, and despite the Jews' developing attachment to their diaspora homes, consciousness of being in a state of exile remained a central element in Jewish identity. Those who stayed in Judea, as well as those who scattered throughout the world, understood that the nation was in "time out" from the ideal harmony of God-Torah-people-land. This sense of temporariness and the expectation and hope of restoration became central to Jewish belief.

Another legacy of the Great Revolt was the flowering of the western Diaspora. Although there was no mass forced exile, the decline of Judea and the development of its links to Rome led many Jews to resettle within various territories of the empire in North Africa and Europe. (In the course of the coming millennium, these communities would grow and prosper, so that by 1000 CE the centers of Jewish life would be in Europe, North Africa, and Babylonia—and not Jerusalem.)

Memory

Joseph ben Mattathias, an aristocrat of priestly descent from Jerusalem, was charged with organizing and commanding the struggle against Rome in the Galilee. As he attests, he had mixed feelings about the wisdom of rebelling, but he did his job, commanding the resistance at the fortified village of Yodfat, the first major battle of the war, in 67 CE. When Vespasian's forces overran the town, Joseph surrendered. Enslaved and then freed by Vespasian, he took on Vespasian's family name, becoming Josephus Flavius. He then proceeded to write a detailed and carefully researched history of the Jews, retelling the biblical account from Creation to Ezra, then continuing through the Hasmonean and Roman periods, up to his own time. While he had an apologetic agenda, and not always reliable sources, on the whole scholars consider him to be a serious and trustworthy historian, and his works constitute our main source of information on his era.

Written in Greek, his works were not in the Jewish library until the modern period, though bits and pieces of them found their way into medieval Jewish texts. The story of the siege of Masada, for example, so much a part of modern Jewish consciousness, is found only in Josephus's history, not in any Rabbinic text. The Jews of the Middle Ages wouldn't have known about it.

Titus erected a triumphal arch containing depictions of his troops carrying off the sacred objects of the Temple, in Rome—where it still stands. There is a Jewish folk tradition of refusing to walk under that arch.

When Herod rebuilt the Temple, his engineers erected the structure on a large platform supported by retaining walls of massive cut stones. After the Temple was leveled, churches and later mosques were built on the holy spot, on top of the platform. The one clearly visible remnant of the original Herodian Temple complex today is the retaining wall, accessible on both the southern and western sides. Since the Middle Ages, many Jews have considered "the Western Wall" (*hakotel hama'aravi*, the Kotel) a holy place, a sacred symbol of attachment to this place and its history. It is a pilgrimage destination.

The tradition folded its mourning for the destruction of the Second Temple into the mourning for the First Temple. It is said that both events took place on the same date, and the various days and customs of mourning—including the fast on the Ninth of Av (see chapter 7)—relate to the two destructions as if they were one event.

TEXT FOR DISCUSSION

The traditional liturgy articulates the "official" ideology: the Jewish people were exiled because of their sins, and they expect, when God is ready, to return and reestablish the sacrificial cult. It is interesting to consider: Is traditional imagery being used here to express a utopian hope for national restoration? Do Jews today indeed hope to restore the sacrifices?

> On account of our sins were we exiled from our country and driven from our land, and we are unable to make the pilgrimages and to worship before You, to fulfill our obligations in Your chosen house, the great and holy Temple upon which Your name is called, because of the hand that was sent forth against Your sanctuary. May it be Your will, Lord our God and God of our ancestors, the merciful King, that You, in Your abundant mercy, will relent and have pity upon us and upon Your sanctuary, and that You will rebuild it speedily and that You will increase its glory.
>
> Our Father, our King, reveal soon the glory of Your kingdom upon us; appear and be exalted over us in the sight of all the living. Bring home our scattered people from among the nations, and gather our exiles from the ends of the earth; bring us to Zion Your city in joy, to Jerusalem Your sanctuary in eternal happiness. There we will perform our obligatory sacrifices for You.
>
> —From the *Musaf Amidah*, in the traditional festival liturgy

FURTHER READING

Cohen, Shaye. *From the Maccabees to the Mishnah*. Philadelphia: Westminster, 1987. A survey of the development of the beliefs and institutions of Judaism against the historical background of the Second Temple and early Rabbinic periods.

Finkelstein, Louis. *The Pharisees*. Philadelphia: Jewish Publication Society, 1961, vol. 1, chap. 2. A survey of the internal divisions in the Jewish nation during the Roman period.

Hayes, John, and Sara Mandell. *The Jewish People in Classical Antiquity*. Louisville KY: Westminster John Knox Press, 1998. Chapters 3 and 4 give a detailed chronology of the Roman period through the Great Revolt.

Josephus Flavius. *The Wars of the Jews*. The most commonly used translation, by Whiston, published in 1732, is available free online. There is also a modern translation by G. A. Williamson (London: Penguin, 1970) and another in progress (by Steve Mason, published by Brill).

Schurer, Emil. *A History of the Jewish People in the Time of Jesus*. Edited by Nahum Glatzer. New York: Schocken Books, 1961. A translation of a classic nineteenth-century study of the period. A compact and straightforward narrative.

11. Finding a Messianic Equilibrium

THE BAR KOKHBA REVOLT, 132–135 CE

HISTORY

Life after the Great Revolt

The decades after the war seem to have been relatively quiet, a time of rebuilding and recovery. Neither the Romans nor the Jews were interested in provocations. The presence of the Roman Tenth Legion and their construction activities—especially roads—contributed to improving commerce and quality of life.

A famous story from the Talmud highlights Jewish ambivalence about these contributions: "Rabbi Yehudah said, 'How wonderful are the works of this people [the Romans]! They have established markets, they have built bridges, they have built baths.' Rabbi Yose was silent. Rabbi Shimon bar Yochai answered, 'They established markets—for prostitutes to work there; they built bridges—in order to collect tolls; they built baths—to pamper themselves'" (Babylonian Talmud, *Shabbat* 33b).

Traditionally, Jews have seen this period as the time in which Rabbinic leadership was established as the successor to the old hierarchies of priesthood and monarchy. These Rabbis—heirs of the Pharisees and of Rabbi Yochanan ben Zakkai, and "graduates" of the academy he founded at Yavneh (see chapter 10)—have long been depicted as the core of a structure of Jewish autonomy that developed after the Temple's destruction. In this view, the Rabbis/scholars became a kind of self-perpetuating elite based on their knowledge of the accumulated oral interpretation of the Torah. Through their individual authority and in their collective institutions (academy, Sanhedrin), they determined the operative Torah law for the Jewish community in the Land of Israel and for diaspora communities.

However, our knowledge of this process is almost entirely based on literature written by rabbis at least two centuries later. Thus, we face a dilemma of "myth versus history" similar to what we encountered in the chapters on biblical events.

Current scholarship tends to see the Rabbis' assumption of central authority in the first two centuries of the Common Era as a projection backward of a reality that only took shape in the third century and later. The situation was probably more disorganized than the Rabbinic literature suggests. More likely, the Rabbis were indeed a leadership group during this time who did develop and perpetuate methods and traditions for interpreting and applying the Torah. However, they constituted one approach among many. Research on Roman provincial governance suggests that their formal autonomy would have been unlikely. Archaeology suggests that other approaches to the Torah (for example, mystical approaches) were not preserved for inclusion in later Rabbinic texts (such as the Talmud) and hence dropped out of collective memory.

Thus, the rich plurality of approaches to Torah interpretation that characterized the Second Temple period (see chapter 9) appears to have continued after the destruction. The processes of centralization that led to what came to be called Rabbinic Judaism likely became significant only from the third century onward.

The Bar Kokhba Revolt

Meanwhile, in 115–117 CE, tensions between Jews and gentiles in Libya, Egypt, Cyprus, and Mesopotamia during Emperor Trajan's reign led to riots, open rebellions, and many thousands of casualties. This may have had echoes in Palestine, although we do not have clear evidence. We do know that Trajan's successor, Hadrian, managed to provoke serious unrest in Palestine, perhaps by first offering to support rebuilding Jerusalem and the Temple and then reneging. In any case, his policies were not as laissez-faire as those of his predecessor. And once Hadrian specifically forbade circumcision (for everyone, not just Jews) as a form of mutilation, the fuse was lit for rebellion—which exploded in 130 CE when Hadrian ordered that a pagan temple be built on the site of the Temple.

Unfortunately, there was no successor to Josephus, so we have no contemporary historical account of these decades. Our sources are Rabbinic texts (compiled in the fifth century or later); Roman historians who lived after the events, especially Dio Cassius (155–235) and Eusebius (263–339); and a collection of military correspondence and related documents written by the rebels, discovered near the Dead Sea in 1960.

Shimon bar Kokhba (or Kozba, or Koziba), referred to as *nasi* (patriarch) on the coins minted by his followers, led the revolt. We know nothing of his life, background, or family. He headed what appears to have been an organized military campaign that experienced some early success in pushing back the Roman troops. However, the Romans sent reinforcements, the rebel army was overwhelmed, and Bar Kokhba and his forces were cornered in the fortress of Beitar, near Jerusalem.

Ultimately the three-and-a-half-year rebellion resulted in massive deaths among the fighters and the civilian population and destruction of infrastructure. Moreover, during the years after the defeat, Hadrian's regime continued to enforce harsh anti-Jewish policies, such as prohibiting Sabbath observance, Torah study, and circumcision.

The Bar Kokhba debacle—coming just sixty-five years after the last defeat—was even more devastating economically, socially, and spiritually. It seems to have led to a kind of resignation—a consciousness that living under foreign rule was the new normal and that the nation would have to develop institutions to cope with this long-term reality. It undermined hopes for restoration.

Nonetheless, Jewish life slowly recovered and continued. The focus of Jewish life moved away from the center of the country to the Galilee and Golan in the north. Jews remained a majority of the population, and Jewish cultural creativity flourished in the context of accommodation with Roman rule. And the community in Palestine remained central for the diaspora Jewries. Out of this substrate grew the structure of leadership and law that ultimately came to dominate Jewish life, Rabbinic Judaism (see chapter 12).

The Messianic Idea and its Impact

The trauma associated with the destruction of the First Temple had confirmed the Deuteronomic ideology (see chapter 7) that the history of the nation reflected its relationship with God. Sin on the national level had led to punishment in the form of destruction and exile—but God's promise was eternal, so God's favor would be restored. The Temple's rebuilding just fifty years later supported the belief that this cycle of sin-punishment-forgiveness-restoration could take place in the people's lifetime. But then, full restoration never came: the Temple was built, but foreigners and usurpers occupied David's throne, one after another.

During the Second Temple period, this dissonance and frustration gave rise to a new genre of popular literature: apocalyptic writings. Apocalyptic writers utilized visions, mystical contemplation, and symbolic interpretation of texts and events to try to understand the map of history. As they saw it, if history is the playing out of a divine-human drama, it would be useful to know the script; then they could recognize the signs of the coming messianic redemption—and know how long they'd have to wait. Apocalyptic literature sought to locate the current experiences of the nation on the map of history—on the script of redemption.

This literature was deeply influential. It not only reflected the thoughts of the people and their leaders; it led to a ripeness, an openness if not a willingness to believe that current events indicated the approach of the restoration.

One of the many apocalyptic works then in circulation was accepted into the Hebrew canon: the book of Daniel. Daniel 12:9–12 tells us:

> [9]Go, Daniel, for these words are secret and sealed to the time of the end. [10]Many will be purified and purged and refined; the wicked will act wickedly and none of the wicked will understand; but the knowledgeable will understand. ([11]From the time the regular offering is abolished, and an appalling abomination is set up—it will be a thousand two hundred and ninety days. [12]Happy the one who waits and reaches one thousand three hundred and thirty-five days.)

Apocalyptic ferment did not necessarily lead to messianic activism. For many who wrote and studied such literature, it remained in the realm of contemplation, of theory. It was an attempt to understand the world and God's plan for it—to find meaning in history.

However, it did provide fertile ground for the germination of messianic speculation and even messianic activism. For those who believed it was possible to read the map of history, it could be tempting to step on the accelerator in order to get to the ultimate destination sooner. In this context we can understand the Jews who believed the claims that Jesus of Nazareth was the Messiah—claims that certainly did not sit well with the ruling power whom the Messiah was expected to overthrow, nor with Jewish leaders anxious not to provoke that power.[6]

A century later, the situation had gotten even more desperate. The fall of Jerusalem and the Temple had moved the nation backward, away from the prospect of restoration, and Hadrian's policies had brought matters to a new low. How could the end not be near? And so some evidence indicates that Bar Kokhba's attempt to overthrow Roman rule—which, from a rational point of view, should have seemed doomed from the start—arose out of a belief that he was the Messiah, destined to rebuild and restore the Jewish kingdom with divine support.

When Bar Kokhba's endeavor crashed and burned, the messianic fever was quenched. Apocalyptic speculation retreated back into the world of mystical contemplation. The nation could not afford any more such misreadings of the map of history.

While the messianic idea that originated with the prophets remained a central and powerful element of Jewish belief, from Bar Kokhba onward the leaders of the nation tried (usually—but not always—with success) to remove its apocalyptic sting. They disavowed it as a short-term action plan. They retained it only as a long-term hope in the face of a sober view of current reality.

Timeline: 70–~200 CE

70	Jerusalem is destroyed and then converted into a base for the Roman Tenth Legion. Caesarea (on the coast) becomes the official Roman provincial capital.
73	The annual tax that had been collected to support the Temple in Jerusalem is henceforth collected to support the temple of Jupiter Capitolina in Jerusalem.
~75	The Gospels (accounts of the life of Jesus of Nazareth) are written/edited.
96	The Flavian dynasty in Rome (Vespasian, Titus, Domitian) ends. Rabban Gamaliel (son of a leader of the revolt) replaces

---

6. Most Jews rejected Jesus's messianic claim. However, his followers re-imagined "redemption," moving it from the national sphere to the personal, spiritual realm. In so doing they created a new religion, uncoupled from Jewish national identity, and thus able to spread among the gentile population of the region—and beyond.

	Rabbi Yochanan ben Zakkai as head of the academy and Sanhedrin in Yavneh.
115–117	While Emperor Trajan is off fighting in Mesopotamia, the Jewish colonies in Libya, then in Egypt and Cyprus, and finally in Mesopotamia riot against their pagan neighbors and rise up in revolt against Rome. All outbreaks are defeated at great cost to both sides.
117	Hadrian succeeds Trajan as emperor.
117	General Lucius Quietus is rewarded for suppressing the revolt in Mesopotamia with the governorship of Judea. Some evidence indicates that the new emperor, Hadrian, promised to rebuild Jerusalem and the Temple but then had a change of heart. The nation attempts rebellion once again; Lucius Quietus puts it down.
130	Hadrian prohibits circumcision as a form of mutilation. Then, on a visit to Jerusalem, he decrees that a new city, Aelia Capitolina, be built there, with a pagan temple on the site of the Temple.
132	After Hadrian leaves the area, Shimon bar Kokhba (also known as bar Koziba or bar Kozba) leads a violent uprising. The Romans send in reinforcements. Massive destruction and dislocation ensue.
135	Bar Kokhba's last stronghold, Beitar (seven miles south of Jerusalem), falls; Bar Kokhba is killed; the rebellion ends. Jerusalem is indeed rebuilt as Aelia Capitolina, and Jews are forbidden to enter the city. Judea is renamed Syria Palaestina. Many Jews abandon their identity.
138	Hadrian dies. His successor, Antoninus Pius, relaxes some legal restrictions; for example, he now allows Jews (only) to practice circumcision. The economy begins a slow, two-century recovery. The center of gravity of Jewish life in Palestine moves to the Galilee and Golan.
~200	Under the *nasi* (patriarch) Rabbi Yehudah (grandson of Gamaliel), the academy and Sanhedrin move to Zippori, in the lower Galilee—a large, mixed (Jewish and Roman) city and a Roman regional capital.

PRIMARY TEXT

The two texts that follow are both Rabbinic. The midrash *Eikhah Rabbah*, edited in the fifth century or later, is a collection of interpretations and teachings based on the biblical book of Lamentations. This passage is one of the few in Rabbinic literature that discuss the Bar Kokhba revolt. The excerpted passage from the Babylonian Talmud, edited in the fifth century, is from a collection of Rabbinic sayings about the conditions necessary for the coming of the Messiah.

1. *Eikhah Rabbah* (Vilna) 2:4

"The Lord has destroyed without mercy all the habitations of Jacob" [Lamentations 2:2], such as Rabbi Yishmael, Rabbi Shimon ben Gamaliel, Rabbi Yeshvav, Rabbi Yehudah ben Bava, Rabbi Hutzpit the translator, Rabbi Yehudah the baker, Rabbi Haninah ben Teradion, Rabbi Akiva, Rabbi Shimon ben Azzai, and Rabbi Tarfon; and some leave out Rabbi Tarfon and include Rabbi Elazar ben Harsom. . . .

This is the origin of the tradition that the Romans executed ten leading rabbis at the time of the Bar Kokhba revolt. Accounts elsewhere in the Rabbinic literature describe the torture and execution of a few of these rabbis.

Rabbi Yochanan said: Rabbi [Yehudah HaNasi] used to teach: With respect to the passage "a star will come forth out of Jacob" (Numbers 24:17), read it not as "a star," but as "a deceiver."

When Rabbi Akiva saw Bar Kozba, he said: Behold, King Messiah!

Bar Kokhba's real name is not clear. Sometimes he is referred to as Bar Kokhba ("son of a star") and other times as Bar Kozba or Koziba ("son of deception"). One of these may have been his given name and the other a nickname applied by his supporters/detractors.

Rabbi Yochanan ben Torata said to him: Akiva, grass will grow out of your cheekbones before the Messiah comes. . . .	Rabbi Akiva, one of the leaders of his generation, seems to have supported Bar Kokhba and even believed that he was the Messiah. Not all of his colleagues agreed.
Hadrian besieged Beitar for three and a half years. . . . He killed so many that a horse was up to its nostrils in blood; and the current of blood was strong enough to carry a stone weighing fifty selas, and to flow four miles out into the sea.	Beitar is nowhere near the sea. The authors want it to be clear that Bar Kokhba and his followers caused a disaster.

This passage (along with others that describe the martyrdom of individual rabbis) suggests that a number of prominent rabbis, including Rabbi Akiva, supported the revolt or at least engaged in activities that asserted autonomy in opposition to government policy—support based on Bar Kokhba's messianic expectations.

Unlike the case of Jesus of Nazareth, after Bar Kokhba's defeat and death, there was no attempt to argue that he was still the Messiah. Later generations viewed Bar Kokhba in a negative light and perceived his Rabbinic supporters as misguided, even while their martyrdom made them heroes.

2. Babylonian Talmud, *Sanhedrin* 97a–98a

Rabbi Zeira, whenever he chanced upon scholars calculating the time of the Messiah's coming, would say to them: I beg of you, do not postpone it, for it has been taught: three come unexpectedly: the Messiah, a found object, and a scorpion. . . .	A watched pot never boils. If you think you know when the Messiah will come, that is when he will not come.

Calculating the end is a recipe for sure disappointment and disillusionment. |
| Rabbi Shmuel ben Nachmani said in the name of Rabbi Yonatan: | |

Blasted be the bones of those who calculate the end, for they would say: since the predetermined time has arrived and he has not come, he will never come. . . .

Rabbi Yehoshua ben Levi met Elijah . . . and asked him, "When will the Messiah come?"

According to a popular interpretation of 2 Kings 2, Elijah the prophet never died, but periodically reappears to reveal information about God's thoughts and plans.

"Go and ask him," was the reply.
  "Where is he sitting?"
  "At the gate of the city."
  "How will I recognize him?"
  "He sits with the poor lepers; they all unbind and re-bandage all their wounds at once; he unties and re-bandages his one by one, so that he won't be delayed when he is called."

Rabbi Yehoshua found him and greeted him: "When will you come?"
  "Today."

The coming of the Messiah is not determined by some cosmic plan, but is conditional on the nation's return to living according to the covenant, to Torah.

Rabbi Yehoshua returned to Elijah and said, "He spoke falsely to me, stating that he would come today, but he has not."

Elijah answered him: "This is what he said to you: 'Today, if you will hear his voice' [Psalm 95:7]."

Recoiling from messianic speculation and activism in the wake of the Bar Kokhba revolt, the Rabbis say that such conjecture and crusading is not only pointless but actually dangerous—and hence forbidden. The nation's role is to tend to the covenant, to live according to the Torah. God will bring the Messiah—and the restoration—when God is ready. There is no way we can know when that will be until it happens.

LEGACY

Impact

The Bar Kokhba revolt created a new equilibrium regarding the place of messianism in the mainstream tradition. From this point onward, messianism was, for the most part, "controlled."

On the one hand, the idea that God's promise to David would be fulfilled, and full restoration would come, was institutionalized in the liturgy as a core belief; much later, Maimonides, writing in the twelfth century, would declare that one who denied this expectation was as if he denied the whole Torah. Indeed, one of the secrets of the Jewish nation's survival through centuries of powerlessness and persecution is, arguably, life in the constant hope of national restoration.

On the other hand, the experience had demonstrated the danger lurking in messianism for a powerless nation. As Michael Walzer would write, centuries later, in *In God's Shadow*, "Political activists possessed by a messianic faith are cut loose from all the normal constraints on political action. They don't have to calculate their chances, cultivate popular support, prepare for a long march, build alternative institutions." And so, the messianic expectation was kept in a protective envelope of "later, not now"—confined to mystical speculation and liturgical formulas.

A key legacy of Bar Kokhba was the institutionalized maintenance of a delicate balance between hope as a core of belief and even of identity—and patience. This tension—between the difficulty of waiting while suffering and the reluctance to get drawn into a false-messianic disaster—has been an almost constant concern of Jewish leadership and literature ever since.

At certain times, holding that balance was a great challenge. Messianic speculation and activism continued to appear throughout the centuries and lands where Jews lived. Although these episodes almost never involved military insurrection, in many cases they nonetheless ended in major disillusionment if not apostasy. For example:

- In 1295, the Jews of Avila (Spain) gathered in the synagogue to welcome the Messiah, on the date predicted by mystic and messianic hopeful Abraham Abulafia. They waited in vain and went home heartbroken.
- In 1502, a German Jew, Asher Lammlein, proclaimed himself the Messiah. Rabbis decreed fast days to prepare for the imminent redemption—which failed to materialize.
- In the 1660s, a wave of messianic enthusiasm centered on a Turkish Jew, Sabbatai Zevi, swept the Jewish world (see chapter 18). Thousands of Jews sold their property and prepared for the ingathering, only to learn that the "messiah" had converted to Islam to save his life.

Memory

The one explicit reference to the Bar Kokhba revolt in the traditional liturgy is the *Eileh Ezkerah* (These I will remember), recited on Yom Kippur. This poem is intended to inspire repentance—and God's mercy—by recalling the self-sacrificing faith of the ten Rabbinic martyrs.

A folk tradition links Lag ba-Omer, the thirty-third day of the counting of the Omer between Passover and Shavuot (the Feast of Weeks, Pentecost; see Leviticus 23:9–21), to the Bar Kokhba revolt. While the significance of the specific date is not clear, traditionally it was observed as a kind of field day when children would go on excursions into the countryside, armed with bows and arrows, building bonfires and "pretending" not to be studying Torah (to avoid Roman persecutions). In the twentieth century, Zionist educators rehabilitated Bar Kokhba, presenting him as a brave military leader, a national hero—a suitable model for a nation engaged in a violent struggle for independence. Thus, Lag ba-Omer has become elevated to a more significant holiday; in Israel, schools are closed and the country covered by a pall of bonfire smoke. Tens of thousands of people participate in a pilgrimage to the grave of Rabbi Shimon bar Yochai (associated with the Hadrianic persecutions; but see chapter 15 for the later significance of this rabbi) in the Galilean village of Meron.

TEXT FOR DISCUSSION

Gershom Scholem, credited with founding the modern academic study of Jewish mysticism, also wrote much about messianism. Generally the messianic hope is seen as a positive force for the Jewish people's survival; here Scholem suggests a flip side. Could it be that the messianic hope is a force for passivism, for a disengagement from the world?

> There is something grand about living in hope, but at the same time there is something profoundly unreal about it . . . [T]he Messianic idea has compelled a life lived in deferment, in which nothing can be done definitively, nothing can be irrevocably accomplished . . .
>
> —Gershom Scholem, *The Messianic Idea in Judaism*, p. 35

FURTHER READING

Cohen, Shaye. *From the Maccabees to the Mishnah*. Philadelphia: Westminster, 1987. A survey of the development of Judaism's beliefs and institutions against the historical background of the Second Temple and early Rabbinic periods.

Hammer, Reuven. *Akiva: Life, Legend, Legacy*. Philadelphia: Jewish Publication Society, 2015. A biography of perhaps the best-known rabbi of second-century Palestine, based on current scholarly views of the sources.

Levine, Lee. *Visual Judaism in Late Antiquity*. New Haven: Yale University Press, 2012. A major examination of archaeological evidence for a plurality of traditions of interpretation and belief.

Scholem, Gershom. *The Messianic Idea in Judaism*. New York: Schocken Books, 1971, pp. 1–36. A classic essay by a pioneering scholar in the field.

Silver, Abba Hillel. *A History of Messianic Speculation in Israel*. Gloucester MA: Peter Smith, 1978. A catalogue of messianic calculations and movements throughout Jewish history.

Steinberg, Milton. *As a Driven Leaf*. 1939; repr., New York: Behrman House, 2015. A classic historical novel about the lives of the second-century Rabbis and the issues they faced.

12. The Oral Law Becomes Literature

THE MISHNAH, ~200 CE

HISTORY

Life after the Bar Kokhba Revolt

The Bar Kokhba revolt wrought significant devastation. Many towns were destroyed, in some cases permanently. Religious persecution continued, and some Jews abandoned their religion entirely. Agriculture and trade were disrupted; the resulting economic depression motivated a wave of emigration.

However, in the course of the second and third centuries, commerce and culture recovered. Jewish communities continued to strive to live according to the laws of Torah, interpreting and applying the Written Torah to contemporary needs. As we saw in the preceding chapters, from the Hasmonean period through the third century CE, various interpretive approaches competed for dominance. Over the next two centuries—until the compilation of the Talmud—the Rabbis gradually consolidated their control of the interpretive process, so that ultimately "Judaism" came to mean Rabbinic Judaism. The compilation of the Mishnah can be seen as symbolizing this transition.

The Hadrianic persecutions had shut down the Rabbis' center at Yavneh (see chapter 10). Slowly, with the progress of social and economic reconstruction and the subsiding of Roman persecution, the Rabbis regrouped. Toward the end of the second century, they reestablished the Sanhedrin in Usha, a small Galilean village (see chapter 10). After convening in several villages in the north, around 200 CE the Sanhedrin moved to Sepphoris (Zippori), a large mixed city and Roman regional capital—which suggests that the Jews no longer feared Roman suppression of their institutions. Rabbi Yehudah, the son of Shimon, became the *nasi* (patriarch), and in the course of a few decades, he succeeded in transforming this position from simply head of the Rabbis' internal hierarchy to the recognized head of the entire Jewish community.

This transformation was pivotal. When Rabbi Yehudah, who embodied the Rabbinic approach to the Torah, became the political leader of the Jews of Palestine—recognized as such by the Romans—the foundation was laid for the dominance of Rabbinic Judaism for the next fifteen hundred years.

The same time period saw the creation of the first major systematic compilation of the Oral Law: the Mishnah. Traditionally credited to Rabbi Yehudah HaNasi, the Mishnah was foundational for Rabbinic Judaism, becoming the organizing structure for most later discussions and compilations.

Rabbi Yehudah HaNasi

Rabban Gamaliel II assumed the leadership of the Rabbis from Yochanan ben Zakkai around 80–90 CE (see chapter 10). The Hebrew Bible's canonization and the formulation of the basic norms of Rabbinic Jewish liturgy are generally attributed to the period of Gamaliel's leadership in Yavneh. Stories about him suggest he was a charismatic and at times authoritarian leader whose relationship with other rabbis was not always smooth. He had an impressive pedigree as a descendant of the early Pharisaic leader Hillel—and, according to later traditions, of King David. After the Bar Kokhba revolt, his son Shimon succeeded him. Toward the end of the second century, Shimon's son, Yehudah, assumed the mantle of leadership.

The traditions about Yehudah emphasize his scholarship—that his colleagues received his legal determinations with respect. However, his high status and recognized authority were more likely a result of his friendly relationship with the Roman administration and his great wealth (it is not clear which led to which). Repeatedly throughout Jewish history (for example, Joseph in Genesis; Esther and Mordecai in the book of Esther), having "connections" with the rulers conferred political power within the Jews' own society.

Yehudah lived an aristocratic life in his estate in Bet She'arim (in the western Jezreel Valley, not far from Haifa today). The Rabbinic literature contains a number of stories about his close relationship with the emperor (which may or may not be true, but probably reflect how he was seen and the cultural milieu in which he moved). He was proactive in enforcing and building his authority, traveling about the country to observe, supervise, and in general make his presence felt. While the title of *nasi*—patriarch—was also carried by his father and grandfather, during Rabbi Yehudah's tenure this office developed from an internal leadership role among the Rabbis to a position of real authority—for example, to appoint local rabbinical leaders and to enforce halakhic rulings.

The Rabbinic sources about Rabbi Yehudah (often simply referred to as "Rabbi") suggest the Rabbis felt a certain ambivalence toward him. On the one hand, they emphasized his scholarship and his "rabbinical" qualities: "Beauty, strength, riches, honor, wisdom, old age, and children are fitting for the righteous and fitting for the world. . . . Rabbi Shimon ben Menasya said: These seven qualities that the sages listed for the righteous were all realized in Rabbi Yehudah HaNasi and his sons" (*Mishnah Avot* 6:8).

On the other hand, they evinced a certain discomfort with his Roman connections, his aristocratic lifestyle, and his authoritarian leadership. For example, the Babylonian Talmud (*Sanhedrin* 38a) recounts an awkward conversation in which the sons of Rabbi Yehudah's colleague and rival Rabbi Hiyya apply to him the following verse in Isaiah (8:14): "He shall be . . . a stumbling block and a stone of offense for both the houses of Israel."

In later generations, first in Babylonia and later in other diaspora communities, there would be a separation of powers between "lay" authority (usually oligarchic, based on relations with the gentile rulers) and rabbinic authority (based on knowledge of Torah and its interpretation). At this time, Rabbi Yehudah seems to have represented both—and thus helped move the Rabbis and their ideology into a central position in the nation, relative to other models of leadership and approaches to Torah.

The Rabbis' ideology held that their interpretations actually originated at Mount Sinai (see "Text for Discussion" below) and that prophecy had ended in the first generations of the return to Zion (see chapter 8), so the Rabbis' teachings were the closest we could now get to revelation. Thus, it is telling that traditionally Rabbi Yehudah was seen not as a descendant of the priests or of Moses the prophet, but as a scion of the royal house of David. As a rabbi and the Rabbis' leader we would expect him to have priestly or prophetic antecedents, and yet his royal pedigree ascribed to him political, not intellectual/spiritual, authority. This "crossing over" made his role unique.

The Mishnah

Until Rabbi Yehudah's time, the Oral Law had remained a growing collection of oral traditions: remembered discussions of textual interpretations and legal precedents (some of which may have been transcribed) on a large variety of topics. The Rabbis had long believed that the Oral Law had to remain oral, to distinguish it from the Written Law. They saw the benefits—its flexibility, its sustaining the sanctity and ultimate authority of the original Written Law and the authority of those who remembered and transmitted the Oral Law—as significantly outweighing the potential "costs" of this ideology: transmission breakdowns, inconsistency, and disunity.

According to the traditional view (see "Primary Text" below), with the passage of time and changes in the political and economic realities of life in the land, these oral traditions accumulated in quantity and diversity. Eventually, repeated upheavals due to wars, persecutions, and migrations called the cost-benefit equilibrium into question. The Rabbis finally decreed that the Oral Law had to be written down in order to preserve it. Thus, the Mishnah emerged.

The word *Mishnah* comes from the Hebrew root *sh-n-h*, meaning "to repeat" (referring to study as recitation of the oral tradition). The Mishnah was written in Hebrew, even though the vernacular in Palestine at the time was Aramaic (a Semitic language similar to Hebrew). Aramaic was the "English" of the period, uniting the Middle East from Palestine to Persia, while Hebrew, the language of the Bible, was a marker of Jewish identity, used for prayer and Torah study. Originally the Mishnah was divided into sixty tractates (some were later subdivided, so today there are sixty-three). Each of these was further divided into chapters and individual *mishnayot* (verses).

The tractates are grouped in six topical "orders":

1. *Zera'im* (seeds)—agricultural laws, tithes, prayers, and blessings
2. *Mo'ed* (festival)—laws regarding the Sabbath and holidays
3. *Nashim* (women)—laws relating to marriage and personal status; also to vows and to the Nazirite

4. *Nezikin* (damages) — civil and criminal law
5. *Kodashim* (holy matters) — laws regarding the sacrifices and the Temple service
6. *Tohorot* (purity) — laws relating to ritual purity and impurity

While Rabbi Yehudah is credited with decreeing the transcription of the Oral Law into the Mishnah, this picture may be oversimplified. Various collections of Rabbinic traditions, both oral and written, existed before him, and the oral process of reciting and interpreting tradition continued for centuries after him. Moreover, while the Mishnah has a clear topical structure, it was not a law code; it often set forth multiple opinions on a question and left some disputes unresolved.

It seems, therefore, that Rabbi Yehudah's contribution was more modest — but in a way more far-reaching — than the traditional view suggests. It appears that he used his authority to create a unifying scaffolding, an all-encompassing organizational structure with categories and subcategories, that served as the conceptual basis for the Rabbis' ongoing work in developing the Oral Law. His achievement can be seen not in having written a book, but in having invented a conceptual framework to guide all future discussion. The actual compilation of the book, the Mishnah, apparently occurred over the next few generations.

The Synagogue

During the same period that the Oral Law was crystallizing into a concrete document, another important institution continued its development and assumed new significance in the post-Temple reality: the synagogue. Apparently the synagogue (from Greek, "place of meeting"; in Hebrew *beit knesset*, "house of assembly") had its origins in the Diaspora, where, after the First Temple's destruction, Jews had needed a location to serve as a center of communal life. To what extent these synagogues / gathering places served as loci of public prayer, and to what extent they were limited to study and communal affairs, is unclear. With the Second Temple's destruction, a similar need arose among the Jews of Palestine. Just when and how the synagogue developed into the institution we know today, combining the functions of prayer, study, philanthropy, social life, and communal governance, is not known. We do know, from a rich third- to sixth-century archaeological record of buildings identified as synagogues, that the model probably began to crystallize in second- to third-century Palestine.

The Rise of the Babylonian Center

The rise of Christianity—and its adoption by the Roman empire in the fourth century—diminished the possibility of pluralism that had existed in a pagan environment, as the new religion saw itself as superseding Judaism: coexistence would have meant admission of the possible truth of Judaism, which would imply a denial of the truth of Christianity. Hence, Palestine under Christian Rome became increasingly inhospitable; the emperor abolished the patriarchate around 425 CE. The center of gravity of Rabbinic scholarship—and hence of the development of the Oral Law—began to shift to the center that had been developing in Babylonia. The carrying of the Mishnah to Babylonia, as the basis for the continuation of the Oral Law process there, preserved the centrality of Palestine, even as the Babylonian center became dominant.

By the second half of the first millennium CE, Babylonian Jewry numbered as many as a million, a flourishing and innovative community (even while it experienced political vicissitudes such as the Sasanian [Zoroastrian] conquest in 229 CE). Several major yeshivot (rabbinical academies) were functioning in the area between the Tigris and Euphrates rivers, the dominant ones at Sura and Pumbeditha. Because the community needed both a mechanism for internal governance according to Torah law and an outward-facing authority for dealing with the gentile authorities, it was in Babylonia in this period that a dual-track authority structure became institutionalized: the Ga'on ("exalted one": the head rabbi of the yeshiva, or chief rabbinical authority) functioned in tandem with the Resh Galuta ("head of the Diaspora," often translated as "Exilarch"—a lay leader whose authority was oligarchic-political). The Ga'on, appointed by the community for his scholarly attainments, represented the authority of Torah; the Exilarch, appointed by the king based on connections and wealth, served as liaison between the royal court and the Jewish community. Usually this separation of powers worked harmoniously, though at times it gave rise to community conflicts (e.g., who had to obey whom). This structure became the model for diaspora Jewish communities throughout the world.

Rabbinic Literature

The compilation of the Mishnah was the first blossom in the flowering of a rich legal and interpretive literature over the course of a millennium. The categories into which this literature is generally divided can be confusing. Here is a brief overview.

The word *midrash* (from the root *d-r-sh*, "explicate" or "preach") is a general term used for a specific exegetical or homiletic interpretation of a biblical verse. However, the same term also denotes the entire genre of textual interpretation and is sometimes used as the title for a specific collection of such interpretations. This entire body of midrashic interpretation (oral and then written) is divided into two overall categories:

1. *Halakhah* (way): law—whether laws derived explicitly from laws in the Torah, or laws that developed in the course of historical experience and were found a "root" in Torah text.
2. *Aggadah* (telling): narrative, explanation—philosophical, historical, and theological explanations of biblical text—and tales that come to fill in "gaps" in the Bible narrative.

Some collections of rabbinic literature maintain the distinction between these two; e.g., the Mishnah is almost entirely *halakhah*; the Midrash Rabbah collections are almost entirely *aggadah*. On the other hand, some-like the Talmud—contain both, intermingled.

The following Literature Timeline lays out the best-known timing of the most important works.[7]

---

7. The Aramaic form of the root of the word *Mishnah* (*sh-n-h*, "repeat") is *t-n-h*. The Rabbis of Palestine of the first two centuries CE, whose teachings are recorded in the Mishnah and Tosefta, are generally referred to as the *tannaim*; these centuries are thus the tannaitic period.

The Rabbis of the next three centuries, until the compilation of the Talmuds in both Palestine and in Babylonia, are identified as *amoraim* (from the root *a-m-r*, "say"). They were followed by a generation or two of *sevoraim* (from *s-v-r*, "reason") in sixth-century Babylonia, credited with bringing the Talmud text to its final form.

The period from the compilation of the Babylonian Talmud until the eleventh century is traditionally called the gaonic period, for the Rabbinic leaders of the communities of Babylonia.

A Literature Timeline

Dates are approximate.

<400 BCE	Torah and Prophets: The text of the Torah (Pentateuch) is generally thought to have attained its present form by the time of Ezra (see chapter 8). The latest of the books categorized as Prophets (Nevi'im) date from the same period.
<100 BCE	Writings: The latest books of the Bible, in the Writings (Kethuvim; e.g., Daniel), were written during the Hasmonean period.
<200 CE	Bible: The closure (canonization) of the Hebrew Bible apparently took place during the first two centuries CE. The modern Hebrew term for the Bible is the acronym Tanakh (Torah, Nevi'im, Kethuvim).
~200 or later	Mishnah: The first organized collection of Oral Law traditions, which served as a basis for subsequent discussions and compilations.
~200 or later	Tosefta: A collection of additional Oral Law material from before ~200 CE, not included in the Mishnah, but following the same organizational structure (not to be confused with the Tosafot, medieval French/German commentaries on the Talmud).
<300	Tannaitic midrashim: Collections of Rabbinic explications and expansions of biblical texts — primarily legal sections — from the same period as the Mishnah: *Mekhilta* — on Exodus; *Sifra* — on Leviticus; *Sifrei* — on Numbers and Deuteronomy.
~425	Palestinian Talmud: A collection of further discussions of the Oral Law, organized according to the structure of the Mishnah. It is called the Jerusalem Talmud in Hebrew, although it was apparently compiled in Tiberias.
~500 or later	Babylonian Talmud: A collection of further discussions of the Oral Law, apparently compiled between 500 and 700 CE in Babylonia. It follows the structure of the Mishnah.
~500–1200	Other collections: Over the centuries after the compilation of the two Talmuds, a number of collections of

Rabbinic explications, expansions, and sermons were assembled, generally by anonymous editors. Among the most familiar are the following:

- *Tanchuma* — on the whole Torah.
- *Midrash Rabbah* — separate compilations on each book of the Torah and the Five Scrolls in the Kethuvim (Writings).
- *Pesikta* — two collections of sermons on public readings from the Torah and Nevi'im (Prophets).

PRIMARY TEXT

In the late tenth century, Rav Sherira ben Hanina served as *Ga'on* of the yeshiva of Pumbeditha (now in Baghdad). A creative and prolific scholar and respected leader, he played an important role in maintaining his yeshiva's authority over communities that were becoming established in North Africa and Iberia. It could take several generations for an outpost of Jewish life to grow to a size sufficient to attract and support its own rabbi.

Responding to a question from a North African rabbi, he wrote a historical account of the development of *halakhah* and its literature. "The Epistle of Rav Sherira Ga'on," as it is now known, is an important document of early Jewish historiography. The Rabbis hardly ever composed narrative history, so this text is unique. It is the primary source for the tradition that Rabbi Yehudah compiled the Mishnah.

The Epistle of Rav Sherira Ga'on

"When was the Mishnah compiled? In the days of Rabbi [Yehudah HaNasi]" (Bab. Talmud, *Yevamot* 64b).

This constitutes the only close-to-contemporary reference to Rabbi Yehudah's redaction of the Mishnah.

. . . Throughout his father's life, Rabbi Yehudah grew in scholarship, . . . [learning from all the important rabbis of his father's generation].

And in those years, all the matters that had been undecided were explained and decided, on account of the fear that they would be lost in the chaos following the destruction of the Temple....

[But] not one of the earlier rabbis wrote down his knowledge, until the end of the days of the holy Rabbi Yehudah. And while there was not unanimity in reading and interpretation, still, each knew the reasoning and agreed upon it, knowing which matters were unanimous and which were disputed, which were minority and which were majority opinions. But they did not have an ordered formulation, a known articulation of the teaching ("Mishnah") that everyone could teach in identical language. Rather, the reasoning and the traditions, even though all knew and agreed upon them, were taught by each rabbi to his pupils in any combination he wished, in whatever order he wished, in the degree of detail he deemed suitable; sometimes presenting opinions with attribution to their authors—and sometimes not....

And when Rabbi Yehudah saw that there were such great differences

Rav Sherira explains that the process of organizing and presenting the Oral Law in a coherent way had begun earlier, in the days of Yavneh. While there were different versions of what was remembered and what was passed down, still the basic structure and the applicable legal conclusions were matters of consensus. However, since in legal discussions the formulation of the decision, links to precedents, and references to earlier authorities are not just questions of style but of substance, the lack of uniformity in formulating the tradition posed a clear danger of disorder and schism. This danger inspired Rabbi Yehudah's act of compilation and editing.

among the rabbis' teachings, even
though they were in agreement, he
felt that this would cause a great
loss of truth, for he saw that the
hearts were diminishing, that the
fountain of wisdom was stopped
up, and that the Torah was disap-
pearing. . . .

Rabbi Yehudah was granted by
heaven Torah and power, and all
accepted his authority . . . as it
was said (Bab. Talmud, *Gittin* 59a),
"From the days of Moses until
Rabbi Yehudah we had not seen
Torah and power together [like
this]."

And the rabbis were free of oppression during Rabbi Yehudah's time,
because of the friendship between
Rabbi Yehudah and Antoninus.

In the days of Rabbi Yehudah . . .
the circumstances were right for
him to explain *and to write down
[the law]*, and the words of the
Mishnah were like those that
Moses heard directly from God, a
sign and a wonder. And Rabbi did
not invent these words in his heart,
but rather, they were the teachings of the earlier rabbis who came
before him. . . .

The rabbis' being free of oppression
during the time refers to the traditions about Rabbi Yehudah's friendship with a certain Roman named
Antoninus. We don't know who he
was. The stories imply that he was
the emperor, but we have no evidence.

There are two manuscripts of this
text. In one the words "write down"
are not present. So we don't know
what Rav Sherira intended to say.

And when everyone saw the form
of the Mishnah, the truth of its
contents and the precision of its
language, they gave up their previous teachings, and this law spread
throughout the land of Israel . . .
Israel relied upon this law, and . . .
received it in faith, and no one disputes its authority.

—A. Neubauer, *Seder Hachamamim Vekorot Hayamim*, part I (Oxford: Claren-
don, 1888), pp. 6–12

In this chapter and in previous ones, the development of the Oral Law
has been presented as a rational historical process whereby the Rabbis
interpreted the words of the Written Law according to the consciousness
and circumstances of their own age—since, of course, the reality of their
lives was different from the biblical context. This approach sees the oral
tradition and its written compilations (e.g., the Mishnah) as human works,
created by a leadership elite in order to preserve the relevance and sanctity
of the Written Law in their time. Rav Sherira's account seems to fit with
this view. However, he takes pains to disavow it, giving Rabbi Yehudah
credit for his innovation but emphasizing that he actually wasn't inno-
vating, just putting things in order.

In other words, the traditional view of the Oral Law is not historical.
Both the Written Law and the Oral Law were traditionally seen as one
inseparable unit, of divine origin (*Shemot Rabbah* 28:4):

"And God spoke all these words . . ." (Exodus 20:1): Rabbi Isaac said,
"Everything that the prophets prophesied in the future, throughout the
generations, they received at Mount Sinai, as Moses said to Israel, 'to him
who is standing with us here today and to him who is not here with us . . .'
(Deuteronomy 29:14). And not only did the prophets receive their prophecy at Mount Sinai, but all the scholars who arise in every generation—
each one of them receives his knowledge from Mount Sinai."

The tension between historical and traditional views found expression in a number of rejections of rabbinical authority across the centuries—for example, the Sadducees during Second Temple times (see chapter 9), the Karaites in eighth-century Babylonia, and the modern Reform movement (see chapter 20). Indeed, Rav Sherira's account of Rabbinic literature likely had a polemic purpose: to refute the Karaites' claims that the Rabbis did not have authority to interpret the Torah. Like the Sadducees, the Karaites insisted that the Torah must be understood in its literal meaning, without human interpretation. However, any reading, no matter how literal, involves some degree of interpretation, so these rejecters of Rabbinic authority were actually just substituting their own interpretation for that of the Rabbis.

The Karaites persisted, on the fringe of Judaism, in various locations, mainly in Muslim regions. Today several Karaite communities continue in locales throughout the world, the most substantial ones in Israel, where they number around thirty thousand people.

LEGACY

Impact

As the first authoritative compilation, created in the Land of Israel, the Mishnah became the foundation of all future development of Jewish law. Embedded in the Talmud, it served as the basic text of Jewish literacy, law, and life, across centuries and continents. It was the universal platform for applying the Torah to everyday life, through Rabbinic interpretation. Its authoritative status has not diminished over time.

The Mishnah's creation and its elevation to the status of a central text can be seen as concrete expressions of the "rabbinization" of Judaism, wherein the Rabbis' approach to the explication and expansion of the biblical text became dominant. In other words, "traditional Judaism" as we know it originated with this turning point.

Memory

The Talmud is formatted as a sentence-by-sentence interpretation and expansion of the Mishnah text. Thus the Mishnah has been studied for centuries in that embedded form, as a part of a larger whole. However, it has also been studied as a book in its own right. Many commentaries on the Mishnah itself have been produced over the ages, including in our own time.

Written in the Land of Israel, in Hebrew, the Mishnah has served, through the generations, as a link to the land. When it speaks of agriculture, or seasons and other natural phenomena, or places, it reflects the reality of life in first- and second-century Palestine. Thus, those in the Diaspora who studied it experienced life in that land vicariously through their immersion in the text. Moreover, the Rabbis, the very flesh-and-blood inhabitants of the land who starred in the Mishnah, became important figures in the Jewish imagination—in many cases, at least as well-known and admired as biblical characters, not just as teachers/leaders, but as heroes and exemplars.

TEXT FOR DISCUSSION

A famous Rabbinic legend, a midrash on the story of Moses's ascent into the cloud on Mount Sinai (Exodus 34:28), addresses the tension between the immutability of the Torah and the historical development of the tradition. What do you think of the way it resolves the tension?

> Rabbi Yehudah [not Rabbi Yehudah HaNasi, but a Babylonian *amora*] told, in the name of Rav: When Moses went up into heaven [to receive the Torah] he found the Holy One sitting and making crowns [= traditional calligraphic decorations in Torah scroll script] for the letters. He said to Him, "Master of the universe, who is preventing you from giving the Torah without this?"
>
> He answered him, "There will come a man many generations from now, Akiva ben Yosef, who will expound mountains of laws from each of these decorations."
>
> [The *tanna* Rabbi Akiva lived in the second century CE, about fourteen hundred years after Moses.]
>
> "Master of the universe, show him to me."
>
> "Turn around."
>
> And Moses went and sat in the eighth row [of the academy of Rabbi Akiva] and could not understand what was being discussed. His strength failed him. Then, at one point, the students said to Rabbi Akiva, "Rabbi, how do you know this?"

He answered them, "It is a tradition from Moses at Sinai."
And Moses recovered.

—Babylonian Talmud, *Menachot* 29b

FURTHER READING

Blackman, Philip. *Mishnayoth*. New York: Judaica Press, 2000. The Mishnah in English. Available at http://hebrewbooks.org.

Cohen, Shaye. *From the Maccabees to the Mishnah*. Philadelphia: Westminster, 1987. A survey of the development of Judaism's beliefs and institutions against the historical background of the Second Temple and early Rabbinic periods.

Levine, Lee I. *Visual Judaism in Late Antiquity: Historical Contexts of Jewish Art*. New Haven: Yale University Press, 2012. A major presentation of research on non-Rabbinic traditions from the Roman period.

Rabinowich, Noson D. *The Iggeres of Rav Sherira Gaon*. Jerusalem: Moznaim, 1988. The full text of the Epistle of Rav Sherira Ga'on, translated; several extended excerpts are in L. Schiffman, *Texts and Traditions: A Source Reader for the Study of Second Temple and Rabbinic Judaism* (New York: Ktav, 1997).

Urbach, Ephraim. E. *The Sages: Their Concepts and Beliefs*. Translated by Israel Abrahams. Jerusalem: Magnes, 1975, pp. 593–603. A brief account of the development of Rabbinic leadership and the patriarchate after 70 CE, within a comprehensive study of the Rabbis' thought, by a leading twentieth-century scholar.

13. The Golden Age of Iberian Jewry

MAIMONIDES, 900–1200 CE

HISTORY

The Rise of Islam

The religion of Islam arose in the Arabian desert in the early seventh century. Its prophet, Muhammad, taught that Islam had preceded both Judaism and Christianity and that they were actually subsumed within Islam; the holy text attributed to him, the Qur'an, contains many references to characters and events found in the Jewish Bible, the New Testament, and associated commentaries and folklore.

The new religion spread among pagan desert tribes but failed to make the inroads it had expected among Jews and Christians. Thus, Muslims developed a kind of resentful sibling rivalry with both "sister religions," just as Christians felt a certain kinship for Judaism — coupled with anger at the Jews for casting doubt, by their very existence, on Christian truth.

In its early years, Christianity spread through missionizing; only after the Roman emperor Constantine converted (apparently in 337 CE) did it enter the phase of being spread "from above," by the decrees of kings, and hence by military conquest. With Islam, however, the religious and the political were integrated from the beginning. Revered as a prophet, Muhammad was also a political/military leader, uniting many tribes in the Arabian Desert. His successors, the caliphs (deputies of the Prophet), ruled as monarchs and served as the ultimate authority for religious doctrine and practice. And their campaigns of conquest were extremely successful. Within a century of Muhammad's death in 632, the Muslim caliphate ruled a vast swath of land, from Spain in the west to Persia in the east.

A great deal has been (and continues to be) written regarding the "true nature" of the relationship of Islam — and of Muslims — to Judaism and the Jews. It remains unclear if such a "true nature" can be articulated. Muhammad himself seems to have been ambivalent, the Qur'an is ambiguous on the topic, and the historical record contains a broad spectrum of different relationships, ranging from cruel persecution — including forced conversion, expulsion, and massacre—to examples of close cooperation, shared values and culture, and mutual respect.

The great twentieth-century historian of Islam Bernard Lewis expressed it this way:

> Two stereotypes dominate most of what has been written on toler-
> ance and intolerance in the Islamic world. The first depicts a fanati-
> cal warrior, an Arab horseman riding out of the desert with a sword in
> one hand and the Qur'an in the other, offering his victims the choice
> between the two. . . . The other image . . . is that of an interfaith, inter-
> racial utopia, in which men and women belonging to different races,
> professing different creeds, lived side by side in a golden age of unbro-
> ken harmony. . . . Both images are of course wildly distorted; yet both
> contain . . . some elements of truth.
>
> —Bernard Lewis, *The Jews of Islam*, p. 3

Relevant for our purposes is the reality of inconsistency: The treatment of the Jews varied from place to place and time to time, depending on cultural and spiritual currents, political and economic factors, and personal relationships. At times, it suited the needs of Muslim rulers to allow Jews to prosper and to hold positions of power; at other times, such prosperity and power were perceived as threats. The same was true for intellectual inquiry and artistic expression. At times, the flowering of thought and creativity was seen both as strengthening Islamic culture and as support-ing economic development; at other times, it was seen as undermining Muslim faith and "traditional values." Religious texts and traditions were interpreted in the light of the needs of the hour.

Such pendulum swings were not, of course, unique to Islam and indeed were less drastic than under Christianity, where the theological tension with Judaism was far more acute. To the Muslims, the Jews were just infe-rior, benighted; to the Christians, they were a theological threat. And from the Jewish perspective as well, cooperation with Muslims was easier than with Christians; Christianity's emphasis on religious images always gave off a faint odor of idolatry, whereas Islam came under no such suspicion.

Under the caliphs in Babylonia, the Jews experienced ups and downs in their status and fortunes—one notable "down" being the requirement to wear distinctive Jewish garments, a mandate originating under the Muslim rulers in Baghdad. In general, though, they were allowed to prosper and maintain their institutions. The prevailing caliph recognized and honored the Exilarch (see chapter 12), treating him as a member of the court and assigning him responsibility for collecting the Jewish community's taxes.

The Mongol conquest in 1258 was a major blow to the community, leading to significant emigration and the decline of communal institutions. The Mongol ruler Tamerlane finally eliminated the Exilarch position in 1401.

The Golden Age

When an army of Muslim Berbers from Morocco conquered Christian Visigothic Spain in 711, they passed their conquest on to the caliph in Damascus. Faced with a mixed, mostly Christian population, the new governors of the land imposed somewhat symbolic restrictions on both Christians and Jews—such as prohibiting construction or repairs of churches or synagogues and barring Christians and Jews from holding public office—while allowing a high degree of vocational and economic freedom.

A few decades into Muslim rule, dynastic struggle roiled the center of the empire in Baghdad. Abd ar-Rahman, a scion of the losing side (the Umayyads) made his way to Spain, attracted local support, and became king of Muslim Spain (Andalusia). He then seceded from the caliphate, so that for the next four hundred years Andalusia was an independent caliphate, with its capital at Cordoba.

Abd ar-Rahman I and his successors presided over a period of great economic growth, accompanied by a flowering of culture. A new approach to Islam now prevailed in the Cordoba caliphate: non-Muslims were tolerated and protected, and a rationalistic intellectual climate allowed science and philosophy to flourish. While non-Muslims remained second-class citizens, they were welcome to participate in cultural and economic life.

From approximately 900 to 1200 CE (to the extent we can date the Golden Age), Jews were able to engage in all aspects of economic life in Muslim Spain, as farmers, craftsmen, physicians, merchants, and public officials. The Jews' involvement in agriculture was particularly significant, as this was often restricted in Christian Europe; owning and working land has always been an expression of belonging in a place.

The Jews also partook in the rich cultural life of the Muslim world in general—and of Andalusia in particular—that was nourished by exposure to Greek and Persian texts and ideas that the Muslims encountered in the lands they conquered. Fascinated by Aristotelian philosophy, the Jews created their own major philosophical works. They also practiced medicine, researched mathematics and astronomy, wrote popular poetry, and served as advisors and administrators to kings and nobles (see "Leading Jewish Personalities of Muslim Spain" below). The Arabic language was a unifying force; Jews in Iberia and throughout Muslim lands studied and wrote in Arabic, in Hebrew, and in Judeo-Arabic (parallel to Yiddish in Eastern Europe).

The Golden Age began to lose its luster in 1030, when the unifying rule of the Cordoba caliphate splintered into a patchwork of smaller states. The decline became steeper when Berber armies from North Africa, encouraged by the caliphate's political weakness, invaded Andalusia in 1086. Espousing a fundamentalist Islam, they not only opposed granting privileges to religious minorities, but ushered in a regime of persecution, community destruction, and forced conversions. In the early thirteenth century, Christian powers finally expelled these interlopers as part of their campaign of reconquest that had begun at the time of the First Crusade (see chapter 15). The Christian reconquest was essentially completed in 1248; only the city-state of Granada in the southeast held out as an independent emirate until 1492.

Timeline: The Jews in Muslim Spain, 507–1248 CE

Jews lived in Iberia since Roman times, though we have little information about their communities.

507	The Visigoths (Christians from Germany) conquer most of the Iberian Peninsula.
630	King Sisebut decrees that all Jews must convert to Catholicism or emigrate. Under subsequent Visigothic kings the policy is enforced inconsistently. The Jewish position remains difficult.
622	The Hejira: Muhammad and his followers migrate from Mecca to Medina.

634–644   Umar ibn al-Khattab, the second caliph, builds a Muslim empire from Libya to Persia (including Palestine—the Mosque of Omar in Jerusalem is named for him—and Babylonia). In most cases, subject peoples are granted a high degree of autonomy.

711   The Muslims pursue conquest of Iberia. Seeing the Muslims as liberators, the Jews support the invaders, who in turn use them to garrison conquered cities as they move northward. Many Jews who had fled under the Visigoths return from North Africa.

756   A survivor of the Umayyad dynasty, Abd ar-Rahman I, sets up a semi-independent emirate in Cordoba.

882   Rabbi Saadiah Ga'on is born; a scholar, philosopher, and charismatic leader of Babylonian—and world—Jewry, he dies in 942.

929   Abd ar-Rahman III unites Muslim Spain under a strong central government and declares the kingdom an independent caliphate.

1030   The Cordoba caliphate breaks up into a mosaic of quarreling city-states.

1066   A power struggle between a Jewish vizier and his Muslim rival leads to anti-Jewish riots in Granada, resulting in hundreds of casualties.

1086   A Berber (North African) dynasty, the Almoravides, conquers Muslim Iberia, bringing an era of religious intolerance.

1148   The Almohad conquest begins. Under their rule, a period of extreme intolerance and persecution ensues.

1212   Christian forces expel the Almohads.

1248   Christian forces conquer all of Muslim Iberia except Granada.

Leading Jewish Personalities of Muslim Spain

Dates are approximate.

Hasdai ibn Shaprut (910–75)   A physician at the court of Abd ar-Rahman III, he rose to prominence as an advisor and diplomat for the king and an intercessor for Jewish communities throughout the world.

Menachem ibn Saruk (920–70) Poet and pioneering scholar of Hebrew grammar.

Dunash ibn Labrat (920–90) A poet, he brought Arabic models of rhyme and meter to Hebrew and also pioneered the study of Hebrew grammar.

Samuel ibn Nagrela, "Hanagid" (993–1056) Vizier to the king of Granada and poet.

Isaac Alfasi (1013–1103) Talmud scholar; his "Book of Laws" is still studied as an important early codification of talmudic law.

Solomon ibn Gabirol (1021–58) Philosopher and prolific poet, some of whose works have entered the traditional liturgy.

Isaac ibn Giyat (1038–89) Talmud scholar and poet.

Bahya ibn Pakuda (1050–1140) Poet, Bible scholar, and philosopher; his *Duties of the Heart*, a systematic moral philosophy, is still widely studied.

Moses ibn Ezra (1055–1138) Poet and literary scholar.

Judah Halevi (1075–1141) Poet and philosopher; his *The Kuzari* is considered one of the major Jewish philosophical works of all time.

Abraham ibn Ezra (1089–1167) Poet, Bible scholar, and astronomer; his commentary on the Bible is still widely studied.

Benjamin of Tudela (1130–73) World traveler whose journal is an important source for Jewish and general history of this era.

Moses ben Maimon (1135–1204) Also known as Maimonides or Rambam; philosopher, physician, and legal scholar (see following text).

Maimonides

While the Golden Age produced many great works of liturgy, poetry, philosophy, and scholarship, one scholar's contribution was unique in its scope and lasting impact. If the Golden Age was a turning point because it presented a model for balance between distinctiveness and integration, the life and work of Rabbi Moses ben Maimon epitomizes this model. For this reason (among others), his works have remained central in Jewish intellectual and spiritual life ever since.

A Brief Biography of Moses ben Maimon

1135   Moses ben Maimon is born in Cordoba to a long-established family of rabbis. Later, he will be known to the Jews as Rambam, the acronym of Rabbi Moses ben Maimon. The Latin form of his name is Maimonides.

1148   The Maimon family flees Cordoba to escape Almoravid persecution. They wander in Spain and Morocco, spending about six years in Fez.

1165   Maimonides travels to Crusader-ruled Palestine and wanders south, finally settling in Cairo. There he becomes the physician to the sultan and leader of the large Jewish community.

~1168   Maimonides completes his commentary to the Mishnah (in Arabic). This comprehensive and wide-ranging work also represents the first complete commentary directly on the Mishnah (without the Talmud). Throughout his life, he also writes hundreds of responsa (legal opinions) for communities around the world, as well as shorter philosophical, legal, and political books, several of which still hold an important place on the Jewish bookshelf along with his three major works listed in this table.

1173   Maimonides's brother David, a successful merchant who had supported the whole family, dies at sea. Maimonides strongly opposes receiving payment for Torah study. Without David's support, he has to spend his days working as a physician, relegating his Torah scholarship to "after hours."

~1178   Maimonides completes the Mishneh Torah, his code of Jewish law (in Hebrew). For this he creates his own organizational structure, not following that of the Mishnah/Talmud. This work has served as a major resource—and a focus of controversy—ever since.

~1190   Maimonides completes Guide of the Perplexed, a work seeking to reconcile rationalist philosophy with Jewish texts, beliefs, and practices. He addresses it (in Arabic) to Jews who are "perplexed" by the challenge of living in two cultures.

1204   Maimonides dies.

PRIMARY TEXT

The depth and breadth of Maimonides's erudition in all the Jewish literature that came before him, his knowledge of the surrounding culture, his ability to question and analyze, and his gift for clear and graceful expression—all these qualities have kept his works on the best-seller list for eight hundred years. Moreover, another important factor seems to have been his courage: his willingness to tackle, head-on, what he saw as the key spiritual and intellectual challenges of his age.

A mark of this courage was his taking on the challenge of preparing a codification of Jewish law. The act of codification implies the authority to choose among the multiple legal opinions on any given topic, found in the Talmud and later commentaries, declaring which are binding. Such an act requires not just erudition, but hubris — and the willingness to stand up to rejection. Since no institution could formally grant Maimonides this authority, he took it upon himself.

His *Mishneh Torah* (Repetition of the Torah) is divided into fourteen books (hence its nickname *Yad Chazaka*, "strong arm": the letters in the word *yad*, Hebrew for "arm," have the numerical value 14; and note the conclusion of the Torah, Deuteronomy 34:10–12: "Never again did there arise in Israel a prophet like Moses . . . for the *strong arm* and the great awe that Moses displayed before all Israel"). Each book is divided into topical sections, and these into chapters and verses — similar in structure to the Mishnah, but using a different order and hierarchy of topics and subtopics. It is written in a clear Hebrew that might be seen as emulating the Mishnah.

In its opening pages (excerpts to follow), Maimonides touches upon three themes that were central to all of his work: the importance of creating a systematic articulation of Jewish belief; the need for codification even with its price; and the necessity to address rationalist concerns regarding the many biblical texts that seem to personify God.

To Maimonides, the conditions of life in Muslim Spain required all three. Integration and cultural interchange necessitated clearer self-definitions. Jewish practices and beliefs had to be articulated in accessible ways and in terms that made sense in the cultural milieu — holding their own with the competition in the marketplace of ideas.

Excerpts from Maimonides, *Mishneh Torah*

Introduction (pp. 39–40)
In our days, severe vicissitudes
prevail, and all feel the pressure of
hard times. The wisdom of our wise

men has disappeared; the understanding of our prudent men is hidden. Hence the commentaries of the Geonim and their compilations of laws and responses, which they took care to make clear, have in our times become hard to understand so that only a few individuals properly comprehend them. . . .

On these grounds, I, Moses the son of Maimon the Sefardi, bestirred myself, and, relying on the help of God, blessed be He, intently studied all these works, with the view of putting together the results obtained from them in regard to what is forbidden or permitted, clean or unclean, and the other rules of the Torah—all in plain language and terse style, so that thus the entire Oral Law might become systematically known to all. . . . Hence, I have entitled this work *Mishneh Torah* (Repetition of the Law), for the reason that a person who first reads the Written Law and then this compilation, will know from it the whole of the Oral Law, without having occasion to consult any other book between them.

Maimonides is casting himself as a latter-day Yehudah HaNasi, trying to save the Oral Law from being lost on account of historical dislocations and the lack of proper scholarly leadership. Note he is also insinuating that the current authorities, the *Ge'onim* in Babylonia, are not effective.

In the Middle Ages, the biblical term "Sepharad" or "Sefarad" (Obadiah 1:20) came to mean Spain. Maimonides, writing in Egypt, is emphasizing his Spanish roots.

Maimonides was influenced by the code of Rabbi Isaac Alfasi but was much more ambitious; Alfasi saw his work as a tool for Talmud study, not as a replacement for it. Some of Maimonides's contemporaries perceived Maimonides's claim that his work would replace all other texts of the Oral Law, including the Talmud, as evincing unwarranted arrogance. And of course it did not override all that had come before it, but it did become an almost indispensable aid for anyone studying the Talmud and other legal texts. Maimonides's language was indeed terse and clean, and his organization logical and clear. Moreover, he covered all areas of Jewish

Book I, Knowledge:
Basic Principles of the Torah,
Chapter 1 (pp. 43–45)

1) The basic principle of all basic principles and the pillar of all sciences is to realize that there is a First Being who brought every existing thing into being. All existing things, whether celestial, terrestrial, or belonging to an intermediate class, exist only through His true existence.

4) . . . He alone is real, and nothing else has reality like His reality. The same thought the Torah expresses in the text: "There is none else besides Him" (Deut. 4:35); that is: there is no being besides Him, that is really like Him.

6) To acknowledge this truth is an affirmative precept, as it is said, "I am the Lord your God" (Ex. 20:2; Deut. 5:6). And whoever permits the thought to enter his mind that there is another deity besides this God, violates a prohibition; as it is said, "You shall have no other gods before Me" (Ex. 20:3; Deut. 5:7), and denies the essence of religion—this doctrine being the great principle on which everything depends.

law, including those that were only applicable within the Land of Israel and those that were no longer applicable in the absence of the Temple.

Another important—and controversial—Maimonidean innovation was placing statements of belief in a code of law, even to the point of stating (v. 6) that belief in God's uniqueness is a positive commandment, and doubting it is a violation of a negative one.

One of Maimonides's great challenges in defending Jewish belief from rationalist criticism was explaining the many biblical texts that seem to personify God. His insistence that these are all metaphors aroused opposition in those who,

9) . . . What is the meaning of the following expressions found in the Torah: "Beneath His feet" (Ex. 2:10); "Written with the finger of God" (ibid. 31:18); "The hand of God" (ibid. 9:3) . . . and similar phrases? All these expressions are adapted to the mental capacity of the majority of mankind who have a clear perception of physical bodies only. The Torah speaks in the language of men. All these phrases are metaphorical.

uninterested in harmonizing with rationalism, deemed this approach as undermining belief in the truth of the Torah.

—From Isadore Twersky, *A Maimonides Reader*

LEGACY

Impact

Maimonides's wide-ranging contributions have informed and challenged the discourses of Jewish thought and law in every generation since. The *Mishneh Torah* is indispensable for students of Jewish law. *Guide of the Perplexed* remains a foundational work in Jewish philosophy, a landmark contribution to the effort to harmonize Jewish and Western culture. A poetic version of his "Thirteen Principles of Faith," in which he attempted to condense all of Jewish belief into thirteen beliefs (Maimonides's commentary to the Mishnah, Tractate *Sanhedrin*, chapter 10), is a popular hymn, "Yigdal."

In his own time Maimonides was not universally revered, as he largely is today. His rationalist approach was highly controversial, especially in Jewish communities whose cultural and religious environment leaned not toward the rationalism of Muslim Iberia, but toward the mysticism of Christian France. The controversy raged in literature and sermons and reached a nadir in public book burnings in the thirteenth century (see chapter 15).

The *Mishneh Torah* also stirred some opposition, particularly from scholars in France, who saw it as an attempt to supersede the Talmud. On the one hand, the *Mishneh Torah* acquired an authoritative status due to Maimonides's erudition, clarity, and reasonable persuasiveness. On the other hand, within a generation it had begun to generate commentaries containing opposing views. As these accumulated, they were studied and ultimately printed alongside Maimonides's text. They "softened" the *Mishneh Torah* from an authoritative code into a useful tool for legal deliberation, which it remains to this day.

The Christian reconquest in 1248 put an end to the Golden Age, and the expulsion in 1492 (see chapter 16) put an end to Jewish life in Iberia altogether. Nevertheless, the experience of this period continues to resonate on a number of levels:

- Subsequent generations saw the model of mutual respect that characterized the Golden Age as unique and worthy of emulation. This understanding became a model for their own approach to the world. In other words, ever since the biblical patriarch Abraham, Jews had been challenged to find the balance between maintaining their distinctiveness and integrating into the surrounding culture. The Golden Age appeared to demonstrate that such a balance was possible.
- The Jews also established a new model of deep rootedness in a diaspora homeland. Despite the ideology of living in exile, the Jews of Iberia had unpacked their bags and put down roots, the pulling up of which would prove highly traumatic (see chapter 16). Despite the trauma, this model continued to influence Jewish life in Western Europe and North America.
- The division of world Jewry into Sephardic and Ashkenazic (see chapter 14) originates with the creation of a distinctive Sephardic Jewish culture—another outcome of this Golden Age. During the centuries of the Golden Age, the majority of the Jews in the world lived in Muslim countries (Iberia, North Africa, Mesopotamia) and dominated Jewish culture. After Jews emigrated from Iberia to escape Christian oppression, they created vibrant centers of Sephardic Jewish culture all around the Mediterranean and beyond.
- The rich cultural creations of the Golden Age are still very much with us. Many—among them Abraham ibn Ezra's popular Torah commentary and the poems of both Judah Halevi and Solomon ibn Gabirol that have entered the liturgy—have become classics of Hebrew culture.

Memory

The continued existence of Sephardic Jewish culture means that the memory of the Golden Age is very much alive.

Today we encounter this heritage in a number of places. For example:

- Hundreds of synagogues throughout the world follow Sephardic liturgical customs, such as positioning the leader's podium in the center of the synagogue and housing the Torah scrolls in a portable, cylindrical wooden or metal case.
- Communities, cantors, orchestras, and individual performers continue to perform religious and secular Sephardic music, including many Ladino songs.
- The spoken Hebrew of modern Israel uses the Sephardic pronunciation.
- Communities and families throughout the world, including Israel, Turkey, Latin America, New York City, and London, continue to pass on Sephardic traditions in holiday and life-cycle observance, music, and food. For example, in Sephardic communities, legumes and rice are eaten on Passover; Ashkenazic tradition forbids this. Some Ashkenazic families have taken on the Sephardic custom of holding a "seder" on Rosh Hashanah eve—eating and explaining a sequence of symbolic foods.

Maimonides himself holds a place of honor in Jewish collective memory. Hospitals, schools, and synagogues around the Jewish world—as well as streets in Israel—are named for him. And his tomb (according to tradition) in Tiberias is a pilgrimage site (although, being a rationalist, he probably would not have approved of prayers for divine intercession being offered at his tomb).

TEXT FOR DISCUSSION

The twentieth-century scholar Jacob Guttmann articulates a question raised by Maimonides's efforts: Is "harmonization" between revealed religion and rationalist philosophy really possible, or must one system "surrender" to the other? What do you believe?

Despite Maimonides' keen awareness of the differences between Judaism and the Aristotelian schools . . . the relationship between [religion and philosophy, for him] . . . is essentially one of identity. . . . For Maimonides, this is not merely a matter of congruence of the objective contents of revelation on the one hand and of philosophic knowledge on the other. Philosophy is rather a means, in fact the sole means, for the internal appropriation of the content of revelation. Religious faith is a form of knowledge. . . . Here we have an intellectualist concept of faith which . . . makes religious inwardness dependent upon the deepening of philosophic understanding. Philosophy not only has religion as its object, but it is the central element of religion itself, the royal road that leads to God.

— Julius Guttmann, *Philosophies of Judaism*, trans. David Silverman
    (Philadelphia: Jewish Publication Society, 1964), p. 155

FURTHER READING

Ashtor, Eliyahu. *The Jews of Moslem Spain*. 3 vols. Translated by A. Klein and J. M. Klein. Philadelphia: Jewish Publication Society, 1973–1984. A detailed history.

Gorsky, Jeffrey. *Exiles in Sepharad: The Jewish Millennium in Spain*. Philadelphia: Jewish Publication Society, 2015. A compact survey of Spanish Jewish history. See especially pp. 1–69.

Halbertal, Moshe. *Maimonides: Life and Thought*. Princeton: Princeton University Press, 2014. Analysis of Rambam's work in the context of the history of *halakhah* and Jewish thought—and his cultural milieu.

Kraemer, Joel. *Maimonides: The Life and World of One of Civilization's Greatest Minds*. New York: Doubleday, 2008. A biography, with emphasis on historical and cultural context.

Lewis, Bernard. *The Jews of Islam*. Princeton: Princeton University Press, 1984. A classic study of Jewish-Muslim relations.

Twersky, Isadore. *A Maimonides Reader*. New York: Behrman House, 1972. An anthology of excerpts from Rambam's works, with informative introductions.

14. The Rise of Eastern European Jewry

THE CRUSADES, 1100–1300 CE

HISTORY

The Rise of Ashkenaz

As the scattered Jewish communities of Iberia were gaining in numbers and self-confidence under Muslim rule, a similar process was occurring to the north and east, in what became France and Germany, the region the Jews called Ashkenaz. Technology advanced, populations grew, cities developed, and the Jews began to organize communities governed by local lay and rabbinical leadership—and to assert independence from the authority of the Geonim in Babylonia. Jews engaged in various professions (the great biblical and talmudic commentator Rashi, for example, was a vintner), and some attained positions of wealth and power. They also established autonomous communal institutions for education, governance, and social welfare.

However, overall there was a qualitative difference between life under Christianity and life under Islam during this time. The Muslim conquerors were often content to tolerate religious minorities for the sake of stability and economic growth. While at select times the church and Christian rulers adopted similarly pragmatic policies, the relationship of Christianity to Judaism was more fraught. The competition between Christianity and Judaism was seen as a zero-sum game, so the pressure to "prove" the truth of Christian faith by perpetuating Jewish suffering was constant. This general ideology of Jewish inferior status translated into requirements to wear special garments and to pay special taxes, restrictions on where Jews could live, and prohibitions against holding public office and participating in trade. Jews were excluded from manufacturing, because the craft guilds were closed to them. They were excluded from agriculture, because they were not allowed to own land. And whatever status and stability they did attain were always at risk, for there was nothing to prevent a local ruler from expelling them and confiscating their property.

For their part, the Jews intrinsically felt more comfortable under Muslim rather than Christian rule. The language of Islam was Arabic, a Semitic language with a relationship to Hebrew and Aramaic; the language of Christianity, on the other hand, was the language of Rome, which evoked bitter memories of destruction and exile. Islam, like Judaism, forbade even the appearance of worshiping images, while Christian churches were crowded with figurative art. From this vantage point as well, the prospects for the Jews' stable integration into the surrounding society and culture were much slimmer in Christian than in Muslim lands.

Nevertheless, despite obstacles and setbacks, Jews found a home in Ashkenaz. Their communities and institutions grew, and these produced scholars and leaders whose contributions transcended their time and place. Among them are Rabbenu Gershom (~960–1040), the first Ashkenazic rabbi known to have issued halakhic decrees accepted across the whole region (for example, the prohibition of polygyny and of divorcing a woman against her will); and Rabbi Solomon Yitzchaki of France (1040–1105), known as Rashi, who authored commentaries on both the Bible and the Babylonian Talmud that have served as key resources throughout the Jewish world ever since.

Because the Jews maintained greater cultural distance from their environment in Ashkenaz, Jewish scholarship was generally not in dialogue with non-Jewish thought, as it often was for the Jews in Muslim lands. It was, rather, an internal conversation among texts and voices within the body of Jewish traditional literature.

The Crusades

With the launch of the First Crusade in 1096, Jewish "outsiderness" and Christian antisemitism erupted into a major catastrophe for Ashkenazic Jewry.

The year before, Alexius, the Byzantine emperor, had requested Pope Urban II's assistance against the Turks, who had conquered Jerusalem and other parts of his realm. Soon thereafter, Urban, presiding over a major church council, called for a large-scale military campaign that would unite Christian forces from across Western Europe both in helping Byzantine Christians in their struggle with the Turks and in "rescuing" the Church of the Holy Sepulchre in Jerusalem. Participant fighters were promised a "plenary indulgence," the release from obligation of acts of penance for sins confessed (or, as many believed, release from time in purgatory after death). The response was enthusiastic; armies were raised across the continent.

In the meantime, however, the call also brought forth disorganized mobs who, without military discipline, plundered their way across Europe until they were stopped by armies of the Christian countries they sought to pass through in the east. Along the way, the despised Jews the mob encountered in the Ashkenazic communities stood in for the far-off infidel enemy, serving as a vulnerable target and an easy source of plunder. Notably, the church and various local rulers denounced such behavior and tried to protect the Jews. Occasionally these efforts succeeded, but more often they did not, because the church and rulers lacked the strength—or the will—to stand against the mob.

In the course of two centuries, from 1096 to the fall of the Crusader Kingdom of Jerusalem in 1303, there were at least seven (historians quibble over the number) European military campaigns to conquer the Holy Land or to defend Christian rule there. The largest of these, and the one causing by far the most damage to European Jewish communities—due to its unintended mobilization of mob violence against local Jews—was the first. Thousands of Jews were massacred, and a number of communities were crippled or decimated.

However, as terrible as they were, the Crusades were passing phenomena. They may have temporarily united European Christian rulers against a far-off common enemy, but Christian Europe remained politically fragmented and often unstable, riven by dynastic conflicts and territorial disputes, so anti-Jewish measures tended to be local and short-term. And so, even in the midst of considerable turmoil, Jewish life went on. In various times and places during these two centuries, many individuals and communities even thrived, economically and culturally. For example, the Tosafists (= those who add), rabbis who developed a major new approach to talmudic analysis, were active in France and Germany during this period.

Nevertheless, these extreme events demonstrated to both the Jews and their neighbors the reality of Jewish vulnerability. And the First Crusade would inaugurate four centuries of insecurity and oppression, punctuated by violent attacks, confiscations, and expulsions.

Migration to the East

While Jewish communities and institutions did regroup and continue to function through the Crusades and centuries after, many Jews sought a more secure environment. Between approximately 1200 and 1500, thousands migrated toward the "wide open spaces" to the east, to Poland.

Small colonies of Jews had previously resided in Poland—immigrants from the south and east, from Byzantine territories and the Khazar kingdom in the Caucasus (whose king converted to Judaism in 740, taking the whole kingdom with him; it lasted almost three centuries). In addition, small numbers of Jewish merchants from Germany had traded and then settled in western Poland. But after the first century of the Crusades, the movement eastward grew significantly and continued through the next three centuries. Poland was rich in natural resources but underpopulated and underdeveloped, and its secular rulers saw German (Jewish and Christian) immigration as a means for developing trade and industry. Thus they issued charters that accorded the immigrants protection in their persons, their property, and their freedom to live according to their religion and culture.

The Jews' reception in Poland was nonetheless mixed. Poland had converted to Catholicism in 966, and the church was less enthusiastic about welcoming or even tolerating Jews than were the nobles and kings. Hence, Jewish life there was lived in the tension between religious persecution and economic and cultural flowering.

The particular circumstances of Jewish migration from the more "advanced" west to the more "primitive" east had several consequences:

- The temptations—and the opportunities—to integrate with the surrounding culture were minimal. The Jews tended to live apart and even to speak their own language, which they had brought with them. Yiddish was Judeo-*German*, not Judeo-*Polish*.
- The Jews also brought with them Ashkenazic Jewish culture: ritual practices, such as dressing the Torah scroll in a cloth mantle; an approach to Torah study based on internal analysis of the text (the Tosafists' method); and foods, such as the triangular filled pastries (hamantashen) eaten on Purim. Moreover, they preserved their connection to their "roots" by continuing to rely on the halakhic author-

ity of rabbis in Western Europe until a local leadership developed, around 1500.

- Jews were generally not allowed to own agricultural estates, which in any case were worked by the peasants (serfs) living on the land. Hence, Jews moved into managerial positions or certain skilled trades that they themselves needed in their own communities. For example, they became estate managers for the noble landowners (mediating between the owners and the peasant tenants), tax and toll contractors for the government, moneylenders, and traders (cloth, wood, metal, manufactured goods). To serve Jewish needs, they became tailors, brewers/winemakers, innkeepers, and butchers and then served non-Jewish customers as well.
- Immigration plus a high natural rate of increase led to rapid Jewish population growth, reaching perhaps 20 percent or more of an estimated one million world Jewish population by the sixteenth century.

As a result, by the mid-sixteenth century, Poland had become a major center of Jewish life and culture, characterized by an elaborate structure of autonomous self-government (national as well as local), vibrant institutions of scholarship and education (yeshivot), and great scholars, such as Rabbi Moses Isserles (1520–72), who wrote a code of *halakhah* parallel to the Sephardic code, the Shulchan Arukh, and Rabbi Solomon Luria (1510–73), whose commentary is included in all standard editions of the Babylonian Talmud.

Timeline: Medieval Ashkenaz, 800–1600 CE

Jews were living scattered from France to Russia, from Roman times. The Jews gave this region the biblical name Ashkenaz (Genesis 10:3).

960–1040?   The life of Rabbenu Gershom ben Yehuda, "Maor Hago-
            lah" (Light of the Exile) of Mainz (Germany); a scholar
            and leader whose authority was recognized through-
            out Ashkenaz, he led the region's move toward indepen-
            dence from Babylonian authority.

963–66   Mieszko organizes Poland as a kingdom, establishes
            the Piast dynasty, and converts the kingdom to Catholi-

	cism. The kingdom would remain fragile and often fragmented over the next thousand years.
987	Hugh Capet becomes king of France; his descendants rule in Paris until 1328.
~1100	For the next three centuries Germany has a weak central government, with many semiautonomous territories.
1040–1105	The life of Rabbi Solomon Yitzchaki, "Rashi," of Troyes (France); he was a prolific scholar and teacher whose clear and comprehensive commentaries on the Bible and Talmud remain central texts on the Jewish bookshelf.
1085	Alphonso VI of Castile and Leon conquers Toledo from the Muslims; the Christian reconquest of Spain has begun.
1095	Pope Urban II calls on European Christians to march eastward to help Byzantine Christians in their struggle with the Turks and to reassert Christian rule over Jerusalem.
1096	The Crusader mobs (the "People's Crusade") massacre and plunder Jewish communities across Germany until they reach Hungary, where the army stands against them.
1099	The Crusaders take Jerusalem, massacring the Muslim and Jewish populations.
~1100–1300	The Tosafists (= those who add on), a school of talmudic analysis, are active, primarily in France.
1145–49	Second Crusade. Ashkenazic immigrant communities in Poland begin to grow.
1150–1217	Life of Rabbi Judah "the Pious" of Regensburg, who led the pietistic movement Hasidei Ashkenaz (not to be confused with the Hasidic movement that would arise in Eastern Europe in the eighteenth century).
1182	German emperor Frederick I defines the Jews as "property of the Imperial Chamber," a concept that spreads throughout Christian Europe. Meanwhile, French king Philip Augustus orders the expulsion of the Jews from his lands (he allows them to return in 1198).
1187	Saladin leads a Muslim victory over the Crusaders and retakes Jerusalem.

1189–92	Third Crusade.
1202–1303	Several more Crusades, mostly unsuccessful; the last Crusader fortress finally falls in 1303.
1215	The Fourth Lateran Council, a major gathering of Catholic leadership, decrees that Jews throughout Catholic Europe must wear a distinctive Jewish badge and forbids them to hold public office, among other restrictions.
1241	Anti-Jewish riots break out in Frankfurt. Meanwhile, the depredations of the Tatars in Poland leave the country in need of population and skills, leading to large-scale immigration from Germany, both Christian and Jewish.
1264	Duke Boleslav of Kalish issues his *Statuta Judeaorum*, defining the rights and obligations of the Jews in his territory; this becomes the model for defining the status of Jews throughout Poland.
1298	Approximately twenty thousand Jews are massacred in Bavaria and Austria.
1306	King Philip the Fair orders the expulsion of all Jews from France.
1348–49	Blamed for the Black Death (bubonic plague), thousands of Jews are massacred across Europe (including Spain, but especially in the German Empire). The plague itself made no distinction between Jews and Christians.
~1400–~1500	Jews are repeatedly expelled from various cities and states of Western and Central Europe.
1470–1541	Life of Rabbi Jacob Pollack of Lublin, the first major Torah scholar known to us from Poland; he is credited with bringing knowledge and methodology from Germany that served as the foundation for the rise of Jewish scholarship in the east.

PRIMARY TEXT

Several Jewish accounts of the Crusades were found in the late nineteenth century. The most coherent as a historical narrative is a manuscript by Solomon bar Simson, about whom we know nothing except that he probably lived a generation after the events. Most likely he assembled and edited his narrative from reports he received. Christian historical sources corroborate many of the events he describes, but not all the specific local details can be verified. In any case, his dramatic rendition reflects important aspects of the medieval Ashkenazic experience.

Chronicle of Solomon bar Simson

As [the Crusaders] passed through the Jews' towns, they said to each other, "We are setting off on a long journey to reclaim our house of idols and to take revenge on the Ishmaelites — but living right here among us are the Jews, whose ancestors killed and crucified [Jesus] for nothing. So first let's take vengeance on them and eliminate them from among the nations so that the name of Israel will no longer be remembered — or else let them become like us and accept the son of prostitution [impurity]."

The narrator first describes the gathering of French and German "hordes" as they set forth to conquer Jerusalem.

The Jews knew the Christians' anti-Jewish arguments and were unsparing in their mockery of the Christians' faith.

... On the eighth day of Iyar, on the Sabbath, the enemies rose up against the community of Speyer and killed eleven holy souls who sanctified the Creator's name on the holy Sabbath and refused to be defiled by the filth [of the Christian faith]. There was an important and pious woman who slaughtered herself for the sanctification of [God's] name. She was the first in all those communities to slaughter herself. The rest [of the Speyer com-

A recurrent theme in this document: choosing death—even suicide—over baptism.

Apparently in a number of cases clergy or nobles/kings tried (not always successfully) to save the Jews from the mob, whether to assert their authority amid chaos, or out of humanity, or because of economic interests.

munity] were saved by the bishop without defilement (baptism).

... [In Mainz], on the third day of Sivan [local Crusader leader] Emicho the evil one ... came to the gate with all his forces, and the townspeople opened the gate for them. ... The holy God-fearing ones were loyal to their creator: From old to young, they put on armor and took up weapons ... and fought against the Crusaders and the townspeople at the gate. But on account of their sins the enemy overcame them and took the city. ...

And when the children of the holy covenant saw that the decree had been decreed and that the enemies had entered the courtyard, they all cried out ... to their father in heaven, and cried for themselves and for their lives, and accepted the divine judgement, and said to each other, "Let us be strong and suffer the holy yoke of reverence for God, for it is only temporarily that the enemies kill us—and death by sword is the least painful of the four forms of execution ... but we will live forever, our souls in paradise. ..."

And when the enemies entered the courtyard they found there

This was war. Sometimes the Jews attempted armed resistance, but they were generally overwhelmed by the mob. Martyrdom then became a kind of psychological warfare, a public put-down of Christianity: Christian faith is so detestable that it is better to be dead than Christian.

This is the thinking behind the concept of dying for *kiddush ha-Shem*, the "sanctification of God's name": in showing that belief is more important than life itself, the martyr brings honor to that belief and to God— and shows disdain for those trying to "save" him or her through an "abominated" religion.

Note the Deuteronomic view: the people's sufferings were punishment for their sins.

The Talmud describes four methods of execution: sword, fire, stoning, strangulation.

Note that the burghers ("townspeople") are specified among the mob. The rising class of urban merchants

some of the pious ones with Rabbi Yitzchak ben Moshe . . . he presented his neck and they cut his throat first . . . and those who were hiding in the rooms saw these things and cried, "There is nothing better for our God than to sacrifice our souls." And women rose up in strength and slaughtered their children and themselves, and many people had the courage to slaughter their wives and their children . . . and they cried out in a great voice, "O God, look and see what we are doing to sanctify Your great name, in refusing to exchange You for the disgusting, crucified one, despised in his own generation, the bastard son of a menstruating, promiscuous woman."

. . . The whole community of Regensburg were forcibly converted, for they saw that they couldn't be saved. The Crusaders and the mob gathered all [the Jews] who were in the city and pushed them into the river and made the sign of evil over the water — "the warp and weft" [i.e., the cross] — and thus baptized them all at once in the river, for there was a [great mass of] people there. But they all returned to follow the Lord; as soon as God's ene-

saw the Jews as unwelcome competition, so the Crusades were useful to them.

Martyrdom was not the only option. Insincere conversion followed by repentance was possible. To situations like this Rashi applied the talmudic statement "A Jew, even though he has sinned, is still a Jew." Therefore, no conversion process was required to return to Judaism (see chapter 16).

Note that the Regensburgers did not commit suicide, and they are not criticized for their choice. Perhaps this indicates a certain ambivalence about what constituted the "best" response. Suffering conversion under duress and then doing penance is also, perhaps, a form of *kiddush ha-Shem*, but one that allows life—and Jewish life—to go on.

mies had passed by they did a great
penance. For what they had done,
they had done on account of great
force, unable to stand against the
enemies; moreover, the enemies
had not wanted to kill them. May
God forgive us our sins.

—A. Neubauer and M. Stern, *Hebraische Berichte uber die Judenverfolgungen
wahrend der Kreuzzuge* (Berlin: Leonhard Simion, 1892), pp. 1–2, 6–7, 28

The dynamic present in the massacres of the First Crusade would recur
throughout Christian Europe. While the church officially tried to protect the
Jews from violence, its teachings appeared to give the common folk license
to kill. Catholic doctrine presented the Jews both as rejecters of Christianity
who must survive—but suffer—as witnesses to the falseness of their belief,
and also as Christ killers, agents of the devil who posed an ongoing threat.
Hence, when the Jews were pushed into unpopular and vulnerable economic
niches (moneylenders, tax collectors, merchants), explosions of anti-Jewish
mob violence came to serve as useful releases for social and class tensions.

Solomon bar Simson's text describes several important—and not necessarily congruent—Jewish responses to this harsh reality:

· The Jews are being punished collectively for their own sins.
· Jews should fight for their lives when they can.
· Judaism is true; Christianity is "false" and "disgusting"; it is important to demonstrate to the Christians that Jews would rather die than
be baptized.[8]
· On the other hand, if one is baptized under duress, one is still Jewish, and return is possible.

8. Solomon bar Simson's stories of Jews committing suicide to avoid baptism represent an extreme
understanding of the talmudic dictum (*Sanhedrin* 74) that faced with the choice of idolatry or
death, one must choose death—but death at the hand of the oppressor, not at one's own hand.
We do not have examples of such behavior attested after these Crusader-period accounts. Later,
the model of false conversion became dominant (see chapter 16).

LEGACY

Impact

The Jews' calamitous experience during the Crusades became a prototype for Jewish-Christian relations in Europe. The Crusades' demonstration of Jewish vulnerability made that vulnerability a part of European culture. Thus, even if Solomon bar Simson's manuscript was unknown to most Jews and Christians, the experience it described became a black cloud that darkened European Jewish history for eight hundred years.

After the Crusades, many Jews took on the profession of moneylending. One contributing factor seems to have been that given the prospect of expulsion—and the danger to merchants transporting goods on the roads—it was prudent to keep one's assets compact and portable. Moreover, as the European economy developed, there was a growing need for credit—just at the time the church was ratcheting up its opposition to moneylending by Christians.

The Crusades were also a turning point in inaugurating the migration of the Ashkenazic center eastward, facilitating the great flowering of Polish Jewry, an impact that is still felt throughout the Jewish world (see chapters 17, 18, 21, and 24). In the nineteenth- and twentieth-century migrations, the Jewish communities of North and South America and Palestine became outposts of Polish-Ashkenazic culture. In the case of Palestine, Ashkenazic dominance lasted until the mass migration from North Africa and the Middle East to newly independent Israel (see chapter 27). In North and South America, what generally passes for "Jewish culture"—foods, holiday and life-cycle customs, liturgy—is actually Ashkenazic culture.[9]

Memory

Surviving literary narratives from the Crusades period include a body of poetry written for inclusion in public prayer. Most of the works were not included in printed prayer books and so have dropped out of Jewish lit-

9. Interestingly, once the State of Israel adopted the Sephardic pronunciation of Hebrew, this pronunciation became standard in most diaspora communities—even those that are in all other respects heirs of Ashkenazic traditions. Today, the Ashkenazic pronunciation of Hebrew is only heard in those Orthodox communities who are committed to preserving Ashkenazic custom in its entirety as a religious obligation.

urgy. One exception is the *Av harachamim shochen bam'romim* (Father of mercies who dwells on high) prayer, recited in Ashkenazic synagogues on certain Sabbaths and festivals. In addition, the beloved Ashkenazic *piyyut* (hymn) that is sung during Hanukkah candlelighting, *Maoz Tzur* (Rock of Ages)—a narrative of God's repeated saving of the Jewish people from persecution—dates from this period.

The Crusades experience and aftermath colored many historians' writings, giving rise to what the twentieth-century historian Salo Baron dismissively called "the lachrymose theory" of Jewish history. The succession of massacres, expulsions, extortions, and so on experienced in medieval Europe came to be seen as the main event, and not as a series of interruptions in a history not merely of survival, but of autonomy, prosperity, and cultural creativity. Baron's argument is important; calamities had significant impact, of course, but if they were the whole story, there would be no story.

TEXT FOR DISCUSSION

During the period of the Crusades, the Muslim Almohads subjected Jews to forced conversion in North Africa and Spain (see chapter 13). When asked about the obligation of martyrdom, Maimonides gave the following answer. How do you believe his analysis might have been received by his Ashkenazic contemporaries?

> Remember that in all the difficulties that occurred in the time of the sages, they were compelled to violate commandments and to perform sinful acts. . . . But in this persecution they are not required to do anything but say something, so that if a man wishes to fulfill the 613 commandments secretly he can do so. He incurs no blame for it. . . . This compulsion imposes no action, only speech. They [the Muslims] know full well that we do not mean what we say, and that what we say is only to escape the ruler's punishment and to satisfy him with this simple confession. . . . But if anyone comes to ask me whether to surrender his life or acknowledge, I tell him to confess and not choose death.
>
> —Abraham Halkin, trans., *Epistles of Maimonides: Crisis and Leadership* (Philadelphia: Jewish Publication Society, 1985), p. 30

FURTHER READING

Chazan, Robert. *In the Year 1096: The First Crusade and the Jews*. Philadelphia: Jewish Publication Society, 1996. An analysis of the Jewish accounts of the First Crusade and their place in Jewish thought and historiography.

Eidelberg, Shlomo, trans. and ed. *The Jews and the Crusaders*. Hoboken NJ: Ktav, 1996. Translations of the Hebrew chronicles of the Crusades.

Katz, Jacob. *Exclusiveness and Tolerance*. New York: Schocken Books, 1961, pp. 3–130. A classic analysis of Jewish-Christian relations in medieval Europe.

Parkes, James. *The Jew in the Medieval Community*. New York: Hermon Press, 1976, pp. 19–92. A description of Jewish-Christian relations up to and through the Crusades period.

Weinryb, Bernard. *The Jews of Poland*. Philadelphia: Jewish Publication Society, 1973, pp. 3–106. A survey of developing Jewish life in Poland until 1500.

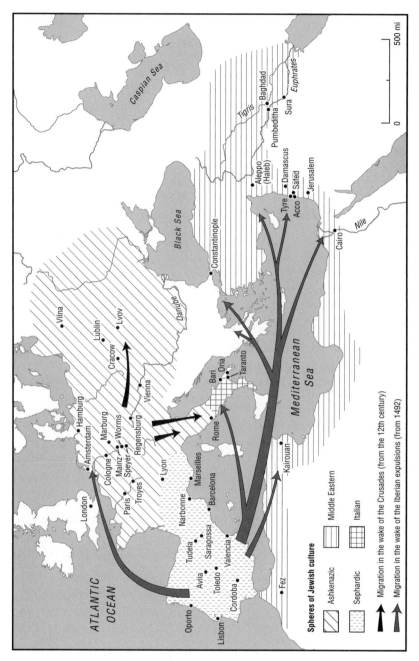

Map 3. Medieval Jewish cultures, ca. 1500 CE

15. Kabbalah Enters the Mainstream

NAHMANIDES, ~1300 CE

HISTORY

Life in Christian Spain

As the Christians expanded and consolidated their rule of Iberia in the twelfth, thirteenth, and fourteenth centuries, they encountered Jewish communities and Jewish leaders who saw them as deliverers from Almohad persecution (see chapter 13)—ironically, just as the Jews had seen the Muslim conquerors as deliverers from Visigothic oppression in the eighth century. Meanwhile, the Christian rulers needed the Jews for their skills (especially literacy), trade and diplomatic connections, and capital. Thus, a dynamic developed that was similar to the one in Poland (see chapter 14): the church wanted the Jews to survive but to suffer; the rulers wanted the Jews to thrive but not to feel too secure. In the *modus vivendi* that evolved, Jews lived in protected communities with a high degree of autonomy; for example, their internal court system, based on Torah law, had the authority to adjudicate matters of personal status, business disputes, damages, and crimes of property. Yet, Jews were circumscribed by a variety of restrictions—barred from craft guilds and landowning, required to live in the "Jewish street," obligated to wear the Jewish "badge," burdened with special "Jew taxes"—and the general awareness that their fortunes depended on the whims of the current ruler.

Nonetheless, the Christian reconquest of Iberia did not bring the kind of suffering the Jews of Ashkenaz experienced during the same period. Many communities thrived, and individual Jews rose to positions of power despite church opposition; for example, King James I of Aragon issued a decree prohibiting Jews from holding public office but then appointed a Jew, Judah de la Cavalleria, as his state treasurer.

Jewish cultural life flourished. As the neutral cultural meeting ground of the former Golden Age—secular poetry, philosophy, and science—was significantly reduced under the new regime, Jewish intellectual and spiritual creativity turned more inward: to halakhic (legal) scholarship and engagement in spiritual matters. Jews in Christian Spain developed a new approach to mysticism, Kabbalah, which became important to the intellectual and spiritual life of the people and, in subsequent centuries, would have far-reaching influence throughout the world.

Kabbalah

Two events embody the spiritual foundation upon which Judaism was later constructed: Abraham's discovery of God (see chapter 1), and the Revelation of the Law to the entire people Israel at Mount Sinai (see chapter 3) — both of which later generations remembered as unique, direct, personal encounters between humans and God. In each generation, Jewish leadership considered how to interpret and institutionalize these revelations. The sum total of these accumulated interpretations — both as literature and as law — is what we know as Judaism.

However, a tension is built into this developmental process. On the one hand, subsequent generations are intended to "reenact" the Revelation through their living the law and studying the texts; on the other hand, such reenactment is only "the next best thing to being there." As the original event recedes into the past, the experience of studying and remembering it may feel distant, ritualized, archaic. The spirit may feel petrified — and this can lead to chafing at the restrictions of tradition and attempting to escape the bonds, by somehow getting closer to the original experience.

The waves of Jewish mysticism over the centuries can be seen as manifestations of such rebellion. Mysticism generally refers to various text study methods and meditative practices that allow the mystic to experience close contact, or communion, with God. In Judaism it has taken different forms, including ecstatic experiences based on meditation, asceticism, or music and dance; elaborate symbolic interpretations of traditional texts and rituals; and activist modes that on occasion have spilled over into magic or messianism. The mystic argues: Why must we accept that direct encounters with God were restricted to ancient times and are not available to us?

Here, another built-in tension arises: between mystical experience and traditional stability. Just as mysticism may revitalize tradition, it may also endanger it. If everyone had equal access to direct divine revelation, then everyone could claim prophetic authority; each new prophet could then offer "a new Torah," as it were, undermining the authority of Moses's Revelation and the tradition grounded in it.

That seems to be why mystical approaches to Judaism have always been present but never became dominant. Their products—liturgical poetry and practices, commentaries, great scholars—were often absorbed into the tradition but "kept in place," never radically redirecting it.

Several factors may have contributed to the flowering of a new school of mysticism in Spain and Provence starting in the thirteenth century. Mystical thought was well developed in medieval European Christianity, and despite the cultural distance between Christians and Jews, Jewish thinkers were likely influenced by their surroundings to pursue the study of theosophy (knowledge of God). Jewish mysticism may have also flourished as an expression of dissatisfaction with the establishment leadership—rabbis and oligarchic lay leaders. In any case, this new school, Kabbalah, developed during the Reconquest, with Girona, in the northeast, as its first center.

Kabbalah had a strong intellectual-theosophical component. Its students imagined a series of ten emanations, together constituting an invisible structure (reminiscent of the electron orbitals of modern physics) mediating between the infinite God and the finite universe. Finding expressions of these emanations and the relations among them, kabbalists believed they could influence these relations, through understanding and concentrating on symbolic interpretations of classical texts and everyday ritual.

The primary text of Kabbalah was the Zohar ("Splendor"—perhaps based on the prophet Ezekiel's use of the word to describe his vision of God, in Ezekiel 8:2). The kabbalists believed that the Zohar originated in Rabbi Shimon bar Yochai's circles in second-century Palestine (see chapter 10), because it presented itself as a collection of teachings by Rabbi Shimon and his fellow *tannaim* (Rabbinic sages) and stories about them, written in Aramaic. However, the presence of Spanish words and sentence structure, the references to medieval historical events, and the fact that neither the Talmud nor any other medieval texts ever refer, even indirectly, to the ideas, stories, and halakhic decisions contained in the Zohar have led modern scholars to see it as a much later work. Today it is thought to be a product of thirteenth-century Spain, compiled by Rabbi Moses de Leon of Avila (~1240–1305), a prolific writer of kabbalistic texts, several of which have survived in manuscript form.

The Zohar went on to become a best seller, apparently because of the "authority" of its attribution to Rabbi Shimon. Reprinted many times, it gave rise to a whole literature of commentary.

From this period forward, while intensive scholarship in Kabbalah remained the province of elite circles of experts, its influence spilled over into the mainstream. Its terms and symbols became part of the liturgical texts, practices, and Torah study of the wider community. An important conduit for this dissemination was the Torah commentary of Rabbi Moses ben Nahman, or Nahmanides.

Nahmanides

As Maimonides (Rambam) was to the Golden Age, so was Rabbi Moses ben Nahman (Ramban, Nahmanides) to Christian Spain of the Reconquest. Both were intellectual and creative giants whose written works immortalized aspects of the Jewish interaction with a particular cultural and political environment, by folding that interaction into the ongoing accumulation of Jewish tradition.

Nahmanides, also a physician, spent most of his life in Christian Spain. Born in Girona in 1194, he was influenced by teachers from different cultural origins — Spain, Provence, and Ashkenaz — and by the kabbalistic scholarship of his home community. He went on to bridge different approaches, especially the Andalusian rationalist tradition represented by Maimonides and the mystical and pietistic approaches of Provence and Ashkenaz.

He wrote a number of halakhic works, including a critique of Maimonides's *Sefer ha-Mitzvot* (a mapping of the 613 commandments), and practical legal treatises on topics such as death and mourning, and marital relations. His magnum opus was his commentary on the Torah, in which he responded to and expanded upon two major commentators who preceded him — Rashi (of France) and Abraham ibn Ezra (of Muslim Spain) — and introduced kabbalistic thought into his explication of the biblical text (see below). Because of his very accessible style and wide-ranging knowledge, his commentary became and remains very popular and influential, included in most editions of the Hebrew Bible with traditional commentaries.

Nahmanides is also remembered for his involvement in two significant public events that shed light on the reality of Jewish life and culture in Christian Spain:

1. The Maimonidean Controversy: When Maimonides's writings seeking to reconcile rationalist philosophy with Jewish belief made their way into Christian Spain and France, they ran up against an unsympathetic cultural milieu. In those communities, where both Jews and Christians held beliefs in mysticism and pietism, rationalism had never been an issue, and Maimonides's suggestions that traditional descriptions of God and God's actions could be understood allegorically were seen as blasphemous, a denial of the Torah's truth. In the 1220s, supporters and opponents of Maimonides's approach attacked each other in letters, sermons, appeals for communal support, and decrees of excommunication. Nahmanides, recognized as a rabbinical authority by this time, sided with the critics of rationalist philosophy but tried to defend Maimonides's intentions and his scholarship, arguing that Maimonides was only doing what was required by the needs of the hour in his particular setting. His counsel of dialogue and respect was not heeded, however, and the discourse became increasingly strident. In 1233 the church got involved, publicly burning Maimonides's books in several French towns. At this point both Maimonides's opponents and defenders realized that things had gotten out of hand, and the controversy died down—for the time being.

2. The Disputation of Barcelona: In 1263, instigated by the apostate Pablo Christiani, King Alphonso X ordered Nahmanides to engage in a public debate with Pablo on whether the Messiah had come and on the nature of the Messiah predicted by the prophets. After four days, the king commented to Nahmanides, "Let the debate be adjourned, for I have never seen a man who was wrong argue his case as well as [you]." While Nahmanides emerged honorably from the fray, in the end he was tried for blasphemy and found guilty. The king commuted his sentence from death to banishment, and he left Spain for Palestine, where he spent his last years.

Timeline: The Period of the Reconquest, 1015–1270 CE

1015	Christian forces finally conquer Catalonia (northeastern Spain), a long-contested borderland between Muslims and Christians.

1085	Christians conquer Toledo, in the center of the peninsula.
1145–49	The Second Crusade includes campaigns against the Muslims in Iberia.
1194	Nahmanides is born in Girona, in Catalonia. He goes on to study medicine as a profession. Rabbis from Spain, Provence, and France are his teachers in Jewish studies.
1204	Maimonides dies.
1210	Nahmanides begins his first work of scholarship: a defense of Rabbi Isaac Alfasi's legal code (see chapter 13).
1231	The Inquisition is established to root out the Cathar heresy in France.
1232	Nahmanides intervenes in the dispute over Maimonides's philosophical works, trying to make peace between the factions.
1233	Church officials burn Maimonides's books in several French cities.
1248	Christians complete the reconquest of Iberia (except Granada).
1252–84	Reign of King Alphonso X of Castile. He issues a code of law that both supports the autonomy of local Jewish communities and restricts Jewish life. This code becomes widely imitated throughout Iberia.
1263	The Disputation of Barcelona: Nahmanides is ordered to defend Judaism before the king and court.
1267	Banished by the king, Nahmanides emigrates to Palestine, where he goes on to complete his commentary on the Torah.
1270	Nahmanides dies in Palestine.

Timeline: Jewish Mysticism

~100	First texts of Merkavah (Chariot) mysticism—visions and mystical experiences based on the description of the chariot in chapter 1 of Ezekiel. Originating in Palestine and spreading to Babylonia—and later to Europe—these experiences and texts were known to the Rabbis of the

Mishnah and Talmud but did not enter the mainstream of Rabbinic literature.

~1150–1250   The emergence of Hasidei Ashkenaz (the Pious Ones of Ashkenaz) in the Rhineland communities. Absorbing ideas from Merkavah mysticism and the Christian environment, this popular movement taught that a mystical understanding of the Torah gave rise to a life—or at least acts—of altruism and asceticism.

~1180   The beginning of the rise and spread of Kabbalah, an approach to Jewish mysticism emphasizing speculation on the emanations of the divine in the world and understanding classical texts and laws as expressing—and influencing—these emanations.

~1280   Rabbi Moses de Leon compiles the Zohar (Splendor), to become the central text of Kabbalah.

~1500–1600   Safed, a town in northern Palestine settled by many exiles from the Spanish expulsion (see chapter 16), becomes a center for a new, activist version of Kabbalah: "Lurianic" Kabbalah (for Rabbi Isaac Luria), whose influence would radiate throughout the Jewish world.

~1750   The beginning of the rise and spread of Hasidism in Poland. A popular movement influenced by various previous strands in Jewish mysticism (both ecstatic and contemplative), it would spread rapidly and become a mass movement (see chapter 18).

PRIMARY TEXT

Nahmanides uses Rashi's commentary as a basis for his commentary on the Torah. Rashi, the "foundation stone" of medieval commentary, focused mostly on explaining the plain meaning of the text, often by referring to interpretations found in the Rabbinic literature (Talmud and midrash). Nahmanides often quotes from Rashi, occasionally disagrees with his commentary, but more often adds other layers and nuances onto the basic explanation. He frequently refers to kabbalistic interpretations, draws on his knowledge of the sciences, and brings in rational-philosophical understandings (in order to reject or reintepret them).

Note that Nahmanides is known not as a great original scholar of Kabbalah, but as a popularizer of it. He produced a rich and useful popular work that, on account of his broad learning and eclectic approach, helped bring kabbalistic concepts and symbolism out from the esoteric realm and into general Jewish discourse for everyone.

Nahmanides, Introduction to Commentary on Genesis

We have a true tradition that the whole Torah consists of names of the Holy One blessed be He, and that if the division into words is changed from the traditional division, the letters form names of God. . . . This is why we may not use a Torah scroll in which even one letter is added or subtracted in error [even if the error has no consequence for the meaning of the verse]. . . .

So it seems that when the Torah was given, "written with letters of black fire upon a background of white fire," the letters were contiguous, without spaces between words, so it could be read as a series of divine names, or it could be read in our normal reading, giving the plain meaning of the Torah and law. It was given to Moses our teacher in writing using the normal division, and orally divided according to the divine names. This is like the practice of those who are knowledgeable in Kabbalah, who write God's great name [of seventy-

This is an example of a kabbalistic explanation for a well-known law. A Torah scroll must be perfect. Even if a mistake is trivial in terms of content, it renders the scroll unusable. Nahmanides's comment expresses an important kabbalistic concept: the letters and words of the Bible have meanings that transcend their normal denotation; those with the training and commitment can find new meanings through recombinations of the letters, among other methods.

The image of the Torah as black fire on a background of white fire is found in a number of parallel Rabbinic midrashim.

two letters] contiguously and then divide them into words of three and other combinations. . . .

. . . I am writing this commentary for those who read the weekly Torah portion, to satisfy their curiosity and to draw them close to the plain meaning of the text—as well as to provide edification for those who are versed in Kabbalah. . . .

Nahmanides is explicit about writing on two levels: for the layman, and for the kabbalist. He urges the uninitiated to pass over his kabbalistic allusions.

I earnestly request and advise all who read this book not to try to interpret and understand for themselves any of the hints that I have written regarding mystical meanings of the Torah. I assure you that nothing of these matters can be understood using logical reasoning, but only from the mouth of a wise kabbalist speaking into a receptive ear. Trying to understand them logically is foolish . . . and can only cause great harm. . . .

Nahmanides, Commentary to Genesis 1:1: "In the Beginning God Created . . ."

. . . The act of creation is a deep mystery that cannot be understood from the plain text, and it cannot be fully known except through the tradition going back to Moses our teacher who received it from the mouth of God; and those who know it are obligated to conceal it. . . .

The first words of Genesis are *Bereishit bara Elohim* (In the beginning God created). *Reishit* appears many times in the Bible in various contexts, with the connotation of first or best; e.g., Exodus 23:19; Deuteronomy 33:21; Jeremiah 2:3.

[Nahmanides then presents Rashi's explanation that the Torah began with the creation of the earth in order to affirm God's prerogative to divide the earth as He saw fit—granting Israel possession of the Land of Israel. He goes on to quote a Rabbinic midrash linking several appearances of the word *reishit* in the Torah.]

Here Nahmanides connects a rabbinic sermon based on recurrence of *reishit* in different contexts with the kabbalistic concept of the divine emanations (*sefirot*). One of these emanations, wisdom (*hokhmah*), is at the top of the flowchart in the kabbalistic imagination. (See Psalm 111:10: *Reishit hokhmah*, "The first [or: best] wisdom" or "Wisdom is first.")

The Rabbis' intent [in the above texts] is as follows: The word *bere-ishit* hints at the creation of the world by the ten emanations, and alludes in particular to the emana-tion of wisdom, which is the foun-dation of everything, as it is said [Proverbs 3:19], "The Lord founded the earth by wisdom."

... A man counts ten measures [of produce] and sets aside one mea-sure as a tithe: This is an allusion to the ten emanations—for wise men contemplate the tenth emanation [wisdom] and speak about it. ...

The law of tithes requires that the offering come from the first, or best (*reishit*) produce (Deuteronomy 18:4).

[Returning to the explication of the opening words, *bereishit bara:*]

Now listen to the simple, direct, and clear explanation of the text: The Holy One blessed be He created all the creations from absolute nothing-ness. The only Hebrew expression

In returning to discuss the explica-tion of the opening words, *bereishit bara*, Nahmanides engages with the rationalists, arguing that the Hebrew text implies a rejection of the Aris-totelian view that matter is eternal: God created the unformed primeval

we have for this creation *ex nihilo* is *bara* (created). And there is nothing under the sun or beyond it that did not arise originally out of nothingness. But God extracted from this absolute and total nothingness a very tiny foundation, nothing but the creative force itself, ready to take on form, to go from potential to reality. This was the primeval matter, which the Greeks called *hyle*. And after the *hyle* God created nothing further, but merely formed it into everything that exists.

matter, *hyle*, imagined by the Greeks to be eternal, out of absolute nothingness, and then built the world out of it. Here Nahmanides is co-opting contemporary philosophical/scientific concepts while rejecting their religious implications.

LEGACY

Impact

The flowering of Kabbalah that radiated out of Christian Spain had significant impact on Jewish belief and practice around the world. Mysticism moved out of the ecstatic, esoteric fringe into the mainstream, by focusing on theosophy: "a mystical doctrine, or school of thought, which purports to perceive and to describe the mysterious workings of the Divinity, perhaps also believing it possible to become absorbed in its contemplation," as Gershom Scholem, the pioneering twentieth-century scholar of Jewish mysticism, wrote in *Major Trends in Jewish Mysticism* (p. 206).

Through the structure of the *sefirot*, the divine emanations, Kabbalah offered a way to concretely imagine the spiritual. Through this imagery, Jews could find spiritual meanings in the everyday laws of Judaism as well as in biblical and Rabbinic texts, thereby revitalizing these practices and texts. The texts of Spanish Kabbalah—the Zohar, Nahmanides's commentary— made this revitalization widely accessible, facilitating its popularization (see "Timeline: Jewish Mysticism") and development.

Of course, just as the Oral Law developed in pendulum swings between codification and expansion, a similar dynamic has characterized the relationship between Kabbalah and the legal tradition. For example, kabbalists in sixteenth-century Safed introduced the *Kabbalat Shabbat* (welcoming the Sabbath) service on Friday evenings (before the obligatory evening service), and in their eyes the popular hymn *Lekhah Dodi* in that service was a mystical text. Today, *Kabbalat Shabbat* is standard in Jewish liturgy, and everyone sings *Lekhah Dodi*, usually with no consciousness of mystical symbolism.

Memory

As soon as printing was invented, Nahmanides's Torah commentary became a beloved staple of the Jewish bookshelf. For many people throughout the centuries and in the present, his interpretations (along with Rashi's and Abraham ibn Ezra's) have been seen as inseparable from the biblical text itself. His warm, "teacherly" style and his wide-ranging, eclectic approach to the Torah engaged generations of Jews in text study, and his work thereby moved kabbalistic language and symbolism into the general vocabulary of Judaism.

TEXT FOR DISCUSSION

Here, Isadore Twersky, a leading modern scholar of medieval Jewish history and philosophy, offers his concise appraisal of Nahmanides's approach to *halakhah* and Kabbalah. Considering it is often said that Judaism is a religion of law based on the Sinai covenant, how do you think Nahmanides would have responded to Twersky's appraisal?

> His intense, simultaneous preoccupation with halakhah and kabbalah is also emblematic of the "law and spirituality" theme in Judaism—a creative, authoritative Talmudist of the first order, Nahmanides insisted with great pathos that study of Talmud must be supplemented by study of kabbalah whose concepts and symbols infuse the normative system with spirituality and theological vision.
>
> —Isadore Twersky, *Rabbi Moses Nahmanides (Ramban): Explorations in His Religious and Literary Virtuosity* (Cambridge MA: Harvard University Press, 1983), p. 7

FURTHER READING

Baer, Yitzhak. *A History of the Jews in Christian Spain*. Vol. 1. Philadelphia: Jewish Publication Society, 1961. A detailed history.

Chavel, Charles. *Ramban: His Life and Teachings*. New York: Feldheim, 1960. A brief biography that includes Nahmanides's teachings on a number of topics.

Chazan, Robert. *The Jews of Medieval Western Christendom, 1000-1500*. Cambridge: Cambridge University Press, 2006, pp. 90-115. A concise chronology and analysis of the Jewish experience in Christian Spain.

Finkel, Avraham Y., trans. and ed. *Sefer Chasidim—The Book of the Pious*. Northvale NJ: Jason Aronson, 1997. The major text of Hasidei Ashkenaz.

Gorsky, Jeffrey. *Exiles in Sepharad: The Jewish Millennium in Spain*. Philadelphia: Jewish Publication Society, 2015. A compact survey of Spanish Jewish history. See especially pp. 70-96.

Maccoby, Hyam. *Judaism on Trial*. Portland OR: Vallentine Mitchell, 1993. Documents from the Barcelona disputation, among others.

Moses ben Nahman. *Ramban: Commentary on the Torah*. 5 vols. Translated by Charles. Chavel. New York: Shilo, 1971-76. A modern translation of Nahmanides's commentary on the Torah.

Scholem, Gershom. *Major Trends in Jewish Mysticism*. New York: Schocken Books, 1961. A survey of the development of mysticism by the scholar who founded its study as a discipline in the twentieth century. See especially chapters 1 and 6.

16. The End of Iberian Jewry

CONVERSION, EXPULSION, DIASPORA, 1300–1600 CE

HISTORY

Developments in the Christian Kingdoms of Iberia

In the early 1300s, as the Christian monarchs expanded and consolidated their rule over Iberia, they found the Jews—engaged in various professions and in the bureaucracy—useful to them as suppliers, bankers, advisors, administrators, and diplomats. Hence, Jewish life continued to thrive.

By the middle of the fourteenth century, however, the Jews' situation deteriorated. Certain social groups, particularly nobles and burghers, resented the competition for resources and influence. At the same time, the church became increasingly militant in its efforts to prove the absolute truth of Christian belief by demonstrating the falseness of the competition. Such demonstration required Jews to convert—or to suffer for their refusal.

As the century drew to a close, the condition of the Jews grew increasingly precarious. Popular preachers and church officials incited against the Jews, often resulting in mob violence. The kings and their officials responded inconsistently, sometimes protecting the Jews (the kings' assets) and other times going with the flow of religious persecution or popular anger.

A breaking point came in 1391, when the king of Castile died. In the ensuing interregnum, the lack of a strong central government facilitated attacks on Jews that spread through all of Spain. Thousands of Jews were killed, and some communities, such as Barcelona, were completely destroyed.

The next century saw some rehabilitation, as the rulers reasserted their authority and ordered that Jewish communities be reestablished and protected (not all of them; for example, Barcelona's Jewish community was not restored until the twentieth century).

Yet things were falling apart. As the Christian rulers consolidated their rule, they brought Spain into the cultural and religious orbit of Europe, where the church's theological "problem" with the Jews (see chapters 14–15)

strongly influenced public policy. The church's missionary activities escalated. Jewish functionaries still served at the highest level of government—
for example, as court physicians and financial managers—but pressure
from the church as well as from Spanish nobles and middle-class citizens
who resented Jewish economic and political competition made their position precarious. In the course of the fourteenth and fifteenth centuries,
both local and national governments acted (sometimes reluctantly) to
restrict Jewish economic freedom and to remove Jews from public office.
And increasing religious zealotry among the Christian nobility weakened
the Jews' access to royal protection.

When King Ferdinand of Aragon married Queen Isabella of Castile
in 1469, their marriage represented the political unification of Spain.
"The Catholic Monarchs" (as they were known) decided to purify the
kingdom of Jewish and Muslim influence. They established a Spanish
branch of the Inquisition in 1480 to root out Judaizing heresy. Then in
1492, with the conquest of Granada, the last Muslim enclave in the Iberian Peninsula, they ordered the expulsion of any Jews (or Muslims) who
refused to convert.

After centuries of rootedness, acculturation, and integration, the edict
was a huge shock and trauma for the Jews. Mass conversions and mass
migrations followed. The nearest destination, Portugal, allowed many Jews
to enter, but five years later would join the Spanish kingdom and adopt
an even crueler policy: forced conversion with no option of emigration.

Over the course of the sixteenth and seventeenth centuries, emigrants
spread around the Mediterranean (North Africa, Palestine, Turkey, Greece,
the Balkans, Italy) as well as the Netherlands. Their migration was fraught
with danger (storms, pirates, disease) and the trauma of uprooting.

The Jews' outlook improved with the fortuitous rise of the Ottoman
Empire in Turkey. From 1453 onward, the Ottoman dynasty extended
its territory into southern Europe, Egypt, and the Middle East. Like the
developing Polish kingdom three hundred years earlier (see chapter 14),
the Ottomans welcomed the Jewish refugees, recognizing their skills, connections, and resources as useful for economic development. Vibrant Sephardic communities sprang up throughout Ottoman lands.

It would take until the twentieth century for the Spanish edict of expulsion to be repealed. And it would be another century before descendants

of the expellees were granted the right to apply for Spanish or Portuguese citizenship (in 2015).

Conversion, Heresy, and the Inquisition

However, the story of the end of Iberian Jewry is more complicated than a simple narrative of expulsion and migration (as described in Don Isaac Abarbanel's account later in this chapter). Already before the 1391 catastrophe, conversion was not uncommon. Some Jews made the decision out of a true crisis of faith or were convinced by missionary claims. Others converted out of expediency, for from the moment of baptism, all Jewish restrictions and special obligations were canceled, and there was no limit to the convert's opportunities in business, government, and even the church.

From 1391 until 1497 (the decree of forced conversion in Portugal), conversion expanded into a large-scale phenomenon. It's estimated that toward the end thousands of Jews underwent symbolic conversion with no true religious conviction. Disbelieving in the Christianity they practiced publicly, they observed Jewish ritual in secret, waiting for a change in policy or the chance to emigrate and openly return to Judaism.

The neutral term for all of these categories is "Conversos." At the time, Christians who were suspicious regarding the sincerity of the Jews' conversion used the pejorative term "New Christians" and the even more pejorative "Marranos" (swine). Meanwhile the Jews referred to forced converts sympathetically as *anusim* (forced ones)—as distinct from *meshumadim* (destroyed ones), those who were perceived to have converted voluntarily. Today, descendants of *anusim* who maintained their Jewish identity in secret are referred to as "crypto-Jews."

From the Christians' vantage point, the increasing number of Jewish converts to Christianity entering Iberian society soon became problematic. In many cases, Jews who had resources, skills, and connections and had previously been denied social integration and positions of authority rose quickly to full integration upon conversion—and even to high positions. Born Christians competing for the same jobs, social status, and resources resented this instant advancement and suspected the conversions were insincere. Adding to these suspicions, Jews who converted retained their previous social and business connections—and often their residency—within the Jewish community, and many continued to display Jewish behavior (e.g., refraining from eating pork, a mainstay of the Spanish diet and economy). Thus, by the end of the fourteenth century, popular resentment of the converts—and the church's realization that forced conversions are by their very nature suspect—led to popular violence, legal measures restricting the converts (forbidding them from socializing or living with Jews or even from leaving the country, to prevent their reverting to Judaism), and finally the establishment of an institution for finding and rooting out insincere converts: the Inquisition. Since doubts prevailed about New Christians' Christian commitment, "purity of blood" became a criterion for public office. In other words, the perceived unreliability of conversion led to institutionalizing a racial definition of Judaism.

Meanwhile, the converts were so numerous and so ubiquitous that the church itself began to feel threatened. It was impossible to know who "really" was a Christian, as Conversos had made their way into the Catholic clergy and even into the church hierarchy.

Hence, from the mid-1400s, the Inquisition became a dominant force in public life. No one was safe from its reign of terror. Ostensibly a court system with orderly proceedings of gathering evidence to find "Judaizers" and ensure their repentance, it developed into a powerful, corrupt, and cruel institution that used unreliable informers and torture to obtain "evidence," confiscated property, and carried out public executions. The public ceremonies of "repentance" gained through suffering and death were known as *autos-da-fé*, "acts of faith."

Note that Inquisition authorities had no interest in or authority over Jews per se. The Inquisition's sole purpose was to purify the church from heresy and insincere conversion. Jews were supposed to be Jews and Christians, Christians, each having a clear identity with a defined status. The Inquisition was to enforce this clarity, to prevent the blurring of boundaries and the confusion over divinely ordained status that the Converso phenomenon had created.

Inquisition activity peaked in Portugal in the sixteenth and seventeenth centuries as the church persecuted descendants of the forced converts of 1497. Ultimately, church doubts regarding forced conversion, pressure from world public opinion, and modernization in Spain and Portugal led the respective monarchs to close the Inquisition—in Portugal in 1820 and in Spain in 1834. By then, the Inquisition in Spain and Portugal had publicly executed more than thirty thousand "Judaizers."

Conversion and the Jewish Community

The prevalence of conversion was problematic for Jews as well as Christians. By this time, the Jews of Iberia were deeply integrated socially and economically in the land and culture and couldn't imagine another home (at least until the messianic redemption). Hence, the persecutions and expulsions brought their Spanish and Jewish identities into conflict. While some saw conversion as a betrayal, as the century wore on (especially after 1497) it became a fact of life. Converts who left the peninsula—or their descendants—often reverted to Judaism in their new homes. This raised difficult legal questions; for example: if a Converso man refused to join his Converso wife in emigrating and returning to Judaism, was she free to remarry in her new home, or was she still legally married? Rabbis in North Africa and Ottoman lands struggled with many such painful cases involving family relationships torn by conversion and emigration.

In most cases, when the Conversos emigrated to other lands, the official Jewish position was as to repentant sinners—that is, they were accepted automatically, with no "reconversion." On the other hand, those who stayed in Spain and Portugal were unable to transmit their Jewish identity openly, through the generations. While various romantic anecdotes about "secret Jews" endure—locals wittingly or unwittingly observing vestiges of Jewish customs generations after the expulsion (and indeed, there certainly were such cases)—the vast majority of the converts, true or false, ultimately disappeared into the Christian population.

The Sephardic Diaspora

Suddenly, between 1492 and 1497, the largest (at least three hundred thousand), proudest, culturally and materially richest Jewish community of the Middle Ages disappeared from the Iberian Peninsula.

Still, over the years about one hundred thousand Jews from Spain and Portugal (Portugal would later relax the prohibition of converts' emigration) were able to emigrate and bring their culture with them. They established important communities in North Africa, Palestine, Syria, Turkey, the Balkans, Italy, the Low Countries, and, later, outposts in the New World.

For the most part the émigrés did not assimilate into their new Jewish communities, but maintained their own institutions, customs, and cultural activity, encompassing *halakhah*, Kabbalah, philosophy, liturgy, and music. Many of these communities would develop into vibrant, self-sustaining centers of Jewish life and culture that lasted until the Holocaust or until the mass migration to Israel after 1948.

Thus, the expulsion/conversion erased Sepharad, the Jewish "province" of Iberia, from the map, but Sephardic culture continued to flourish, in new locales, with pride.

Timeline: 1263–1654

1263	Disputation of Barcelona (see chapter 15).
1306	Expulsion of Jews from France (see chapter 14). Many Jews flee to Navarre in northern Spain, including converts to Christianity who seek to return to Judaism and are pursued by the Inquisition.
1328	Riots against the Jews in Navarre.
1340–1412	Life of Hasdai Crescas, a widely respected halakhic authority who authored anti-Christian polemics as well as a critique of Maimonides's Aristotelian philosophical approach. He was also a communal activist with close ties to the royal administration, which he sought to exploit—with some success—to protect Jewish communities in a difficult period.
1348	Riots against the Jews in various locations, in the wake of the Black Death.
1354	A conference of Jewish communities in Aragon asks the king to call on the pope to take action against the persecution of Jews. Pope Clement VI later issues a bull rejecting the popular accusation that the Jews had caused the plague by poisoning the wells.
1391	After over a decade of antisemitic incitement by a popular preacher, riots and violent attacks on the Jewish community break out in Seville. At a time of interregnum in Castile, the attacks spread throughout Spain, leading to widespread conversions and the destruction of many Jewish communities. Many communities are soon rehabili-

tated; but some, such as Barcelona and Valencia, disappear from the map of Jewish history.

1393   King John I of Aragon enacts laws preventing new converts to Christianity from socializing or living with Jews and from leaving the country (ostensibly in order to return to Judaism).

1413–15   Disputation of Tortosa. Pope Benedict orders all Jewish communities of Aragon to send leaders to participate in a public "disputation" whose explicit goal is to discredit Judaism (and the Talmud) and to encourage conversion. Many conversions — and new persecutions of those who refuse — ensue.

1449   Toledo experiences the first major outbreak of popular violence against converts to Christianity, who are seen as having "parachuted" into positions of power with their conversion. Later laws prohibit converts from holding positions of authority.

1469   Queen Isabella of Castile marries King Ferdinand of Aragon. As they consolidate their rule, they institute policies to persecute insincere converts.

1480   The Inquisition, which had functioned in various European cities locally since the thirteenth century, is instituted as a Spanish national institution.

1482–98   Term of Tomas de Torquemada as Grand Inquisitor. A Dominican who served as personal confessor and advisor to Isabella, he oversaw the Inquisition's expansion into an all-powerful and brutal national court system for the persecution of converts — ultimately executing more than thirty thousand "Judaizers."

1491   Ferdinand and Isabella conquer Granada, the last Muslim enclave in Iberia.

1492   Ferdinand and Isabella issue an edict of expulsion to all the Jews in the kingdom. The Jews scatter around the Mediterranean and the Low Countries; many go to Portugal. Ottoman sultan Beyazid II welcomes the refugees and assists them in reaching and settling in Turkish territories.

1497   Ferdinand and Isabella's daughter becomes betrothed to the king of Portugal — on the condition that he remove all the Jews there. He decrees expulsion but then decides to convert them all, by force if necessary, and forbids them to emigrate. The ban on leaving the country is lifted in 1507, leading to a large wave of emigrants.

1516   Palestine comes under Ottoman control, facilitating Jewish migration there.

1654   The Portuguese conquer Recife (Brazil) from the Dutch. Forced to flee, the Jews who had settled there put down new roots at the nearest Dutch outpost, New Amsterdam.

PRIMARY TEXT

Don Isaac Abarbanel's eyewitness description of the expulsion is often quoted in histories of the period.

Abarbanel (sometimes spelled Abravanel) was born in Portugal in 1437 to an "aristocratic" family (wealthy and learned). He held a number of high positions in the financial administrations of the lands where he lived and became very wealthy through these posts and his private business dealings. In addition, he was a respected rabbi and a prolific and creative scholar, whose commentary on the Bible is still popular.

Don Isaac Abarbanel, Introduction to Commentary on Kings

At the beginning of the year 5244 (1484), as I was about to begin writing my commentary on the book of Kings, I was called to the house of the king of Spain, highest of the kings of the land, the ruler of the kingdoms of Castile, Aragon, Catalonia, Sicily, and the rest of the islands; I came to the court of the king and his wife, and I was with them many days. God gave me favor in their eyes and in the eyes of the highest officers of the kingdom, and I was busy with

Abarbanel had been treasurer to the king of Portugal; political instability there impelled him to flee to Spain in 1483, where he entered the royal service as an advisor and tax contractor.

their work for eight years. Meanwhile, I acquired wealth and honor on my own, not in their courts and in their palaces. Therefore Torah [study] stopped and my writing was halted. Because of my work for the gentile kings . . . I abandoned my heritage, the kingdoms of Judah and Israel, and the commentary on their [history].

In the ninth year, the year of "He who scattered Israel" [Jeremiah 31:10], the king of Spain captured the kingdom of Granada with the great city Granada and its environs. In his victory his heart was uplifted and his spirit changed, and he credited his power to his God. So "Esau" said in his heart, "How can I please the God who girded me with strength in war and how can I thank my Master who has given this city in my hand, if not by bringing under his wings the people who walk in darkness, the scattered sheep of Israel, and by bringing the wayward daughter to his religion and his belief? Or else to send them to another land, . . . so that they will no longer dwell in my land nor remain in my sight." And so the word of the king went forth, like the laws of Persia and Media [Esther 2:19], decreeing: "All the families of the house

The word *mezareh*, "scattered," has the numeric value of 252. The Hebrew year 5252 was 1492.

Since Roman times, "Esau" was the Jewish pejorative "code" for Romans and then Christians.

Though Abarbanel doesn't mention it, the order of expulsion applied to Muslims as well.

of Israel who are baptized and bow down and worship the god of the gentiles will eat of the fruit of the land like us and dwell in the land and trade in it. And if you refuse and rebel and do not mention my god's name and do not worship my god, then get up and depart from among my people, from the lands of Spain, Sicily, Majorca, and Sardinia that are under my rule, so that after three months there shall not remain one trace of him who is called Jacob or Israel in all the lands of my kingdom."

As I was present in the king's court, I exhausted myself with words to the king; three times I pleaded with him, "Won't you save us O King? Why are you doing this to your servants? Ask of us a high price; gold and silver and anything anyone of Israel owns they will give for their land." I called upon my friends, who were close to the king, to plead for my people, and nobles gathered to speak to the king forcefully to reverse the wrathful decree and his plan to destroy the Jews, but he, like a "deaf viper that stops its ears" [Psalm 58:5], would not respond; and the queen stood at his right hand to urge him on to complete the work he had begun. We struggled but were not suc-

It seems that the king and queen were indeed driven by religious zeal. They were unmoved by appeals of the rich and powerful and even by the offer of bribes.

cessful. I did not rest and was not
silent, but the day of wrath came.
And the people heard the terrible
news and mourned; everywhere
that the king's decree arrived there
was heavy mourning, and a great
fear and sorrow such had not been
seen since the day Judah was exiled
from his land. . . . Each man said to
his brother, "Be strong for our religion and for the Torah of our God,
against the voice of the slanderer
and the blasphemer, the enemy
and the avenger. If he lets us live
we shall live, and if he kills us we
shall die, but we will not profane
our covenant. Our hearts will not
retreat, and we will walk in the
name of the Lord our God."

To the Jews of Spain this seemed a
calamity on the order of the Babylonian exile.

Powerless, three hundred thousand of the people, I among them,
from young to old, infants and
women, on one day all departed
from the lands of the king, to
wherever the wind [or spirit; Ezekiel 1:12] took them, and they went
out with [God] their King at their
head. . . . Some went to the nearby
kingdoms of Portugal and of
Navarre, where they encountered
trouble and darkness, and the evils
of violence and hunger and disease. Some of them set to sea, and
there too the hand of God was
against them to strike and destroy

Abarbanel does not mention the
many Jews who chose to remain
and be baptized, whether as a
sham or as a sincere conversion.

them, for many miserable ones were sold as slaves in the lands of the gentiles, and many "sank like lead in the mighty waters" [Exodus 15:10]; others were burned with their ships by the fire of God. No one was spared from His harsh judgment, who by sword and who by captivity. . . . As our fathers said [Numbers 17:27]: "We perish; we are lost, all of us lost." May the name of the Lord be blessed.

I too chose the route of a ship at sea, and I, with other exiles, arrived with my household here in the glorious city of Naples, whose kings are kindly.

Abarbanel and his family sailed to Naples, where he entered the service of the king. When the French invaded Naples in 1495, he fled once again, ending up in Venice, where he died in 1508.

Abarbanel is a classic representative of a certain "type" then common in Iberian Jewry: the wealthy, educated businessman and public servant who moved comfortably among kings and nobles—and at the same time a rabbi who devoted significant energy and talent to serious Torah scholarship.

Interestingly, Abarbanel gives the story "spin" like a traditional tale of woe—from the Babylonian exile to the Crusades: the Jews condemn the cruel enemy but see God's hand in the disaster; they fight but then accept their fate. He mentions exile and martyrdom but not conversion, an option chosen by thousands. His comparison of the expulsion to the Babylonian exile is a common theme in literature from the period. Jews saw their exile as a disaster of cosmic proportions.

LEGACY
Impact

The date 1492 is etched in Jewish collective memory. The expulsion from Spain has universally been seen as one of the key turning points in Jewish history—a unique and terrible trauma for individuals, communities, and Iberian Jewry at large and the sad end of a glorious era.

At the same time, the expulsion was also a beginning, as Sephardic culture flowered in new footholds around the world. The great Jewish civilization that developed in North Africa (see chapter 27), the rise of Lurianic Kabbalah in Safed (see chapter 18), the vibrant communities of Amsterdam, Saloniki, Izmir/Smyrna, and ultimately New York and Philadelphia—all had roots in the 1492 edict.

A major center of Jewish life also developed in the Netherlands, which welcomed the exiles. Protestantism had gained a foothold there, and from 1568 the country was in a state of ongoing rebellion against Spanish Catholic control. With Dutch cities offering a refuge from the Inquisition in the sixteenth century and thereafter, Amsterdam became a vibrant, thriving Jewish cultural center. Among its more famous luminaries are the following:

- Manasseh ben Israel (1604–57) was a rabbi, community activist, and printer who established the first Hebrew press in Amsterdam.
- Uriel da Costa (~1580–1640) was a Portuguese refugee who published rationalistic critiques of Judaism (and religion in general) that the Amsterdam Jewish communal leadership judged heretical. After repeated excommunications and humiliations, he committed suicide.
- Baruch Spinoza (1632–77), from a Portuguese Converso family, arrived in Amsterdam, after several migrations, in 1627 and reverted to Judaism. Excommunicated at the age of twenty-three for his heretical views, Spinoza spent the rest of his short life quietly setting forth his philosophical system, which included rationalistic critiques of the Bible and religion. At the time, both Jews and Christians banned these writings. Today Spinoza is recognized as one of the founding fathers of modern Western philosophy.

Memory

The fast day the Ninth of Av, commemorating the destruction of the First and Second Temples, came to commemorate additional disasters over the years, including the expulsion from Spain. Otherwise, there is no liturgical commemoration of the expulsion.

Today elements of Sephardic culture echo its origins: the Ladino language—Judeo-Spanish, spoken by the exiles for generations; poetry and music; foods, holiday customs, and liturgy.

Over the past century and a half, descendants of Conversos have been "discovered" in villages in the Portuguese countryside, Mexico, and elsewhere. These families seem to have preserved Jewish memories or vestiges of observances. Some of them are unaware of their connection to current Judaism; others seek to return and join a community. The authenticity of these memories and the mechanisms of their preservation are subjects of ongoing research (and controversy).

According to Muslim folk tradition, the *aqal*, the rope holding the keffiyeh head-scarf in place, is always black, as a sign of mourning for the 1492 expulsion. Like the Jews, many Muslims underwent insincere conversions to Christianity; these converts were called *Moriscos*. Ultimately, as many as two hundred thousand managed to emigrate, mostly to North Africa.

TEXT FOR DISCUSSION

The Jews saw the expulsion not only as a catastrophe, but as one of cosmic significance. Is it possible to avoid seeing the events we ourselves experience as having historical—or even cosmic—significance? What are the costs and benefits of attempting to "understand" the map of history?

[Soon after the expulsion there appeared] numerous epistles, tracts, homilies, and apocalyptic writings in which the repercussions of the catastrophe reached their most vigorous expression. In these writings, whose authors were at great pains to link up the Expulsion with the ancient prophecies, the redemptive character of the 1492 catastrophe was strongly emphasized. The birthpangs of the Messianic era, with which history is to "end" . . . were therefore assumed to have set in with the Expulsion.

—Gershom Scholem, *Major Trends in Jewish Mysticism* (New York: Schocken Books, 1967), p. 147

FURTHER READING

Baer, Yitzhak. *A History of the Jews in Christian Spain*. Vol. 2. Philadelphia: Jewish Publication Society, 1961. A detailed history.

Chazan, Robert. *The Jews of Medieval Western Christendom, 1000–1500*. Cambridge: Cambridge University Press, 2006, pp. 90–115. A concise chronology and analysis of the Jewish experience in Christian Spain.

Gorsky, Jeffrey. *Exiles in Sepharad: The Jewish Millennium in Spain*. Philadelphia: Jewish Publication Society, 2015. A compact survey of Spanish Jewish history. See especially pp. 97–356.

Roth, Cecil. *A History of the Marranos*. New York: Schocken Books, 1974. A detailed account of the converts, expulsion, Inquisition, and development of the diaspora communities.

Yerushalmi, Yosef. *From Spanish Court to Italian Ghetto*. New York: Columbia University Press, 1971, pp. 1–50. A concise survey and analysis of the converts' experiences.

17. The Rise and Collapse of Polish Jewry

THE COSSACK REVOLT, 1648 CE

HISTORY

The Flowering of Polish Jewry

By about 1500, Poland was becoming a significant center of Jewish life and culture, with well-developed local communal governance, both oligarchic and rabbinic leadership elites, and a growing populace, which by the seventeenth century would reach half a million, over 50 percent of the total Jewish population worldwide.

The sixteenth century might well be called a "golden age" for Polish Jewry. Like the Golden Age of Iberia, the cultural creativity of this period was rich and influential, and its impact extended well beyond Poland's borders and the historical period. Yet the two periods were very different. In the welcoming environment of Muslim Iberia, Jewish creativity flourished from cross-cultural dialogue; in the insular environment of Christian Poland, the creative dialogue was internal, and its products primarily works of *halakhah* and Kabbalah. Rabbi Moses Isserles of Krakow authored the Ashkenazic response to the Shulchan Arukh, the halakhic code written by Sephardic rabbi Joseph Karo. Rabbi Meir of Lublin was among those who wrote significant commentaries on the Talmud. (More examples of creative scholarship appear in "Leading Jewish Personalities of the Polish 'Golden Age'" later in this chapter.) The growth of large-scale, national institutions of Jewish autonomy (see "Communal Autonomy" below) added to the authority of Torah law and to the status of those who studied and taught it

Another manifestation of this inwardness can perhaps be seen in the rise of the *pilpul* approach to text study in Polish yeshivot. The Hebrew word *pilpul* is a form of the word for pepper, connotating something pungent or sharp. In talmudic times it referred to incisive logical analysis of a text, but it came to be associated with Rabbi Jacob Pollack's system of intensive textual analysis, made popular in Polish yeshivot, wherein scholars sought ostensible logical contradictions in a text and then went to great lengths, by comparative analysis of other texts, to reconcile the contradiction (for a sacred text may not contain an actual contradiction). Some rabbis criticized his method as artificial, encouraging a halakhic approach that was detached from real-life concerns. The word *pilpul* is often translated pejoratively as "talmudic casuistry."

Communal Autonomy

A significant factor in both the rise and the fall of Polish Jewry was the Polish Jews' unique position as an "interstitial" element in Polish society. However the Jews had entered Poland — as migrants, pioneers, invited/protected guests — they remained "other" in relation to the existing social order. They were neither nobles/landowners nor peasants/serfs. The burghers of the towns — merchants and craftsmen — saw them as competitors, resented their intrusion, and made social and legal efforts to avert their success.

As a result, many Jews moved into a middle-management stratum. They managed the rural estates of landowners who lived in the city; served as tax agents for local and national authorities; operated stills and taverns; traded wholesale in timber, grain, and other goods; and became moneylenders, both serving as bankers for nobles and extending credit to peasants.

On the one hand, since Jews had minimal opportunities to integrate economically or socially, this "outsider" socioeconomic position helped strengthen the autonomous Jewish society and keep its boundaries clear. On the other hand, it made the Jews particularly vulnerable as scapegoats for all the discontent and resentment of those whose crop shares, taxes, and interest they were charged with collecting. Jews were seen as representing power, when in fact, being caught in the middle, they had none.

During medieval times, a dual leadership structure — rabbis and oligarchs — governed the typical Jewish "city within a city," presiding over an internal taxation system that supported Jewish educational and social welfare institutions, as well as a system of courts, empowered to judge almost every civil or criminal matter within the community. In addition, they apportioned and collected external taxes levied upon the Jews as a group (thus governments had an interest in allowing Jewish communal self-government).

Jewish autonomy within Poland went significantly beyond this. Already early in the sixteenth century Poland had a chief rabbi recognized by the government. Then, in 1580, the community established the Council of Four Lands (Great Poland, Little Poland, Podolia/Galicia, Volhynia, later joined by a fifth, Lithuania): a body of rabbis and leaders from constituent communities who would meet twice a year, at the large commercial fairs in Lublin and Yaroslav, to serve as a supreme court, addressing matters between communities as well as appeals. This "state within a state" gave the Jews the power of a united voice when negotiating rights and obligations with the government, as well as unprecedented unity and the authority this engendered. The larger Jewish community could apportion resources and obligations among local communities and adjudicate personal and business legal matters on a national scale. Stronger communities could be compelled to help weaker ones. One could not simply flee one's debts—or one's family—and innocently start anew in a different city. Standards could also be enforced in local rabbinical appointments, as the council provided an address for appeals regarding questionable credentials or practices.

For two centuries, the hierarchy of local, regional, and national governing councils and rabbis imparted to Polish Jewry a mechanism for living a life largely governed by Torah law; a sense of unity, pride, and security; and collective bargaining power vis-à-vis the government.

The Cossack Revolt and Its Aftermath

The impressive autonomy of Polish Jewry resulted from several characteristics of the Polish state that had other, less positive results over time:

- Poland was weak and unstable internally. While it was a monarchy, the king was elected by—and often at the mercy of—an unruly, heterogeneous congress of hereditary nobles, many of them wealthy landowners, but many others possessing nothing but a title.
- In part, perhaps, because of that weakness, Poland was constantly beset by enemies around her borders. At various times, the country was at war with Sweden, Russia, Prussia, and Austria. (At the end of the eighteenth century, Poland would be partitioned by its neighbors and disappear from the map of Europe until after the First World War.)
- As a Catholic country that bordered on Orthodox Russia, the church was often in a defensive mode, focused on protecting its interests, power, and faith from challenges to the east.

Interestingly, another group within Polish society that lived with perpetual outsider status was the Cossacks. These autonomous bands of warriors who originated in the sparsely inhabited regions along the Don and Dnieper Rivers (Ukraine) became a constant factor in Poland starting from around 1500. Living in border areas where Poland, Russia, and Turkey met, they operated as outlaws until, at various times, one kingdom or the other would buy their support and engage them as border militias. In general, they were a thorn in the side of the Polish monarchy, which struggled to keep them under control. And they seemed to speak for the large numbers of Russian Orthodox peasants in the plains of the Ukraine who resented being ruled by absentee Polish Catholic landlords.

In 1648 this unstable volcano erupted. A Cossack warlord, Bogdan Chmielnicki, led a rebellion in the countryside against the Polish nobility he accused of oppression and betrayal. The nobles, though, were ensconced in their palaces in the cities; their representatives in the countryside were the Jews.

Weak and disunited, the Polish central government could not mount a serious military campaign against the Cossacks; only limited confrontations ensued. In any case, the Jews—perceived as immediate agents of Polish Catholic oppression—were convenient, powerless scapegoats for peasant resentment and simultaneously expendable to the government. Therefore the vicious raids largely attacked Jews (and Catholic clergy, who similarly offered a powerless target with goods to plunder).

The rebellion went on intensively for a few years, after which fighting continued on and off. Meanwhile, the Cossacks massacred, raped, and pillaged, expelled whole Jewish villages, and kidnapped Jews for ransom or to be sold into slavery.

Finally, in the 1667 Treaty of Andrusovo, Poland agreed to cede control over part of the Ukraine to the Cossacks (under Russian sponsorship). This loss of valuable territory and admission of powerlessness was a disaster for Poland, reducing and weakening the kingdom. For the Jews, though, it was worse—the end of an era. Thousands were killed. Jewish communities and their governing, educational, and cultural institutions were destroyed and dispersed. Fortunes were also lost.

The persecutions, destruction and dispersal of communities, and loss of fortunes led to the people's impoverishment, which in turn led the Jewish institutions of self-government to collapse.

Timeline: 1264–1795

1264	Boleslav of Kalisz (in central Poland) issues a charter detailing the rights and obligations of the Jewish communities and guaranteeing them a high degree of autonomy in governance.
1538	Parliament, meeting in Piotrkov, passes a constitution containing extensive restrictions on Jewish commerce and residence.
1543	Polish astronomer Copernicus publishes his theory that the earth revolves around the sun.
1569	Union of Lublin unites Poland and Lithuania.
1576	Last king of the Polish Yagiello dynasty dies. The newly elected king, Hungarian Stephen Batory, removes many commercial restrictions on the Jews and forbids trying Jews for ritual murder or host desecration.[10]
1580	First meeting of the national Jewish council that will come to be called the Council of the Four Lands.
1623	First meeting of the national Jewish council in Lithuania.
1648	Bogdan Chmielnicki leads Cossack uprising in Poland.
1655	Sweden invades Poland. Most of Poland becomes divided, with control shifting among Sweden, Russia, and the Cossacks.
1666	The movement (based in Turkey) acclaiming Sabbatai Zevi as messiah attracts many Polish Jews as followers (see chapter 18).
1667	Treaty of Andrusovo divides the Ukraine between Russia and Poland and brings two decades of chaos and violence to an end.

10. Two widespread medieval Christian folk beliefs about Jews were the "blood libel," accusing Jews of murdering Christian children to use their blood in the Passover ritual; and the "host desecration libel," the belief that Jews stole communion wafers from churches and deliberately desecrated them. Both are based on the idea that in addition to the Jews murdering Jesus, they are committed to reenacting the crime generation after generation.

1698, 1736, 1747 Ritual murder trials are held in various locations around Poland.

1720 Polish church synod forbids repairing synagogues or building new ones.

1755 Jacob Frank, a Polish follower of Sabbatai Zevi's cult, presents himself as Zevi's reincarnation, attracting a limited following.

1764 Councils of Lithuania and the Four Lands are abolished when the Polish government shifts the responsibility for Jewish taxes to local communities.

1772 First partition of Poland: Austria, Russia, and Prussia seize border regions from the weak Polish government (in Russia's case, with violent Cossack support).

1793, 1795 The second and third partitions: The remainder of sovereign Poland is divided among Austria, Russia, and Prussia, removing it from the map until 1918.

Leading Jewish Personalities of the Polish "Golden Age"

Rabbi Solomon Luria (1510–67) Leading halakhic authority; founded an influential yeshiva in Lublin (no connection to his contemporary, Rabbi Isaac Luria of Safed—see chapter 18).

Rabbi Moses Isserles (1525–72) The recognized halakhic leader of his generation; rabbi of Krakow; wrote the Ashkenazic response to the Shulchan Arukh, the halakhic code written by Sephardic rabbi Joseph Karo.

Rabbi Mordecai Jaffe (1530–1612) Widely learned in the natural sciences, philosophy, and Kabbalah; wrote popular commentaries on the Shulchan Arukh.

Rabbi Samuel Eidels (1555–1632) Known for his exhaustive commentary on the Talmud.

Rabbi Meir of Lublin (1558–1616) Served several large communities; wrote a significant commentary on the Talmud.

Rabbi Isaiah Horowitz (1560–1630) Known for his major work *Shenei Luchot ha-Brit* (*The Two Tablets of the Covenant*), a unique compilation integrating Kabbalah, halakhah, and ethics.

Rabbi Joel Sirkes (1561–1640) Leading halakhic authority. His commentary on the *Tur*, the fourteenth-century code of Rabbi Jacob ben Asher (Germany/Spain), remains an influential halakhic resource.

PRIMARY TEXT

The Polish rabbi Nathan Neta Hanover witnessed the Chmielnicki rebellion firsthand. Fleeing across Europe, he ended up in Italy, where he published his chronicle of the events. While other such chronicles have been published, his clear, succinct, and coherent account has been the most studied and quoted. The title, *Yeven Metzulah*, is taken from Psalm 69:3, "the slimy depths." *Yeven*, "muck" or "slime," is a pun on the Hebrew word *Yavan*, "Greece," referring to the Orthodox Christian religion of the Cossacks (Russian Orthodoxy is a part of the Greek Orthodox Church).

Rabbi Hanover went on to write several other works—collections of sermons, kabbalistic studies—most of which have not survived. He served communities in Central Europe until his death in 1683.

Nathan Neta Hanover, *Yeven Metzulah*

It is well known . . . that there was never so much Torah study in all of the Diaspora of Israel as there was in the land of Poland. In every community they would maintain a yeshiva, and pay the head of the yeshiva well, so that he could maintain the yeshiva without worrying about his livelihood, and the Torah could be his profession. He would not set foot outside all year except to attend the house of study or the synagogue. He sat night and day studying Torah. Each community would support advanced students, providing a weekly stipend so that they could learn the *halakhah* itself

These sections describing the glorious civilization of Polish Jewry come at the end of the book, as a eulogy for the devastated community.

Advanced students often came from towns far away, attracted by a particular rabbi and his approach.

as well as the skills needed for
analysis and innovation. . . .

In the summer they would go to the
fairs at Zaslav and Yaroslav, and in
the winter to the fairs at Lvov and
Lublin. There the students were
free to go and study at any yeshiva
they wanted to. At each of these
fairs there were hundreds of yeshiva
heads, and thousands of students
and tens of thousands of youth and
Jewish merchants, and gentiles like
the sand of the sea, because people came from the ends of the earth
to the fairs. Whoever had a son or
daughter eligible for marriage went
to the fair to make a match, for
there everyone could find a suitable
partner. Several hundred matches
were concluded at each fair, sometimes thousands. The Jews, men
and women, would go about at the
fair in royal dress, for they were
respected in the eyes of the kingdom and the gentiles. The Jews were
as numerous as the sand of the sea,
but now we have diminished due to
our sins, may God have mercy. . . .

In the land of Poland it was as in
Jerusalem before the destruction
of the Temple: they would establish
courts in every city . . . and in each
of the four lands that made up the
kingdom there was a high court. . . .

The commercial fairs were also, it
seems, yeshiva fairs, matchmaking
fairs, and meeting opportunities for
judicial and legislative bodies of the
community.

In cases when heads of two communities were adversaries, they would go before the Council of Four Lands, who would sit twice a year [at the Lublin fair in the spring, and the Yaroslav fair in the fall]. Each community would send one representative [to this council] and they would add to these six leading rabbis. . . . This council was like the Sanhedrin in the Temple; they had the power to judge all of Israel in the kingdom of Poland, to set limits, to make rules, and to administer punishments as they saw fit. . . . A Jewish case was never brought before the gentile courts . . . and if a Jew were to bring a case before the gentile court he would be punished [by the Jewish communal leadership]. . . .

It came to pass in 1648 that there was a Cossack officer named Chmielnicki (may his name be blotted out) . . . who was extremely wealthy, cunning, and a brave warrior.

[There follows a detailed description of the escalating tension between Chmielnicki's Cossacks and the Polish government, and the Cossacks' alliance with the Tatars from the Crimea. The Cossack-Tatar alliance achieves a major victory over the Polish army.]

The exclusive jurisdiction of Jewish communal courts in Jewish life was considered the ideal in most medieval Jewish communities.

Many Jews in communities who could not flee . . . were killed for the sanctification of God's name, cruel and harsh deaths. Some were skinned alive and their flesh thrown to the dogs, some had their hands and feet cut off and were thrown in the road to be trampled by horses. . . . Some were buried alive. Children were slaughtered at their mothers' breast. . . . There was no bizarre means of murder that they did not inflict on them. And many were taken prisoner by the Tatars. . . . Women and girls were raped and carried off to be servants and concubines.

Thus they did in all the places they reached, and also to the Polish gentiles—especially priests and monks. Thousands of Jews were killed east of the Dnieper, and hundreds were forced to convert. Torah scrolls were torn and made into sacks, and shoes.

These are a sampling of the many descriptions that fill the book, as the attackers move from community to community, wreaking havoc.

—Nathan Neta Hanover, *Yeven Metzulah* (1653; Hebrew) (Tel Aviv: Hakibbutz Hame'uchad, 1945), pp. 24, 31–32, 83, 86–87, 90

From this account, Rabbi Hanover seems to have been conscious that he witnessed a turning point. His description of the glory of Polish Jewish life is presented as a picture of "a world that was but is no more." Even though Jewish communities still existed after the massacres and the Council of Four Lands continued to function for another century, a sense prevailed that what remained was merely a remnant. The golden age was over.

Rabbi Hanover's idyllic description of pre-1648 Jewish life is somewhat idealized. As in the case of the Golden Age in Iberia, all the cultural and social successes, the autonomy, and the wealth existed in the context of a vulnerable religious minority subject to constant social and economic restrictions and waxing and waning threats of expulsion and violence.

LEGACY

Impact

The year 1648 marked the beginning of the end of Poland as well as the end of the golden age of Polish Jewry. While the survivors regrouped and rebuilt their homes and communities, the economic life of the Jews, and their social and religious institutions, never recovered from this blow. From then on, until Poland was partitioned in 1772–95, the Polish government's weakness allowed popular and church antisemitism to unleash ritual murder and host-desecration trials, riots, expulsions, and massacres. Under pressure from clergy, nobles, and burghers, each of whom had a particular anti-Jewish motivation, in 1764 the government reformed the Jewish community's taxation process, moving from a system in which the Jews apportioned their collective tax burden internally as they saw fit to a direct, personal levy. In addition, the Council of Four Lands was ordered to disband. Together, the weakening of Poland, Jewish economic collapse, and the disbanding of Jewish self-government meant the end of the golden age and the beginning of a new reality.

By 1795, after three partitions, the large majority of Polish Jews—at least a million—found themselves suddenly in Russia, a country that had until this time forbidden the settlement of Jews within its borders. Already after the first partition, Tsarina Catherine enacted laws removing the Jews from certain professions, especially the production and sale of alcoholic beverages (a highly profitable industry then dominated by Jews, whose dietary laws prohibited them from drinking wine made by gentiles). In 1790 the Russian government, reluctant to accept Jews into the country and pressured by merchants and contractors threatened by Jewish competition, began to impose residential restrictions: Jews could not live outside of cities or migrate beyond their original provinces. The defined regions permitted for Jewish residence came to be called in Yiddish "Tehum Hamoshav" (boundary of residence—often rendered as "Pale of Settlement" in English, "pale" referring to an enclosure or boundary).

Thus, the heritage of 1648 was the creation of a dense, ghettoized, impoverished Jewish population that came to be called "Russian Jewry" because of the Partition of Poland. And, at the end of the nineteenth century, Russian Jewry would serve as the substrate for major movements that would shape the coming century—mass migration, socialism, and Zionism.

By no means, however, did the catastrophe of 1648 lead to the erasure of Polish Jewish culture. Even in adversity, yeshivot functioned and local Polish communities supported a vibrant communal and liturgical life, producing great scholars and important works of commentary, research, and creativity. Local communal self-government regulated daily living, yeshivot trained rabbinical scholars, and itinerant preachers visited local synagogues, bringing popular (often kabbalistic) calls to repentance and promises of redemption. Lithuania, in the north, became a center of halakhic study; its capital, Vilna, became known as "the Jerusalem of Lithuania." Rabbi Elijah ben Solomon, the "Vilna Gaon" (1720–97), a towering figure in eighteenth-century intellectual and spiritual life, wrote notations and commentaries on the Bible, the Mishnah, the Babylonian Talmud, and the Shulchan Arukh; his legacy also includes kabbalistic and mathematical works as well as oral traditions recording his pious personal behavior.

It was out of this milieu—and perhaps as an indirect consequence of 1648—that the Hasidic movement would arise in Poland a century later (see chapter 18), as well as other spiritual and intellectual developments, such as the Musar movement in nineteenth-century Lithuania. And, ultimately, Polish Jewish culture was carried in migrations to Western Europe and Palestine, where it became and remained dominant through the middle of the twenthieth century, and to the Americas, where it continues to set the Jewish cultural tone.

Memory

In Jewish traditional literature the 1648 uprising became known as *gezerot tach vetat*, "the evil decrees of 5408 and 5409" (the Hebrew chronology for 1648–49). Victims and observers wrote liturgical poetry and dirges commemorating the events. While these did not enter the standard liturgies, after historians published the collections and chronicles of the events, modern authors such as Shaul Tschernichovski and Shalom Asch incorporated the material into their poems and novels (*Bat ha-Rav* and *Kiddush ha-Shem*, respectively). For these and other pre-Holocaust Hebrew and Yiddish authors, the 1648 massacres came to symbolize the heroic faith—and pathetic powerlessness—that characterized Jewish life in the Eastern European diaspora.

TEXTS FOR DISCUSSION

How do you believe the "interstitial" position of the Jews in pre-modern Poland relates to the position of the Jews in modern democracies?

> Thus the Ukrainian Jew found himself between hammer and anvil: between the *pan* (landowner) and the *khlop* (peasant), between the Catholic and the Greek Orthodox, between the Pole and the Russian. Three classes, three religions, and three nationalities, clashed on a soil which contained in its bowels terrible volcanic forces—and a catastrophe was bound to follow.
>
> —Simon Dubnow, *History of the Jews in Russia and Poland*, vol. 1, p. 142

> What was typical of seventeenth-century life in Poland is also relevant to twentieth century America. Just as surely as the Jew then was caught between peasant and pan, so is he caught today between many forces competing for power: black and white, Catholic and Greek Orthodox, Catholic and Protestant, business and labor, blue-collar workers and white-collar workers. In every way, the Jew is interstitial.
>
> —Robert J. Marx, "The People In Between" (1968), http://www.jcua.org /document.doc?id=1

FURTHER READING

Asch, Sholem. *Kiddush ha-Shem: An Epic of 1648*. Philadelphia: Jewish Publication Society, 1926. Translation of a Yiddish novel set at the time of the Cossack uprising, based on a popular folktale of Jewish martyrdom.

Dubnov, Simon. *History of the Jews in Russia and Poland*. Vol. 1. Philadelphia: Jewish Publication Society, 1916, pp. 66–219, 306–20. The classic account of the period.

Hanover, Nathan. *The Abyss of Despair (Yeven Metzulah)*. Translated by Abraham Mesch. Piscataway NJ: Transaction, 1983. A translation of the Hebrew chronicle of the 1648 uprising.

Polonsky, Antony. *The Jews in Poland and Russia*. Vol. 1. Oxford and Portland: Littman Library of Jewish Civilization, 2010, pp. 7–159, 322–54. A recent socio-historical perspective on this period.

Weinryb, Bernard. *The Jews of Poland*. Philadelphia: Jewish Publication Society, 1973, pp. 107–203. A survey of events leading up to the uprising and its aftermath.

Map 4. The partition of Poland, 1795 CE

18. The Rise of Hasidism

THE BAAL SHEM TOV AND HIS DISCIPLES, ~1750 CE

HISTORY

A Crisis of Leadership

Despite massacres, dislocations, and a climate of persecution, Polish Jewry carried on, in ways the Jews of Iberia could not. Its culture and institutions continued to function. Yet the ongoing economic decline undermined the community's leadership structure, in two ways:

1. Traditionally, the wealthy stratum of the Jewish community served as the interface between the community and the government. Their assets and business connections enabled them both to generously support communal institutions and to advocate for the Jews with local and national governments. After 1648, a time of scarce resources and great insecurity, the Jewish people came to see these oligarchs more as oppressors than as champions, more as self-interested than as intercessors for the masses.

2. The people also lost respect for the office of the rabbinate. Even in the preceding century, people knew of corruption in the awarding of rabbinical posts. A rabbi seeking the authority and honor (and remuneration) of a communal post could cultivate a relationship (especially marriage) with an oligarchic family to secure one. Sometimes rabbis—sitting as judges—were beholden to wealthy merchants for their jobs, which pressured them to favor those merchants in their rulings. Such conflicts of interest occasionally led to glaringly inappropriate rabbinical appointments. In the wake of the 1648 catastrophe, several factors exacerbated this problem: the weakening and ultimate breakup of the Council of Four Lands (which had the authority to enforce professional and procedural standards), increased oligarchic power in an increasingly impoverished population, and the chaos resulting from the destruction of some communities and the influx of refugees into others.

Outside forces contributed to this loss of faith in communal leadership. The imposition of a direct head tax, a modernizing move asserting the direct authority of the state, was a blow to the authority of communal institutions. Apportioning and collecting the state's taxes had been a significant element of the leadership's power and its commitment to implementing Torah law: wealth-based apportioning of the tax burden institutionalized the obligation of the strong to aid the weak.

Activist Kabbalah and Messianism

Meanwhile, the traumatic sense of dislocation and loss that set in after the Iberian expulsion of 1492 (see chapter 16) had led many Jewish exiles to question the classic Deuteronomic understanding of the covenant (see chapter 7). It was hard to accept the simple reward-punishment model in the face of such massive and seemingly undeserved suffering.

One popular response was a mystical interpretation of this mismatch. In the sixteenth century, the Galilean city of Safed (under Ottoman rule), home to a community of a few thousand Iberian exiles, became a major center of kabbalistic scholarship. One of its leading lights, Rabbi Isaac Luria (known as the Ari—the lion—an acronym for Ashkenazic Rabbi Isaac), is credited with formulating a new, activist approach to Kabbalah. Lurianic Kabbalah emphasized that study and ritual practice, when performed with the proper mystical intention to "repair the world," would move the messianic clock forward toward redemption. In his eyes, Kabbalah was therefore not merely a way for the individual to find deep spiritual meaning, to commune with God, in texts and practices, but a practical tool for intervening in the flow of history, a means for "forcing" the coming of redemption. Luria's disciples scattered around the Jewish world. His teachings were enthusiastically received, especially in Italy and Poland, where in 1649 Rabbi Isaiah Horowitz published his popular *Shenei Luchot ha-Brit* (*The Two Tablets of the Covenant*), a Lurianic perspective on ritual practice and matters of ethics and belief.

Messianic activism carries with it the temptation of messianic expectation. Hence, with the spread of Lurianic Kabbalah, the ground was fertile for such expectations to germinate into a messianic movement. In 1665, the thirty-nine-year-old Sabbatai Zevi of Smyrna (on the Aegean coast of Turkey; today known as Izmir) proclaimed himself the Messiah. A charismatic figure who had been ordained a rabbi at eighteen and had studied Kabbalah on his own, he taught that ascetic practices such as fasting and frequent ritual baths, as well as penitential prayers, could move God to bring the redemption in the immediate future. According to Gershom Scholem's biography of Sabbatai Zevi, his "magic" may have come from severe, perhaps pathological mood swings—Zevi alternated between charismatic intensity and depressed, otherworldly silence. Attracting a small circle of disciples, he wandered among Jewish communities in Greece, Turkey, Egypt, and Palestine for over a decade before his "revelation" in 1665. Apparently, some saw him as a holy man; most just saw him as strange.

The echo of this proclamation was heard throughout the Jewish world—by the descendants of the Iberian exiles, awaiting redemption, and by the still-bleeding Jews of Poland. Rumors spread about Jewish military victories in the Middle East. Thousands of Jews, rabbis and common folk, received the news with joy.

This enthusiasm was not universal, however. When the messianic claimant arrived in Jerusalem, the rabbis of the city deemed him a heretic, excommunicated him, and expelled him. He moved on to Aleppo, where he was received with great enthusiasm.

By the end of 1665, thousands of Jews throughout the world were reciting special penitential prayers and selling their property to be ready to leave for Palestine.

In 1666 Sabbatai Zevi arrived in the Ottoman capital, Constantinople, where he was immediately arrested and imprisoned as "a madman, pretending to be the messianic king" (the sultan would brook no competition). Later that year he was summoned to an audience with the sultan, when his followers expected him to place the sultan's crown on his own head. Instead, the sultan ordered him to convert to Islam, which he did.

The crushing disappointment darkened the lives of a generation. Some of Zevi's followers converted to Islam or Christianity. Others continued to believe Sabbatai Zevi really was the Messiah, formulating a belief in a Sabbatean "second coming." Most returned to their lives, living with the painful knowledge that redemption was, apparently, still far off.

After the crash of the movement, the communal strife between "believers" and "nonbelievers" continued to roil European communities for a century. Sabbatai Zevi died in internal exile in Turkey, in 1676. In Poland in 1755, Jacob Frank, who claimed to be his successor, attracted a small following and considerable attention before he and his followers, rejected by the Jews and pressured by the church, converted to Catholicism in 1759.

Hasidism

The combination of economic depression, ongoing persecution, the collapse of communal leadership, and the disappointment of the messianic expectation left the Jews of Poland in a sort of spiritual depression—and with a leadership vacuum. When a new movement arose that responded creatively to all of these challenges, it spread from a small circle to a mass movement in the course of just two generations.

The founding of Hasidism (the Hebrew *hasid* is usually translated as "pious") is generally credited to Israel ben Eliezer. An itinerant teacher, laborer, and mystic of southeastern Poland (~1700–1760), he was also a healer, using incantations and amulets containing names of God; hence he was known as a *baal Shem* (master of the Name), a term not unique to him. As his reputation as a charismatic teacher grew, though, he came to be called the Baal Shem Tov (the good master of the Name)—or, in acronym, the Besht.

The Besht left no writings, but his disciples and their disciples recorded many stories about him (see text later in the chapter). According to the stories, he lived a life of asceticism and contemplation until around 1740, when he settled in Medzibozh and began to teach his doctrines and attract followers. His students spread his teachings both in writing and through their own teaching, and their students scattered, primarily in the east and south of Poland, founding local Hasidic communities. From then on the leadership of Hasidism was in large part dynastic: local rabbis passed their leadership on to their sons or sons-in-law, and each community developed its own particular dress, prayer and holiday customs, melodies, and so on. To this day, one cannot be a generic Hasid—wherever Hasidim now live in the world, the various communities continue to bear the names of their towns of origin (e.g., Gur, Belz, Lubavitch, Satmar).

Key elements in Hasidic thought underlie the historical role—and success—of the movement:

- Hasidism developed a model of religious leader that differed from the traditional rabbi. While his Torah knowledge was important, more important were his spirituality and charisma. Moreover, on account of his personal qualities, kabbalistic meditation, learning, and divine favor, the Hasidic rebbe (Yiddish for "rabbi"), or tzadik (righteous one), was able to intercede between his congregation and God. He was able to see into the heart—and into heaven. Thus the rebbe was not only a teacher, a preacher, a prayer leader, and—only sometimes—a halakhic authority (especially in the early generations, the Hasidic leaders' desire to be "other" than traditional rabbis led to a certain anti-intellectualism). The rebbe was also a healer, a spiritual counselor, and a prophet. This model was particularly attractive at a time when many people had lost confidence in the authenticity of the traditional rabbinate.
- While Hasidism continued traditions of Lurianic Kabbalah and concerned itself with the link between human action and redemption, it pulled back from the messianism of the Sabbateans. Its kabbalistic activism focused on the individual's attainment of a state of closeness to God. Having been "burned" by messianic activism on a national level, the people turned to a more personal approach to redemption.
- Hasidism emphasized serving God through savoring the pleasures of the world (opposing asceticism) and through experiencing joy (turning away from depression). Music and dance were important means to achieve mystical ecstasy—and hence, closeness to God. Perhaps this was a natural response to the dismal reality experienced over the preceding century.
- Because of its emphasis on the personal, the real world, and the mystical, charismatic leader, Hasidism gave rise to an extensive literature of stories and parables. This genre, together with Hasidic liturgical music and wordless melodies (nigunim), contributed richly to Jewish culture. Both the parables and the melodies functioned on two levels: as simple forms of pious expression comprehensible to anyone, while at the same time holding deeper, mystical meanings for those able to fathom them. This layered approach helped bridge

the divide between traditional scholars and the common people, engaging a broad spectrum of the Jewish community.

While these doctrines and practices characterized Hasidism, it was and is by no means a united, uniform movement. Each community developed unique customs and practices, from melodies to dress. For example, nowadays Lubavitch Hasidic men wear fedoras on the Sabbath and holidays, while other communities wear fur hats (*streimel* in Yiddish). Some communities favor black coats, but the Toldos Aharon Hasidim, originating in Vizhnitz, don distinctive gray and white striped coats on most days (gold coats on the Sabbath).

Every community also established distinctive doctrines and theological and social approaches, such as the Lubavitch community's openness to the world and the Satmar Hasidim's emphasis on isolation. Sometimes these differences have led to strident polemics, as in the case of the conflict between Belz and Satmar Hasidim over participation in Israeli politics (Belz favors; Satmar opposes).

Responses to Hasidism

Unsurprisingly, the traditional rabbinate often took a dim view of the new movement, viewing it as anti-intellectual, vulgar, undermining Jewish law, messianic, and, of course, a threat to rabbinical authority and status. The leader most associated with this opposition, the halakhic scholar and exemplar of extreme piety Rabbi Elijah ben Solomon of Vilna (Lithuania), known as the Vilna Gaon (see chapter 17), took an uncompromising, outspoken position: total rejection of Hasidism as heresy, and insistence that it be rooted out. He and others who opposed Hasidism, known as *Mitnagdim* (opposers; in Ashkenazic pronunciation, *Misnagdim*), denounced early leaders such as the Besht, issued edicts of excommunication against them, ordered their books burned, and prohibited social and religious contact with them.

While these measures had some impact locally in Lithuania, for the most part they were to no avail. Hasidism spread and grew in strength, and by the early nineteenth century it would become a powerful presence in the life and culture of Polish Jewry. A century later, through migration, it would also develop strong roots in Israel and North America. In Lithuania and Western Europe it would make fewer inroads, its center of strength remaining in eastern and southern Poland and the Ukraine.

Among the rabbis who opposed Hasidism were some who nevertheless understood that the new movement arose in response to a real need. The dry, authoritarian, and sometimes even corrupt traditional rabbinate was failing to address the people's need for spiritual leadership, for a revitalization of the tradition (and would provide an opening for the new threat to all of Orthodoxy arising in the west—modern enlightenment; see chapter 19). To respond to the people's needs and take the wind out of the rebels' sails, they modified the existing institutions of prayer, leadership, and study. Rabbi Israel Salanter, as one example, founded the Musar (moral development) movement of late nineteenth-century Lithuania. Musar rejected the perceived anti-intellectualism of Hasidism, retained the centrality of halakhic study, and added a focus on refining traits of the inner life or soul. To accomplish this, the movement encouraged meditation, chanting, studying and discussing Musar texts, and keeping a daily journal of moral development.

Perhaps it was the rising common threat of modernization that helped avoid a complete schism between Hasidism and its opposition.

Timeline: 1572–1795

1572	The Safed kabbalist Rabbi Isaac Luria dies.
1648	Chmielnicki massacres.
1649	Rabbi Isaiah Horowitz's *Shenei Luchot ha-Brit,* a popular work of thought and practice influenced by Lurianic Kabbalah, is published in Poland.
1665	Sabbatai Zevi declares himself the Messiah.
1722	A council of rabbis gathered in Lvov issues an edict of excommunication for all followers of Sabbateanism.
~1740	The Besht settles in Medzhibozh; he begins to preach and gather disciples.
1755	Jacob Frank's messianic movement appears.
1764	The Council of Four Lands is dissolved.
1772	First partition: sections of Poland are annexed by Russia, Austria, and Prussia.

1772	The Vilna (Lithuania) Jewish community, led by the Vilna Gaon, issues a decree of excommunication against the "heretical" Hasidim.
1780	Publication of Rabbi Jacob Joseph of Polonnoye's collection of Hasidic sermons spreads the teachings of the Besht and his disciples.
1790	Russian law limits areas of Jewish residency.
1793, 1795	The final partitions of Poland; the area with the largest Jewish population is annexed to Russia.

Important Early Hasidic Rabbis (Disciples of the Besht and of His Disciples) and Their Contemporaries

Rabbi Jacob Joseph of Polonnoye (1710–84) A scholar of Lurianic Kabbalah, he became a disciple and published the first book of Hasidic thought, *Toldot Ya'akov Yosef*, as well as sermons expressing the Besht's teachings.

Rabbi Dov Ber of Mezeritch (?–1772) "The Maggid of Mezeritch" (*maggid* = preacher). A close disciple, he "inherited" the leadership from the Besht and moved the center from Medzhibozh to Mezeritch. His students scattered throughout Poland, establishing communities and dynasties.

Rabbi Abraham Gershom of Kitov (1701–61) The Besht's brother-in-law, he first opposed him but later joined the movement. As one of the first Hasidic immigrants to Palestine, he helped found the Hasidic community in Jerusalem.

Rabbi Menachem Nachum Twersky of Chernobyl (1730–97) He published a book of sermons that became a popular Hasidic text; his children and grandchildren became the heads of various Hasidic dynasties throughout the region.

Rabbi Levi Yitzchak of Berditchev (1740–1809) A disciple of Rabbi Dov Ber of Mezeritch, he became famous and popular for the stories he told about interceding with God on behalf of the suffering Jewish people.

Rabbi Shneur Zalman of Liady (1745–1812) A disciple of Rabbi Dov Ber of Mezeritch, he founded what became known as Chabad, or Lubavitch, Hasidism.

Rabbi Nachman of Breslov (1772–1810) A grandson of the Besht, he
   emphasized contemplative study of Kabbalah.
Rabbi Elijah ben Shlomo of Vilna (1720–97) "The Vilna Gaon." The pre-
   eminent halakhic and kabbalistic scholar of his generation, he led
   the opposition to Hasidism.
Moses Mendelssohn (1729–86) A scholar of Jewish and general philosophy and a leading figure in the German Enlightenment, he sought
   integration of the Jews into European culture (see chapter 19).

PRIMARY TEXT

First published in 1815, *Shivchei ha-Besht* (*Praises of the Besht*) is the most
complete and best-known collection of stories about the founder of Hasidism. While it is difficult to discern the boundary between myth and history
in these accounts, the stories offer insight into the beliefs and practices
that came to characterize Hasidism.

Shivchei ha-Besht

---

1. [The Besht's brother-in-law, Rabbi
Abraham Gershom, was appalled
by the match that had been made
for his sister.] He invited the Besht
to study Torah with him, that the
Besht might learn something; but
the Besht kept his knowledge secret
and acted as if he understood nothing. Rabbi Gershom said to his
sister, "He is indeed an embarrassment; if you want to divorce him,
go ahead; if not, I'll buy you a horse,
and you can go live wherever you
want (but not here). She agreed,
and they went and found a place to
live. The Besht went off to meditate
alone in the mountains. Their livelihood was thus: Two or three times a

Note that the Besht married into a
rabbinic family. According to Hasidic
tradition, the Besht was a great
scholar, but he kept his learning
secret so as not to be associated with
the dry, authoritarian image of the
traditional rabbinate.

week his wife would come out with
horse and wagon, and he would
dig clay and fill the wagon, and she
would go back and sell it in town.
He would fast extensively, wandering alone among the high mountains. (p. 47)

2. [It was told that] once, in
Medzhibozh, Rabbi Abraham of
Tzubosor was leading the service on a Passover morning, and
the Besht was praying at his seat.
It was the custom for the Besht to
lead the *Hallel* section of the service. And during the repetition of
the *Amidah* [just before *Hallel*], the
Besht was seized by a great trembling, as always happened when
he was praying, as anyone who
saw him praying would know. But
when Rabbi Abraham finished his
part, the Besht did not come forward but stood trembling at his
seat. His disciple Rabbi Wolf Kitzis
came and looked him in the face,
and his eyes were burning like
torches, protruding, not moving—
like a dying man's (God forbid!)....
Rabbi Wolf and Rabbi Abraham
took his hands and led him to the
lectern; he stood there and trembled for a while, and then recited
the *Hallel*, and continued to stand
there and tremble, so that they had
to wait for his tremor to subside

Many Hasidic stories feature ecstatic
prayer, trembling, and trance. In
addition, a popular motif is the simple, "authentic" prayer from the heart
of a child or someone uneducated in
all the halakhic rules of prayer, which
is said to open the gates of heaven.

before they could proceed with the Torah reading. (p. 103)

3. Rabbi Joel of Nemirov told: Once Sabbatai Zevi came to the Besht to ask of him redemption. . . . And redemption can be achieved by drawing near, life to life, spirit to spirit, soul to soul, so the Besht began by drawing near very cautiously, out of fear, for Sabbatai Zevi was very wicked. Once, while the Besht was asleep, Sabbatai Zevi tried to tempt him . . . , and the Besht hurled him away with such force that he fell to bottom of hell. And the Besht peeked and saw that he had landed on a large table next to Jesus. The Besht [later] said that Sabbatai Zevi had in him a holy spark, but that Satan had caught him in his net. (p. 125)

Could it be that the Besht himself was tempted either by Sabbateanism or by messianic pretentions? This story of Sabbatai Zevi coming to the Besht to ask him for redemption suggests a struggle, which ends with the total rejection of both temptations.

4. Once, at the assembly of the Council of Four Lands the chairman was the well-known leader Rabbi Abraham Abba. He brought up the question of how to respond to the claims that the Besht had the gift of prophecy, when it was said that he was an uneducated man; for "a common [ignorant] man cannot be truly pious" [Mishnah Avot 2:54]. The assembly sent for the Besht to appear before them immediately. When he arrived,

Many Hasidic stories tell of the contest between the charismatic rebbe and the traditional rabbi. The pure faith of the "uneducated" Besht trumps the imperfect practice of his self-righteous inquisitor.

the chairman, Rabbi Abraham, addressed him, "According to your behavior it seems as though the Holy Spirit rests upon you, and yet they say you are an ignorant man; so, let us hear from you if you know *halakhah*. Here is the case: In the service of Rosh Hodesh [New Month], what is the rule for one who, in reciting the daily prayer, forgot to insert the special prayer for Rosh Hodesh?"

Regarding the Rosh Hodesh discussion: the rule is that if one realizes that one has forgotten to insert the special addition for the new month in the silent prayer, one must go back to the beginning.

The Besht answered, "This question is irrelevant both to your honor and to me, for in your case, even if you went back and repeated the whole prayer again you would again forget to recite the addition (which was in fact what had happened); and in my case, I would not forget the first time." And when Rabbi Abraham heard that the Besht knew his secret, he was greatly frightened. (pp. 152–53)

Another important theme is the rebbe's ability to know the secrets of the heart.

—*Shivchei ha-Besht* (Hebrew), ed. S. Horodetzky (Tel Aviv: Dvir, 1947), pp. 47, 103, 125, 152–53

While the *Shivchei ha-Besht* is neither a scientific biography nor a formal, canonical statement of Hasidic belief, its many stories about the founder articulate all of the movement's central themes and ideas. Just this brief selection of four tales expresses the following:

· Outsiderness to the established community and its leadership

- The importance of mystical contemplation
- The role of ecstasy in prayer
- The disavowal of Sabbateanism and the sublimation of messianism
- The rejection of the traditional rabbinate as "halakhic pedantry"
- The rebbe's special powers

LEGACY

Impact

Especially in Lithuania, the traditional rabbinate's hostility toward Hasidism never subsided. Western European Jews who later sought acceptance in the modernizing societies around them also developed a hostile view of Hasidism as a primitive folk religion unworthy of an enlightened age. Meanwhile, the movement moderated over time, clarifying its commitment to *halakhah* and scholarship alongside its charismatic leadership and spiritual and ecstatic take on religious practice.

In the end, Hasidism became established as a major force in Jewish life, its communities becoming ubiquitous all over the Jewish world. Two leading liberal Jewish thinkers of the twentieth century, Martin Buber and Rabbi Abraham Joshua Heschel, who were fascinated by it themselves, popularized its concepts to a wider audience. Rabbis Zalman Schachter-Shalomi (who called himself a "neo-Hasid") and Arthur Green continued this process, seeking to enrich and revitalize liberal Judaism by incorporating elements of Hasidic thought and practice. This approach that seeks to synthesize Hasidic mysticism with post-halakhic Judaism is often referred to as Jewish Renewal.

Many Hasidic practices also trickled down into settings wholly disassociated with Hasidic communities. Nowadays, Hasidic melodies, dancing, stories, and parables can be found across the Jewish spectrum.

Memory

Today, the world population of Hasidim numbers approximately a million, with communities in Israel and in major cities elsewhere. For the most part they live sequestered lives, typically dressing in a manner inspired by eighteenth-century Polish nobility; participating in their own institutions of education, culture, and social welfare; and generally limiting their interactions with non-Jews and the non-Hasidic Jewish community, to protect themselves against the temptations of modern secular culture. In many communities, Yiddish is the vernacular. In Israel, Hasidim form the core of the ultra-Orthodox population, which opposes Zionism and the creation of a secular Jewish state, but puts up with the state in order to live, by their own lights, in the Holy Land.

A partial exception to this inwardness and insularity is the Lubavitch community, also called Chabad (an acronym for three of the kabbalistic emanations; see chapter 14). Taking an activist position, Chabad reaches out to Jews outside its boundaries, attempting to "return" them to traditional belief and practice, and thus hasten the messianic redemption.

Ironically, many people today view Hasidism as the heart of the Orthodox mainstream, unaware that its origin was in a rebellion against Orthodoxy.

TEXT FOR DISCUSSION

Solomon Maimon (1754–1800) grew up in Poland, received a traditional education, but ultimately "discovered" the Enlightenment and migrated to Germany. He left an autobiography describing his experiences in the traditional community through his "enlightened" eyes. His critical account of a visit to a Hasidic court is typical of the cynicism with which many modernizing Jews viewed Hasidism. The question arises: Is his cynical outsider's view a fair judgment of the rebbe's authenticity as a spiritual leader?

> On Sabbath I went to this solemn meal. . . . At length the great man appeared, his awe-inspiring figure clothed in white satin. Even his shoes and snuff-box were white. . . . After the meal was over, the superior struck up a solemn inspiriting melody, held his hand for some time upon his brow, and then began to call out [the names of the guests]. . . . Each as he was called recited some verse of the Holy Scriptures. Thereupon the superior began to deliver a sermon for which the verses recited served as a text. . . . Every one of the newcomers believed that he discovered in that part of the sermon which was founded on his verse something that had special reference to the facts of his own spiritual life. . . . However . . . I observed. . . . By means of correspondence and spies and a certain knowledge of men, by observing a man's physiognomy and by skillful questioning, the superiors were able to elicit indirectly the

secrets of the heart, so that among these simple men they succeeded in obtaining the reputation of inspired prophets.

—Solomon Maimon, *Solomon Maimon: An Autobiography*, ed. Moses Hadas (New York: Schocken Books, 1967), pp. 54–55

FURTHER READING

Buber, Martin. *The Legend of the Baal-Shem.* New York: Schocken Books, 1969. A concise discussion of Hasidic thought and a retelling of a selection of Hasidic stories.

———. *Tales of the Hasidim: The Early Masters.* New York: Schocken Books, 1947. Includes translations of many stories from *Shivchei ha-Besht.*

Green, Arthur. "Typologies of Leadership and the Hasidic Zaddiq." In *Jewish Spirituality*, ed. Arthur Green, vol. 2, pp. 127–36. New York: Crossroad, 1987. An analysis of the unique qualities of the Hasidic leader.

Polonsky, Antony. *The Jews in Poland and Russia.* Vol. 1. Oxford and Portland: Littman Library of Jewish Civilization, 2010, pp. 136–57. A concise account of developments in religious life in Poland, from 1648 through the rise of Hasidism.

Scholem, Gershom. *Major Trends in Jewish Mysticism.* New York: Schocken Books, 1941, pp. 325–50. An analysis of Hasidic thought as a manifestation of mysticism.

———. *Sabbatai Sevi.* Princeton NJ: Princeton University Press, 1973. The definitive biography.

19. The Challenge of Emancipation

THE NAPOLEONIC SANHEDRIN, ~1780–1880 CE

HISTORY

The Medieval Status Quo in Western Europe

In Western Europe (between the Pyrenees and the Oder River), from the Crusades until the late eighteenth century, crises were local and scattered. Wars, plagues, famines—and new technologies—swept across the land and had impact on everyday life. Local Jewish communities experienced periods of prosperity and calm—and expulsions and attacks. The center of mass of Ashkenazic Jewry moved eastward into Poland (as we saw in chapter 14); still, life went on in the west, great scholars contributed innovations in Jewish spiritual and intellectual life, and the basic structure of society and the Jews' place in it remained constant. In a society composed of semi-autonomous communities, the Jews' self-contained community, living according to *halakhah*, existed as a natural parallel to the other corporate bodies—clergy, nobility, burghers, peasantry. Parallel, but not equal: on the one hand, this corporate social structure provided a natural place for the Jewish community to maintain its autonomy and thus live by its own lights; on the other hand, the dominant Christian ideology required that this natural place be inferior. So, while the Jews were happy to live in a closed community where they could to a large extent govern themselves, the price of this privilege was an extensive array of social and economic restrictions, special taxes, public humiliations, and a general status of powerlessness, which meant they were usually defenseless against confiscations and expulsions.

Catastrophic external political events disrupted or destroyed the stable equilibrium of the autonomous community in both Iberia and Poland (see chapters 16 and 17). In Western Europe, the traditional communal structure also collapsed, but the process was more gradual, driven by both external and internal forces.

The Modern State and Jewish Emancipation

While some might attribute the roots of this latter process to the humanism of the Renaissance, a more proximate and clear-cut turning point would be the Thirty Years War (1618–48), an exhausting and destructive series of conflicts involving just about every political entity in Western Europe. While various different nationalistic and political interests came into play, the overall conflict has generally been seen as a religious war, the competition between Catholicism and Protestantism for dominance.

Perhaps it was the shock of experiencing such prolonged and vicious violence in the name of salvation that gave rise to the idea that religion should be a matter for the conscience of the individual and not for the coercive apparatus of the state. By the late seventeenth century this idea had found important expression (notably in John Locke's *A Letter Concerning Toleration*), and thinkers and religious rebels echoed it throughout the next century. However, for most of the eighteenth century, those in power rejected such ideas. It took until 1782—when the emperor of Prussia issued his "Edict of Toleration" conferring a degree of equality upon his Jewish subjects—for a government to act accordingly. And then it took another century, with a number of fits and starts along the way, for the concept of individual religious freedom to be normative in the states of Western Europe. In France, for example, while the Declaration of the Rights of Man became law in 1789, two more years of difficult debate ensued before the National Assembly finally agreed that these rights applied to Jews as well.

The Christians of Western Europe spent two centuries (1700–1900) struggling to formulate a new understanding of the state and the individual's place in it. The result was the dissolution of the medieval corporate social structure and the rise of the modern state, composed of citizens who had individual rights and a direct relationship to the state without the mediation of religious or class corporate identities.

Moving religion to the sphere of individual freedom liberated the Jews from their collective oppression. At last, there were no special Jew-taxes, or Jewish badges, or Jewish occupational restrictions, or Jewish streets. However, the end of the autonomous Jewish community meant . . . the end of the autonomous Jewish community. When the ghetto walls came down, the Jews were emancipated not only from external restrictions, but from their ability to govern themselves as a community and to sustain a halakhic society.

Thus, just as Christian Europe worked on emancipation for two centuries, so too the Jews spent those two centuries and beyond struggling to create new theories and institutions that would sustain them in the modern world. How could *halakhah* survive without a closed community authorized to enforce its norms? Could Judaism be based on something other than *halakhah*?

The term "Enlightenment" is used to describe the rationalistic and humanistic currents that stirred European thought and politics in the eighteenth century. This was not a monolithic, straightforward phenomenon, but a broad intellectual/spiritual trend that included different and sometimes conflicting strands. In particular, with respect to its impact on the Jews, the Enlightenment included ideas of tolerance and individual freedom of conscience (e.g., John Locke) but at the same time encompassed a rationalist rejection of all "revealed" religions (e.g., Voltaire). The French revolutionaries viewed religion—the Catholic Church in particular—as a prop of the old order, to be rooted out. And so, to the extent that the Enlightenment promised the end of Catholic hegemony and the creation of a "neutral society" where Jews would be equal citizens, to many Jews it felt almost messianic. But to the extent that it sought the delegitimation and even suppression of all religion, it posed both philosophical and practical threats. The Jewish philosopher Spinoza can be seen as an early harbinger of the rationalist rejection of religion that became a central Enlightenment theme (see chapter 16); leaders of his own community excommunicated him. Moreover, with respect to antisemitism, even enlightened, rational humanists had their limits; they found no irony in debating whether Jews were inherently unproductive and parasitic or whether their persecuted status had forced these characteristics upon them.

Jewish Ambivalence regarding Emancipation: Moses Mendelssohn

Just as emancipating the Jews began to be discussed and enacted in Europe, the Jews themselves began what became a noisy public discourse on the implications of this possibility for their communal—and individual—life.

German Jewish philosopher Moses Mendelssohn (1729–86) was one of the first in a long line of thinkers and leaders who attempted to formulate an "enlightened" approach to Judaism and to articulate a new balance between maintaining a traditional Jewish way of life and accepting the modern reality of the individual living in a secular state. Mendelssohn's own biography was a case study in the difficult encounter between tradition and modernity. A product of a traditional Jewish education, he was deeply knowledgeable in the classical sources but also at home in German culture, writing popular philosophical works. In his life, as in his writings and his communal leadership, Mendelssohn conveyed the message that life in "both worlds" was not only possible but desirable. He believed that Jewish religious commitment and German identity were not contradictory, and a Jew could live by Jewish law without sacrificing enlightenment and emancipation. His project of translating the Bible into German (with a Hebrew commentary) epitomized his approach; its purpose was to reawaken Yiddish-speaking Jews' direct encounter with the Bible, to instruct them in proper German—and to teach them Hebrew. For Mendelssohn and many who were inspired by him, enlightenment meant a literate, loving connection to Jewish roots together with an open-minded yet critical approach to modern European culture. He lobbied government officials, engaged in epistolary debates with Christian thinkers, and sought to strengthen his fellow Jews' commitment to tradition through enlightenment.

A case study: In 1772 the German community of Schwerin wrote to Mendelssohn with a halakhic question. The local authorities had decreed that all dead bodies be held for three days' observation, to make sure the death was real and not some kind of deep coma (apparently there had been some cases of surprising revivals), but this decree seemed to violate the Jewish custom of immediate burial. An attempt at enlightened, scientific governance collided with time-honored custom. Mendelssohn offered a number of halakhic arguments to demonstrate that there was no conflict. For example, if the *halakhah* itself allowed delayed burial for less significant reasons (such as waiting for relatives to arrive at the funeral), how much the more so for this one.

This minor incident foreshadowed the wave of the future. As government increasingly concerned itself with its citizens' rights, obligations, and welfare, the Jewish community correspondingly experienced its own authority in these areas as being overruled and undermined. Believing such encroachment was just another evil decree by gentile rulers, community leaders often sought to circumvent or undo imposed regulations. Mendelssohn, however, did not perceive such encounters as all-or-nothing. In his view, it was both possible—and necessary—to be loyal simultaneously to the Jewish tradition and to the modern state, without conflict. For this, the state would have to understand and accept the Jews, and the Jews would have to understand and accept aspects of modernity.

Timeline: 1689–1870

1689	John Locke publishes *A Letter Concerning Toleration*, arguing that states should not engage in religious discrimination.
1744	The Jews are expelled from Prague (for four years).
1776	Declaration of Independence of the thirteen colonies.
1781	Christian Wilhelm von Dohm publishes *On the Civic Improvement of the Jews*, suggesting that liberating—and integrating—the Jews would "improve" them morally.
1781	The Jewish Free School opens in Berlin, teaching general as well as Judaic subjects—and arousing strong opposition within the Jewish community.
1782	Prussian emperor Joseph II issues the Edict of Toleration, removing a number of restrictions on Jewish economic and social integration, but requiring Jews to educate their children in German.
1783	Moses Mendelssohn completes the first German translation of the Torah and publishes *Jerusalem*, calling for preservation of *halakhah*—as well as civic emancipation and integration into the modern state.
1789	The French Revolution.
1791	The French National Assembly grants full civic rights to all Jewish citizens.
1806–7	Napoleon convenes the Assembly of Notables and the Grand Sanhedrin to clarify the place of Jews in the state.
1810–12	Many restrictions and special taxes on Jews are removed in German lands.

1815	Napoleon falls. Many pre-Emancipation restrictions on Jewish rights across Western Europe are restored.
1819	The Society for *Wissenschaft des Judentums* (the science of Judaism) is founded in Berlin, seeking to integrate the Jewish tradition of study with modern scientific, historical, and critical methods.
1830	The French monarchy falls (again); civic equality is restored in France.
1848	Democratic revolutions in Germany fail; many Jews emigrate to America.
1858	Civic equality is legislated in England.
1867	Civic equality is decreed in the Austro-Hungarian Empire.
1870	Civic equality is decreed in newly united Italy.

PRIMARY TEXT

In 1806 (twenty years after Mendelssohn's death), Emperor Napoleon, intent on consolidating his rule and responding to anti-Jewish agitation in the era of Emancipation, ordered Jewish communities in his realm (which at this point included much of Germany and Italy as well as all of France) to convene and respond to questions concerning the Jews' suitability for inclusion as equal citizens. The "Assembly of Notables," 122 lay and rabbinical leaders representing the various communities, were asked these twelve questions:

1. Is it lawful for Jews to have more than one wife?
2. Is divorce allowed by the Jewish religion? Is divorce valid, although pronounced not by courts of justice but by virtue of laws in contradiction to the French code?
3. May a Jewess marry a Christian, or [may] a Jew [marry] a Christian woman? Or does Jewish law order that the Jews should only intermarry among themselves?
4. In the eyes of Jews are Frenchmen not of the Jewish religion considered as brethren or as strangers?
5. What conduct does Jewish law prescribe toward Frenchmen not of the Jewish religion?

6. Do the Jews born in France, and treated by the law as French citizens, acknowledge France as their country? Are they bound to defend it? Are they bound to obey the laws and follow the directions of the civil code?
7. Who elects the rabbis?
8. What kind of police jurisdiction do the rabbis exercise over the Jews? What judicial power do they exercise over them?
9. Are the police jurisdiction of the rabbis and the forms of the election regulated by Jewish law, or are they only sanctioned by custom?
10. Are there professions from which the Jews are excluded by their law?
11. Does Jewish law forbid the Jews to take usury from their brethren?
12. Does it forbid, or does it allow, usury in dealings with strangers?

These challenging questions forced the notables explicitly and publicly to confront the quid pro quo of integration: the relinquishing of Jewish autonomy. Their deliberations were not easy. As they considered their answers to almost every question, they twisted and turned in order to satisfy Napoleon's obvious intent while remaining loyal to their own identity. Questions six and eight poignantly exemplify the painful price emancipation exacted from Jewish communities.

The Jewish Notables' Answers to Napoleon's Questions 6 and 8

Sixth Question:

   Do Jews born in France, and treated by the laws as French citizens, consider France their country? Are they bound to defend it? Are they bound to obey the laws and to conform to the dispositions of the civil code?

This question addresses the concern that the Jews pray constantly for return to their ancestral homeland of Israel and have traditionally lived in communities governed by their own laws. No one had ever expected otherwise.

Answer:

   Men who have adopted a country, who have resided in it these many

But now, the state demanded direct and explicit loyalty; if the Jews wanted equal treatment, they would be

generations—who, even under the restraint of particular laws which abridged their civil rights, were so attached to it that they preferred being debarred from the advantages common to all other citizens, rather than leave it—cannot but consider themselves as Frenchmen in France; and they consider as equally sacred and honorable the bounden duty of defending their country.

Jeremiah (chapter 29) exhorts the Jews to consider Babylon as their country, although they were to remain in it only for seventy years. He exhorts them to till the ground, to build houses, to sow, and to plant. His recommendation was so much attended to, that Ezra (chapter 2) says, that when Cyrus allowed them to return to Jerusalem to rebuild the Temple, forty-two thousand three hundred and sixty only, left Babylon; and that this number was mostly composed of the poor people, the wealthy having remained in that city.

The love of the country is in the heart of Jews a sentiment so natural, so powerful, and so consonant to their religious opinions, that a French Jew considers himself in England, as among strang-

expected to declare allegiance to the French homeland only and to its laws.

The notables chose to ignore the dilemma of having to choose state over religion. This was not entirely dishonest, as indeed, regardless of their long-term messianic hope of

ers, although he may be among Jews; and the case is the same with English Jews in France.

To such a pitch is this sentiment carried among them, that during the last war, French Jews have been seen fighting desperately against other Jews, the subjects of countries then at war with France.

Many of them are covered with honorable wounds, and others have obtained, in the field of honor, the noble rewards of bravery.

Eighth Question:
    What police jurisdiction do Rabbis exercise among the Jews? What judicial power do they enjoy among them?

Answer:
    The Rabbis exercise no manner of Police jurisdiction among the Jews . . . It is only in the Mishnah and in the Talmud that the word Rabbi is found for the first time applied to a doctor in the law; and he was commonly indebted for this qualification to his reputation, and to the opinion generally entertained of his learning.

When the Israelites were totally dispersed, they formed small com-

national restoration, an important principle in Jewish law was *dina d'malkhuta dina*, "the law of the kingdom is the law." The Jews were prepared to be law-abiding citizens of France or any other state that accepted them. In this sense, dual loyalty was a false issue.

As a result, this dilemma would lead some Jews to disconnect from an explicit hope of return to Israel and to interpret the messianic goal allegorically. Others preferred to "pass" on emancipation if this was its cost.

The eighth question addresses the conflict between the modern state and the continued existence of an autonomous Jewish community.

The notables describe the "suppression" of rabbinical courts in neutral language, as simply a historical fact to which the Jews were happy to adapt. This covers up deep distress and somewhat distorts the reality that for many Jews, the rabbi was still a figure of great authority. Bottom line: The autonomous community was being converted to a voluntary association with minimal authority to enforce its norms.

munities in those places where
they were allowed to settle in certain numbers.

Sometimes, in these circumstances, a Rabbi and two other
doctors formed a kind of tribunal,
named [Beth Din], that is, House of
Justice; the Rabbi fulfilled the functions of judge, and the other two
those of his assessors.

The attributes, and even the
existence of these tribunals, have,
to this day, always depended on
the will of government under
which the Jews have lived, and
on the degree of tolerance they
have enjoyed.

Since the revolution those rabbinical tribunals are totally suppressed in
France, and in Italy. The Jews, raised
to the rank of citizens, have con-
formed in every thing to the laws of
the state; and, accordingly, the functions of Rabbis, wherever any are
established, are limited to preaching
morality in the temples, blessing marriages, and pronouncing divorces.

—Diogene Tama, ed., and F. Kirwan, trans., *Transactions of the Parisian Sanhe-drim* [sic] (London: Charles Taylor, 1807)

Before the notables concluded their deliberations, they were informed of the emperor's intention to convene a Sanhedrin, also composed of lay and rabbinical leaders from across the empire, that would confirm the notables' answers as "binding." Napoleon then used the Sanhedrin's enactments to justify laws regulating Jewish life—laws that largely vitiated Jewish communal authority, establishing government-sponsored Jewish governing bodies called "consistories."

Indeed, the Jews of Western Europe faced a difficult dilemma as they moved from their medieval "state within a state" to the modern model of the state encompassing all its citizens. On a case-by-case basis, harmonization was often possible. However, on the systemic level, the rejectionists had a point: if the state would not brook an intermediary authority, would not allow autonomous communities to exist, then the rabbis' authority was in fact undermined, and Judaism moved into the realm of a voluntary affiliation, just like any professional, civic, or philanthropic association.

With Napoleon's questions/demands, the state's inability to tolerate rabbinical authority—and Jewish national identity—was made explicit. The notables fought, squirmed, and chose their words carefully. Many, but not all of them, believed that harmony was possible. And indeed, we now know that the Emancipation changed the rules of the game, forever.

LEGACY

Impact

The Emancipation of the Jews in Western Europe had several overlapping effects:

a) The end of the autonomous community: The rise of the modern state, with its demand of direct individual citizenship, made the Jewish community's traditional position as a "state within a state" untenable. Individual Jews were now free to interpret for themselves how to live their Judaism and how far to go in accepting the cultural norms of the majority society. This facilitated the flowering of a rich variety of interpretations, compromises, and syntheses, which found expression in Jewish practice and in the vast literature of modern Jewish thought. And the rabbi's role significantly changed. Without a hierarchical community, the rabbi became a teacher, preacher, and counselor. Most were henceforth invested in upholding some kind of boundary definition of Jewish identity and trying to keep the Jews involved in the now voluntary and loosely defined community.

b) The integration of the Jews into European society: From this point on (with setbacks and lapses along the way), Jews could aspire to positions of wealth and power, social status, intellectual and artistic achievement—based on skills and talents, and not limited by religious commitment or ethnic identity. A whole new world opened. However, integration was a two-edged sword, and the destructive effects were soon obvious: unlimited possibilities meant unlimited ways of redefining identity. Many Jews chose to reduce their commitment to Jewish learning, ritual observance, philanthropy, children's education, and more. What came to be called assimilation, which had been almost impossible in the closed medieval community, now became a threat to Jewish survival.

c) A positive impact on Jewish intellectual and spiritual life: Just as during the Golden Age in Spain, extensive contact and serious dialogue with gentile culture gave rise to significant creativity within the Jewish community, so too, the age of Emancipation and Enlightenment in Europe stimulated new ways of studying and understanding the tradition among Jewish scholars, leaders, and even ordinary Jews. The challenge of articulating and defending a position regarding adaptation (or refusal to adapt) to modern culture became—and remains—a central theme in Jewish thought.

The traumas and triumphs of the Emancipation thereby set the stage for the fundamental challenges the Jewish people face today.

Memory

Some Jewish leaders saw the Assembly of Notables and the Sanhedrin as a positive step: a formal undertaking to accept the Jews into the new European society. The lay (i.e., largely oligarchical) leaders tended to welcome the opportunity. The rabbis, on the other hand, were more skeptical and concerned about the price. Indeed, the event bore a certain resemblance to disputations of earlier centuries (see chapter 15), when Jewish leaders were forced to defend themselves in a contest best described as "you can't win; you can't break even; you can't get out of the game." Napoleon's questions/demands did not constitute a gesture of honor for the Jews, the deliberation process was not of their own making, and the answers could not be open and candid. In the end, this was not an experience worthy of rejoicing.

The opening of Jewish culture to Western ideas and general knowledge in eighteenth-century Western Europe is also referred to as "Enlightenment," or Haskalah (Hebrew for "wisdom" or "learning"). One who pursued such studies or advocated for them was called a *maskil*. The *maskilim* discussed their ideas on adapting Judaism to modernity in *Hame'assef* (the gatherer), a literary journal published intermittently from 1784 until 1811. The first Hebrew periodical, *Hame'assef* championed Hebrew as a pure, classical language and criticized the use of Yiddish as a "bastard" language embodying medieval backwardness.

Mendelssohn is remembered as a seminal figure in the Enlightenment. Other notable figures include the following:

- Naphtali Herz Wiesel (or Wessely; 1725–1805), a recognized Jewish scholar whose controversial book *Divrei Shalom ve-Emet* (*Words of Peace and Truth*) argued for combining secular and traditional education.
- Aaron Halle-Wolfssohn (1754–1835), a member of Mendelssohn's circle, contributor to his German Bible translation project, playwright, and editor who developed the strand of Jewish internal criticism of "unenlightened" Jews. He thus gave early expression to a tension between "enlightened" Western European Jews and their "traditionalist" coreligionists in Eastern Europe that would permeate Jewish consciousness for the next century and more.

TEXT FOR DISCUSSION

Here, Mendelssohn expresses the sense that "the enlightened" are always embattled and generally at a disadvantage. Is this the case? If so, why does it seem to be an eternal predicament?

> We dreamed of nothing but enlightenment and by the light of reason hoped to find the environs so lit up that fanaticism certainly would no

more show itself. But we see that already from the other side of the horizon night with all of its ghosts is again ascending. The most dreadful part of it is that the evil is so active, so effective. Fanaticism *acts* while reason is satisfied to *speak*.

—Moses Mendelssohn, letter to Johann Zimmermann, quoted in Michael A. Meyer, *The Origins of the Modern Jew* (Detroit: Wayne State University Press, 1967), p. 53

FURTHER READING

Jospe, Eva, ed. and trans. *Moses Mendelssohn: Selections from His Writings*. New York: Viking, 1975. Annotated selections, with an introduction surveying Mendelssohn's life and thought.

Katz, Jacob. *Out of the Ghetto: The Social Background of Jewish Emancipation, 1770–1870*. Syracuse NY: Syracuse University Press, 1973. The story of Jewish Emancipation by an eminent social historian.

———. *Tradition and Crisis*. New York: Schocken Books, 1961, pp. 233–74. A classic account of the breakdown of medieval Jewish society in response to modernity.

Mahler, Raphael. *A History of Modern Jewry, 1780–1815*. New York: Schocken Books, 1971, pp. 53–77, "Napoleon and the Jews"; pp. 129–228, "Enlightenment, Jews, and Jewish Enlightenment." Detailed accounts of the Napoleonic Sanhedrin and the European Enlightenment's impact on the Jews.

Maimon, Solomon. *Solomon Maimon: An Autobiography*. New York: Schocken Books, 1947. The remarkable autobiography of a Jew who grew up in Poland in the late eighteenth century and then made his way into Enlightenment circles in Germany.

20. Reform and Reaction

THE HAMBURG TEMPLE, 1818 CE

Responses to Emancipation

Not every Jew in nineteenth-century Western Europe was as wise, learned, and sure of his or her own belief as Moses Mendelssohn. But every individual was challenged by the breakdown of the community and the demands/temptations of emancipation. The responses were accordingly varied:

- The belief that traditional belief and practice could be, with minor adjustments, harmonized with integration into the modern, neutral, secular society: Mendelssohn's approach.
- The rejection of all suggestions for modernization and integration as threatening to the tradition: the position of much of the rabbinical leadership.
- The nonideological, practical framework of simply making personal compromises in order to get by: the perspective of many individual Jews, who started keeping their shops open on the Sabbath or who stopped strictly observing the dietary laws, in order to "make it" economically and socially in enlightened Europe.
- The relinquishing of harmonization, and conversion to Christianity. Many Jews chose to be baptized, out of the belief that for enlightened people religion shouldn't really matter, and Judaism was only an obstacle, so one might as well join the majority. Moses Mendelssohn's son Abraham converted to Lutheranism together with his family, including his son Felix (who became a prominent composer).
- The modification of traditional Jewish belief and practice to facilitate integration into the surrounding society. This approach stood behind what became the Reform movement.

Reform and Its Evolution

In its early stages, those Jews who sought the modification — reform — of Jewish observance saw their efforts not as rebellion, but as a modest attempt at harmonization. They viewed their changes as cosmetic, assuming they were modifying popular custom, not violating *halakhah*.

The first such effort occurred in 1796, in Amsterdam, when a small group split off from the main Ashkenazic synagogue (enabled by the French conquest and the disabling of the communal government) to found the "New Community" (later, Adat Jesurun), where dignity, decorum, and an "edifying" sermon were introduced into public worship. Later, the Consistory—the Jewish communal administration Napoleon had sanctioned in the Kingdom of Westphalia (Northern Germany)—ordered similar changes throughout its territory, prohibiting or at least discouraging such "superstitious" and disruptive behaviors as breaking a glass at weddings, beating willow branches on Hoshana Rabbah (the seventh day of Sukkot), and wild noisemaking while reading the Scroll of Esther on Purim. The Amsterdam and Westphalian Consistory reforms lasted only until the fall of Napoleon. However, the possibility of reforming Jewish practice, especially public liturgy, had been demonstrated.

The president of the Consistory was Israel Jacobson (1768–1828), a wealthy businessman who had studied for the rabbinate before choosing a commercial career. Inheriting a rabbinical position as well as a government job from his father-in-law, he became an activist leader both in lobbying the government for full Jewish emancipation and in "modernizing" the Jewish community.

In 1810 Jacobson built a synagogue to serve the Jewish trade school he had founded in the small community of Seesen. The building was designed with the leader's stand near the front of the hall—not in the middle, as was traditional. There was also an organ—and even a bell tower—both familiar features of Christian churches, and heretofore foreign to Jewish worship.

When the Consistory collapsed (after a coalition of European powers defeated Napoleon), Jacobson moved to Berlin, where he found many like-minded Jews. In 1815 he began holding a private Sabbath service in his home, with German sermon and hymns. This proved so popular—up to four hundred worshipers—that it was transferred to the larger home of Jacob Herz Beer, where it continued until it was shut down by king's order in 1823.

Meanwhile, the ideas of the Berlin Reformers spread to Hamburg, a free city and the largest Jewish community in Germany. There, a new synagogue could be opened without government interference. The Hamburg Temple, dedicated in 1818, incorporated the liturgical innovations that had been tested in Seesen and Berlin. In that year, one Eliezer Liebermann published two booklets giving the halakhic basis—and rabbinical letters of support—for the Hamburg liturgical reforms. The rabbinical establishment published a scathing rebuttal (see "Primary Texts" below). More rebuttals and counter-rebuttals followed.

These polemical publications were significant in expressing the Reformers' transition from "cosmetic" to ideological. Their attempts to make changes they believed were permissible by law and desirable for the community—for example, German sermons and hymns, moving the reader's stand to the front, the rabbi's wearing a robe—were met by outrage and outright refusal to even be considered. Losing their respect for the tradition and for its authorities who were blatantly unwilling to join them on their quest to modernize Jewish liturgy, they just kept on walking, leaving the rabbis and the *halakhah* behind. Thus, after public confrontations over the Berlin and Hamburg experiments, the Reformers increasingly abandoned the effort to stay within the confines of the halakhic community. This course was also consonant with the overall direction of the European Enlightenment, toward individualism and secularism (see chapter 19).

From Experiment to Movement

Meanwhile, the encounter between tradition and modernity found expression in intellectual realms as well. The Mendelssohn model of rabbinical scholarship combined with secular learning (science, philosophy) produced two important developments:

1. A shift in defining Judaism from law (action) to belief, as seen in works by Reform rabbis such as *The Religious Philosophy of the Jews*, by Samuel Hirsch, and *The Religion of the Spirit*, by Solomon Formstecher. This was both an expression of rebellion against halakhic authority and a reflection of the European environment. Christian scholarship of the time was largely devoted to theology, and rabbis were now drawn to this field, which had not been part of the intellectual world of Ashkenazic Jewry. They began writing books of religious philosophy, rather than *halakhah*.

2. The rise of *Wissenschaft des Judentums*, "the science of Judaism."
   Its best-known pioneer, Leopold Zunz (1794–1886), started out as
   a preacher at the Beer home synagogue in Berlin and went on to
   become a widely respected scholar. He taught that the modern, scientific, critical study of classical Jewish texts could yield historical
   knowledge that could provide guidance for current Jewish life and
   renew the relevance of the texts. If one sought to revise the prayer
   book, for example, researching the history of the liturgy could help
   clarify obscure prayers, demonstrate that the prayer book had a
   history (i.e., it had undergone changes over time—it was not fro-
   zen), and offer alternative texts based on past formulations. The
   renowned scholar and radical Reformer Abraham Geiger (who typ-
   ified early Reform rabbis in having received both a traditional and
   a modern secular academic education) went on to unite Reform
   and *Wissenschaft* by creating a renewed Judaism that synthesized
   these two authorities. In order to maintain the Torah's centrality
   despite its history of human composition and editing, he asserted
   that Reform must embrace modern scientific biblical criticism and
   develop its own interpretive methods and traditions.

In the decades after the Hamburg Temple's dedication, the initial focus
on modernizing synagogue aesthetics shifted to more substantive issues,
such as whether and how to maintain major practices such as circumcision, the dietary laws, and the Sabbath. In the first stage of Reform, up
until now, these topics had not been discussed. However, once it became
clear that Orthodoxy would not consider any changes and that Reform
was moving toward rejecting the authority of *halakhah*, all the "pillars"
of traditional observance were open to question

The Reformers' ideas and practices found receptive audiences in many
communities. Local experiments multiplied across Germany and beyond.
By 1869 at least sixty congregations in Germany identified with Reform
Judaism.

At first the rabbis serving the various new congregations were all the
products of traditional education. They brought to their work as innovators
deep familiarity with both *halakhah* and traditional worship. However, as
the generations passed, the leadership stratum began to include preach-

ers, teachers, and assertive lay leaders without grounding in traditional studies. Growth in numbers, this generational shift, and the development of intellectual and ideological frameworks led to more radical innovations (e.g., communities that observed the Sabbath on Sunday) and to a consciousness that the new approaches could be seen as a coherent movement.

This consciousness found expression in three rabbinical conferences, in 1844, 1845, and 1846, each attended by a few dozen rabbis who identified with the Reformist direction. The spectrum from conservative to radical was very broad. It was agreed that the rabbis' decisions would have moral force but no binding authority.

Many pioneering resolutions were passed. The rabbis expressed their definition of Judaism as a religion — not a nationality — by eliminating prayers for the return to the Land of Israel, arguing that the emancipated Jew's homeland was his or her country of citizenship. They elected to retain Hebrew for key prayers but encouraged use of the vernacular in the service, because many Jews no longer understood Hebrew. They sanctioned use of an organ to beautify Sabbath worship, despite its Christian associations. They relaxed the prohibition against traveling on the Sabbath and reduced Passover, Shavuot, and Sukkot observance from two days to one, to harmonize Sabbath and holiday observances with the needs of emancipated life. They also modernized circumcision practices to conform to modern sanitary procedures and discouraged certain mourning customs, such as tearing garments, which they saw as undignified.

Changes to reflect gender equality would take longer in coming. In 1846 a proposal for declaring women's religious equality was submitted to the Breslau conference; while it seemingly reflected most participants' views, the conference adjourned without discussion of the matter. Gender-mixed seating was introduced into American Reform synagogues at mid-century, but separate seating would remain the rule in Europe well into the twentieth century. And the first Reform woman rabbi would not be ordained until 1972 (see chapter 29).

Overall, the conference debaters encountered great difficulty in reaching consensus on any issue. This heterogeneity was in fact inherent in an ideology that gave precedence to beliefs/values over law and to individual autonomy over communal authority.

Responses to Reform

As the early experiments in reforming traditional worship developed into a movement that explicitly rejected the authority and relevance of *halakhah*, several responses took shape, providing alternatives that themselves came to be movements:

- Orthodoxy (a term first used around 1800 to refer to traditional Judaism), exemplified by the Hamburg rabbinical court's total rejection of any innovation, even the most trivial or desirable, so as not to undermine the authority of *halakhah*.
- Neo-Orthodoxy, a direction quietly pursued by many traditional rabbis who permitted various modifications and compromises they saw as beneficial to their communities, without ascribing ideological significance to them. This approach crystallized into the neo-Orthodox movement under Rabbi Samson Raphael Hirsch (1808–88), who taught *Torah im derekh eretz* (Torah with secular learning); he believed it was possible to live fully committed to *halakhah* without forgoing Western dress, aesthetics, and culture.
- Positive-historical Judaism: At the Frankfurt rabbinical conference in 1845, when the rabbis voted that Hebrew was not necessarily central to Jewish worship, Rabbi Zachariah Frankel, head of the Jewish Theological Seminary of Breslau (the first modern professional school for training rabbis, in contrast to a yeshiva) walked out, arguing that while changes are needed, certain root historical commitments may not be tampered with. He called his approach "positive-historical"; it is generally seen as the precursor of the movement known today as Conservative Judaism.

Timeline: 1786–1886

1786	Moses Mendelssohn dies.
1796	An alternative synagogue with "modern" decorum opens in Amsterdam.
1806–7	The Napoleonic Assembly of Notables and Sanhedrin are convened.
1810	Israel Jacobson's temple in Seesen is dedicated.

1812	Frederick William III of Prussia grants the Jews civil rights and citizenship with some limitations.
1815	Napoleon falls. The Congress of Vienna allows individual states to rescind emancipatory laws.
1815	Israel Jacobson begins to hold Reform services in his home in Berlin.
1818	The Temple, the Reform synagogue in Hamburg, is dedicated.
1824	The first Reform congregation in North America opens, in Charleston, South Carolina.
1844–46	Rabbinical conferences are held annually in Brunswick, Frankfurt-am-Main, and Breslau, respectively.
1846	After a six-year (occasionally violent) struggle, the Breslau community officially recognizes two congregations: Reform and Orthodox.
1846	Rabbi Isaac Mayer Wise immigrates to the United States, where he becomes a leading figure in developing Reform institutions.
1848	The failure of democratic revolutions in Central Europe leads to a wave of Jewish migration to North America.
1868–69	A national Jewish congress in Hungary splits into two communal organizations: traditionalists and "Neologs" (~Reform).
1875	Rabbi Isaac Mayer Wise founds the Hebrew Union College in Cincinnati, for training rabbis.
1885	Reform rabbis, assembling in Pittsburgh, draft the Pittsburgh Platform, articulating the movement's key principles.
1886	The Jewish Theological Seminary in New York is founded by Sephardic Orthodox rabbis and lay leaders. It would develop into the rabbinical school and intellectual center of the Conservative Movement.

PRIMARY TEXT

Nothing is known about Eliezer Liebermann, who in 1818 published twin pamphlets in defense of the Hamburg reforms: *Or Nogah* (*Lights of Splendor*), an extended essay by Liebermann, quoting various traditional sources; and *Nogah ha-Tzedek* (*The Splendor of Justice*), containing responsa (answers to halakhic questions) from three rabbis—two Sephardic rabbis from Italy, and a Hungarian rabbi who became an outspoken Reformer. The Sephardic respondents dealt with the halakhic questions out of context—they were not part of the German rabbinical establishment who felt threatened by the changes. Hence, they were able to give permissive answers to theoretical questions. Liebermann's own essay marshals traditional sources to support the reforms but is clearly a polemic, not a halakhic determination.

The Hamburg rabbinical court fought back by publishing a collection of responsa from a number of Ashkenazic rabbis using halakhic arguments to reject all of Liebermann's claims.

Eliezer Liebermann, *Or Nogah*

Why should we not draw a lesson from the peoples among whom we live? Look at the Gentiles and see how they stand in awe and reverence and with good manners in their house of prayer. No one utters a word, no one moves a limb. Their ears and all their senses are directed to the words of the preacher and to their prayers. Now judge please, you blessed of God, people of the Lord, seedlings of the faithful, how very much more there is for us to do. Are we not obligated to be the most discreet and to guard our steps and the utterances of our lips when we go to the House of God? . . . Will it occur to a man of intelligence that we should distance ourselves from a good and righteous act because we do not esteem he who performs it . . . ? Such an opinion could not but evoke derisive laughter.

The opposition to liturgical reform made much of the prohibition against imitating gentile religious practices (Leviticus 18:3), taking it well beyond the original intent of preventing syncretism with paganism. Liebermann advocates for a common-sense understanding, rejecting the application of the verse to all foreign customs.

[In Hamburg] they utter their prayers in an intelligible and lucid manner. They have chosen for an advocate between them and their Father in heaven an upright man, a rabbi eminent in Torah and wisdom and an accomplished orator. His prayer is pleasant and becoming to everyone that hears it. All join together with him to praise and glorify in a pleasant and becoming fashion, verse by verse and word by word. No one speaks nor are any words exchanged; the irreverent voices of frivolous conversation are not heard. . . .

Liebermann criticizes the prevalent custom of simultaneous prayer, aloud and not in unison, as cacophony. The ideal model, he says, can be seen in the Protestant church's dignified proceedings.

[The Hamburg preachers] preach the word of God every Sabbath and festival. They inform the congregation of the ways of the Lord and His statutes according to the righteous law of our holy Torah, so that they may fulfill all that is contained in the Written and Oral Torahs. The preachers inflame their hearts with the fear of God, blessed be He, so that they may observe His commandments. . . . They also arouse the love of our brethren, the inhabitants of our land, even if they not be Jewish, and instill love of the land of our birth, so that we should give our lives for it and always pray for its safety. For the prayer for the land of our birth precedes in

Note that the purpose of the reforms is to enhance the people's loyalty to the *halakhah*.

The priority of love for the German homeland and its gentile inhabitants meant, both in the eyes of Reformers and of their opposition, a rejection of the messianic prayers for restoration of Israel.

time the prayer for the land of our fathers, the land of Israel. . . .

If in former times there had been [such] teachers of righteousness to our people, the children of Israel, who had illuminated the good and beneficial path as contained in our holy Torah and had preached the word of God mingled with sap and nectar, then we would not be an object of ridicule and scorn for the peoples and a figure of strife and contention among the nations. Moreover, many of our people who have left our religion in this generation because of our numerous iniquities would not have done so. For what profit have the people from the sermons of preachers who build fortresses for them, hewn stones and columns, which they ascend by means of homiletics to the heights of sharp-wittedness and erudition. Through casuistry they weave complicated and fine-spun embroideries. All the people (including the women and children) hear the voices, but they do not understand one word. . . . When the ministers and sages [of the Gentiles] come to our places of worship to observe our customs and to hear the words of our teachers . . . they hear merely the sound of noise in the camp of the Hebrews and do not understand anything.

Here we have a key claim of the Reformers: that traditional Jewish practice has made the Jews a laughingstock in the eyes of their neighbors, seen as primitive—and that this unaesthetic, crude practice has even caused many Jews to leave the fold.

Liebermann argues that the common people are alienated from the pilpulistic (see chapter 18) homiletic style of the traditional rabbinate.

Eileh Divrei ha-Brit, by the Hamburg Rabbinical Court

1. It is forbidden to change the worship that is customary in Israel from the Morning Benedictions to the *Aleinu*, and all the more so to make any deletions in the traditional liturgy.

2. It is forbidden to pray in any language other than the holy tongue. Every prayer book that is printed improperly and not in accordance with our practice is invalid and it is forbidden to pray from it.

3. It is prohibited to play a musical instrument in the synagogue on the Sabbath and on the festivals even when it is played by a non-Jew.

These rather extreme halakhic proclamations are questionable in terms of precedents and theory, but the rabbis felt that it was essential to stop up every possible breach, in order to prevent the whole wall from collapsing. This is the conceptual underpinning of what came to be called the "Orthodox" position.

—From Eliezer Liebermann, *Or Nogah* (Dessau, 1818), pp. 22–25; *Eileh Divrei ha-Brit*, by the Hamburg Rabbinical Court, Altona, 1819, p. 1; translations from P. Mendes-Flohr and J. Reinharz, eds., *The Jew in the Modern World: A Documentary History* (New York: Oxford University Press, 1980), pp. 146–53

Liebermann's essay is a classic expression of a recurring theme in the Jewish response to modernization: As the Jews became—or aspired to become—more a part of the surrounding society and culture, they began to imagine they could see themselves through the eyes of their gentile neighbors and adopted what they perceived to be the gentiles' critical view of Jewish customs. Thus, they became embarrassed by traditional behaviors and sought ways to make them more "acceptable"—or to abandon them.

In its response, the rabbinical court assumed that all the Reformers' suggestions to imitate gentile practices were driven purely by this embarrassment, and not by a sincere desire to revitalize Jewish worship.

LEGACY
Impact

Reform represented a radical transformation in two dimensions:

1. Prior to the nineteenth century, a Jew who chose to live outside the
   halakhah was simply a sinner, in his or her own eyes and those of the
   community (before the Emancipation and the emergence of secular
   society, the only way to leave the Jewish community was to convert to
   another religion). Reform redefined Jewish identity, separating it from
   halakhah. In the eyes of Reform Judaism, one could be a committed,
   normative Jew without accepting the norms of *halakhah*. One could be
   Jewish in belief, self-perception, identification with the Jewish people,
   and consciousness, even if one did not live according to *halakhah*.
2. Reform also disentangled Judaism from nationality. Since the Emancipation demanded that Jews demonstrate loyalty to their nation of
   residence, continued loyalty to a Jewish nation and homeland seemed
   to conflict with this demand. The new Reform model of Judaism par-
   alleled the Protestant one, in which an individual joined the religion
   by profession of religious belief and not via a structure of community
   and law that could clash with distinctive national identity.

The debate articulated in the preceding text continues to divide the
Jewish world. Many different approaches seek to find the balance between
tradition and modernity, and some of them have been institutionalized
into movements (e.g., Conservative, Reconstructionist, Lubavitch, Modern Orthodox, Humanistic). But schematically, the opposing positions on
the ends of the spectrum can be summarized as follows:

- The autonomous individual is the ultimate authority with regard to
  personal moral behavior and acceptance of religious rituals to ground
  it. Jewish texts and the accumulated tradition can offer guidance, but
  the individual is sovereign. Jewish and universal values overlap in
  many areas, and Jews can live fully both as Jews and as participants in
  the wider society and culture. The Reform option has provided a path
  to continued Jewishness for many who desire the richness of both

Judaism and secular society and might otherwise have assimilated fully or even converted. According to Reform Judaism, the Torah was not written by God, but divinely inspired, and throughout the generations Judaism has changed in response to new circumstances; therefore, in every generation a Jew is to study the tradition and personally consider how to integrate it into his or her life. The birth of Reform Judaism in Germany thus represented a turning point, in leading to a Judaism that can survive and flourish in the new era.

- Judaism cannot be separated from *halakhah*; the covenant at Sinai is what makes the Jew Jewish, and the *halakhah* is the expression of the covenant. The ultimate authority is the "chain of tradition" as expressed in the halakhic rulings of the rabbis of each generation. Attempts to define Judaism differently are only justifications for sin and have provided a waystation for Jews who wish to abandon their Jewish identity and assimilate into the wider society. The birth of Reform Judaism thus represented a turning point in threatening the ability of Judaism to survive and flourish.

Memory

Reform congregations multiplied in nineteenth-century Western Europe; however, the great expansion of the movement took place in North America. The German immigrants of the mid-nineteenth-century wave to America— having escaped the failure of the 1848 democratic revolutions in Europe— now often found themselves living in isolated communities where they were distant from Jewish educational and ritual resources and pressured to "fit in." An individualistic, often attenuated relationship to the tradition became commonplace. This reality fit Reform ideology, which rejected halakhic authority and focused on both individual autonomy and belief.

The Reform leaders who organized the movement in America saw their work as creating a truly American Judaism, one suitable for the needs of a new life in a new, free land. They established a rabbinical school, Hebrew Union College, late in the century, and an association of congregations (the Union of American Hebrew Congregations—predecessor of the Union for Reform Judaism), founded in 1873 with twenty-eight congregations. Thus the movement was already established among the German immigrant community and "ready" when the mass migration from Russia began in 1881 (see chapter 21).

As Jewish life in Europe recovered after the Holocaust and then the fall of the Iron Curtain, Reform communities have again sprung up across the continent. The movement has grown in Israel too. However, the great center of Reform Judaism remains North America, where about 35 percent of Jews identify themselves as Reform.

TEXT FOR DISCUSSION

Rabbi Jakob J. Petuchowski, a professor at the Reform seminary, articulated the difficulty of transmitting the revolutionary consciousness of a first-generation Reform Jew to subsequent generations. How is it possible to educate children for free choices that their parents have already made?

In order to be able to make his individual choice [of what mitzvoth to observe] the Reform Jew must have at his disposal a knowledge of the material from which this choice is to be made, a knowledge of the mitzvoth handed down by Tradition. This, in turn, necessitates an intensive study of that Tradition. In theory, a Reform Jewish education would have to be much more intensive than an Orthodox one.

—Jakob J. Petuchowski, *Heirs of the Pharisees* (New York: Basic Books, 1970), p. 172

FURTHER READING

Hirsch, Samson Raphael. *The Nineteen Letters*. Jerusalem and New York: Feldheim, 1969. A classic document: a brief manifesto of neo-Orthodoxy.

Meyer, Michael A. *The Origins of the Modern Jew*. Detroit: Wayne State University Press, 1967, pp. 115–182. Spotlight on the evolution from Enlightenment to Reform—and to *Wissenschaft des Judentums*.

———. *Response to Modernity: A History of the Reform Movement in Judaism*. Oxford and New York: Oxford University Press, 1988. The definitive, comprehensive history of the movement.

Plaut, W. Gunther. *The Growth of Reform Judaism: American and European Sources until 1948*. Philadelphia: Jewish Publication Society, 2015. A volume of annotated source excerpts tracing the Reform movement's development.

———. *The Rise of Reform Judaism: A Sourcebook of Its European Origins*. Philadelphia: Jewish Publication Society, 2015. A volume of annotated source excerpts tracing the Reform movement's development.

21. The Rise of North American Jewry

THE GREAT MIGRATION, 1881–1924 CE

HISTORY

Deterioration in Russia

With Poland's various partitions in 1772–95, the Russians, who had prohibited Jewish entry into their kingdom, suddenly found themselves with a large Jewish population. Over the next century, they implemented different policies aimed at "solving the Jewish problem," encouraging assimilation, conversion, or emigration.

The century saw a crescendo of anti-Jewish measures, from economic and educational restrictions to blood libel trials, expulsions, and pogroms. Meanwhile, the kingdom itself was increasingly unstable, and the winds of revolution and counter-revolution never blew fair for the Jews. The serfs' emancipation in 1862 created a mass of indebted and impoverished peasants seeking an outlet for their frustration. After a terrorist assassinated Tsar Alexander II in 1881, a wave of pogroms swept the country. The Jews, it seems, were blamed by all sides for all ills.

This dynamic continued and intensified until the revolution of 1917 and beyond (see chapter 30). Generally the Russian government responded to violence against the Jews by blaming the victims (for their exploitation of the peasants, among other things), winking at the perpetrators, and enacting new restrictive laws against the Jews. Throughout the 1880s, Western Jews, horrified by these persecutions, held protest demonstrations (for example, the Guildhall meeting in London in 1890) and successfully lobbied their governments to intercede diplomatically. British and American ambassadors protested to the tsarist government, which consistently stonewalled them.

In response to their situation, some Russian Jews joined revolutionary movements or the Zionist movement. Others sought to apply the Western European experience of the Enlightenment and Emancipation to Russian reality, supporting government policies requiring Jewish schools to include secular subjects (as of 1844)—and even government-sponsored rabbinical seminaries (which operated in Vilna and Zhitomir, 1847–73), requiring science and liberal arts courses along with Jewish studies. The graduates were qualified to be "crown rabbis"—that is, state functionaries—but most communities rejected them as religious or halakhic authorities.

However, after the 1881 pogroms, such long-term solutions lost their appeal. Emigration became the path of choice and quickly developed into a mass phenomenon.

Mass Migration

Between 1880 and 1930, more than 2.2 million Jews left Russia for North America, Western Europe, Palestine (see chapter 24), and Latin America. Three-quarters of them came to the United States. They were just one tributary to the great river of immigrants to America: German, Italian, Irish, and others (gentiles and Jews), fleeing oppression and poverty, were also drawn by America's liberal immigration policy and the promise of freedom and opportunity. When the United States enacted severe immigration restrictions in 1924, the flow was cut off, deflected to Latin America and elsewhere.

The big cities, especially those on the Eastern Seaboard, absorbed most of the immigrants, benefiting from the influx of manpower and culture—and suffering from the burdens of absorption (education, social welfare, culture clash). New York, the main port of entry, came to symbolize the American value of being a haven for the "homeless, tempest-tossed." In this vibrant, diverse metropolis, the squalor of the tenements was legendary, but the freedom and sense of opportunity were magnetic.

For the Jews, the concept of a land whose national identity was based on ideology, not on ethnicity or religion, was revolutionary. In all the eras and sites of Jewish life throughout the ages, there had never been such a place. There was something almost messianic in the prospect of a new life in this new world. And so, despite the risks and uncertainties, the disruption of family and community and tradition, the stories of privation and loneliness—the worse things got in Russia, the better immigration to the United States appeared.

After the 1881 pogroms, immigration numbers to the United States began to grow significantly, between 1900 and 1910 reaching an average of eighty-two thousand Russian Jews per year. Recognizing the phenomenon already in the early 1880s, Jewish organizations in Western Europe (such as the Russo-Jewish Committee, established in London in 1882) and in the United States (such as HIAS, the Hebrew Immigrant Aid Society, founded in New York in 1881) began organizing to help the immigrants arrive safely at their destinations and be absorbed upon arrival. But as the numbers grew, this effort became both more necessary and more difficult, as gentile immigrants were also pouring into the East Coast cities and affecting their economies, schools, and social services.

By 1881, about two hundred thousand Jews were already living in the United States, most of them immigrants (or their children) from the mid-century Central European wave. Many were well-established and integrated; some had become wealthy. They responded to the new influx with ambivalence. On the one hand, they felt obligated to help their suffering, impoverished, uprooted fellow Jews, and so they generously built and supported institutions to assist the immigrants in education, training, health, and social welfare. At the same time, they viewed the massive immigration of poor Jews from a premodern setting as an embarrassment and even a threat to their accepted status. Hence, some tried to prevent or restrict the entry of impoverished Jews who wished to immigrate, or to disperse them far from the crowded East Coast even before they arrived on U.S. soil (the Galveston Plan). Established American Jews also supported efforts to build institutions that would speed the immigrants' Americanization.

The Rise of the North American Jewish Community

Three interrelated aspects of American society had significant impact on how Jewish life developed in the new setting:

- Mobility: Despite the continued existence of some class, ethnic, and religious barriers, the prospects for social and economic mobility were infinitely greater in the United States than in Russia (or anywhere else). To the immigrants it was an article of faith that a family sewing piecework in a sweatshop could see its children become doctors, lawyers, and captains of industry. And indeed, so it came to pass. For the large majority of immigrants, within a generation or maybe two, the American dream came true: the Jews were (on the whole) middle class and above, well educated, and influential in the larger society.

- Freedom: In the absence of both a hierarchical Jewish community with its social controls and an authoritarian government, the individual faced an unlimited choice of spiritual, social, political, and intellectual pursuits and affiliations. One could define oneself as Orthodox, Reform, socialist, atheist, Zionist, any idiosyncratic combination, or none of the above. This freedom was exhilarating but also at times frightening; without an anchor, it was easy to feel adrift.
- Openness: The diversity and lack of central authority meant that, for better or worse, no one could speak for the Jews, internally or externally. The flip side of variety was a high degree of disunity. Jewish life in the United States was totally voluntary and individualistic. As a result, the community's ability to enforce moral norms, demand participation, collect *tzedakah* (funds for social welfare), and take a political stand were all significantly attenuated.

Thus, while the Jews prospered, integrated, enjoyed security and pride, and otherwise thrived in the new environment, these benefits came at a cost: the weakening of many beliefs, commitments, and institutions that had been central to Jewish identity in the Old World. And especially in the generations after immigration, geographical dispersal away from the intense cultural environment of the immigrant neighborhoods contributed to this dilution of commitment and involvement.

In Europe it was different. Even in places where emancipation had come, the old Jewish community as a hierarchical structure, mediating between the Jews and the outside world (and the state), continued to function in some form.

But in the United States, where the individual, autonomous citizen was the baseline ideal, attempts to create any kind of communal structure with "teeth" consistently failed—or failed even to get off the ground. Suddenly rabbis were no longer authorities, but marketers. And so a rich and variegated spectrum of local and national Jewish organizations, all voluntary, replaced the traditional community.

The Jews adapted to the voluntariness of American society by enthusiastically volunteering, pursuing distinctly Jewish interests and causes in every sphere: worship, social welfare, social change, education, the arts,

Zionism, and more. This sometimes contentious, cacophonous communal life was a distinctively American response to the new Jewish reality.

And thus, the immigrants of the great wave created a new and powerful world center that would have significant, even dominant impact on every aspect—philanthropy, scholarship, liturgy, education, spirituality—of world Jewish life and culture to this day.

Timeline: 1862–1924

1862	The serfs are emancipated in Russia.
1881	Tsar Alexander II's assassination unleashes pogroms throughout the Jewish Pale of Settlement. Jewish migration from Russia to the United States jumps from an annual average of about four thousand to about thirteen thousand.
1881	HIAS—Hebrew Immigrant Aid Society—is founded in New York.
1882	The Russian government promulgates the "May Laws," imposing new economic restrictions on Jews.
1886	Etz Haim Yeshivah opens in New York. The precursor of (neo-Orthodox) Yeshivah University, it offered traditional studies along with some secular subjects.
1888	The Jewish Publication Society is founded, the oldest not-for-profit, nondenominational Jewish publisher in North America.
1891	A government decree expels all Jews from Moscow, creating thousands of refugees. A coalition of American Jewish organizations establishes the American Committee for Ameliorating the Condition of Russian Exiles.
1892	Baron Maurice de Hirsch, a German Jewish millionaire, agrees to finance the transfer of three million Jews to Argentina. In the end, about ten thousand migrate there.
1895	The Federated Jewish Charities of Boston is founded—the first Jewish federation.
1897	The first Russian census numbers 5.2 million Jews, the largest Jewish community in the world.
1897	The *Jewish Daily Forward* begins publication in New York.
1900	Average annual Jewish immigration from Russia to the United States reaches eighty-two thousand.

1903–4	In severe pogroms, several thousand Jews are killed in the Ukraine.
1906	The "Galveston Plan," to redirect immigrant arrivals away from the East Coast, is inaugurated. By 1914, when it ceases operations, it will have dispersed about ten thousand Jews to southern and midwestern cities.
1908	New York Police commissioner Theodore Bingham states that the city's Jews (20 percent of the population) are responsible for 50 percent of the crime, leading to a huge outcry — and a retraction — but stimulating the Jewish community to organize itself to improve social services.
1909	More than two hundred Jewish organizations in New York agree to establish a communal governing structure, "The Kehillah," under the leadership of Rabbi Judah Magnes. It lasts until 1922.
1912	Henrietta Szold founds Hadassah, the Women's Zionist Organization
1913	In a highly publicized trial in Kiev, Mendel Beilis is acquitted of a ritual murder charge.
1913	The United Synagogue of America, the organization representing Conservative Judaism, is established.
1914–18	World War I.
1917	The Communist revolution in Russia.
1918–20	Russian civil war gives rise to major pogroms, especially by Ukrainian nationalists and the White army; approximately fifty thousand Jews are killed.
1924	In response to growing popular opposition to immigration, based on fears and perceived economic interests, the Johnson-Reed Act passes, imposing strict quotas on immigration from Southern and Eastern Europe; Jewish immigration drops from 119,000 in 1921 to 10,000 in 1925.

PRIMARY TEXT

One of the flagship institutions of the immigrant community was the Yiddish daily newspaper, the *Jewish Daily Forward*, founded by editor Abraham Cahan in 1897. Moderately socialist in tone, the paper was an important community builder as well as a vehicle for Americanization. Letters in its popular advice column, "A Bintel Brief," often clearly and painfully reflected the immigrant experience. Here is one example.

"A Bintel Brief," 1909

I was born in a small town in Russia, and until I was sixteen I studied in Talmud Torahs and yeshivas, but when I came to America I changed quickly. I was influenced by the progressive newspapers, the literature, I developed spiritually and became a freethinker. I meet with freethinking, progressive people, I feel comfortable in their company and agree with their convictions. But the nature of my feelings is remarkable. Listen to me: Every year when the month of Elul rolls around, when the time of Rosh Hashanah and Yom Kippur approaches, my heart grows heavy and sad. A melancholy descends on me, a longing gnaws at my breast. At that time I cannot rest, I wander about through the streets, lost in thought, depressed.

When I go past a synagogue during these days and hear a cantor chanting the melodies of the prayers, I become very gloomy and my depression is so great that I cannot endure it. My memory goes back to my happy childhood years. I see clearly before me the small town, the fields, the little pond and the

Like so many immigrants, the writer is unable to maintain his faith and practice amid the open climate—and lack of institutional moorings—he finds in New York.

And yet, there is a dimension in his identity that his atheism, and the openness of the environment, cannot suppress. Interestingly, for all the injustice, poverty, and insecurity of life in Russia, it is still possible to be nostalgic for it—even if one has intellectually and socially distanced oneself from the beliefs and traditions of one's youth.

woods around it. I recall my childhood friends and our sweet child-
like faith. My heart is constricted,
and I begin to run like a madman
till the tears stream from my eyes
and then I become calmer.

These emotions and these moods
have become stronger over the
years and I decided to go to the
synagogue. I went not in order to
pray to God but to heal and refresh
my aching soul with the cantor's
sweet melodies, and this had an
unusually good effect on me.

Sitting in the synagogue among the
landsleit and listening to the good
cantor, I forgot my unhappy weekday life, the dirty shop, my boss,
the bloodsucker, and my pale sick
wife and my children. All of my
America with its hurry-up life was
forgotten.

Landsleit—Yiddish for the "folks"
from the old country.

I am a member of a Progressive
Society, and since I am known
there as an outspoken freethinker,
they began to criticize me for going
to the synagogue. The members
do not want to hear of my personal
emotions and they won't understand that there are people whose
natures are such that memories
of their childhood are sometimes
stronger than their convictions.

The American dream, at the
moment, is not so golden. The synagogue, a link to an idealized past,
provides some grounding and
respite, even absent any sense of religious belief or commitment. Yet the
writer seeks something else . . . perhaps a nontheological Jewish spirituality.

And where can one hide on Yom
Kippur? There are many of us, like
me. They don't go to work, so it
would be good if there could be
a meeting hall where they could
gather to hear a concert, a lecture,
or something else.

—Isaac Metzker, ed., *A Bintel Brief* (New York: Behrman House, 1971), pp. 101–2;
used by permission of Black Star

Like the letter writer, many immigrants experienced spiritual ambivalence in America. The geographical and cultural dislocation of immigration, and the instant emancipation, created a sense of alienation from
traditional belief and practice. To the new American, the synagogue of
the shtetl ("little town" in Yiddish — a Russian Jewish village) felt long ago
and far away. These were "progressive" times, and this was a "progressive"
place. And yet, a clean break was not so simple. The values, memories,
melodies, feelings — significant components of Jewish identity that had
been formed in the shtetl — could not be erased; the disconnect from the
old life left a void.

In this milieu, over the century, new forms of Judaism emerged: new
syntheses between the emotional need for traditional roots and the anti-
traditional intellectual and spiritual currents of American life.

As in the case of the early German Reformers (see chapter 20), the
perceived precariousness of emancipation often influenced the immigrants' self-image and behavior. Imagining that they could see themselves
through the eyes of their more "advanced" brethren — or of the American
environment — they were embarrassed by their own culture — names, religious practice, language, dress, and more. Often they made painful compromises, such as changing their family names to disguise their origins
and distancing themselves geographically from Jewish communal life, in
order to "fit in."

LEGACY

Impact

The great wave of immigration to the United States in the late nineteenth and early twentieth centuries created a new center of Jewish life in the world. To appreciate the magnitude of this change, consider that in 1880 the Jews of the United States represented 3 percent of the world Jewish population; in 1920 they were 23 percent.

The transformation was, however, considerably more than demographic. This new center faced the new and unique challenge of building sustainable institutions of Jewish life in an open society—an ongoing challenge to this day. The Jews' dominant response was to build and support liberal movements (Reform, Conservative, Reconstructionist), which grew, thrived, and created elaborate institutions of religion, social action, and education throughout the country. Orthodoxy in America was strong and vibrant but remained limited to about a 10 percent minority

As generations pass, however, the liberal movements have struggled to maintain their numbers and to support their institutional frameworks in the face of several interrelated challenges:

- Increasing rates of intermarriage: from 17 percent in 1970 to 58 percent in 2013. Once considered an aberration and an anathema, "marrying out" has become so common that many communal institutions have invested major resources in welcoming mixed families and adopting a more inclusive model of Jewish identity—one no longer based on formal recognition of Jewish status (descent or conversion).
- A general process of drifting away: Fewer than a third of American Jews are formally affiliated with a synagogue, and fewer than a quarter attend synagogue regularly. The forsaking of regular involvement in organized Jewish life has led more generally to a diminution of education, familiarity with religious tradition, and Jewish textual knowledge. The ostensible elimination of all barriers—racial, religious, and ethnic—to integration and advancement in American society has allowed Jews to choose "anchors" of identity other than Jewishness, among them professional, political, cultural, and geographical affinities.

- A new cultural trend—the rejection of ascribed identity in general: The traditional model in which gender, ethnic, and religious identities were clear, bounded, and generally determined by birth has given way to a more fluid understanding that grants the individual a much higher degree of freedom to choose and change.

Despite an ongoing, nagging doubt about what Jewish identity means to the younger generations and how Jewish continuity can be ensured in an open society, the "Golden Age" of Jewish life in North America has rivaled all previous such efflorescences (described in earlier chapters) in cultural creativity. Beyond the important institutions of specifically Jewish scholarship under the auspices of the religious movements and non-denominational Jewish colleges, dozens of universities offer programs in Jewish studies, staffed in many cases by leading scholars. It is difficult to keep up with the rich and variegated output of Jewish books, periodicals, music, art, theater, videos, websites, and social media discussions. Isaac Bashevis Singer, Bernard Malamud, Irving Berlin, Saul Bellow, Henry Roth, Chaim Potok, Philip Roth, Leonard Cohen, Steven Spielberg, Elie Wiesel, Leonard Bernstein, Bob Dylan, Barbara Streisand, Kirk Douglas, and Thomas Friedman constitute just a small sampling of the hundreds of artists, editors, and producers in every medium who have examined and processed their experience of being Jewish in America through their creative work and, in so doing, have made significant contributions to both Jewish and general culture.

Another heritage of the immigrant experience, one that has weakened somewhat in the course of the century, is the association of Jews with the left side of the political spectrum. Whether because they brought socialist beliefs with them from the turmoil of pre-revolutionary Russia or whether they were influenced by their experiences of capitalist exploitation in the sweatshops of New York, the Jews became disproportionately active in the labor union movement, in socialist organizations, and, later, in supporting liberal or social-democratic positions, politicians, and parties. Some Jewish thinkers suggest that these leanings derive from "Jewish values" expressed in the Bible and later literature; others attribute them to Jewish alienation from the nationalism and antisemitism associated with right-wing parties in Europe; still others believe that struggling immigrants felt "saved" by the ideas of openness, diversity, and equality that characterized American society and were emblematic of American leftist ideology. In any case, today many U.S. Jews express their "Jewishness" through their liberal politics and social justice activism.

Memory

The great wave of Russian Jewish immigration did not give rise to institutionalized commemoration. There were no additions to the liturgy, nor special days of celebration or remembrance. Old immigrant neighborhoods (such as New York's Lower East Side) that once served as "cultural preserves," worthy of visiting for a vestige of the immigrant experience (complete with Jewish food samplings) have largely transitioned to havens for newer waves of immigrants (e.g., from Asia and Latin America) or gentrified. Anthologies of literature, museums, academic research, chapters in history textbooks, websites, and more continue to record the immigrant experience, but its memory has largely faded with the demise of the immigrants (as well as their descendants' dispersal to the suburbs and, sometimes, their choice to sever connections to their immigrant roots). Meanwhile, Russian Jews—like all American immigrants—saw elements of their culture absorbed into general American culture: from foods such as bagels and knishes to words like *chutzpah* (nerve, arrogance) and *schmaltz* (chicken fat, often connoting "corniness"). For earlier generations, such appropriations were a source of pride; with the passage of time, however, they have largely lost their original significance as markers of Jewish identity.

TEXT FOR DISCUSSION

Writing in 1958, sociologist Ben Halpern seems to be saying that in the contexts of European Emancipation and immigration to America, the only sustainable Jewish identity is religious identity. Is that the case?

At the very outset of the European Emancipation, Jews were brusquely confronted with the price they must pay: for freedom of the individual, virtual dissolution of the group. The immigrant to these shores, too, found that the prize of Americanization was to be won at a price: by unreserved elasticity in discarding everything which America might find foreign. In both cases, only religion was reserved as a sanctuary of Jewish tradition . . . [but] in America there was no urgency about the procedure.

— Ben Halpern, "America Is Different," in *The Jews: Social Patterns of an American Group*, ed. Marshall Sklare (New York: Free Press, 1958), p. 31

FURTHER READING

Feingold, Henry. *Zion in America: The Jewish Experience from Colonial Times to the Present.* New York: Hippocrene, 1974, pp. 113–243. A history of the period encompassing the great migration.

Goren, Arthur. *New York Jews and the Quest for Community.* New York: Columbia University Press, 1970. A detailed account and analysis of the New York Kehillah experiment's rise and fall.

Howe, Irving. *World of Our Fathers.* New York: Harcourt Brace Jovanovich, 1976. A classic study of the Russian Jewish immigrants' political and cultural experiences in New York.

Lipsky, Seth. *The Rise of Abraham Cahan.* New York: Nextbook/Schocken, 2013. A biography of the fabled cultural leader of the immigrant generation — and a window into that generation's experience.

Polonsky, Antony. *The Jews in Poland and Russia.* Vol. 2. Oxford and Portland OR: Littman Library of Jewish Civilization, 2010, pp. 1–86. A detailed account of the Jews in Russia, 1881–1914.

Sorin, Gerald. *A Time for Building: The Third Migration 1880-1920.* Baltimore: Johns Hopkins University Press, 1992. A comprehensive survey of the immigrant experience during the great wave.

22. Jewish Nationalism

THEODOR HERZL, 1896 CE

HISTORY

The Fading Vision of Emancipation

Despite reverses along the way, the progress of emancipation in Western Europe seemed assured in the second half of the nineteenth century. Even after the reaction after the 1848 revolutions, emancipatory laws continued to be enacted, and Jews increasingly found their way into the social, cultural, and economic fabric of Europe. However, two growing shadows darkened this celebration:

- The "price" of emancipation—integration—seemed to pose a threat to continued Jewish life. Leaders and observers of the Jewish community decried the loss of Jews both formally (baptism) and informally (assimilation).
- Expressions of antisemitism not only failed to diminish, as anticipated, but intensified. The hoped-for New Europe failed to materialize. Enlightenment was undermined by the currents of reaction—including the growth of exclusionary, xenophobic nationalism. Religious hatred of Jews morphed into racial antisemitism.

Ironically, it seemed that the harder Jews tried to fit in, and the more they sacrificed to do so, the more they came to be seen as unassimilable. Even Jews who spoke fluent German or French, who were "enlightened," at home in Western culture, insisted on retaining certain identity markers—especially the tendency to in-marry. To the gentiles, this "proved" the Jews were indeed a separate "caste," unwilling or unable to be integrated. Thus, various social frameworks, such as the popular, secular, Freemasons, continued to exclude Jews.

Calling attention to this lose-lose situation, in 1862 the German Jewish socialist Moses Hess proposed that Jews break out of it by establishing a Jewish state in Palestine. In his book *Rome and Jerusalem*, he described the

Jewish "problem" as a national one, which could only be solved by political means—not a religious one, which could be solved by modernization and enlightened rule. But Western European Jews, still in thrall to the dream of emancipation and anxiously awaiting its realization, were not ready for this paradigm shift. Hess's book was largely ignored. In the same year, a Polish Orthodox rabbi, Zvi Hirsch Kalischer, published a Hebrew pamphlet calling for Jewish settlement in Palestine as a means for hastening the messianic redemption. This work, too, made barely a ripple in its time. Today Hess and Kalischer (and a few contemporaries) are often referred to as "proto-Zionists"—who floated "Zionist" ideas before the word had been coined.

Meanwhile, in the East, illusions of emancipation had never really taken hold; after 1881, emigration to the United States and other Western countries became a mass phenomenon (see chapter 21). Influenced by the rising nationalistic consciousness in Europe, some small Jewish circles in Russia began to discuss, plan, and support emigration to Palestine as a preferred destination. After all, if the Jews were going to emigrate, why not to a place deeply embedded in their history, religion, and literature, where they could restore their own culture rather than compromising with other nations' cultures? These groups organized themselves into a loose network called Chovevei Tziyyon (Lovers of Zion).

In 1882 the first group of Chovevei Tziyyon colonists, fourteen students, left Kharkov to sail for Palestine. They settled in the southern coastal plain, founding the farming community Rishon LeTziyyon. Over the next twenty years, successive groups (about twenty-five thousand settlers in all) established a score of other colonies around the country (see chapter 24).

Thus by the last decades of the century, in both Western and particularly in Eastern Europe, emigration to Palestine was "in the air" as a solution to the Jewish "problem."

Herzl and Political Zionism

In 1891 Theodor Herzl, an ambitious young writer from an integrated Budapest Jewish family, was appointed Paris correspondent for the liberal Austrian newspaper *Neue Freie Presse*. Over the next several years, as he covered events in France, his awareness heightened regarding the tension between the dream of emancipation and the reality of rising antisemitism.

A formative point was the Dreyfus trial. In 1894–95 Alfred Dreyfus, a minor Jewish officer in the French army, was accused of passing secrets to the Germans. The evidence was thin, but he was convicted and sentenced to solitary exile on Devil's Island (off the French Guiana coast). While the trial was secret, army investigators revealed enough information to raise doubts and arouse continuing protest from liberal politicians and journalists. In 1898 the novelist Emile Zola published an open letter to the government, "J'accuse," accusing the army and the government of railroading Dreyfus on account of corruption, incompetence, and antisemitism. "J'accuse" set off a political storm. Zola, convicted of libel and facing prison time, fled the country. Those defending the army played the antisemitism card; anti-Jewish demonstrations and publications proliferated. At the same time, the commotion mobilized many intellectuals and politicians to call for a review of the case. Ultimately, the sloppiness and overt dishonesty of the prosecution were revealed—but it took time: Dreyfus was not exonerated until 1906.

In essence, the Dreyfus case demonstrated the Jews' vulnerability as pawns in the struggle by the "old guard"—army and church—to retain power in the face of modernization.

Even before the trial, Herzl had been formulating his analysis of the Jewish situation, working on drafts of the pamphlet *Der Judenstaat* (*The Jews' State*—commonly translated as *The Jewish State* or *A Jewish State*) he would publish in 1896. His central claim (see "Primary Text" below) echoed that of Hess three decades earlier: Hope of emancipation is an illusion; the Jews are a nation and therefore not assimilable into the nations of Europe. The solution must be to remove them from Europe, to a place of their own.

The pamphlet outlined key elements in the preparation and migration process. European rulers would play a major diplomatic role in opening up Palestine for Jewish emigration. Jewish community leaders would take responsibility for organizing the emigration and establishing the state.

Herzl also offered proposals for the new state's social and economic structure. He envisioned establishing a corporation to handle the orderly sale of Jewish property in Europe and land purchase in the new homeland. He called for a "workfare" program to create full employment and a universal seven-hour workday. He expected communities to migrate *en bloc*, settling together in their new home.

Most readers—even Zionist activists in Russia—viewed Herzl's manifesto as the work of an outsider or crackpot. It drew a small number of enthusiasts, mostly students. From the moment of its publication, however, Herzl was transformed from a journalist into an activist. For the remaining eight years of his life (he died in 1904 at age forty-four), he devoted all of his inheritance (his father had been a successful merchant) to feverish activity to realize his vision. By 1898 Herzl had burned through 80,000 marks—at least $9 million in today's value; when he died, his supporters had to take up a collection to provide for his children's education.

With those funds, he founded a Zionist newspaper, *Die Welt* (*The World*). Between 1897 and 1903, he convened six Zionist Congresses, at which activists and community leaders from throughout Europe gathered to debate ideology and strategy and create organizational infrastructure. He shuttled from capital to capital and from millionaire to millionaire, seeking diplomatic and financial support for his plan.

Herzl did not succeed in persuading the world's rulers to do more than nod and smile. He failed to imbue them with moral compulsion to help the Jews—or to convince them that the Jews were a nation—or to show them how their own interests would be served by the plan.

Nor, at the time, did he succeed in convincing the majority of the Jewish establishment. Both Reform and Orthodox leaders opposed Zionism as a secular nationalistic movement. In a sense, Zionism represented the mirror image of Reform: If Reform saw Judaism as primarily a set of beliefs—a religion, not a nationality—Zionism saw Judaism as primarily a nationality, not a religion. And if Reform replaced *halakhah* with ethics, Zionism replaced *halakhah* ("the portable homeland") with the state. The Reform movement would largely oppose Zionism on ideological/religious grounds until the 1930s, when developments in Europe and the rising influence of Russian immigrants led to rethinking this position. Orthodox Jews, meanwhile, were divided. Some found a way to accept Zionism by ascribing messianic significance to it, but others refused to take this step and hence rejected it as false messianism—a division that continues until the present.

Nonetheless, despite opposition and skepticism from every quarter, by dint of Theodor Herzl's overwhelming dedication and a certain personal charisma (many Jews ascribed to him messianic qualities), he did succeed. He created a grassroots movement with an infrastructure that continued to pursue the goal of a Jewish state after his death. Ultimately his role was transformational. In 1917, thirteen years after his death, British foreign secretary Lord Balfour formally declared the British government's support for "the establishment in Palestine of a national home for the Jewish people."

The Development of Zionism

From the beginning, a heterogeneous assembly gathered under the banner of Zionism. Among the significant divisions were the following:

- Political versus practical: Herzl opposed the small-scale colonization supported by the Russian Zionists. He believed it was necessary to wait for diplomatic success that would allow mass migration. The practical Zionists said the need was too immediate to wait, and creating facts on the ground could advance the larger plan.
- Political versus cultural: Herzl's vision of the state was strongly colored by his own roots in middle-class Central Europe, where various European languages were spoken. He was even willing to consider the British proposal to create a temporary Jewish colony in East Africa (Uganda), which the cultural Zionists considered anathema. Other Jews, especially the Russian Zionists, believed that a fundamental goal was to create a center of authentic, revitalized Jewish culture—in Hebrew, in Palestine (see chapter 23).
- Human intervention versus God's plan: The Zionist movement was modeled on other European secular nationalist movements of the late nineteenth and early twentieth centuries. It was not a religious, messianic movement. However, the parallels between the vision of the nationalists and the redemption described by the biblical prophets were hard to miss, and Zionist rhetoric often resonated with messianic references. While some Orthodox leaders saw Jewish settlement in Palestine as a welcome option both for relieving the people's suffering and for fulfilling the commandments related to living in the Holy Land, the majority opposed Herzl's idea as forbidden human intervention in the divine plan for Israel's redemption ("forcing the end"). Meanwhile, the pull of Herzl's vision was

so strong, a number of rabbis were moved to formulate a new position: the Zionist endeavor was indeed messianic, paving the way for
divine redemption. Thus, Orthodox believers could support Zionism
without violating the prohibition against "forcing the end." With this
reading of the map of history, an Orthodox Zionist faction emerged
within the larger movement. This in turn gave rise to endless controversy over the "Jewishness" of the envisioned state: Would/could
halakhah be the law of the land? If the state is a phase in the messianic redemption, what role should the traditional image of that
redemption have in determining boundaries, governance, social policy, and more?

· Socialist versus liberal: The idea that Zionism could be synthesized with socialism became very popular in Eastern Europe, where
  socialist movements were flourishing in response to tsarist oppression (among all Russians but especially among the Jews, whose
  oppression was so acute; see chapter 30). While socialism nominally opposed ethnic and religious division, at this time syntheses between nationalism and socialism were popular, so the idea of
  merging Zionist and socialist visions of redemption attracted many
  Jews, who envisioned a Jewish national state governed by a socialist approach to social justice. Socialist Zionism became a powerful force in the Zionist movement (and, later, in the institutions the
  Jewish immigrants would establish in Palestine). On the other hand,
  liberal Zionists argued that Zionism's aim was not a Jewish proletarian revolt, but a "normal" Jewish nation-state, with the freedom (and
  social classes) found in any modern capitalist society.

These divisions continued to play out over the years, within the Zionist
Organization (the organizational embodiment of the movement, founded
at the First Zionist Congress in 1897), the political parties active among the
immigrants to Palestine, and the State of Israel's party politics from 1948 on.

Timeline: 1862–1922

1862   Moses Hess, a German Jewish socialist, publishes *Rome and
         Jerusalem*, arguing that antisemitism is eternal, and there-

fore acculturation and assimilation hopeless. He proposes a socialist Jewish state in Palestine.

1862   Zvi Hirsch Kalischer, a Polish Orthodox rabbi, publishes *Drishat Tziyyon* (*Seeking Zion*), arguing that the Jews should begin to build their own national state by emigrating to Palestine and living on the land; they should not wait passively for the Messiah.

1881   Pogroms in Russia.

1881–82   Chovevei Tziyyon (Lovers of Zion) groups form in various Eastern European countries to encourage emigration to Palestine. By the early 1890s this movement spreads to Western Europe, where it is especially active among students.

1882   The first Chovevei Tziyyon groups emigrate from Russia and Romania, founding colonies in the north and center of Palestine over the next two decades. This later becomes known as the First *Aliyah*, the first wave of Zionist immigration (see chapter 24).

1894–95   The trial, for treason, of French Jewish army captain Alfred Dreyfus. Convicted and exiled to Devil's Island amid an outpouring of antisemitism, he is ultimately exonerated in 1906.

1896   Theodor Herzl publishes *Der Judenstaat*.

1897   First Zionist Congress convenes, in Basle, Switzerland.

1898   Nachman Syrkin, a young Zionist activist and a philosopher, publishes "The Jewish Question and the Socialist Jewish State," a key document in the development of socialist Zionism. He goes on to be a leader of the socialist stream in Zionism.

1900   Socialist Zionist groups begin to form around Russia.

1902   Herzl publishes *Altneuland* (*Old New Land*), a utopian novel imagining life in the Jewish homeland in the year 1922.

1902   The Orthodox Zionist movement Mizrachi (literally "eastern," but also an acronym: *merkaz ruchani*, "spiritual center") is founded in Vilna.

1903   Pogroms in Russia.

1903   At the Sixth Zionist Congress, in Basle, Herzl's suggestion to consider examining a temporary refuge in East Africa arouses a stormy controversy.

1904   Herzl dies.

1904	A new wave of immigration from Eastern Europe, the Second *Aliyah*, begins, bringing approximately forty thousand Jews to Palestine until the outbreak of World War I.
1908	The revolt of the "young Turks," deposing the Ottoman sultan, unleashes expressions of nationalism within the empire.
1909	Tel Aviv, the "first Hebrew city," is founded.
1917	The British government issues the Balfour Declaration.
1917	With the Ottoman defeat, Great Britain occupies Palestine west of the Jordan.
1921	Arab mob attacks on Jews in Jaffa spread to other towns, until British forces restore order.
1922	The League of Nations (the forerunner of the UN, founded in 1920 in the wake of World War I) ratifies the Mandate for Palestine, formalizing British rule and granting international recognition to the Balfour Declaration.

PRIMARY TEXT

Though Herzl's pamphlet was not a best seller at first, it has since come to be seen as a foundational document of the Zionist movement. He further developed his vision in his 1902 novel *Altneuland* (*Old New Land*), describing a fictional visit to the Jewish state twenty years hence. Interestingly there he explicitly states that the new entity is "not a state," but a voluntary "collective society."

Theodor Herzl, *A Jewish State*

The Jewish question still exists. It would be foolish to deny it. It is a remnant of the Middle Ages, which civilized nations do not even yet seem able to shake off, try as they will. They certainly showed a generous desire to do so when they emancipated us. The Jewish question exists wherever Jews live in perceptible numbers.

It was a common theme in Enlightenment literature to blame antisemitism on the Jews—their clannishness, unproductivity, and primitive customs aroused hostility, and the solution was for them to "improve themselves." Herzl is saying something else—that the Jews, no matter how "improved," will always be outsiders in a world organized by

Where it does not exist, it is carried by Jews in the course of their migrations. We naturally move to those places where we are not persecuted, and there our presence produces persecution. This is the case in every country, and will remain so, even in those highly civilized—for instance, France— until the Jewish question finds a solution on a political basis. The unfortunate Jews are now carrying the seeds of Anti-Semitism into England; they have already introduced it into America.

nations, for the Jews themselves are a nation and can never integrate into others' nations.

I believe that I understand Anti-Semitism, which is really a highly complex movement. I consider it from a Jewish standpoint, yet without fear or hatred. I believe that I can see what elements there are in it of vulgar sport, of common trade jealousy, of inherited prejudice, of religious intolerance, and also of pretended self-defense. I think the Jewish question is no more a social than a religious one, notwithstanding that it sometimes takes these and other forms. It is a national question, which can only be solved by making it a political world-question to be discussed and settled by the civilized nations of the world in council.

Since the Jewish question is national, it must be solved politically among nations, not in the street and community.

We are a people—one people.

We have honestly endeavored
everywhere to merge ourselves in
the social life of surrounding communities and to preserve the faith
of our fathers. We are not permitted to do so. In vain are we loyal
patriots, our loyalty in some places
running to extremes; in vain do we
make the same sacrifices of life and
property as our fellow-citizens; in
vain do we strive to increase the
fame of our native land in science
and art, or her wealth by trade and
commerce. In countries where we
have lived for centuries we are still
cried down as strangers, and often
by those whose ancestors were not
yet domiciled in the land where
Jews had already had experience of
suffering. The majority may decide
which are the strangers; for this,
as indeed every point which arises
in the relations between nations, is
a question of might. I do not here
surrender any portion of our pre-
scriptive right, when I make this
statement merely in my own name
as an individual. In the world as it
now is and for an indefinite period
will probably remain, might precedes right. It is useless, therefore,
for us to be loyal patriots, as were
the Huguenots who were forced to

The heart of Herzl's argument:
Emancipation is doomed to failure.
As long as the Jews are a minority, no
matter how "well-behaved," they will
be considered strangers and exist in a
position of weakness.

In the social circles in which Herzl
grew up, where the vision of an
enlightened society held sway, this
view was considered heresy.

emigrate. If we could only be left in peace. . . .

But I think we shall not be left in peace. . . .

At this point in time, Herzl had not decided that the goal was specifically Palestine. The point was for the Jews to have a land of their own. And here (as opposed to his view expressed in *Altneuland*), the goal is a state.

The whole plan is in its essence perfectly simple, as it must necessarily be if it is to come within the comprehension of all.

Let the sovereignty be granted us over a portion of the globe large enough to satisfy the rightful requirements of a nation; the rest we shall manage for ourselves.

The creation of a new State is neither ridiculous nor impossible. We have in our day witnessed the process in connection with nations which were not largely members of the middle class, but poorer, less educated, and consequently weaker than ourselves. The Governments of all countries scourged by Anti-Semitism will be keenly interested in assisting us to obtain the sovereignty we want. . . .

He assumes that the nations of the world will be only too happy to help, so as to get rid of their Jews.

. . . It might . . . be said that we ought not to create new distinctions between people; we ought not to raise fresh barriers, we should rather make the old disap-

And in conclusion: the dream of a universal, neutral society is a naïve illusion, incompatible with human nature.

pear. But men who think in this
way are amiable visionaries; and
the idea of a native land will still
flourish when the dust of their
bones will have vanished trace-
lessly in the winds. Universal
brotherhood is not even a beautiful
dream. Antagonism is essential to
man's greatest efforts.

— Theodor Herzl, *A Jewish State*, pp. 4–5, 25, 98

The radical seed in Herzl's work was not the idea of a Jewish state, but
the suggestion that not only had emancipation failed, but it was doomed
to continue to fail. The only "normalization" the Jews could and should
hope for was not as normal citizens of France or Germany — but as a nation
like all the other nations with a state of their own.

While this idea did not originate with Herzl and didn't even make a big
splash when he published it, after he devoted his considerable energy and
talent into promoting it, it changed the course of Jewish and world history.

LEGACY

Impact

Herzl can be seen as responsible for a turning point in Jewish history in
three ways:

1. Reconceiving of Judaism as a nationality. This had far-reaching
   impact on the development of Jewish culture and consciousness,
   creating a space for the growth of "secular Judaism" (see chapter 23).
2. Disseminating the idea that integration is useless and emancipation hopeless — a perspective that remained controversial for
   decades but still hovers over practically every discussion about the
   future of the Jewish people.
3. Kick-starting the process of creating a real, non-messianic Jewish
   state, which came to fruition in 1948.

With our twenty-first-century consciousness it can be asked: What gave the European powers the right to carve up Africa, Asia, and the Middle East and, in the process, promise part of Palestine to European Jewish "colonists" (which is indeed what the Zionist settlers called themselves)? Herzl lived at a time when this right went unquestioned, when colonialism was taken for granted, when "the sun never set on the British Empire." And yet, while political Zionism rode this wave, it did not see itself as a colonialist enterprise, but rather as its opposite—an act of national self-determination to restore the exiled Jews to their "native" homeland. When the settlers encountered the local population in Palestine, they discovered that achieving their noble goal would entail dealing with difficult moral dilemmas (see chapter 24), which to this day remain unresolved.

After Herzl's death, the institutions he created and individuals inspired by him continued his work. Among those who led the political struggle for statehood, several figures stand out:

- Chaim Weizmann, who played an important role in the negotiations leading to the Balfour Declaration and served as Israel's first president
- Ze'ev Jabotinsky, who founded the Revisionist Zionist movement, which advocated a more militant, self-reliant—and liberal economic—approach than the dominant socialist Zionist parties
- David Ben-Gurion, who presided over the political process leading to the Declaration of Independence in 1948 and served as Israel's first prime minister

Memory

Theodor Herzl is widely regarded as the "founding father" of the Jewish state. The Israeli national cemetery is located on Mount Herzl in Jerusalem, and his tomb is the most impressive one there. A city, Herzliya (just north of Tel Aviv) and countless streets and schools in the state bear his name. In Israel, Herzl is not uncommon as a male first name. His image, especially the famous profile view of him leaning on a railing in Basle during the First Zionist Congress, is a universally recognized icon of Israeli culture.

While Herzl is not remembered as a great German writer, several of his quotes have become immortal:

In Paris . . . I achieved a freer attitude toward anti-Semitism, which I now began to understand historically and to pardon. Above all I recognized the emptiness and futility of trying to "combat" anti-Semitism.
—Diary, undated, spring, 1895

The Jewish State is a world necessity. They will pray for me in the synagogues. But also in the churches.
—Diary, June 16, 1895

Were I to sum up the Basle Congress [the First Zionist Congress] in a word—which I shall guard against pronouncing publicly—it would be this: At Basle, I founded the Jewish State. If I said this out loud today, I would be answered by universal laughter. Perhaps in five years, certainly in fifty, everyone will know it.
—Diary, September 3, 1897

If you will it, it is no dream.
—Old New Land, 1902

TEXT FOR DISCUSSION

Herzl's futuristic novel Old New Land, published in 1902, imagined Palestine in 1922. He suggests that the Jews of the future will "go beyond" statehood to something more advanced. Do you believe the Jews are a nation equivalent to "the other civilized nations"? What defines a nation? In the light of the past century's events, can you imagine a more advanced reality?

[The words of the fictional host, in the Jewish national home in Palestine in 1922, to a visitor from 1902:] It was only at the end of the nineteenth century, when the other civilized nations had already attained to self-consciousness and given evidence thereof, that our own people—the pariah—realized that its salvation lay within itself. . . . And so the Jewish nation once more raised itself to nationhood.

We have no state, like the Europeans of your time. We are merely a
society of citizens seeking to enjoy life through work and culture.

—Theodor Herzl, *Old New Land*, trans. Lotta Levensohn (Princeton:
Wiener, 1997), 79, 105–6

FURTHER READING

Avineri, Shlomo. *Herzl: Theodor Herzl and the Foundation of the Jewish State*. London: Weidenfeld & Nicolson, 2013. An in-depth study of Herzl's Zionist years by a leading Israeli political scientist.

Bein, Alex. *Theodore Herzl*. Philadelphia: Jewish Publication Society, 1962. The classic biography.

Hertzberg, Arthur. *The Zionist Idea*. Philadelphia: Jewish Publication Society, 1959. A useful anthology of writings by thinkers from various stages and streams of Zionism.

Herzl, Theodor. *The Diaries of Theodor Herzl*. Translated and edited by Marvin Lowenthal. New York: Grosset and Dunlap, 1962. Annotated excerpts from Herzl's personal diary, 1895–1904.

———. *A Jewish State*. Translated by Silvie D'Avigdor. New York: Maccabaean, 1904. Herzl's manifesto, setting forth his analysis and solution for the "Jewish question."

Laqueur, Walter. *A History of Zionism*. New York: Schocken Books, 1972. A comprehensive history of the movement; pp. 3–208 cover up to the Balfour Declaration.

23. The Secular Zionist Revolution

AHAD HA'AM, ~1900 CE

HISTORY

Two Facets of Nationalism

While longing for the restoration of Jewish sovereignty and for the ingathering of the exiles to the Land of Israel was a central and powerful component of Jewish belief through the generations, that longing was not Zionism.

A modern national movement, Zionism came into being when that traditional messianic longing encountered several modern phenomena: secular humanism, the failure of emancipation, and the rise of nationalism in Europe. Herzl's efforts were not inspired by the Bible or the liturgy, but by the social and political realities he saw around him.

Moreover, Herzl's reaction was not the only possible response to this historical moment. Nationalism can be seen as comprising two, not necessarily inseparable strands:

1. The rational, statist strand: Broad, multicultural empires are unsustainable and unnatural. The normative mode of political organization is the ethno-culturally homogeneous nation-state. A nation is defined by various cultural markers (e.g., language, shared history, folk traditions) and a geographical homeland. Therefore, modern Europe would ideally be a peaceful mosaic of sovereign nation-states, each ruled by a distinct ethno-cultural group, attached to its ancestral homeland.

2. The romantic, spiritual strand: A mystical connection links landscape and identity. National identity is not a matter of statehood, but of the deep rootedness of the people (the nation) in the soil of its homeland. There is an intrinsic interrelationship among culture, geography, and personality ("mentality"). "Germanness" or "Frenchness," for example, encompassed not only citizenship in a particular homeland—and language, music, and food—but personality and (often vague) moral traits such as coldness or warmth, rigidity or

flexibility, dourness or joie de vivre, and so on. In time, this perspective would come to include the idea that race is also a central component of national identity.

Zionism — Jewish nationalism — reflected this dichotomy. Two opposing Zionist streams emerged: political Zionism, largely a Western European approach, and cultural Zionism, dominant among Eastern European Jews.

In Western Europe, Theodor Herzl and his followers were dedicated to a rational, political understanding of nationalism. Herzl's influential pamphlet *A Jewish State* analyzed the Jews' social and political position and proposed a state as a feasible solution to a practical problem (see chapter 22). Indeed, Herzl was leery of attempts to define or focus on "Jewish culture," as he feared (correctly, it turned out) that such attempts would only expose schisms and lead to discord, undermining his perceived need for total unity in pursuit of statehood.

On the other hand, for many Russian Jews who were drawn to Zionism, the "Jewish problem" was not the failure of emancipation (for which they never had much reason to hope), but a crisis of identity. Having grown up within the traditional Jewish community, they believed their challenge was to bring their identity into harmony with the modern world that was breaking into Russia. For them, cultural Zionism was the ideal synthesis between maintaining rootedness in the tradition and accepting the freethinking, rational assumptions of modernity. For if Judaism could be seen as a national culture, if the Jewish tradition could be understood as a culture separate from religious belief, then Zionism could sew up the tear in their identity.

Ahad Ha'am and Cultural Zionism

The person whose writings most clearly articulated the cultural Zionist ideology in the early years of the Zionist movement was the writer, editor, and activist Asher Ginsberg, who went by the pen name of Ahad Ha'am ("One of the People").

The pattern of his life's development was typical of his generation. Born into a Hasidic family in the Ukraine in 1856, he received a traditional education limited to halakhic and Hasidic texts. As an adolescent, he discovered, and studied in secret, works of the Jewish Enlightenment in Western

Europe as well as "outside" literature (i.e., general Western history and thought—and languages). He was employed in his family's business, which in 1886 was forced by tsarist economic restrictions to move to Odessa.

There, Ahad Ha'am discovered a large, heterogeneous Jewish community and a center of literary creativity and ideological ferment. Shortly thereafter he began to publish essays analyzing the Jewish "situation," criticizing various Jewish responses to modernity, and articulating and developing the concept of cultural Zionism. While he was uncharismatic and uninterested in either politics or a formal leadership role, his writings alone rapidly propelled him to the stature of a "game changer." Without holding a formal institutional position, he nonetheless became the spokesman and leader of the Chibbat Tziyyon (Love of Zion) movement (whose members were called Chovevei Tziyyon—Lovers of Zion).

Many of Ahad Ha'am's essays on Jewish history and identity, culture, leadership, Zionist thought, and activism (including his criticisms of the settlers in Palestine for lacking commitment to authentic Jewish culture and Jewish values) became classics of modern Hebrew literature and Jewish thought in his lifetime and remain so to this day. He moved to London in 1907, immigrated to Palestine in 1921, and lived in Tel Aviv, where he died in 1927, mourned as a national hero.

Public exchanges between Ahad Ha'am and Herzl were often strident—Ahad Ha'am attacking Herzl's political Zionism and Herzl counterattacking Ahad Ha'am's cultural Zionism. (The tension between the two was apparently more than ideological; each saw the other as a threat to his own personal status and prestige.) In principle, Ahad Ha'am was not opposed to creating the Jewish state that Herzl advocated. Unlike Herzl, though, he believed the state should arise as an organic development—the culmination of a process of revitalizing Jewish culture in its secular, modern context. If the Jewish people's national development were to be jump-started by handing them a sovereign state before they had undergone the process of creating a renewed, sustainable culture, he declared, it would lead to a state that would not be Jewish in any meaningful way; it might save Jews, but it would destroy Judaism. The likely failure of political Zionism would lead to despair and demoralization.

Ahad Ha'am envisioned the slow advance of an immigrant community in Palestine. A Jewish society, taking root there, would grow, creating an indigenous, natural, vibrant Jewish culture — an organic synthesis between the modern world and the Jewish tradition, entirely rooted in the homeland with all its historic resonances. Ultimately, these institutions would give rise to a state.

Ahad Ha'am introduced a significant idea into Jewish thought: Jewish culture could be separated from Jewish religion. In his view, the commanding voice of the covenant was no longer God, but the "life spirit" of the nation. The Jewish people and its culture had their own intrinsic value; the extrinsic factor of divine commandment, of Deuteronomic reward and punishment (see chapters 3 and 7), was unnecessary. Moreover, Jews who rejected Judaism's theological underpinnings could nonetheless remain rooted in traditional practice. One could be an atheist without relinquishing the intellectual, social, and even spiritual benefits provided by participation in traditional observance.

Ahad Ha'am's teachings not only articulated cultural Zionism; they opened up the possibility of secular, cultural Judaism.

The New Jew

As Ahad Ha'am's cultural Zionism encountered other currents in European and Jewish thought at the turn of the century, another new concept emerged: "the New Jew." This new model of Jewish identity would have significant impact on the culture of the growing Jewish immigrant community in Palestine (see chapter 24) and beyond, in these ways:

- Productivization: Throughout the nineteenth century, many Jews had internalized the antisemitic claim that the Jews were unproductive, engaging only in study, moneylending, and trade, but not working the soil or in the crafts — which was a sort of half-truth, reflecting the results of Christian oppression in particular areas and eras. Thus, already around the mid-century efforts were made to "productivize" the Jews by training them in crafts and agriculture. This project became associated with Zionism: life in the homeland was viewed as a means to restore the Jews to their ancient origins as a people of the land.
- Hebrew: In Western Europe, most Jews used Hebrew for prayer but spoke the vernacular of the lands in which they lived. In East-

ern Europe they spoke Yiddish. Cultural Zionists and others therefore advocated for linguistic "normalization" through returning to
Hebrew, the ancestral tongue. Ahad Ha'am and his generation had
pioneered the use of Hebrew in modern literary forms, such as
essays and novels; the natural next stage was for Hebrew to become
the vernacular of renewed Jewish life in the Land of Israel. This
necessitated the explicit — and controversial — decision to secularize
a sacred language. An important mark of the authenticity of the New
Jew would be a natural fluency in Hebrew.

· Strength: Currents in turn-of-the-century European thought, both
east and west, disparaged the "Old Europe" as decadent, weak, and
rootless and esteemed the traits embodying the antithesis — physical
strength, speed, and courage. Similarly, various Zionist leaders and
many young pioneers settling in Palestine attached great value to
courage and strength. These qualities became associated with the
"rehabilitation" of the Jewish people, to be expected with agricultural labor, the return to the land.

The New Jew — strong, self-reliant, fearless, free, and suntanned, working the soil of the Land of Israel, and living his or her life in Hebrew —
became a powerful ideal in the minds of immigrants to Palestine and Jews
throughout the world.

A problematic, unanticipated corollary was the New Jew's alienation from
Jewish tradition. The Old Jew, unproductive and passive, was Orthodox,
so religion came to be seen as a relic of the world against which the Zionists rebelled. Within cultural Zionism, Ahad Ha'am and Chaim Nachman
Bialik, among others (see "Leading Early Contributors to Cultural Zionist Literature and Thought" below), sought to keep the link to tradition
by secularizing it. Others, such as Michah Yosef Berdichevski and Shaul
Tschernichovski, rejected the accumulated postbiblical tradition, seeking to base the new Jewish culture solely on Hebrew, the Land of Israel,
and the biblical epic with its depiction of life in a sovereign national state.

Timeline: 1860–1914

1860   British Jewish philanthropist Moses Montefiore funds the first
        of several residential communities outside the walls of the

Old City of Jerusalem, as well as projects in industry, vocational training, and agriculture.

1878 The first modern agricultural settlement, Petach Tikvah (Gateway of Hope—see Hosea 2:15), is founded in the coastal plain by a few Orthodox families from Jerusalem.

1882 Fourteen Chovevei Tziyyon pioneers set out from Kharkov for Palestine, becoming the first Zionist settlers.

1882 Lexicographer and activist Eliezer ben Yehudah, "father of modern Hebrew," pioneers using immersion to teach spoken Hebrew in a Jerusalem school and resolves (successfully) to raise his son, born that year, completely in Hebrew.

1884 The first conference of Chovevei Tziyyon, in Kattowitz (Russia).

1889 Ahad Ha'am's first published article, "This Is Not the Way," argues that Zionism's successful development depends on educational work to build Jewish identity—and therefore practical efforts at settlement or creating a state are premature.

1898 Speaking at the Second Zionist Congress, Herzl's right-hand man, Max Nordau, declares renewal of the Jewish commitment to bodily vigor and strength—"Muscle Judaism"—as a Zionist goal.

1903 The founding conference (in the colony Zichron Yaakov) of the Teachers' Union, to develop the teaching profession, curricular content, methods, and materials for a Hebrew, Zionist education system, takes place.

1905 Gymnasiah Herzliyah, the first Hebrew high school in the Land of Israel, is founded in Jaffa.

1913–14 "The Language War": The German Jewish philanthropic organization Ezra opens a technical college (which later becomes the Technion) in Haifa, assuming that German will be the language of instruction. After the Teachers' Union and other Zionist activists protest and boycott, the language of instruction is changed to Hebrew.

Leading Early Contributors to Cultural Zionist Literature and Thought

Yehudah Leib Gordon (1831–92) A pioneer in using Hebrew in modern literary forms, in both poetry and prose, he opposed Zionism and supported the Jews' maintaining their culture and pride while finding their place in the European environment.

Chaim Nachman Bialik (1873–1934) He rebelled against his Orthodox upbringing, became active in Chovevei Tziyyon, published his first poem in 1892, and rose rapidly to fame as "the poet of the Hebrew rebirth." He immigrated to Palestine in 1924.

Michah Yosef Berdichevski (1865–1921) From a prominent Hasidic family, he studied in a yeshiva and then German universities. He criticized Ahad Ha'am, arguing that Jews must free themselves from the constraints of tradition and that the New Jews' culture must express basic human drives and emotions, through all the arts.

Shaul Tschernichovski (1875–1943) After receiving a Russian education and studying medicine in Western Europe, he became a prolific and popular Hebrew poet and translator of Western classics into Hebrew. His fascination with nature and criticism of the "Old Jew" helped shape the popular image of the "New Jew." He immigrated to Palestine in 1931.

Yosef Chaim Brenner (1881–1921) In his pioneering Hebrew novels and essays, he darkly criticized the "Old" Jewish life. Immigrating to Palestine in 1909, he became a leader among the socialist Zionists.

PRIMARY TEXT

This brief excerpt from one of Ahad Ha'am's influential essays sets forth the main arguments of cultural Zionism.

Ahad Ha'am, "Political Zionism: The State of the Jews and the Jewish Problem"

It is not just the Jews who came out of the ghetto, but also Judaism. The Jews reached this stage only in certain lands, at the mercy of the nations; but Judaism achieved (or is achieving) this on its own, in every place where it has come in contact with modern culture. This cultural

Ahad Ha'am sees the main challenge facing Judaism not as material— relieving Jewish suffering—but rather as spiritual, in finding a way for Judaism to survive the encounter with modernity. A culture that sees itself as inferior to the cultures around it will self-destruct

current, when it comes into Judaism, destroys its defenses from inside, so that it will no longer be able to close itself off and to live an isolated life.

The spirit of our people longs for further development, for the absorption of the foundations of general culture that come to it from outside, to digest them and to absorb them — as it did at various times in the past.

However, the conditions of life in exile are not appropriate for this. In our time culture everywhere clothes itself in the national spirit of the people of the land, and the stranger who would approach must suppress his distinct identity and be absorbed into the spirit of the ruling nation. Therefore, Judaism in exile will never be able to develop its own essence, in its own way, and thus when it leaves the ghetto it is in danger of losing its independent existence, or, at the least, its national unity; i.e., dividing up into many Judaisms, each with different characteristics and a different life, according to the lands where the House of Israel is scattered.

And since the people sees that it cannot bear any longer the exilic

through assimilation. A strong culture will have the resources and self-confidence to borrow, compromise, and innovate without losing its core. Such strength and self-confidence are not possible in the European environment, in which cultures have hegemony in ethno-cultural nation-states.

In order for Jewish culture to compete on a level playing field, the Jews must have a place where their culture is the dominant, majority culture, and the right place is their ancient homeland. Statehood is only appropriate for a nation that has demonstrated its national existence as a rooted, dynamic culture; once the Jews do that, statehood will follow naturally.

"armor" in which its will-to-live
clothed it when it left its land—
and without which its life is in
danger—Judaism seeks to return
to its historic center in order to live
there a life of natural development;
to engage its powers in every aspect
of human culture; to develop and
to perfect the national assets it has
accumulated thus far; to contrib-
ute in the future to the common
human treasure—as it did in the
past—a great national culture, the
fruit of the free labor of a people
living according to its own spirit.

For this purpose, the people can
get along, for now, with very little, and doesn't need to establish
a state, but rather to create for
itself in its homeland the proper
conditions for its development: a
fair-sized population of Hebrews,
working, unhindered, in every
branch of culture, from agriculture
and crafts to science and literature.
This community, which will assemble gradually, will ultimately serve
as the center of the nation, where
its pure spirit will be realized and
will develop in all directions until
it achieves its full potential. And
from this center the spirit of Judaism will then radiate outward to
all the communities of the exile,
to revitalize them and to preserve

their overall unity. Then, when our
national culture in Palestine will
have reached such a high level,
we can be sure that the community there will produce people who
will know how to seize the right
moment to found there a state—
not just a state of the Jews, but
truly a Jewish state.

This Chibbat Tziyyon, concerned
for the continued existence of
Judaism at a time of Jewish suffering, is strange and incomprehensible to the Western political
Zionists, just as the Yavneh of
Rabbi Yochanan ben Zakkai was
strange and incomprehensible to
the political activists of his time.
Thus, the Zionism of the "state
Jews" cannot satisfy the "Jewish
Jews," who see its spread as a threat
to their aspirations and goal.

The secret of our existence as a
people . . . is what the prophets
taught already in ancient times:
to respect only spiritual strength,
not to worship physical power.
That is why our people, unlike
other nations, did not sink to self-
abnegation in the face of superior
material strength. As long as [our
people] is true to this principle,
there is a solid basis to its life. . . .

The literal translation of the title of
Herzl's manifesto was *The Jews' State*.
Ahad Ha'am plays on this wording to
highlight his criticism: he seeks a "Jewish state" expressing Jewish culture,
not just a state belonging to Jews.

Ahad Ha'am elevates Rabbi
Yochanan ben Zakkai as an exemplar
in being ahead of his time. According to tradition, Rabbi Yochanan
ben Zakkai opposed the rebels who
sought to overthrow Roman rule,
opting instead to focus on cultural
autonomy in the town of Yavneh (see
chapter 10).

But a political idea that is not
founded upon a national culture is
liable to lead the people astray from
its spiritual power, giving rise to a
tendency to seek "glory" by attaining material strength and state sovereignty; thus would be severed the
thread that connects [our people]
to its past, and its historical foundation would be undermined.

—Ahad Ha'am, "On the Questions of the Day, I" (Hebrew), *Hashiloach* 3, no. 1,
Tevet 1898

This text presents the key concepts of cultural Zionism:

- The Jewish question is not only or even primarily a material one, but
  a cultural one—the need to adapt to modernity.
- In a world where the boundaries of national sovereignty are also
  cultural boundaries, the continued natural development of Jewish
  culture and its adaptation to modernity require national life in a historic homeland. Without such a sustaining center, there is no future
  for life in exile.
- It is not necessary for all Jews to live in the homeland; if a critical
  mass resides in the land, their cultural creativity will radiate outward, sustaining Jews wherever they live.
- Settlement and cultural development in the homeland do not require
  formal statehood, though they are likely to lead to it naturally.

LEGACY

Impact

Ahad Ha'am's conception of cultural Zionism has had a lasting impact in
two major spheres:

1. The mainstream culture of the Jewish immigrant community in
   Palestine—and later the State of Israel—stands on the foundation

of his revolutionary idea that it is possible to separate Jewish culture from Jewish religion. Many aspects of traditional practice, including the Hebrew language, traditional texts, and the calendar and holidays, were thereby retained as important elements of Jewish identity even absent the religious beliefs that had previously justified—and been expressed by—these practices. Today, the majority of Israeli Jews are not affiliated with a religious denomination. They view Judaism—as they learned in public school—as a rich culture, with colorful holidays, proverbs and folktales, visual symbols, music, and a vibrant colloquial language that resonates with the poetry of the biblical prophets. Belief in God or commitment to a covenant is not required to access and possess these treasures. In addition, toward the end of the twentieth century, a flowering of local and national efforts to revitalize Ahad Ha'am's heritage has popularized study of classical Jewish texts from a nonreligious perspective in both schools and adult education settings, Israelis thereby "reclaiming" the traditional sources from their Orthodox guardians.

2. As Ahad Ha'am envisioned, Palestine and then Israel became a cultural center for the whole Jewish world. From early in the century, the creativity of the Jewish community in the land played a major role in shaping the cultural life of Jews everywhere—through the revival of Hebrew, literature, music, scholarship, tourism, and much more.

Combining these two elements, Ahad Ha'am's legacy is profound: the existence of cultural Judaism in the Diaspora. Today countless thousands of Jews view their Jewishness as a cultural rather than religious identity—an option that had never existed before the twentieth century.

Strongly influenced by Ahad Ha'am's approach, in 1934 Rabbi Mordecai Kaplan, a teacher at the Jewish Theological Seminary (Conservative) in New York, published his magnum opus, *Judaism as a Civilization*. Rejecting a supernatural god, Kaplan grounded Jewish practice in a cultural, nontheological understanding of sanctity. In his view, Judaism was an evolving civilization encompassing all aspects of life: language, arts, historical memory, philosophy, and social institutions. The Sabbath, the Torah scroll, or the Land of Israel thus took on sanctity not through God's commandment or presence, but because of their centrality in Jewish civilization.

Like Ahad Ha'am, Kaplan saw Israel as a center, but not the physical home, of all Jews. However, unlike Ahad Ha'am, he was particularly concerned with the challenge of sustaining Jewish life in the face of individualism and assimilation in America. Emphasizing the importance of local communities in enriching Jewish life and culture, he advocated creating "Jewish centers" that would go beyond the traditional synagogue model, encompassing arts, sports, social action, and more.

Kaplan's approach was institutionalized in the Reconstructionist movement,[11] a parallel to the Reform and Conservative movements, with its own rabbinical seminary, network of congregations, and so on. His ideas also had impact well beyond the confines of the movement. Congregations of varying denominations expanded their institutions to be more like Jewish cultural centers, and Kaplan's disciples pioneered Jewish summer camps as models of all-inclusive communities. On the other hand, his emphasis on Hebrew as a living language never gained much traction among American Jews, even within the Reconstructionist movement.

Memory

While Herzl is remembered universally as "the founding father" of the State of Israel, Ahad Ha'am sits right next to him in the Zionist pantheon—and in terms of ongoing presence in Israeli intellectual life, he surely outweighs his old rival. A deeply knowledgeable, profound, lucid, and prolific writer, he is still studied in Israeli high schools, and his words continue to be analyzed, debated, and quoted in public discourse and academic research.

And there is no city in Israel without a street and a school named for him.

TEXT FOR DISCUSSION

One of Ahad Ha'am's most quoted statements takes the Sabbath as a case study of the relationship between Jewish religion and Jewish culture. What are its implications for observance of Sabbath laws? Do you agree with them?

Whoever feels in his heart a true connection to the life of the nation through the generations will not be able—even if he rejects belief in the world to come or in the Jewish state—to imagine the reality of the

---

11. Kaplan sought to "reconstruct" American Jewish life and institutions in keeping with his civilizational—as opposed to religious—understanding of Judaism.

Jewish people without "the Sabbath Queen." It can be said without exaggeration that more than Israel has kept the Sabbath, the Sabbath has kept Israel.

—Ahad Ha'am, *Hashiloach* 3, no. 6, Sivan 1898

FURTHER READING

Hertzberg, Arthur. *The Zionist Idea*. Philadelphia: Jewish Publication Society, 1959. An anthology including excerpts of writings of Ben-Yehudah, Nordau, Ahad Ha'am, Bialik, Berdichevski, Brenner, Kaplan, and others.

Kornberg, Jacques. *At the Crossroads: Essays on Ahad Ha'am*. Albany: State University of New York Press, 1983. A collection of essays on different aspects of Ahad Ha'am's thought, writing, and influence.

Laqueur, Walter. *A History of Zionism*. New York: Schocken Books, 1972, pp. 162–71. A brief account of cultural Zionism.

Rubinstein, Amnon. *The Zionist Dream Revisited*. New York: Schocken Books, 1984, pp. 3–49. A concise, scholarly narration of the development of cultural Zionism and the New Jew.

Shimoni, Gideon. *The Zionist Ideology*. Hanover NH: University Press of New England, 1995. Chapter 7 maps the various thinkers and movements that interpreted Zionism as a pathway to secular Jewish identity.

24. Zionist Settlement of the Land of Israel

FIRST AND SECOND *ALIYOT*, 1882–1914 CE

HISTORY

The Jewish World in 1881

The end of the nineteenth century was a time of great ferment and upheaval in the lives of both Western and Eastern European Jews (see chapters 21–23). The sense that emancipation was failing to fulfill its promise, the rise of nationalism, and the collapse of Russia combined to generate broad and deep changes in Jewish life and Jewish identity: the creation of the North American Jewish center, the birth of a Jewish national movement, the reconceptualization of Judaism as a secular culture, and the founding of another major new center of Jewish life, in the Land of Israel.

In the wake of the 1881 pogroms and rising concern for the Jewish future in the empire, masses of Russian Jews either emigrated to the West or joined the revolutionary struggle within Russia. Many, both of those who emigrated and those who stayed to join the struggle, placed their faith in political or cultural Zionism.

Among the many who believed in a Zionist vision—political or cultural—a small number actually set out to fulfill it in person. These "practical Zionists" began trickling into Palestine in 1882; over the three decades until the outbreak of World War I in 1914, around sixty-five thousand arrived. These pioneers had a practical, physical impact on later developments: they created "facts on the ground," laying the foundations for institutions of culture and government that, seen in retrospect, constituted the "state in the making."

Zionist historians periodize Jewish immigration to Palestine up to the Second World War in five "immigrations." Each such wave is referred to in Hebrew as an *aliyah*—an ascension, since traditionally immigration to the Land of Israel was seen as a spiritual ascent (see the five *aliyot* in the timeline below). In particular, the first two *aliyot*, from 1881 to 1914, would serve as a turning point, establishing key cultural and institutional foundations that determined much of what came later.

Palestine in 1881

The Jews in the first wave of immigration did not encounter an empty land. In the nineteenth century, the land the Europeans and the Zionists called Palestine (Eretz Yisrael—the "Land of Israel" in traditional Hebrew parlance) was part of the Ottoman province of Syria, ruled from Damascus. In 1881, before Zionist immigration, its population was 457,000, of whom approximately 400,000 were Muslims, 42,000 Christians, and 15,000 Jews. Most Muslims and Christians were sharecropping peasants who used primitive agricultural methods to work lands owned by landowners living in cities.

The first intercity carriage way (between Jaffa and Jerusalem) had opened in 1869, and the first railroad line (along the same route) began operations in 1892. The Ottomans had signed agreements with Western powers (France, England, Russia, the United States, and others) granting their consuls the authority to look after their citizens' interests, in a climate otherwise permeated by Ottoman bureaucratic corruption and inefficiency. The consuls were able to provide mail and other services and, more importantly, to protect their nationals from Ottoman prosecution and taxation. From the Ottoman perspective, the Jewish settlers were European citizens entitled to their consuls' protection.

The Jewish population was Orthodox, and until the mid-nineteenth century most were Sephardic, descendants of the Iberian exiles of 1492 (see chapter 16). The vast majority lived in the four "holy cities" of Tiberias, Safed, Jerusalem, and Hebron; a minority resided in small communities within Arab farming villages.

After the Sephardic influx of the sixteenth century, there had been a constant trickle of individual and small group immigration, especially from Eastern Europe.

By around 1880—on the eve of the Zionist wave—the majority of Jews in the Land of Israel had shifted from Sephardic to Ashkenazic. The economics had changed as well. While many of the Sephardim had been well integrated into the local economy as craftsmen, farmers, and merchants, the newer Ashkenazic arrivals believed their mission was to live and study Torah in the Holy Land on behalf of Jews everywhere. A bureaucracy called the *chalukah*, (distribution) collected and distributed philanthropic support from abroad to sustain their economy, but it was never enough. Poverty was the norm.

To the Zionists, this population—especially the Ashkenazic majority supported by the *chalukah*—came collectively to be called "the Old *Yishuv*" (*yishuv* = settlement or community), because these Jews fit the stereotype of the "Old Jew"—dependent, unproductive, premodern, pallid, and sycophantic (see chapter 23). In contrast, the Zionist immigrants saw themselves as "New Jews," committed to working the land and building a modern society and culture; their population and its institutions came to be called "the New *Yishuv*."

The tension between these two communities—the New *Yishuv* seeing in the Old *Yishuv* everything they were rebelling against, and the Old *Yishuv* seeing the New *Yishuv* as heretics and threats to their way of life—was a significant factor in cultural and political life and remains so to this day.

The First *Aliyah*

In 1882 a group of fourteen students, members of a Chovevei Tziyyon group (see chapter 23) in Kharkov, set off for Palestine. They called themselves the Bilu—an acronym for the verse from Isaiah 2:5, "*Beit Ya'akov l'chu v'neilchah*," "O house of Jacob let us go" ("v" pronounced "u"). After some brief training and experience in agricultural work, they founded the settlement of Rishon LeTziyyon (First in Zion—Isaiah 41:27). Within a few years, other groups of Chovevei Tziyyon founded another six communities. Every aspect of life, including medical care, transportation, and industry, was poor, primitive, and difficult. The land they bought from Arab landowners was often swampy and malarial. And these middle-class university dropouts had come with idealism but no relevant skills or experience. Many died, went back, or emigrated to the West.

When, already in the first years, it became clear that the difficult conditions, together with the settlers' lack of experience, would likely lead the enterprise to collapse, Baron Edmond de Rothschild agreed to step in. A scion of the French branch of the well-known European banking family, he poured millions of dollars into the Zionist colonies in Palestine, even though he had rejected Herzl's plan for mass emigration. Moreover, over several decades he brought in experts, investment, equipment, training, and supervision to develop agriculture and industry. Some of his innovations took root and had lasting impact (e.g., wineries, citrus culture, malaria research); others flopped (silkworms, glassmaking).

Rothschild's generosity to the colonists did not, however, always give rise to feelings of mutual affection and admiration. The high-handed ways of Rothschild's local administrators—and the settlers' feeling of dependency—led to an intertwining of gratitude with resentment.

Immigration tapered off in the late 1880s, but picked up again in the 1890s, leading to another wave of new settlements. By 1903, more than two dozen communities had been established, scattered from the far north to the northern Negev desert.

The term the settlers of the First *Aliyah* used to describe their community was *moshavah* (colony). They were not embarrassed to be "colonists." Happy to live as well as they could while rooted in the soil of the homeland, they employed local Palestinian Arabs as laborers on their farms—a practice they deemed to be natural and mutually beneficial.

They sought autonomy, productivization, cultural revitalization, even sovereignty—but not revolution from established traditions. Many, in fact, stayed Orthodox or at least, as cultural Zionists, remained strongly attached to traditional texts and practices. The first public institution they built in their communities was the synagogue.

The Second *Aliyah*

Immigration waxed and waned over the last decades of the nineteenth century, in response to fluctuations in tsarist persecutions. But then, in 1903, came a more violent wave of pogroms against Russian Jewry, which gained energy in the coming years from nationalist anger over the 1905 loss of the Russo-Japanese War and the failed Russian revolution that followed. These pogroms led the 1903 Zionist Congress to consider Herzl's proposal for a "temporary haven" in East Africa and stimulated a new, second wave of immigration to Palestine.

The immigrants who composed the second wave—about forty thousand between 1903 and 1914—were largely similar in perspective to those in the first wave, but also included an energetic, activist minority of young Russian socialist Zionists (Nachman Syrkin's "The Jewish Question and the Socialist Jewish State" had appeared in 1897—see chapter 22).

The very nature of "Jewish socialism," a term first used by organized groups around 1880, appeared to be internally contradictory. "Jewish" was a religious or ethnic identity, and "socialist" a universalistic movement seeking to transcend or suppress religious and ethnic divisions. To solve this identity conflict, some Jewish socialists turned to "socialist Zionism," which envisioned the synthesis of two utopian plans: the Jewish return to the Land of Israel and the establishment of a workers' society there. The new movement caught on in Russia, where a number of Jews were disillusioned that despite their revolutionary activities, the country was not progressing toward universalist socialism; rather, the 1905 revolution had failed, only making matters worse. Sensing that the dream of a "neutral" society would not come true in Russia (see chapter 30), they sought to realize their messianic socialist vision in their ancestral homeland, the Land of Israel.

The first groups of these young idealists, about a thousand in number, arrived in 1904. Given their commitment to socialist ideology, they did not see themselves as colonists, but as agricultural proletarians. They and those who followed them did not seek middle-class comfort, but to escape it. Many relished their blisters and fevers and hunger, even as many others couldn't take it; not a few died or emigrated—or committed suicide.

At first the socialist Zionists worked as laborers on the farms of settlers from the First *Aliyah*, idealizing the revolutionary concept of "Hebrew labor"—and competing with Arab workers for jobs. Ultimately, they established their own communities called kibbutzim (collectives), founded on socialist economic principles and self-sufficiency with respect to labor. Their ideology dictated that employing Arab laborers was a form of capitalist exploitation.

Also, they talked a lot, constantly debating points of socialist ideology, strategy, and moral issues: Large-scale communes or small intimate ones? Hegemony in the land or shared power with the indigenous Arab population? Free love or traditional family? Continuity of Jewish culture or a break with the past? Into the somewhat sleepy, bourgeois Palestine of the First *Aliyah*, they brought self-consciousness, vibrancy, impatience, activism, and creativity. In addition to the kibbutz movement, they built the first high school, a self-defense organization, a labor union (which provided a political voice and social welfare services—including an HMO—

for members), a consumer cooperative (supplying both agricultural and everyday needs to the workers at a discount), political parties (e.g., Poalei Tziyyon—"Workers of Zion"), newspapers (e.g., *Hapoel Hatza'ir*—"The Young Worker"), and a city (Tel Aviv).

And so, while the settlers of the First *Aliyah* and their patron established the reality of modern Jewish agricultural settlement and created its infrastructure, the *chalutzim* (pioneers, as they called themselves) of the next wave built the whole range of institutions that became the "state in the making." And when the State of Israel came into being in 1948, these young *chalutzim*, whose leadership had developed within the *Yishuv*, were positioned to become the "founding fathers" of the state. Typical of these was David Gruen, who immigrated from Russia in 1906 at age twenty, took the name David Ben-Gurion (Hebraizing one's name was a kind of Zionist sacrament—becoming a New Jew), worked as a laborer while rising through the socialist Zionist political ranks, and became Israel's first prime minister in 1948.

Religiously, the Second *Aliyah* socialists tended to be atheists or at least to reject traditional organized religion. They sought to ground their continued Jewish identity somewhere on the line between Herzl's statist nationalism and Judaism as culture.

Ambivalence about their Jewish roots was one more aspect of the personal torment many endured as they tried to become New Jews far from home and family. Their relationship to their predecessors from the First *Aliyah* was often antagonistic, as the socialist Zionists disdained and resented the earlier generation's values, comforts, conservatism, and religion. And the antipathy was mutual: the Jews of the First *Aliyah* viewed the newcomers as rebels against time-honored norms, behaviors, and beliefs (from "proper" manners, dress, and sexual mores to religious observance) they considered fundamental to Jewish identity and survival.

The First World War brought great suffering to all the inhabitants of Palestine, regardless of religion or ideology. Hunger, disease, Ottoman expulsions of foreign citizens (which most Jewish colonists were), and emigration reduced the general and Jewish populations significantly. The Jewish population fell from eighty-five thousand to fifty-six thousand, and Zionist settlement and institution-building projects ceased as the focus shifted from building to surviving.

But, after the war and the establishment of British mandatory rule in 1922, a new era dawned. Palestine was now ruled by a modern, Western, democratic power. The League of Nations had charged Britain with administering the land temporarily—preparing it for independence. And the British named the Zionist Organization Herzl had founded at the First Zionist Congress as the Jewish people's agent in administering and developing Palestine; it came to be called the Jewish Agency. Furthermore, it would turn out that the pioneering efforts of the first two waves of immigration had built a firm foundation for the state-building that would ensue over the next three decades.

Timeline: 1881–1939

1881	Pogroms in Russia. Mass emigration begins.
1881	Lexicographer Eliezer ben Yehudah arrives in Palestine and embarks on his life's work: modernizing the Hebrew language.
1882–1903	First *Aliyah*: About twenty-five thousand immigrants establish approximately twenty-five agricultural settlements. Many of these communities, including Hadera, Kfar Saba, Rechovot, Rishon LeTziyyon, and Zichron Ya'akov, are sizable towns in Israel today.
1883	Baron Edmund de Rothschild agrees to support the struggling Jewish settlements in Palestine with funding and training.
1897	First Zionist Congress: The Zionist Organization is created—the official launch of Zionism as a political movement.
1901	The Zionist Organization establishes the Jewish National Fund to collect funds from Jews around the world to purchase land for settlement in Palestine.
1902	The Zionist Organization establishes the Anglo-Palestine Bank, to raise and transfer funds and issue credit, in support of settlement in Palestine.
1903	Pogroms in Russia.
1903	Founding conference of the Teachers' Union in the *Yishuv*.
1904–14	Second *Aliyah*: About forty thousand immigrants, about 10 percent of them young socialists pursuing a vision of revitalization through agricultural work and communal living.
1909	The first "Hebrew" city, Tel Aviv, is founded.

1909	The self-defense organization Hashomer (the Watchman) is founded to protect rural colonists from land and livestock theft and other hostile actions by their Arab neighbors.
1909	Deganiah (Grain of God), the first communal agricultural settlement (kibbutz), is founded in the upper Jordan Valley.
1913	The First Arab Congress, in Paris, calls for political rights for Arabs in the Ottoman Empire: the first formal expression of Arab nationalism, which would develop alongside — and in conflict with — Zionism.
1914–18	First World War: The Jewish population of Palestine falls from eighty-five thousand to fifty-six thousand because of emigration, expulsion, and disease.
1918	Representatives of Jewish settlements and parties in Palestine meet to establish new autonomous institutions under British rule, leading to an elected Assembly of Delegates in 1920.
1919–23	Third *Aliyah*: A second wave of approximately thirty-five thousand primarily ideologically motivated socialist Zionists arrives from Russia.
1921	Palestinian Arabs riot in and beyond Jaffa against Zionist settlement, killing forty-seven Jews. In quelling the riots, the British kill forty-eight Arabs.
1922	As part of the peace process after World War I, the League of Nations divides the Middle East into British and French "mandates," with the British assigned to rule Palestine in preparation for independence.
1924–29	Fourth *Aliyah*: About sixty-seven thousand mostly middle-class, urban immigrants settle in Palestine. Most are from the newly independent Poland, which is experiencing instability and economic hardship. In 1924 the United States closes its borders; immigration to America is no longer an option.
1929	Demonstrations and counter-demonstrations over control of the Western Wall in Jerusalem escalate into a second wave of violent riots around the country by Palestinian Arabs; 133 Jews and 116 Arabs are killed.

1929–39   Fifth *Aliyah*: About 250,000 mostly middle-class immigrants arrive from Germany and other Central European countries, seeking to escape the rising tide of Nazi persecution.

1939   The British White Paper restricts Jewish immigration and land purchase in Palestine.

1939   Outbreak of World War II.

PRIMARY TEXT

Berl Katzenelson (1887–1944) was active in socialist Zionist circles in Russia before he immigrated to Palestine in 1909. By the time the twenty-two-year-old arrived, he was an enthusiastic disciple of two of the most influential writers of that generation: Yosef Chaim Brenner, who harshly criticized the "old" Jewish life and the Zionists' failings; and A. D. Gordon, who articulated a romantic belief in the redemptive power of agricultural labor, of living on the land. He would go on to become one of the dominant political and intellectual leaders of the *Yishuv*: a writer, editor, and activist/institution-builder who helped found the socialist Zionists' consumer cooperative, HMO, and newspaper.

A few days after Katzenelson arrived in the Land of Israel, he went to work in the fields near Petach Tikvah. The text that follows is excerpted from a letter he wrote to his family in Russia just days into his new life.

Berl Katzenelson: First Impressions of the Land *Iggerot Berl Katzenelson*

Before our eyes was the first street of Petach Tikvah. The luxury struck us in the face. Lush green gardens. Avenues of erect young cypress trees stretching from gate to house. Mansions with verandas, balconies. One gate even had a bright brass plate bearing the owner's name, with a lantern nearby. This is not the stable, solid wealth of the farmer of Sarona, but the glitz of the "*paritz*," or perhaps of

Sarona, a community of German Protestant Templers founded in 1871 near Jaffa, served as a model of modern, individual, entrepreneurial agriculture for the Jewish settlers.

merchants who have tasted the life of a *"paritz."*

Paritz—pejorative Yiddish term for "landowner."

It was suggested we walk to Ein Ganim. This is the settlement founded last year by workers. . . . The plan was for every worker to receive a dwelling and a plot of land for vegetables and milk, so that he would be able to stay at work. We hadn't yet left Petach Tikvah when we could already see from the hill the new little houses of Ein Ganim scattered across a wide expanse. It was a beautiful afternoon. From the dense air of the hotel and the spiritual air of Petach Tikvah we entered the small, free republic that had sprouted next to it. Whoever couldn't find his place in Orthodox Petach Tikvah could find fulfillment here. Here was a free world.

The Ein Ganim model: a proletarian village, where the wife would tend a small farm to help sustain the family of the worker.

Katzenelson refers to "free" in the sense of "freethinking."

As I was walking, I wondered just how real this all is; I know that in the Land of Israel one must be cautious, for we are always rich in lovely fantasies here, so my enthusiasm was tempered. Still, the view itself, the broad horizon, the mountains of Judah in the distance surrounding the place, the new little houses, some of one room, some of two or even three, the recognition that almost (almost!) the

He articulates the ideal of "Hebrew labor."

entire *moshavah* had been built
by Jewish hands, the well with its
pump in the middle of the road—
the pride of Ein Ganim—all these
filled the heart with joy and light.
Newness, freshness, youthfulness
fill everything here.

The earth has almost not been
worked yet, but here and there
something comes up. Around one
of the houses there are real crops.
It appears that here lives a serious
farmer. The question of where his
seriousness lies—in money or in
the work of his hands—I will leave
for another time.

I ask my host how many years he
has been in the land. He answers,
"Six years." How different is the
sound of the words here from in
Jaffa. The road, the houses, the
people, the horizon—everything
welcomes you with a certain
warmth and joy. . . .

Brenner takes me to Gordon. So
easily, in such a short time, I am
already privileged to meet these
two men, who occupy such an
important place in my heart. I
never would have imagined Gordon thus: Outside, near the house,
on a torn mat, sits a Jew of about

The pioneers were influenced by the
narodniki of Russia, socialists who
idealized and idolized the traditional
peasant village where life was simple, earthy, and authentic.

Note the cynicism regarding a Jew
from the First *Aliyah*: Was his an
authentic Jewish garden, or one
whose owner could afford an Arab
gardener?

Jaffa was the urban center and port
of entry.

The *Yishuv* of this period was intimate and exciting. Only two days in
the country and the young green-
horn was already hobnobbing with
his two idols.

fifty . . . barefoot, bare-headed,
in patched trousers. . . . "This," he
announces, "is my parlor, which
can hold countless guests. Its only
drawback is that the roof leaks."
He likes this joke and frequently
repeats it.

. . . And on everything rests the
Shekhinah. . . .

Shekhinah—traditional term for the
Divine Presence. For Katzenelson, the
settlement, the pioneers, Gordon—
all are manifestations of holiness.

Neighbors see us and come over.
From the distance we hear the
singing of a group of teenage boys
and girls, who also draw near. In
short, an idyll of the Land of Israel.

—Berl Katzenelson, *Iggerot Berl Katzenelson*, vol. 1, ed. Yehudah Sharett (Tel
Aviv: Am Oved), p. 119

This brief letter touches on a number of important themes of the Second *Aliyah*:

· The antagonism between the First and Second *Aliyah* settlers with
  respect to lifestyle and ideology
· The romanticization of the land, of the simple life, of labor
· The ideal of "Hebrew labor"
· The replacement of traditional religion by a secular religion of land
  and labor
· The sense of possibility, wide-open spaces, liberation, rebirth

Interestingly, Berl Katzenelson went on to be an outspoken (and sometimes lonely) critic of socialist Zionism's rejection of Jewish tradition. He
advocated for a thoughtful and organic process of building a new culture
on the firm foundation of Jewish tradition, as envisioned by Ahad Ha'am.

LEGACY

Impact

The pioneers of the First and Second *Aliyot* translated the Zionists' political and cultural visions into solid foundations for future development.

Physical: The pioneering work of settling the land, draining swamps, building towns and roads, developing agriculture and industry and commerce—all established the foundation of a renewed, modernized center of Jewish life.

Political/social: On a certain level, the Jewish state was not founded in 1948, but much earlier: during the period of the two original waves of immigration, when so many of the state's ideological and organizational foundations were set in place. After all, the state was not created overnight; it formalized a reality that had been developing organically for over half a century.

Moreover, the tension between the middle-class colonists of the First *Aliyah* and the socialist pioneers of the Second *Aliyah* came to underlie Israeli political life dividing liberal (i.e., capitalist, nationalist) Zionists ("the right") and utopian socialist Zionists ("the left"). Today's political camps in Israel are the successors of these original ideological streams.

In addition, an ambivalent and complicated relationship emerged between the settlers and the Palestinian Arab population. Some of the factors first seen in the First and Second *Aliyot* and still present include mutual fear, mutual benefit and shared interests, mutual envy, cultural misunderstanding, class conflict, interference by outside political forces, idealism, and historical memories and myths. This is a large and complex topic; see chapter 26 for further discussion.

Cultural: The establishment of Hebrew as the language of the state-to-be was not a foregone conclusion: The Old *Yishuv* resisted the secularization of the sacred language, and many Western European Zionists (such as Herzl) expected that the language of the Jewish national home would be the language of science and enlightenment: German. And of course, the local vernacular was Arabic. Eliezer ben Yehudah's widely publicized efforts to modernize Hebrew and institute it as the language of the land resonated with the romantic nationalism of the pioneers, for whom the rebirth of Hebrew symbolized reconnection with their ancient roots in the soil.

Memory

In the Jewish world at large, the painful and heady days of the pioneers are relegated mostly to history books and the occasional novel or memoir. They are not memorialized in ritual.

However, in Israel, reminders of this early period are inescapable. Many communities large and small trace their origins to this period and continue to express pride in their history, founders, and original buildings. Nationwide, reconstructions, historical parks, living history programs, markers, and monuments memorialize the pioneers. Literature about the period—history and biography, but also fiction, poetry, and drama—is rich and growing. And of course, the music of those days has become Israeli "folk music." Schoolchildren visit the sites, read the memoirs, sing the songs.

That said, the attention paid to the Second *Aliyah*, in particular, waxes and wanes depending on the government in power. Since the labor parties lost dominance of the body politic in 1977, public adulation of the socialist pioneers has been somewhat attenuated.

One unique heritage of the Second *Aliyah* that remains a pillar of Israeli popular culture (though it has wilted somewhat with globalization) is the folk dancing tradition. The pioneers' enthusiastic, sweat-drenched dancing into the night after grueling days in the fields was their secularized ritual of Jewish spiritual elevation. Based on romantic notions of European peasant life (and perhaps on Hasidic memories), and often based on Russian dances, "folk songs" were composed and "folk dances" choreographed—and then taught from community to community and from generation to generation. Both amateur and professional folk dancing are still popular cultural expressions in Israel today.

TEXT FOR DISCUSSION

Nachman Syrkin (1868–1924) was a leading theoretician of the Zionism and socialism synthesis. Do you agree that the two naturally fit together as expressions of striving for a messianic utopia?

> For a Jewish state to come to be, it must, from the very beginning, avoid all the ills of modern life. . . . The Jewish state can come about only if it is socialist; only by fusing with socialism can Zionism become the ideal of

the whole Jewish people. . . . The messianic hope, which was always the greatest dream of exiled Jewry, will be transformed into political action.

—Nachman Syrkin, 1898 (in Hertzberg, *The Zionist Idea*, pp. 349–50)

FURTHER READING

Elon, Amos. *The Israelis: Founders and Sons*. London: Weidenfeld and Nicolson, 1971, pp. 82–147. An account detailing the background and experiences of the immigrants composing the First and Second *Aliyot*.

Frankel, Jonathan. *Prophecy and Politics*. Cambridge: Cambridge University Press, 1981. A comprehensive history of Russian Jewish socialism, including socialist Zionism and the Second *Aliyah*.

Hertzberg, Arthur. *The Zionist Idea*. Philadelphia: Jewish Publication Society, 1959. An anthology including excerpts of various socialist Zionist writings, including Gordon and Katzenelson.

Laqueur, Walter. *A History of Zionism*. New York: Schocken Books, 1972, pp. 270–95. A brief account of socialist Zionism and the Second *Aliyah*.

Morris, Benny. *Righteous Victims*. New York: Random House, 1999, pp. 3–66. A close examination of Jewish-Arab relations in Palestine up to 1914.

Shapira, Anita. *Berl: The Biography of a Socialist Zionist*. Cambridge: Cambridge University Press, 1985. A window on Katzenelson and his time.

———. *Israel: A History*. Translated by A. Berris. Waltham MA: Brandeis University Press, 2012, pp. 27–64. A leading contemporary historian's account of this period.

25. The Destruction of European Jewry

THE HOLOCAUST, 1933–45 CE

HISTORY

The Jews in the New Europe

The First World War and its aftermath confirmed that Herzl had correctly interpreted the handwriting on the wall (see chapter 22). The breakup of the old multinational empires into a mosaic of ethnic nation-states essentially led to the undoing of emancipation, and worse. The sparks of exclusivist, xenophobic nationalism that Herzl had glimpsed at the Dreyfus trial grew to a singeing bonfire in the 1920s and '30s across Europe and then exploded with unimaginable destructiveness with the rise of Nazism in Germany.

The new governments established after the end of the First World War were not based on established democratic traditions. Many of them were unstable and gave way to dictatorships (e.g., Italy, Yugoslavia, Portugal, Poland, Hungary). Moreover, it was impossible to draw boundaries that precisely matched the lines between the various ethnic communities that had constituted the empires, so the new states were nominally based on particular cultures—but in reality contained significant minorities of other ethnic groups. While setting the postwar borders, the 1919 Treaty of Versailles did guarantee minority protections, but these were often implemented grudgingly and were essentially toothless in the face of the new states' sovereignty. Meanwhile, ethnic resentments provided ripe fruit for demagogues and dictators to pluck and exploit. For example, from his ascent to power in 1926, Jozef Pilsudski, the "father of modern Poland," became increasingly dependent on support from nationalist, antisemitic parties; Poland renounced minority rights in 1934. Meanwhile, Lithuania had already done so in 1924, followed by Turkey in 1926 and Latvia in 1934.

And then, in the 1930s the Great Depression caused great suffering around the world. Jobs evaporated and incomes fell, resulting in masses of angry people lacking an obvious, logical target for their rage. In the new states of Europe, the people directed their fury vaguely at the new "enlightened" European order—and concretely at "the usual suspects": ethnic and religious minorities, especially the Jews.

In this new environment, the nineteenth-century liberal promises of emancipation, integration, and normalization crashed and burned. And antisemitism was unleashed, both from Enlightenment ideals and from any premodern frameworks of empire and church that had kept it under some degree of control.

Each country's story is different, but overall the Jews of Europe experienced an intensified antisemitism during the interwar years, both official and unofficial—and occasionally violent. Meanwhile, in the decade following the 1917 Russian revolution, the brutal civil war between Red forces (fighting for Bolshevik socialism) and White forces (comprising various capitalist, monarchic, and socialist factions) repeatedly placed the Jews in harm's way. To the Reds, the Jews were petty capitalists; to the Whites, they were socialist sympathizers. There was probably some truth in both stereotypes. Individually the two sides, especially in the Ukraine, seized on the Jews as convenient scapegoats and targets.

A corollary to the rise of ethnocentrism in the collapsing Old Europe was a new focus on defining identity through race. National culture became romantically associated with its familial and geographical roots; the people venerated the deep, mythic, even biological bond between blood and soil. Linking a nation's primeval ancestors, landscape, and culture may have helped European leaders trying to forge new realms in the states spun off by World War I; it certainly found a resonance in cultural Zionism. But for the Jews living in those new states, it was fraught with danger.

Already in the second half of the nineteenth century, various theories of racial inequality were being published, some by "mainstream" European intellectuals. A commonality was the disparagement of the Jew: Jews were portrayed as morally inferior (dishonest, predatory), threatening (controlling the banks and the media), or both. Already in 1879 the slogan *"Die Juden sind unser Ungluck"* ("The Jews are our misfortune") had become popular in Germany.

Nazism and the Third Reich

All of the above factors came into play in Germany, only more so. Germany's punishment at the Versailles Conference (harsh reparations, demilitarization, loss of territory) gave rise to a simmering resentment aimed at the Allies, but more generally at the liberal, universalistic vision of a "new Europe" that the Versailles Treaty sought to implement at the expense of German power and pride. Leaders who spoke in terms of the sacred German blood and soil, the ancient myths, the purity of the race, the betrayal by the world and by the outsiders within, found ready listeners. Jewish integration—and Jews in general—came to symbolize the "new Europe" and hence came to be seen as Germany's "misfortune."

Germany had become a democracy after the war, but as in many other postwar European states, some of its ethnic and class groups were unwilling to share power. The government founded in Weimar in 1919 was fractious and unstable, beset by violent challenges from extra-governmental militias and struggling to cope with hyperinflation. By 1933 public discontent was at such a fervor that pro-democracy parties failed to form a ruling coalition in the parliament, and Adolph Hitler was able to assemble a right-wing coalition. Then, within months, he employed popular support, coalition maneuvering, and his party's private militia (to violently suppress opposition) to create a one-party dictatorship with no rivals.

In 1925–26 Hitler had set forth his views in his autobiography, *Mein Kampf* (*My Struggle*), and it had become a best seller. He offered a unique response to the apparent weakness and decadence of Weimar democracy: an ideology based on German racial superiority and on the threat the Jewish race posed to that superiority. As a result, once he came to power, Germany became driven by two missions intended to restore its lost glory: (a) dominate the world and (b) eliminate the Jews.

Within the same year the government began enacting laws to force the Jews out of German culture, government, and economy. The 1935 "Nuremberg Laws" canceled Jews' German citizenship and prohibited Jewish marital relations with gentiles. Three years later, on November 9, 1938 (*Kristallnacht*—"the night of broken glass"), the government unleashed "popular" pogroms: paramilitary forces and civilians throughout Nazi Germany smashed the windows of Jewish-owned stores, hospitals, schools, and synagogues; ransacked their interiors; and killed hundreds of Jews. Hitler had escalated his war on the Jews from legal persecution to violence.

During much of the 1930s, the Nazi government favored Jewish emigration (leaving behind property, of course). However, once the military expansion phase—German conquest of other European states—began in 1939, Jewish emigration came to be seen as "impractical." As the Nazis conquered Poland and then the rest of Europe, their territory came to include millions of Jews. The Western democracies had demonstrated clear unwillingness to grant Jewish refugees safe harbor on their shores. In 1939, for example, the United States, Canada, and Cuba had all refused to accept 937 German Jewish refugees fleeing for their lives aboard the ss St. Louis; Great Britain accepted a few hundred, and the rest were returned to mainland Europe, where most would later perish in Nazi-ruled countries. Since Nazi ideology would not accept the presence of a Jewish population and emigration was not an option, Nazi leaders rapidly developed and implemented a policy of ethnic cleansing by mass murder.

In 1938 Germany annexed Austria; a year later it conquered Poland. Within three years most of Europe—from the French coast to the Soviet border, from Scandinavia to Greece—was under its control. In each country it occupied, Germany introduced its policies of persecuting Jews and other minorities such as Roma (Gypsies) and homosexuals. In many cases, these policies reinforced the agendas of various local antisemitic groups and leaders, gaining their cooperation and support for Nazi rule.

The Nazis' obsession with elimination of the Jews would continue to drive policy even when it conflicted with their own self-interest in pursuing the war effort, as the tide turned against them in 1944–45.

The Holocaust

Historians argue over the trajectory of the idea to annihilate European Jewry. Did Hitler intend it from the beginning? Did it arise because emigration failed to "solve the problem"? Was it born out of the momentum of conquest?

In any case, Jews in conquered areas were expelled and/or concentrated into ghettos and there subjected to humiliation, dispossession, starvation, torture, and murder, primarily by ss units accompanying the army.[12] In 1941 "special forces" units of the ss began systematic mass murder of Jewish populations by bullets or mobile gas chambers. A year later the Nazis began to establish eleven extermination camps, all located in Poland (Auschwitz, Tre-

---

12. The ss (Schutzstaffel—protective squadron) started out as Nazi militias; after 1933 it became institutionalized as a governmental agency, separate from the army, responsible for enforcing racial policies and running concentration (i.e., prison) and extermination camps.

blinka, Sobibor, and others). Throughout the war, the rail network of Europe continuously moved Jews from the conquered territories to the camps.

The Nazis employed large-scale industrial methods—gas chambers—to kill their victims. By the end of the war, approximately six million Jews had died—67 percent of the prewar population.

Jews Murdered in the Holocaust, by Country

Country	Number of Jews Murdered (% of Prewar Jewish Population)
Poland	3,000,000 (90%)
Latvia, Lithuania, and Estonia	228,000 (90%)
Germany and Austria	210,000 (90%)
Bohemia and Moravia	80,000 (89%)
Slovakia	75,000 (83%)
Greece	54,000 (77%)
The Netherlands	105,000 (75%)
Hungary	450,000 (70%)
Belgium	40,000 (60%)
Yugoslavia	16,000 (60%)
Rumania	300,000 (50%)
Norway	900 (50%)
Conquered areas of the USSR	1,252,000 (44%)
France	90,000 (26%)
Bulgaria	14,000 (22%)
Italy	8,000 (20%)
Luxemburg	1,000 (20%)
Denmark	0
Finland	0

—Lucy S. Dawidowicz, *The War against the Jews, 1933–1945* (New York: Holt, Rinehart, and Winston, 1975), p. 403

The human dimension of the Holocaust cannot be described with statistics. The monstrous synthesis of human evil and modern social and technological engineering placed human nature itself under an x-ray microscope, exposing unprecedented cruelty—and indifference to it—but also remarkable resilience and heroic resistance to evil. On the one hand, Western democracies closed their borders to refugees, antisemitic locals eagerly collaborated with the Nazi rulers, and many Jews denied the reality around them—or lost hope. But on the other hand, thousands of European gentiles risked (and often lost) their lives resisting the Nazis or protecting Jews, from Western consuls forging emigration papers to peasants hiding Jews in their cellars. Meanwhile, Jews engaged in both physical resistance (e.g., the 1943 Warsaw Ghetto revolt) and spiritual resistance. Even in the camps, many Jews continued to maintain their culture and their human dignity.

The "lessons" of the Holocaust are still being explored and debated (see "Legacy" below). What is certain is that in the course of one decade, European Jewish life—human, material, cultural—was largely extinguished.

Timeline: 1855–1945

1855   Arthur de Gobineau publishes *The Inequality of the Races*, articulating a racial theory of history, one of many such works that would appear from 1848 onward.

1873   Germany's boom economy crashes in the context of a world depression; many citizens blame the Jews and the liberals (many of whom are Jews).

1878   Adolph Stocker founds an explicitly antisemitic political party in Berlin.

1879   The prominent German historian Heinrich von Treitschke begins to publish essays on the Jewish question, coining the phrase "*Die Juden sind unser Ungluck*" ("The Jews are our misfortune").

1890   Antisemitic parties begin to gain representation in local and national legislatures in Europe.

1919   The Treaty of Versailles that ends World War I imposes significant punitive measures against Germany, including territorial losses, demilitarization, and substantial reparations.

1919   The new Weimar constitution grants full equal rights to the Jews, just as popular expressions of antisemitism reach new heights in the press and in political and social organizations.

1925   Adolph Hitler publishes *Mein Kampf* (*My Struggle*), a manifesto of the ideas that will form the basis for his National Socialist (Nazi) Party: hatred of the Jews and the need to expand Germany's borders.

1933   As a result of a parliamentary stalemate, a coalition of right-wing parties forms a government in Germany. Adolph Hitler's National Socialist Party is dominant. Hitler is named chancellor. The National Socialists' private militia violently suppresses all opposition, enabling Hitler to establish a one-party dictatorship.

1933   The German government begins dismissing Jews or forcing them out of positions in public service, education, and culture and eventually from business and social life.

1935   The Nuremberg Laws ban intermarriage with Jews and cancel Jews' citizenship in Germany.

1938   November 9: *Kristallnacht*, a day of government-sanctioned mob violence against Jews and Jewish institutions.

1938   Germany annexes Austria.

1939   Germany annexes the Czech Republic and invades Poland.

1940   Germany invades Denmark, Norway, France, Belgium, Luxemburg, Netherlands, Romania, and Greece and conducts air raids over Britain.

1940   The first ghettos are created and sealed off in Polish cities.

1941   Germany invades Yugoslavia and the Soviet Union.

1941   German ss *Einsatzgruppen* begin the systematic murder of Jews in Poland and Russia.

1941   The first extermination camps become operational.

1941   The United States enters the war after Japan attacks Pearl Harbor.

1942   At the Wannsee Conference, the German government adopts a plan to systematically murder the Jews of the conquered territories.

1943   The liquidation of ghettos begins.

1943   The Warsaw Ghetto uprising occurs.

1945   Germany surrenders; Hitler commits suicide.

PRIMARY TEXT

When the Germans entered Vilna, Lithuania, in the spring of 1941, about sixty thousand Jews (locals and refugees) resided in the city. By the time the Nazis sealed off the ghetto that September, more than twenty thousand Jews had been murdered, mostly at Ponar, a killing site in the nearby forest. The ghetto was liquidated in the fall of 1943. Only a few hundred Jews escaped and survived.

Abba Kovner and Ruszka Korczak were leaders of the local Hashomer Hatzair socialist Zionist youth movement. Reporting on a group meeting in late December 1941, this passage from Korczak's memoir highlights the frustration, depression, and paralysis engendered by the realization of total powerlessness — and the efforts to retain some sense of autonomy nonetheless.

Ruszka Korczak, "Flames out of Ashes"

[Ruszka Korczak:] A bloody catastrophe is overwhelming our people. Its main part, the Jewry of Europe, is facing extinction. No matter how tragic this fact may be for us, objectively speaking there is still hope that not all our people will go down to the grave. What will the coming generations learn about? From what springs will they draw? According to what values will our youth in Eretz-Yisrael, which will be fruitful and flower, be brought up, if our people's history consists only of slaughter, extermination, and ineffectuality?

Our task is to give that history a new note and a different content. Our history should not contain

The Germans used various methods of disinformation to keep their killing operations unknown to the next victims—and even when evidence got out, many Jews couldn't or wouldn't believe it. By this point, in Vilna, it was no longer deniable.

only tragedy. Let it have heroic
struggles, self-defense, war for
a worthwhile life, and death in
honor as well. . . .

Someone said: None of those who
have spoken up to now have mentioned one important problem. I
refer to the collective responsibility which has been placed on the
Jews of the ghetto. In our situation,
how can we consider a struggle and
the preparations for armed combat, when we know very well that
they are liable to bring about the
end. We have no assurance that we
are not facing immediate liquidation of the ghetto and the extermination of its inhabitants. The
moment our activities begin, shall
we not be endangering the whole
ghetto? We are not discussing our
readiness. We personally are ready
and willing; but have we the right
to assume responsibility for all the
Jews in the ghetto, to endanger
their lives and—should we fail—to
be accomplices, in fact, to their
extermination. . . . The collective
responsibility of all for the actions
of the few hangs over our heads
like a sword. . . .

Abba Kovner: . . . We should
remember that the possibilities
and conditions for the rescue of

Without hindsight, and in a fog of
uncertainty and disinformation, any
action that might provoke the Germans to greater cruelty imposed an
excruciating moral responsibility on
the actors.

One of the most horrific aspects of
the Nazi methodology was using
their absolute power to force their
victims into situations wherein their
own moral compass was smashed—
compelling betrayal under threat of
communal or family punishment;

individuals are extremely difficult as a result of the organized hunt for Jews and the anti-Semitism of the general population. The conditions are so difficult that the rescue of individuals will demand the basest means, such as pretending to be an anti-Semite when other Jews are being led to slaughter; viciousness — each man for himself at his neighbor's expense; and treachery — serving the enemy in order to save one's life. . . .

Someone here mentioned collective responsibility: How can we take responsibility for others, the outcome of which will be the sacrifice of thousands? This collective responsibility will be one of the most difficult problems in our lives. But in the final analysis, what does it mean? Our activity may bring the end closer — but that end will come in any case. What I demand to know is: who will take the responsibility for all of us going to our deaths like sheep to slaughter?

It was asked too how we could resist when the forces are so tragically unequal. We have no hope of winning. There are no chances of a real fight. In our ghetto, the conditions are such that every attempt of ours will be foiled before it

allowing survival in return for collusion. The reprieve or reward was always a fraud.

The opposition between "sheep to the slaughter" and "death with honor" became an important theme in Israeli culture after the Holocaust. The "New Jews" were ashamed of the seeming passivity of the Holocaust victims, and hence glorified Kovner and those like him. Later, this stance became controversial. It was asked: How does anyone have the right to judge behavior under such circumstances? Moreover, based on accumulating research, some historians now ask: Is the "sheep to the slaughter" image even justified? Perhaps Israelis' need to distance themselves from the powerlessness of the Holocaust experience caused them to overlook the phenomenon of spiritual resistance—and instances of physical resistance—leading to a myth of pas-

even begins. But our actions cannot depend on the answer to this question. . . . The chief thing is — how can we not defend ourselves? . . . The action which we are about to take is not an act of despair. It is not the end of everything. In practice, that is what may happen, but anyway, today we must make our choice.

The tasks ahead of us are very difficult. Firstly we must get rid of all illusions. We must develop a consciousness of the situation in ourselves and in our fellows too. We must understand the danger completely. The youth which is confused and depressed after the latest German actions must have its faith in itself revived: it must have national pride and hatred of the enemy instilled in it. Then it must be prepared for battle and for struggle as an organized group.

sivity that does not reflect historical reality.

The question also arose as to whether "instilling hatred of the enemy" is itself not a form of surrendering the moral high ground.

—Ruszka Korczak, *Lehavot b'Efer* (Givat Haviva: Moreshet, 1965), excerpt published in English as "Flames out of Ashes," in *The Massacre of European Jews* (Ramat Efal: World Hashomer Hatzair, 1963), pp. 261–73; used by permission

---

Acts of violent resistance were indeed organized in Vilna and other ghettos, but massively outnumbered and outgunned—and often not supported by their fellow Jews, who feared Nazi reprisal—they never became mass movements, with significant impact on the Nazis. When the Vilna Ghetto was liquidated, some of the resistance members, including Abba

Kovner, managed to flee through the sewers and join the Lithuanian underground resistance ("partisans") in the forest. Kovner survived, fought in the Israeli War of Independence, and became a well-known poet and activist. He also helped found the Diaspora Museum (now the Museum of the Jewish People) in Tel Aviv.

LEGACY

The Holocaust eliminated a significant, fertile, and historical center of Jewish life. In addition to unimaginable human suffering and loss of life, vast cultural resources, human and material, were obliterated.

The experience also gave rise to major developments in Jewish thought and consciousness. Among the issues and questions that continue to exercise Jewish (and gentile) thinkers are the following:

- The covenant: The Jews managed to come through the destruction of the First and Second Temples, the Crusades, the expulsion from Iberia, and the Chmielnicki massacres without seriously questioning the original understanding of the covenant—the inextricable link between the Jews' observance of the law and their fortunes. Until then, it was possible to accept that each punishment was somehow deserved and that it might even help purify the people and bring redemption closer. The immensity, the cruelty, and the illogicality of the Holocaust severely strained that understanding of the world. Is there any sin, personal or national, that could justify the murder of a million children? Is it even possible to believe in a God of history if this is the reality of history?

    For most Jews and Jewish thinkers, the Holocaust experience has made the traditional understanding of the covenant untenable without a new layer of interpretation, such as emphasizing God's hiddenness and/or human free will. For many others, no new interpretation can suffice; faith itself is impossible. Only a secular, cultural conceptualization of Judaism is imaginable (see chapter 23).
- A possible revelation: Deep discussions have also arisen concerning whether the Holocaust was "revelatory." Was it another, albeit extreme, historical example of the terrible things people to do each other, or is it a profound revelation about the nature of the world, of history, of humanity?

- "Owning" the Holocaust: In seeking the "meaning" of the Holocaust, a related tension arises around who "owns" it. Is the "lesson" of the Holocaust universal, encompassing the "banality of evil," the potential depths of human suffering and heights of heroism, the dangers of nationalism, and the bystander's responsibility? Or is the Holocaust an essentially Jewish event, an expression of the particular, unique situation of the Jews: the eternity of antisemitism?
- Enlightenment is naive: To some Jews, the Holocaust is proof that however much the Jews might feel safe in diaspora societies, Enlightenment and Emancipation are ultimately wishful thinking, with no anchor in long-term reality. If antisemitism is simply part of the genome of European and other diaspora cultures, then the Jews should keep their bags packed. Political Zionism is the only guarantee of survival.
- Power and faith: Since the destruction of the First Temple, the Jews lived in a state of powerlessness—without sovereignty or an army representing their interests. They were always guests and often unwelcome. They knew that every sojourn, even of hundreds of years, was temporary; they sustained themselves with the faith in ultimate national redemption. No matter how difficult the times, God would give them the strength to survive without power. The Holocaust raised the question: Is Jewish powerlessness divinely ordained, or merely a function of circumstances? Must the Jews accept this status? Can they afford to? Where should humanist self-reliance, self-defense, and activism meet faith in messianic redemption?

Through the second half of the twentieth century, it seemed that Jewish life in Europe would remain a tattered remnant. However, with the passing of generations, Israel's influence as a cultural center, and the fall of the Iron Curtain (see chapter 30), a number of European cities, both east and west, have witnessed rebirth and modest regrowth of indigenous Jewish culture, such as the following:

- Berlin: More than 40,000 Jews, many of them immigrants from the former Soviet Union (see chapter 30) and Israel; about ten synagogues, as well as various cultural institutions and schools.

- Paris: 350,000 Jews, the majority immigrants or descendants of immigrants from Algeria and other North African colonies (see chapter 27); a rich variety of cultural and religious institutions.
- Italy: 24,000 Jews, primarily living in Rome, Milan, and Florence, including several thousand who immigrated from Libya in 1967. Cultural growth in recent years includes new institutions and a project to translate the Talmud into Italian.
- Warsaw: Most of Poland's 5,000 to 20,000 Jews live in Warsaw, where a renewed interest in Jewish identity and culture sustains a Yiddish theater, a Foundation for the Preservation of Jewish Heritage, as well as synagogues and community centers.

Memory

As of this writing, the world—and the Jews—are still trying to define the place of the Holocaust in their collective memory. Some survivors are still alive; their personal recollections help shape the collective memory as it crystallizes.

Jews throughout the world observe an annual Holocaust Memorial Day, called Yom ha-Shoah; *yom* means "day," and *shoah*, the Hebrew term for the Holocaust, is a biblical word denoting a terrible calamity. The State of Israel chose the commemoration date—the twenty-seventh of Nisan (during the week after Passover)—because it marked the outbreak of the Warsaw Ghetto revolt. Many Orthodox communities prefer to memorialize the Holocaust's victims by reciting memorial prayers on the traditional fast day of the Tenth of Tevet (one of the four fast days associated with the Temple's destruction; see chapter 7). Some liberal congregations recite the *Kaddish* memorial prayer for Holocaust victims at every service.

As the generations pass, it remains to be seen what aspects of the Holocaust will become institutionalized in the liturgy.

Israel maintains a national institute for the study, documentation, and commemoration of the Holocaust: Yad Vashem in Jerusalem. Holocaust research centers and museums around the world—including one on the Mall in Washington DC—also study, document, commemorate, and teach visitors about the Holocaust. There are public Holocaust memorials from Berlin to Shanghai to Miami, as well as Holocaust curricula in public schools. In recent decades, travel to Holocaust historical sites, especially the remains of the extermination camps, has become popular, and many Jewish high schools in Israel and elsewhere sponsor such pilgrimages.

Since the 1950s, a growing body of Holocaust art, memoir, and research—and hybrids among these—have emerged. Holocaust studies is a recognized academic discipline. Yad Vashem and other institutions have accumulated large archives of oral histories, supplementing hundreds of both published and private memoirs. Anne Frank, Elie Wiesel, Andre Schwartzbart, Primo Levi, Claude Lanzmann, Victor Frankl, Leon Uris, Paul Celan, Nellie Sachs, Steven Spielberg, and Roberto Benigni are just a few of the better-known memoirists and artists who have contributed to making the Holocaust a central cultural concern in our time. This creative outpouring has also given rise to the question of if—and then where—to place the boundary between bearing witness and making art for its own sake.

TEXT FOR DISCUSSION

Popular Israeli poet Dan Pagis (1930–86), born in Romania, was eleven years old when he and his grandparents were forced onto a freight car en route to a Nazi labor camp. Thirty years later, he reflected on his experience in the poem "Written in Pencil in the Sealed Railway Car." Note that "man" in Hebrew is *adam*, so the fifth line can be translated as "cain son of adam" (see Genesis 4:1–16). Do you believe the story of Cain and Abel foreshadows the Holocaust? Can the Holocaust be understood as a natural consequence of fundamental and unchangeable human instincts?

Written in Pencil in the Sealed Railway Car

here in this carload
i am eve
with abel my son
if you see my other son
cain son of man
tell him i

—Dan Pagis, *Variable Directions: Selected Poetry*, trans. Stephen Mitchell (San Francisco: North Point, 1989); used by permission of the University of Nebraska Press; English translation © 1982 by The Jewish Publication Society, Philadelphia

FURTHER READING

The volume of literature on the Holocaust is immense. These are respected general histories.

Bauer, Yehudah. *A History of the Holocaust*. New York: Franklin Watts, 2001. Yehudah Bauer is the "dean" of Israeli Holocaust researchers and educators; this is his non-academic historical survey.

Dawidowicz, Lucy S. *The War against the Jews, 1933–1945*. New York: Holt, Rinehart and Winston, 1975. A detailed historical overview with a focus on the Jewish perspective as seen from Jewish sources.

Gutman, Yisrael, and Livia Rothkirchen, eds. *The Catastrophe of European Jewry*. Jerusalem: Yad Vashem, 1976. A selection of scholarly papers on "antecedents, history, reflections."

Hilberg, Raul. *The Destruction of the European Jews*. Chicago: Quadrangle, 1961. The first comprehensive history to be published, dense with factual detail, with a focus on the German bureaucratic mechanism of mass murder.

26. The Jewish State

HISTORY

The Mandate Period: Growth and Development

During the interwar years, practical, political, and cultural Zionism united in the project of building a life in the land, a state among the states, and a renewed Jewish culture. Despite unforeseen obstacles and painful setbacks along the way, the three decades from 1918 to 1948 saw a remarkable transition: from a small, depressed, scattering of communities in Palestine trying to recover from the difficult war years to a full-functioned independent democratic state.

The stream of immigration that had been cut off by World War I resumed in 1919. Together with those who had come before, the new wave of socialist Zionist activists—about thirty-five thousand in number—were instrumental in building infrastructure and institutions, including the Histadrut labor federation, Bank Hapoalim ("the workers' bank"—today Israel's largest bank), and the agricultural settlement of the broad Jezreel Valley in the north. Developing and enriching their community was much easier under Great Britain's rule than it had been under the Ottomans. While the British made only modest investments in Palestine, they introduced Western principles of efficient, honest, public administration, as well as modern methods and standards in education, transportation, and sanitation.

In the mid-1920s, the Fourth *Aliyah*, a wave of about sixty-seven thousand middle-class, urban immigrants, mostly from Poland, injected know-how, capital, and entrepreneurship that advanced the development of Palestinian cities and industry. Tel Aviv grew rapidly, spurring the construction industry and others. The Nesher cement works, Shemen oil mill, and Dead Sea potash mines were all established at this time.

Then, in the 1930s, came the Fifth *Aliyah*—a wave of some quarter million immigrants from Germany, Austria, and other Central European countries. These highly educated arrivals made significant cultural contributions to their new homeland, such as establishing the Palestine Orches-tra (which became the Israel Philharmonic) and turning Tel Aviv into a center of Bauhaus architecture.

The infusion process abruptly came to a halt in 1939 as the British, pres-sured by the Palestinians' violent resistance to growing Jewish numbers and power, imposed severe immigration restrictions—seventy-five thou-sand over five years. The timing could not have been worse; European Jews had now become desperate for a refuge.

Still, during the war years, through confrontation and smuggling, more than one hundred thousand Jewish immigrants managed to reach the shores of Palestine. And so, from 1919 to 1946, the Jewish population in the land grew from sixty thousand to more than half a million.

For much of this period, the economic and security situations in Pal-estine were daunting. Many Jewish immigrants found it overwhelmingly difficult to adjust to the new climate and culture. Until alternatives dried up in the 1930s, many moved back to Europe and even to Russia or moved on to the West. After the United States closed its gates in 1924, Latin Amer-ica became a destination.

During the same period, the gentile population of Palestine rose from 600,000 to 1.2 million. While the British ruled Palestine as a colony—with minimal investment—still, like the Romans before them, they developed a significant transportation infrastructure (ports, roads, and railroads), and they raised standards of education and medical care. This modern-ization attracted illegal Arab immigration from nearby countries and greatly reduced the infant mortality rate, resulting in significant natural population growth.

The Jews and the Arabs approached living in Palestine very differently. Most of the Arabs lived within a traditional, clan-based agrarian society. Not well-organized politically and not driven by an urgent ideological vision, they tended to accept as is the benefits ensuing from the change of empire. The Jews, on the other hand, were not content with what the British offered. Impatient to build up the basis for their future state, they parlayed philanthropic support from abroad into establishing their own autonomous self-government, including an elected assembly, as well as institutions of education and culture, health care, scientific research, immigrant absorption, and self-defense. Some of these activities, such as education, were conducted in cooperation with the British. Others, such as self-defense, were discouraged or prohibited and took place clandestinely. Regardless, when the State of Israel was established in 1948, most state functions had already been in place for years.

The Mandate Period: Interethnic Tensions

The relationship between the Zionist immigrants and the local Arab population of Palestine was complicated, inconsistent, and ambivalent on both sides. These are some factors that contributed to this complex reality:

- As the Ottoman Empire declined, various subject peoples— including the Palestinians—joined the rising tide of European nationalism and began to strive for self-determination. The rise of Palestinian nationalism may have also been fueled by the model and the challenge of Zionist agitation and immigration.
- The Zionists were united in their goal of a "Jewish state" but ambivalent and divided over the Palestinians' place in that future state. They never developed a coherent—or consensus—vision.
- The Jews' settlement and investment brought improved conditions for the local population, such as employment, imported goods, and new infrastructure. However, the Arabs understood that these developments were meant to further Jewish statehood and that this would lead, ultimately, to their disenfranchisement.
- After the Jewish experience of powerlessness in Europe, a strand in Zionist thinking idealized strength, self-reliance, and self-defense. This may have colored Zionists' relations with the local population.
- Palestine had been ruled as a province of a medieval empire. When the British took over, the Arabs did not have any self-government in place except for clan-based leadership in the dozens of villages scattered through the land. The Jews established "national" institutions, including a representative assembly, but no one could claim to speak for the Arabs of Palestine. Thus the Arabs, beset by power struggles between clans, were unable to conduct a symmetrical conversation with the united Jewish *Yishuv*.

- In trying to strike a balance—presiding over the end of colonialism even as they acted like colonialists in taking the Palestine spoils— the British tried to please everyone while still furthering their own interests. To gain support in the First World War, in 1915 the British had promised the Arabs autonomy (the Hussein-McMahon Agreement)—and in 1917, the Jews a "national home" (the Balfour Declaration). When both sides tried to cash in their promises, conflict was bound to ensue.

As all these vectors coalesced and clashed, Palestine experienced a rising curve of violence throughout the Mandate period (1918–48). First, in 1921, the Arabs rioted against Zionist settlement. In 1929 their anger played out in murderous mob attacks on the Orthodox, non-Zionist Old *Yishuv* that were reminiscent of Russian pogroms. In 1936–39 they conducted an armed uprising against the British, demanding a halt to Jewish immigration.

The British tried to calm the Arabs by restricting immigration during the Holocaust, which in turn incited the Jews to violent resistance, through terrorist attacks on both the British and the Arabs and through large-scale smuggling of illegal immigrants. The dominant socialist Zionist parties established a clandestine self-defense organization, the Haganah ("defense"), in 1921; the competing Revisionist Party created its own underground paramilitary organization, the Irgun Tzva'i Le'umi ("national military organization," also called by its acronym, Etzel, or just Irgun for short). The Haganah focused more on self-defense and on preparing for a war of survival when the British would depart. The Irgun employed violent attacks to strike fear into the local Arab resistance and to force Great Britain to withdraw. The clash between these two very different approaches occasionally led to internecine violence within the *Yishuv*.

Partition and Statehood

The rising tide of violence in Palestine led the British to question their role and options as the Mandatory power—to ask, for what cause, exactly, were British boys dying in Palestine? In 1937 a commission of inquiry chaired by Lord William Peel (the Peel Commission) toured the land to gather data and concluded that there was only one way to a peaceful resolution:

divide the land into Jewish and Palestinian states. The Peel Commission suggested dividing lines: The Jewish state would comprise the Galilee and a strip along the coast down past Tel Aviv; the Palestinian state would include the West Bank and the entire Negev. In addition, a corridor from Tel Aviv to Jerusalem (including Jerusalem) would remain under British control.

Many Jews opposed partition. Religious Zionist Jews argued that a political entity was unfit to tamper with a divine promise. Secular nationalists insisted it was unthinkable for a Jewish state to relinquish the biblical heartland of Judea and Samaria, including Jerusalem. A more pragmatic opposition declared that such a small, resourceless, isolated enclave would be neither militarily nor economically viable. Still others believed in the vision of a single, shared binational state. But, ultimately, the Zionist and Yishuv leadership accepted partition—after all, better half a state than none.

On the other hand, most of the Arab populace viewed any "European" state established in Palestine, no matter how small, as just a rerun of the Crusades or as ongoing colonialism—that is, European outsiders continuing their unwelcome and unjust rule of Palestinians. The Palestinian Arabs saw themselves as a native population, entitled to self-determination and self-rule, and the Arabs of surrounding countries supported them; in fact, many were in the process of seeking their own liberation from colonial rule (Iraq 1933, Lebanon 1943, Jordan 1946, Syria 1946). Moreover, as leading Palestinian families (particularly the Husseinis and Nashashabis) struggled for power, fighting the Zionist project served as a useful unifier and outlet for anger.

For another ten years, violence continued. Both sides fought each other and the British (even while the Jews actively supported the British struggle in the Second World War).

By 1947 the British had had enough. Deciding they could not solve the dispute, on February 14 the British cabinet handed the future of Palestine over to the United Nations. On November 29, the UN General Assembly voted by a two-thirds majority to partition Palestine into two states. Throughout the world (excluding the minority of partition opponents), Jews greeted the UN vote with great joy.

The decision did not pacify Palestine. In fact, the violence only escalated. Palestinian Arabs attacked Jewish settlements; the Jewish paramilitary defense organizations carried out violent reprisals. The British confiscated weapons, imprisoned and even executed suspected perpetrators, and tried to keep the two sides from each other's throats—leading each side to accuse the British of favoring the other.

On May 14, 1948, the day the British had set for terminating the Palestine Mandate, the People's Council, the governing council of the *Yishuv*, proclaimed statehood at a festive gathering in Tel Aviv. There was widespread rejoicing—and uncertainty about the new state's military prospects, as the "unofficial" warfare of the preceding months now turned into a full-fledged war. On May 15 the Jordanian Legion invaded from the east, and fighting escalated around the country.

At first an Arab victory seemed assured. Their manpower and resources were far superior—local Palestinian militias had allied with Arabs in the neighboring states of Egypt, Iraq, Jordan, Syria, and Lebanon. However, the Jews had the advantage in leadership, organization, and motivation—and overseas support in funding and military equipment/supplies.

The war was hard-fought and costly, about six thousand dead on each side. A year later, a negotiated armistice set the state's borders. Israel received about 77 percent of Palestine west of the Jordan. The UN Partition Resolution had originally assigned it 56 percent; the extra 21 percent consisted mainly of the western Galilee and the western half of Jerusalem, with a corridor connecting it to the coastal plain.

Of the approximately nine hundred thousand Arabs who lived before the war in territories that became Israel, more than seven hundred thousand fled to neighboring countries during or just after the war. The extent of Israeli forces' active involvement in encouraging this emigration remains a subject of controversy; certainly Israel's leaders had a strong interest in decreasing the Arab population within the new state's borders. The hosting countries viewed the Arab refugees as a burden and a destabilizing force—and believed that absorbing them would amount to de facto recognition of the new geopolitical reality. Thus, except for those who ended up in the West Bank under Jordanian rule (where they constituted the majority of the population), these Palestinians remained stateless, living in refugee camps. Three generations later, many are still there. The Palestinians who remained in Israel became full citizens; by the end of the twentieth century they constituted about 20 percent of the populace.

The land assigned to the Palestinian state did not become a state. Jordan governed the West Bank, and Egypt the Gaza Strip. Meanwhile, armistice was not peace: the Arab nations surrounding Israel made it clear by formal policy and occasional violence that Israel's existence remained unacceptable.

Israel's Most Prominent Founders

Chaim Weizmann (1874–1952) A prominent scientist, he immigrated from Belarus to England, where he became a Zionist leader. He helped negotiate the Balfour Declaration and served as Israel's first president.

David Ben-Gurion (1886–1973) A charismatic and politically astute leader already in his student days in Poland, he filled major leadership positions from his arrival in Palestine in 1906. He served as Israel's first prime minister and continued in the role on and off from 1948 to 1963.

Moshe Sharett (1894–1965) Involved in diplomatic aspects of the pre-state period and known for his negotiating skills, he became foreign minister of the new state for seven years (including a brief stint as prime minister).

Golda Meir (1898–1978) Growing up in the United States, where she became active in socialist Zionism, she immigrated to Palestine in 1921 and then played a major role in fundraising abroad during the War of Independence. Rising through the political ranks, she ultimately served as Israel's prime minister from 1969 to 1974.

Menachem Begin (1913–92) Active in the Revisionist Zionist movement in Poland (the opposition to socialist Zionism), he arrived in Palestine in 1942, becoming a leader of the Irgun (the Revisionist militia). He served as the outspoken head of the opposition to the dominant socialist Zionists in the Knesset from 1948 until he himself became prime minister in 1977 (see chapters 27–28). During his term as prime minister, Israel signed a peace accord with Egypt and invaded Lebanon (1982).

Yitzchak Shamir (1915–2012) Active in the Revisionist Zionist movement in Poland, he immigrated to Palestine in 1935 and became a leader in the Lehi, an underground militia that split off from the Irgun.

Entering the Knesset in 1969, he went on to serve as speaker, foreign minister, and then prime minister (after Begin).

Moshe Dayan (1915–81) Rising through the Haganah underground military
ranks during the pre-state years, he held command positions during
the 1948 war, became Israel's chief of staff in 1953, and later served in
the Knesset and as minister of agriculture. In 1967 he was appointed
minister of defense—in time for the Six-Day War (see chapter 28).

Abba Eban (1915–2002) A South African–born scholar of Arabic literature who was active in English Zionism and a renowned orator, he
became involved in pre-state and post-independence diplomacy.
He served as Israel's ambassador to the UN and to the United States
and subsequently as minister of education and foreign minister.

Yitzchak Rabin (1922–95) Rising through the ranks of the underground
Palmach (elite corps of the Haganah), he went on to hold important command positions during the 1948 war and later became army
chief of staff. Entering politics, he then served twice as prime minister. He signed a peace treaty with Jordan and the Oslo Accord
with the Palestinians. His assassination in 1995, by an extreme
opponent of the partition of Palestine, was a national trauma.

Ariel Sharon (1928–2014) A young soldier in 1948, he rapidly worked his
way up the military ranks, becoming known in the 1956 Sinai Campaign and the 1967 and 1973 wars as a brilliant and courageous
officer whose independence and aggressiveness generated controversy. He went on to become minister of defense and then prime
minister; during his term, Israel withdrew its troops and settlers
from the Gaza Strip (2005).

Timeline: 1915–49

1915   Sir Henry McMahon, acting on behalf of Britain, makes a
           vaguely worded promise to support Arab autonomy (appar-
           ently including Palestine) if the Arabs will revolt against the
           Ottomans. This promise would come back to haunt Great Brit-
           ain when it allowed Jewish immigration and development in
           Palestine after the First World War.

1916   The secret Sykes-Picot agreement between Great Britain and France divides the Middle East into British and French spheres of influence in advance of the expected defeat of the Ottoman empire.

1917   British foreign secretary Arthur James Balfour announces his government's support for "a Jewish national home in historic Palestine."

1918   British troops occupy Palestine.

1919   A Jewish national "department of education" is created to supervise the developing *Yishuv* school system.

1920   Establishment of a coordinated national Jewish self-defense organization, the Haganah.

1920   Twenty parties field candidates in the first elections for a Jewish representative assembly, based on proportional representation. The socialist bloc receives more than 35 percent; ethnic parties, 17 percent; Orthodox parties, 20 percent; nine miscellaneous small parties, 28 percent.

1921   The local Arab population riots against Zionist settlement and the vision of Jewish statehood.

1922   The British remove the area of Palestine east of the Jordan River from the Balfour Declaration provisions. This territory is ruled as a separate mandate, Transjordan, until it becomes the independent kingdom of Jordan in 1946.

1922   Hadassah Medical Organization is formed; it begins to establish hospitals around the country, as well as a nursing school.

1925   The Hebrew University is founded in Jerusalem.

1927   The British high commissioner approves a "constitution" for the *Yishuv*'s self-government, which includes the Assembly of Delegates, an executive committee, and a chief rabbinate.

1929   Arab riots—massacres—against Jews are fueled by a campaign of religious incitement over control of the Temple Mount and Western Wall.

1936–39   The Arabs revolt against the British.

1937   The Peel Commission recommends partition.

1939   A British White Paper sets severe limits on Jewish immigration, land purchases, and settlement construction in Palestine.

1939	The Jewish tactic of *chomah u-migdal* (stockade and watchtower), establishing new settlements overnight on land that had been purchased but not yet settled, reaches a high point with twelve new settlements in May, seven of them on the same night.[13]
1945	After World War II ends, all Jewish underground organizations in Palestine begin direct armed attacks on the British, to force them to withdraw or at least to open the gates for immigration.
1947	The British intercept the *Exodus*, a ship carrying more than five thousand illegal Jewish immigrants, and tow the boat, crew, and passengers to Haifa. From there Britain sends the refugees back to displaced persons (DP) camps in France—which refuses to receive them, so they end up in Germany—a public relations debacle for the British. After Israeli independence, they will ultimately immigrate (legally).
1947	The UN General Assembly passes Resolution 181 to partition Palestine.
1948	The *Yishuv* establishes a full provisional government, to be in place upon British withdrawal.
1948	Britain withdraws. Israel declares independence. War ensues.
1948	In June violence erupts between the provisional government and the Irgun, one of the pre-state underground militias representing Revisionist Zionism (the opposition to the dominant socialist Zionists), when the latter attempts to bring in the *Altalena*, a ship of fighters, arms, and ammunition.
1949	Armistice is negotiated and agreements made with the various warring countries. No agreed borders are set—merely "temporary" armistice lines, as the Arab countries refuse to recognize Israel as a legitimate state.

PRIMARY TEXT

On May 14, 1948, hours before the scheduled British withdrawal, David Ben-Gurion read the provisional government's "Declaration of Independence of the State of Israel" at a brief formal ceremony in the Tel Aviv Art

---

13. British policy prohibited establishing new settlements, but an old Ottoman law prohibited demolishing a completed structure, so this tactic of "instant" construction circumvented the British restriction.

Museum, attended by the members of the Representative Assembly and various dignitaries, and broadcast live on radio. The State of Israel was born.

From the Declaration of Independence of the State of Israel, May 14, 1948

The Land of Israel was the birth-place of the Jewish people. Here their spiritual, religious and politi-cal identity was shaped. Here they first attained to statehood, created cultural values of national and uni-versal significance and gave to the world the eternal Book of Books.

The declaration's agenda disallows any questioning regarding the Jews' bond to the land. Hence, it ignores the fact that the two foundational events—Exodus and covenant—took place elsewhere.

After being forcibly exiled from their land, the people kept faith with it throughout their dispersion and never ceased to pray and hope for their return to it and for the resto-ration in it of their political freedom.

Actually, the Jews were praying for restoration of the Temple cult and the monarchy.

Impelled by this historic and tra-ditional attachment, Jews strove in every successive generation to re-establish themselves in their ancient homeland. In recent decades they returned in their masses. Pioneers, illegal immi-grants, and defenders, they made deserts bloom, revived the Hebrew language, built villages and towns, and created a thriving community controlling its own economy and culture, loving peace but know-ing how to defend itself, bringing

Individuals and small groups immi-grated over the ages, but the effort "to re-establish themselves" was a modern phenomenon.

the blessings of progress to all the country's inhabitants, and aspiring towards independent nationhood.

In the year 5657 (1897), at the summons of the spiritual father of the Jewish State, Theodore Herzl, the First Zionist Congress convened and proclaimed the right of the Jewish people to national rebirth in its own country.

This right was recognized in the Balfour Declaration of the 2nd November, 1917, and re-affirmed in the Mandate of the League of Nations which, in particular, gave international sanction to the historic connection between the Jewish people and the Land of Israel and to the right of the Jewish people to rebuild its National Home.

The catastrophe which recently befell the Jewish people—the massacre of millions of Jews in Europe—was another clear demonstration of the urgency of solving the problem of its homelessness by re-establishing in the Land of Israel the Jewish State, which would open the gates of the homeland wide to every Jew and confer upon the Jewish people the status of a fully privileged member of the comity of nations. . . .

What would have happened to the Zionist vision "without the Holocaust" is an unanswerable question. However, it became a commonplace of Zionist thought that the lesson of the Holocaust was that Jewish survival depended on Jewish power—that is, statehood.

On the 29th November, 1947, the United Nations General Assembly passed a resolution calling for the establishment of a Jewish State in the Land of Israel; the General Assembly required the inhabitants of the Land of Israel to take such steps as were necessary on their part for the implementation of that resolution. This recognition by the United Nations of the right of the Jewish people to establish their State is irrevocable.

This right is the natural right of the Jewish people to be masters of their own fate, like all other nations, in their own sovereign State.

ACCORDINGLY WE, MEMBERS OF THE PEOPLE'S COUNCIL, REPRESENTATIVES OF THE JEWISH COMMUNITY OF THE LAND OF ISRAEL AND OF THE ZIONIST MOVEMENT, ARE HERE ASSEMBLED ON THE DAY OF THE TERMINATION OF THE BRITISH MANDATE OVER THE LAND OF ISRAEL AND, BY VIRTUE OF OUR NATURAL AND HISTORIC RIGHT AND ON THE STRENGTH OF THE RESOLUTION OF THE UNITED NATIONS GENERAL ASSEMBLY, HEREBY DECLARE THE ESTABLISHMENT OF A JEWISH STATE IN THE LAND OF ISRAEL, TO BE KNOWN AS THE STATE OF ISRAEL. . . .

"In the Land of Israel" does not specify borders. This was also controversial. Some of the framers felt that borders should be specified. The dominant position, however, was that since the Arabs had rejected partition, Israel should not obligate itself to the partition borders.

THE STATE OF ISRAEL will be open
for Jewish immigration and for the
ingathering of the exiles; it will fos-
ter the development of the country
for the benefit of all its inhabitants;
it will be based on freedom, justice and peace as envisaged by the
prophets of Israel; it will ensure
complete equality of social and
political rights to all its inhabitants
irrespective of religion, race or sex;
it will guarantee freedom of religion,
conscience, language, education and
culture; it will safeguard the holy
places of all religions; and it will
be faithful to the principles of the
Charter of the United Nations. . . .

WE APPEAL — in the very midst of
the onslaught launched against
us now for months — to the Arab
inhabitants of the State of Israel to
preserve peace and participate in
the upbuilding of the state on the
basis of full and equal citizenship
and due representation in all its provisional and permanent institutions.

WE EXTEND our hand to all neighboring states and their peoples in
an offer of peace and good neigh-
borliness. . . .

WE APPEAL to the Jewish people
throughout the Diaspora to rally
round the Jews of the Land of

Israel is not positioned as a messianic
state, but a modern liberal democracy. Nonetheless, a clause such as

Israel in the tasks of immigration and upbuilding and to stand by them in the great struggle for the realization of the age-old dream — the redemption of Israel.

PLACING OUR TRUST IN THE ROCK OF ISRAEL, WE AFFIX OUR SIGNA- TURES TO THIS PROCLAMATION AT THIS SESSION OF THE PROVISIONAL COUNCIL OF STATE, ON THE SOIL OF THE HOMELAND, IN THE CITY OF TEL-AVIV, ON THIS SABBATH EVE, THE 5TH DAY OF IYAR, 5708 (14TH MAY, 1948).

"the redemption of Israel" may imply messianic overtones

The framers argued about includ- ing a religious reference. Finally they compromised by using the relatively neutral "Rock of Israel."

This text served as the foundational document for the state and for the various "basic laws" that were legislated in lieu of a constitution. Hence, the explicit mention of democratic freedoms is very important. On the other hand, the text doesn't give much guidance regarding the relationship between religion and state or the status of majority and minority cultures. These matters remain unresolved, giving rise to ongoing political struggles.

The state this declaration established included a parliament (the Knesset) of 120 members, chosen every four years by direct election, with a system of proportional representation: citizens voting for a party, rather than an individual. The party gaining a majority — or able to assemble a coalition of parties to create a majority — would then choose the prime minister and all other cabinet ministers. A president, elected by the Knesset and lacking executive powers, would nominally be considered head of state. An inde- pendent judiciary, including a supreme court, would have the authority to reject legislation it deemed to conflict with the "basic laws" rooted in the Declaration of Independence. Local municipal governments would follow a similar structure.

Today, the divisions that characterized the Zionist movement — socialist versus liberal, religious versus secular, messianic versus mundane —

continue to find expression in Israel's political life. Typically, twenty or so parties vie for Knesset seats. None has ever achieved a majority, so coalition jockeying is the rule; the larger parties try to assemble a majority comprising various smaller and special-interest parties. As a result, often a tiny party, serving as the keystone of the coalition, holds veto power over major government policies. Moreover, while elections are scheduled every four years, often they are more frequent, for if a coalition falls apart, new elections are usually called. This system, not unique to Israel (Italy, for example, has a similar multiparty/coalition structure), can serve to protect minorities' rights, but some argue that it disproportionately inflates the power of small population sectors.

LEGACY
Impact

Israel's establishment represented a major change in the historical reality of the Jewish people:

- A state, controlling its own borders and fielding its own army, meant that centuries of Jewish powerlessness and homelessness were over. Jews would no longer be at the mercy of reluctant hosts, nor helpless scapegoats for every local power struggle.
- The state became a culture center for Jews everywhere, reviving the Hebrew language and giving rise to a multifaceted modern Jewish culture open to the world.
- The state became a laboratory for developing the role of the Jewish religion in a modern, democratic Jewish state—a process that remains far from complete.

At least two historical dilemmas continue to trouble those concerned with the state's spiritual and political life:

1. What is the historical/religious meaning of the state? Is it a stage in the progress of messianic redemption, outside of normal history, guided by biblical prophecy? Or is it a normal historical nation-state, required to play by the same rules as other modern states? Is evi-

dence of "normalization" in state life proof of Zionism's success — or
its failure? (See chapter 28.)

2. The early twentieth-century dream of homogeneous ethnic nation-
states controlling their own destinies has proved to be an illusion.
Ethnic purity is not morally possible and probably undesirable, and
no nation can stand alone and dictate its own historical trajectory
solely on the basis of its military and economic strength. What,
then, should be the guiding model of the Jewish state regarding its
internal cultural and religious structure and its relations with the
rest of the world?

Memory

The UN's dramatic vote on November 29, 1947, preserved in newsreels,
remains a moving, emotionally charged "moment in history." Visitors
from around the globe stop at Independence Hall in Tel Aviv, the former
art museum where independence was declared, and listen to the crackly
broadcast radio recording of David Ben-Gurion reading the declaration.

Jewish communities in Israel and throughout the world observe Israel
Independence Day on the fifth of the Hebrew month of Iyar (which coin-
cided with May 14 in 1948). In Israel, there are public celebrations and street
fairs and parties, and it is customary to hike and picnic in parks and nature
preserves. In both the Diaspora and Israel, synagogues ranging from liberal
to Orthodox Zionist hold special prayer services with liturgical additions
that acknowledge the religious/historical significance of the day, marking
reishit tzmichat ge'ulateinu, "the first flowering of our redemption." Israel's
Memorial Day for fallen soldiers and terror victims is observed the day
before Independence Day; although the transition from grief to celebration can be awkward, the logic is powerful.

Many Palestinian Arab citizens of Israel harbor mixed feelings about
Independence Day celebrations. For them, the day's emphasis on the 1948
military victory conjures up memories of loss and defeat. Some groups
hold commemorations of the Nakbah ("catastrophe" in Arabic) on May 15.

Israel's flag features the Star of David, a medieval symbol that somehow came to be a universal Jewish marker. Jewish institutions around the
world generally display it alongside the local national flag.

TEXT FOR DISCUSSION

Holocaust survivor and philosopher Emil Fackenheim believed that the primary significance of independence was the Jewish nation's acquisition of state power. Are there other lenses through which to view this event?

The plain truth is that during the twelve years of the Third Reich . . . , only one form of power counted, and that the Jewish people lacked. In the first period of the twelve years—persecution, expulsion—Jewish victims needed havens, but those only states could provide. In the second period—mass torture and murder—only a state that considered Jewish lives to be a top priority could have mustered planes, bombs, armies, and the other implements of state power that could have made a large difference.

It was therefore an act of world-historical significance when, on 14 May 1948, David Ben-Gurion, on behalf of an ad hoc government of the Jews of Palestine, proclaimed the first Jewish state in 1878 years.

—Emil L. Fackenheim, "The Jewish Return into History: Philosophical Fragments on the State of Israel," in *Contemporary Jewish Theology—A Reader*, ed. Elliot Dorff and Louis Newman (Oxford: Oxford University Press, 1999), p. 226

FURTHER READING

Laqueur, Walter. *A History of Zionism*. New York: Schocken Books, 1967, pp. 209–599. A history from the Balfour Declaration until the Declaration of Independence.

Morris, Benny. *Righteous Victims*. New York: Random House, 1999, pp. 67–258. A recounting from the Balfour Declaration until the Declaration of Independence, with a focus on Jewish-Arab relations.

Rubenstein, Amnon. *The Zionist Dream Revisited*. New York: Schocken Books, 1984, pp. 50–75. A study of the relationship between the Holocaust experience and Zionist thought and action, up to independence.

Shapira, Anita. *Israel: A History*. Translated by A. Berris. Waltham MA: Brandeis University Press, 2012, pp. 66–178. A leading contemporary historian's account of this period.

Shavit, Ari. *My Promised Land*. New York: Spiegel and Grau, 2013, pp. 1–173. A prominent contemporary Israeli journalist interweaves family and historical narratives to explore the costs and benefits of Israel's struggle for statehood.

Silberstein, Laurence, ed. *New Perspectives on Israeli History*. New York: New York University Press, 1991. A collection of papers covering the transition to statehood as well as political and cultural developments during the state's early years.

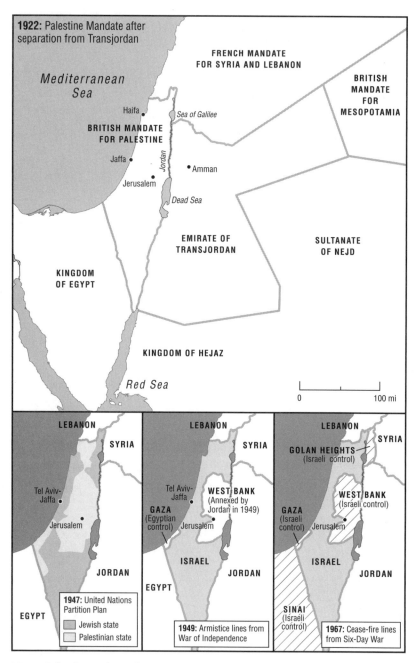

1922: Palestine Mandate after separation from Transjordan

Mediterranean Sea

FRENCH MANDATE FOR SYRIA AND LEBANON

BRITISH MANDATE FOR MESOPOTAMIA

Haifa

Sea of Galilee

BRITISH MANDATE FOR PALESTINE

Jaffa

Jordan

•Amman

Jerusalem

Dead Sea

EMIRATE OF TRANSJORDAN

SULTANATE OF NEJD

KINGDOM OF EGYPT

KINGDOM OF HEJAZ

Red Sea

0   100 mi

LEBANON

SYRIA

Tel Aviv-Jaffa

Jerusalem

JORDAN

EGYPT

1947: United Nations Partition Plan
- Jewish state
- Palestinian state

LEBANON

SYRIA

Tel Aviv-Jaffa

WEST BANK (Annexed by Jordan in 1949)

GAZA (Egyptian control)

Jerusalem

ISRAEL

JORDAN

EGYPT

1949: Armistice lines from War of Independence

LEBANON

SYRIA

GOLAN HEIGHTS (Israeli control)

WEST BANK (Israeli control)

GAZA (Israeli control)

Jerusalem

ISRAEL

JORDAN

SINAI (Israeli control)

1967: Cease-fire lines from Six-Day War

Map 5. Palestine and Israel, 1922–67

27. East Meets West

THE MASS *ALIYAH* FROM NORTH AFRICA AND
THE MIDEAST, 1949–64 CE

HISTORY

Meanwhile, in Africa and Asia . . .

The preceding fourteen chapters (and many general Jewish histories) have dealt almost exclusively with the Jews of Europe or refugees therefrom. However, that emphasis gives a somewhat distorted picture. While momentous turning points seemed to be flashing by in Europe, elsewhere a culturally rich and vibrant Jewish life was quietly being lived by a significant portion of world Jewry. As we know from other fields of culture, the stars of historical narratives written by Europeans tend to be . . . Europeans. Also, numerically, the modern rate of population growth in Europe far outpaced that in the African and Asian communities: in 1650 North African and Middle Eastern Jews were almost 40 percent of the world Jewish population, but over the next two centuries, while their numbers tripled, they fell to 10 percent of world Jewry.

The Jews of North Africa and the Middle East might have remained under the Western radar had it not been for a significant upheaval in their lives: a large-scale and rapid migration from these lands to the newly established State of Israel. The nearly emptying out of important Jewish communities that had existed for centuries created a new and unique cultural reality in Israel: separate, proud, historic, distinctive Jewish communities that had lived largely self-contained for a millennium suddenly found themselves thrown together in the same small space, needing to find a way to live — and flourish — together.

These Jews had all lived in lands that became part of the Muslim world in the seventh to eighth centuries and remained so until the present. Thus their Jewish experience was different from that of Ashkenazic Jewry in Christian Europe (see chapters 14–15). While medieval Jewish life was not easy or secure anywhere, the level of Jewish integration and rootedness was generally higher and more stable in Muslim lands (see chapter 13).

Babylonia (Iraq and Iran)

When King Cyrus of Persia allowed the exiled Jews to return to Judea and rebuild the Temple in 538 BCE, most chose to remain in their new home in Mesopotamia (see chapter 8). This community grew (some estimate the population at over a million), prospered, and served as the center of world Jewish culture for five hundred years (see chapter 12). The chief rabbis (*Ge'onim*) of Babylonia were the halakhic authorities for Jews everywhere. Indeed, the Babylonian Talmud, compiled around 500 CE, remains the "standard" version of the Talmud throughout the Jewish world.

Around 1000 CE the centers in Europe and North Africa began to grow and assert independence, just as invasions and political instability weakened the Babylonian community. Nevertheless, Babylonia continued to sustain strong institutions and a tradition of serious and creative Torah study. It also produced an elite of entrepreneurs and leaders whose influence radiated out to the outposts they established in India and China.

The Maghreb

Since Roman times, Jews had lived in the Maghreb—the area along the Mediterranean coast of Africa, from the Atlantic coast to the Egyptian border. Before mass emigration in the mid-twentieth century, about half a million Jews resided in Maghreb countries.

This was a large and culturally heterogeneous region—cosmopolitan port cities influenced by foreign contacts, isolated Berber tribes in the Atlas Mountains—and Jewish culture reflected this heterogeneity.

The community of Kairouan (in Tunisia), a city founded during the early Muslim period (670 CE) maintained an important yeshiva, which hosted and produced world-renowned rabbis until the community was expelled in the eleventh century. Standard Talmud editions contain the commentary by Rabbi Chananel ben Chushiel, an eleventh-century Kairouan scholar.

Meanwhile, other communities flourished. Maimonides spent time in Fez (in Morocco), as did other important scholars of the Golden Age, most notably the pioneering eleventh-century codifier Rabbi Isaac Alfasi[14] (see chapter 13). The link to Iberia was strong. When Jewish life there began to collapse in the fourteenth century (see chapter 16), a flow of migration

14. The name "Alfasi" means "from Fez" in Arabic.

began, and prominent Iberian rabbis were among the new arrivals. Rabbi Shimon ben Tzemach Duran was one such example. Born in Barcelona and broadly educated in Jewish and general disciplines, he fled to Algiers after the 1391 violence and there became a leading halakhic authority.

After 1492, the flow of Jewish refugees turned into a flood. The Maghreb (along with Turkey and Palestine) became an heir and successor to the Sephardic culture of the Golden Age. Relations between the native Jews and the Jewish immigrants were not easy, however. The exiles, with their European culture and memories of a Golden Age, tended to look down on the locals, who in turn saw them as interlopers and snobs. In some places, such as Tunis, separate communities continued to exist side by side for centuries.

Algeria, Tunisia, and Morocco came under French colonial rule in 1830, 1881, and 1912, respectively, and Italy conquered Libya in 1911. Western governance brought the Jews a degree of modernization — and formal emancipation — but emancipation was a two-edged sword. Until this point, a medieval equilibrium had existed: the Jews were living in their own semi-autonomous communities (the *mellach,* as the ghetto in these countries was called), tolerated yet deemed inferior by the Muslim majority. As the European colonists arrived and imposed their laws and values, among them modernization and emancipation, the local populations rebelled — but not the Jews, who had an interest in supporting the European colonialists. Just two weeks after the French Protectorate of Morocco was established in 1912, riots broke out against the Jews of Fez; sixty Jews were killed, and the *mellach* was destroyed.

Identifying with the French and Italian colonial governments did not help the Jews during World War II, when both governments instituted Nazi-ordered antisemitic measures.

Yemen

A community of ancient (certainly pre-Muslim) and unclear origins that was cut off from other Jewish centers by its geographical isolation, Yemenite Jewry developed under a succession of local Muslim rulers (and, at times, the Ottomans). Gravitating to professions that local Muslims looked down upon, the Jews came to dominate the fields of metalworking, weaving and sewing, pottery, and carpentry. Prior to their mass migration to Israel, the community numbered around fifty thousand.

Many Yemenite Jewish customs and liturgical practices are unique. For example, Yemenite Jews sit on the floor in synagogues; use a closed, decorated room as the *huppah* (canopy) for marriage ceremonies; and pronounce Hebrew in a distinctive way—some argue in a way that preserves biblical pronunciation.

Egypt

Egyptian Jewry also had ancient roots; important colonies existed there already in Hellenistic times (from the third century BCE).

When the Byzantine Christians established rule in 395 CE, they enforced economic and religious restrictions on Jews, so Egypt's Jews welcomed the Muslim conquest in 646. Thereafter, through the centuries, they thrived. At its peak, in the early twentieth century, the Egyptian Jewish population was about eighty thousand strong.

As in other Muslim countries, over the years the Jews remained vulnerable, second-class citizens, while also achieving wealth and high positions. Maimonides, for example, living near Cairo, was the sultan's physician and head of the Jewish community. The attic of Cairo's Ben Ezra Synagogue was an active *genizah*, a repository for discarded sacred books and documents, for a thousand years. The wealth of material discovered there in the late nineteenth century continues to sustain scholarly research on medieval Jewish life in the region.

While the Jews of Arabic-speaking lands had very different historical and cultural experiences, these are a few common threads:

- Language: Arabic was the *lingua franca* (except in Iran, a Muslim nation that spoke Persian). Different, regional versions of Judeo-Arabic (and Judeo-Persian) developed, parallel to the development of Yiddish (Judeo-German) and Ladino (Judeo-Spanish).
- Religion: In comparison to the Christian environment, the relatively smaller degree of theologically based hostility, the higher degree of shared culture, and especially the distance from European enlightenment-emancipation-assimilation largely prevented the development of both a Reform-type rejection of *halakhah* and an anti-modernizing, Orthodox movement (see chapters 19–20). In

short, within the Jewish communities of Muslim lands, there was less religious polarization. Thus, rabbis could render halakhic decisions based on local considerations alone, without being concerned that those decisions would be interpreted ideologically (i.e., as pro-Reform or pro-Orthodox). For example, nineteenth-century Ashkenazic authorities produced several halakhic arguments prohibiting bicycle riding (a new technology at the time) on the Sabbath, seeing it as just one among many innovations threatening to undermine traditional practice. But Rabbi Yosef Haim of Baghdad (1832–1909), a beloved and highly respected halakhist, looked at the specifics of how a bicycle works and found no reason to prohibit its use on the Sabbath.

The Turning Point: 1948

In 1922 the Ottoman Empire fell. The new states-in-formation, such as Syria and Iraq, experienced unstable governments and nationalist xenophobia, together with rapid modernization and the breakdown of traditional communal structures. As was the case in Europe and the Maghreb colonies, this instability and rising nationalism led to the Jews' social and economic exclusion as well as endangerment through occasional violent attacks. The rise of German influence throughout the region then exacerbated this state of affairs. Many Jews viewed the establishment of Israel, with open borders, as a near-messianic opportunity. Mass migration began as soon as the armistice was signed in 1949. Moreover:

- The Israeli government, eager to increase the Jewish population and settle the periphery, actively encouraged this process, helping to organize and transport the immigrants.
- The leaders and masses in the Arab-speaking world, angry over Israel's victory in the War of Independence, often directed their rage at local Jewish populations, precipitating further emigration.

Within the first decade after independence, more than five hundred thousand immigrants from Arab lands (half of these from Morocco) arrived in Israel. Ultimately, the number would reach six hundred thousand.

Significant numbers of Jews also emigrated to the West. The vast majority of Algerian Jews — more than one hundred thousand — moved to France.

Algeria had been a colony, and its Jews were all French citizens and could migrate freely to France. Morocco and Tunisia had been protectorates, whose inhabitants were not French citizens, so their migrations took them to a variety of destinations—mainly Israel, but also Spain, Canada, and South America. By the early twenty-first century, the Jewish communities remaining in Arab lands would range from zero (e.g., Libya, Syria, Iraq) to a few thousand (five thousand in Morocco; nine thousand in Iran).

Middle Eastern and North African immigrants and their descendants are called *Mizrachim*, meaning "Easterners." They are also occasionally referred to as "Sephardim," but this term's more precise meaning encompasses only those Jews who have preserved Iberian Jewish culture—primarily immigrants from communities in Turkey and Greece (who spoke Ladino). The major waves of *Mizrachi* immigration, 1949–52 and 1956–67—together with a higher birth rate among these immigrants than among Ashkenazim— led to parity between these two populations from around 1970 until the major wave of Russian Jewish immigration in the 1990s (see chapter 30). This demographic shift away from historical Ashkenazic dominance was a turning point, changing what was seen as "Israeli culture" and effecting significant political change as well (see discussion in "Legacy" below).

Timeline: 882–1994

882–942	Life of Saadiah Gaon, the world-renowned philosopher and halakhic authority who served as chief rabbi of Baghdad.
1132–50	Jewish communities in the Maghreb (North Africa except for Egypt) are attacked during the Almoravid and Almohad dynasties and especially during the struggle between them.
1258	The Mongols conquer Babylonia.
1391	Thousands of Jews flee anti-Jewish outbreaks in Iberia, arriving in the Maghreb along with prominent rabbis Simon ben Tzemach Duran, his son Solomon ben Simon Duran, and Isaac bar Sheshet. Committed to Maimonides's scholarship, they exert a formative influence on Jewish life in the region.
1492	The Jews are expelled from Iberia; a major wave of migration to the Maghreb and the Middle East follows.
1592–98	Rabbi Israel Sarug, a disciple of the kabbalist Isaac Luria (see chapter 15), travels in the Maghreb spreading his master's

doctrine, helping to establish the major role of kabbalistic study in the region.

1830   France begins the conquest and large-scale colonization of Algeria, which lasts until 1962.

1881   Tunisia becomes a French protectorate (until 1956).

1882   A group of 150 Yemenite Jews immigrate to Palestine, followed by about 2,000 more over the next two decades.

1896   Two English travelers return from Egypt with fragments retrieved from the Cairo Genizah, leading to interest and research; today, libraries in England and the United States hold more than 260,000 documents from the Cairo Genizah, facilitating ongoing research into medieval Jewish life.

1911   Italy conquers Libya from the Ottomans and rules until 1943.

1912   Morocco (which had remained an independent kingdom, not part of the Ottoman Empire) becomes a French protectorate (until 1956).

1920   The League of Nations establishes the British Mandate over Iraq, which holds until Iraq's independence in 1932 (though Britain reoccupied the country from 1941 to 1947).

1922   Egypt, formerly an Ottoman province, declares independence.

1949–50   "Operation Magic Carpet," a.k.a. "Operation Wings of Eagles," airlifts fifty thousand Jews from Yemen to Israel.

1951–52   "Operation Ezra and Nehemiah" airlifts 120,000 Jews from Iraq to Israel.

1948–56   More than sixty-five thousand Moroccan Jews immigrate to Israel. The Moroccan government then forbids emigration to Israel, leading to roundabout routes and clandestine immigration until restrictions are lifted in 1961, and mass immigration resumes.

1959   *Mizrachi* immigrants in Haifa's Wadi Salib slum demonstrate violently over perceived police violence and government discrimination in distributing public housing.

1971   *Mizrachi* neighborhood activists in Jerusalem form the "Black Panthers."

1977   The *Mahapach* (reversal): The socialist Zionists lose their thirty-year hegemony in the Knesset by losing the support of the growing *Mizrachi* population, which perceives them as elitist and supercilious.

1984	"Operation Moses" brings eight thousand Ethiopian Jews to Israel.
1984	Shas (acronym for "Guardians of Sepharad") is founded, an Israeli political party nominally Sephardic–ultra-Orthodox, but actually representing a broad cross section of *Mizrachi* voters.
1991	"Operation Solomon" brings fourteen thousand Ethiopian Jews to Israel.
1994	*Mizrachi* resentment crystallizes under the leadership of Uzi Meshullam, who leads violent demonstrations to demand the truth regarding long-standing rumors that one thousand Yemenite babies were stolen from transit camps in the 1950s for adoption by Ashkenazic Israelis. Investigations are conducted; as of 2016, the results are still classified.

PRIMARY TEXT

Erez Biton was born in Morocco in 1942. Immigrating with his family in 1948, he grew up in Lod, a tough immigrant town where at age ten he was blinded by a stray hand grenade. He became a social worker and psychologist serving Ashkelon, a development town (see "Legacy" below). In 1976 he published his first book of poetry, *Mincha Morokait* (*A Moroccan Offering*), and rapidly became recognized for his artistic grappling with his ethnic heritage and the *Mizrachi* community's struggles. An informal spokesman for the community, he is also the first *Mizrachi* writer to receive the prestigious Israel Prize for literature, in 2015.

Erez Biton, "The Song of Zohara Alfasia" and
"To Speak within a Great Illumination"

"The Song of Zohara Alfasia"

Zohara Alfasia
Was the court songstress of King
  Muhammed V in Rabat, in
  Morocco.
They say of her that when she sang,
Soldiers would fight with knives

Biton met Zohara Alfasia, a hugely popular singer in Algeria and Morocco, and a celebrity in the Jewish community, while he was a social worker in Ashkelon. Immigrating to Israel at age fifty-seven, she lived out the rest of her life in the poor "Atikot

To clear a path through the crowd
To reach the hem of her dress
To place money, a rial, as a sign of
    thanks
Zohara Alfasia,
Today, she can be found
In Ashkelon, in Atikot C, near the
    welfare office,
The smell of leftovers from
    sardine cans
On a wobbly three-legged table,
Glorious royal carpets, piled on a
    Jewish Agency bed,
And she in a faded morning robe
Hours in front of the mirror
With cheap makeup colors
And when she says:
Muhammed V is the apple of
    our eye
At first you don't understand.
Zohara Alfasi has a hoarse voice,
A pure heart, and eyes sated
    with love.
Zohara Alfasia.

C" neighborhood in the development
town of Ashkelon; she died in 1994.

To Biton, her experience represents
that of all the *Mizrachi* immigrants—
from the palace to the welfare office,
from pride and self-respect to mis-
ery and outsiderness (even though,
of course, life in Morocco was not as
romantic as it felt in retrospect).

—Erez Biton, "The Song of Zohara Alfasia," from *Mincha Morokait* (1976), in
Timbisert, A Moroccan Bird (Tel Aviv: Hakibbutz Hameouchad, 2009), p. 46; used
by permission of Erez Biton

"To Speak within a Great Illumination"

—A Morning Prayer for Rabbi
David Buzaglo, One of the Great
Payetanim of Moroccan Jewry

Rabbi David Buzaglo was recognized as one of the leading
twentieth-century *payetanim*—
writers and performers of Moroccan *piyut*, a traditional genre
of songs that were added to
the liturgy but also sung inde-

VERSION I

I will permit myself to say
Something in me is liberated at
    the sound of your name
I will permit myself to say
The nectar of my love flows to the
    threshold of your door
Come from the corner
To the center stage
Rabbi David Buzaglo
Something in me is liberated at
    the echo of your music
For when I followed myself I
    arrived at you
Rabbi David Buzaglo.

VERSION II

Come from the corner
To the center stage
Rabbi David Buzaglo
When I remember you
My heart is a tree planted by
    streams of water
When I followed myself I arrived
    at you
Then I found my own face in
    yours
The name of all my dreams of you
You and I from the ladle of honey
I met you within a great illumi-
    nation.

pendently of it. He immigrated in 1965, at age sixty-two, and died in 1975. In the years after his death, singing, performing, and writing *piyut* became increasingly popular in Israel both among *Mizrachi* Jews and the larger population.

In this poem, Biton's sadness about the uprooting of Zohara Alfasia gives way to the celebration of finding in the voice of Moroccan *piyut* a source of pride and inspiration in the new environment.

—Erez Biton, "To Speak within a Great Illumination," from *Tzipor Bein Yabeshot* (1989), in *Timbisert, A Moroccan Bird* (Tel Aviv: Hakibbutz Hameouchad, 2009), p. 85; used by permission of Erez Biton

Erez Biton was a pioneer in "processing" the complex and ambivalent experience of the *Mizrachi aliyah,* elevating it to serious discourse and artistic expression, and reestablishing pride through reconnecting with the community's cultural roots. "Zohara Alfasia" is now part of Israel's national high school literature curriculum, and Moroccan *piyut* has entered the repertoire of pop singer Kobi Oz, among others. And since Biton began writing, many other *Mizrachim* have joined the conversation.

LEGACY

Impact

With the great migration of Maghreb and Middle Eastern Jews came the almost complete disappearance of a centuries-old Jewish life and culture in those lands. This culture has been largely transplanted to Israel—a not straightforward, often painful process that remains very much in progress.

Geographical isolation and economic stress: The new state was not prepared for the absorption of so many immigrants, together with tens of thousands of European refugees. Most new arrivals were housed in *ma'abarot* (transit camps), where conditions were harsh and support services inadequate. Usually, they were then moved to new "development towns" that had been established in various peripheral and/or border regions in order to disperse the population and settle the whole country. The homogeneous immigrant population and lack of educational and employment resources in these towns often led to stagnation and failure—and resentment. The state is still picking up the pieces from this attempt at social engineering.

Culture shock: The immigrants' conservative, traditional, hierarchical community was suddenly transplanted into a modern, open, secular democracy. They struggled—not always successfully—to reach a balance between assimilation and maintaining their culture, which included their communal and family structures. The first generation especially suffered from a sense of loss and uprootedness, and discord with their offspring, who embraced the dominant Western, secular culture and rejected traditional authority figures. Parents, rabbis, and teachers found themselves humiliated.

Rejection by the established population: The established population's ambivalence regarding the immigrants (like in the United States—see chapter 21) compounded the new arrivals' sense of isolation and loss. The predominantly European society of the new state saw the immigrants as primitive—and their language and culture as unsettlingly similar to that of the Arab enemy. And so both the old and the new inhabitants tried, both consciously and unconsciously, to suppress that culture, resulting in attendant feelings of guilt, regret, and loss.

Slowly, however, the national education system, which promotes a generic Israeli culture, the "melting pot" of the army, and the growing distance from immigrant memories are chipping away at the overlapping barriers of ethnicity, class, and geography. Today, "intermarriage" in Israel is common, and there are many mixed middle-class neighborhoods. Despite economic and educational obstacles, *Mizrachi* Jews increasingly find their way to positions of leadership. Nevertheless, the residue endures in the economic and educational weakness of development towns and *Mizrachi* urban neighborhoods and in the *Mizrachi* population's continued under-representation in the political, economic, and academic elites.

The *Mizrachim* fundamentally changed Israel's political landscape. Until the *Mahapach* (reversal) of 1977, when the election results led to the first right-wing coalition, Israel's Labor Party in its various factions and reincarnations—the heritage of the Second and Third *Aliyah* socialists—had dominated Israeli politics. The early 1970s, however, saw the rise of the "Black Panthers," a movement demanding social justice for *Mizrachi* Jews, and the *Mizrachim*, who now constituted about half the Israeli population, rebelled against the rule of the Ashkenazic elites. Over the years *Mizrachi* activists went on to organize politically. Since 1984 Shas, a party with an explicitly ethnic-*Mizrachi* base, has been a member of almost every ruling coalition.

Religiously, the *Mizrachim* have injected a new, "softer" middle ground into a polarized Israeli landscape. On opposite ends stood Orthodoxy (Zionist and non-Zionist), committed to halakhic authority, and the secular socialist Zionists, who rejected the *halakhah* and the rabbis' authority. The *Mizrachim* introduced a third way: a respect for *halakhah* and rabbis without an all-encompassing commitment. For example, in an Ashkenazic community, a Jew who attends synagogue on the Sabbath would consider it forbidden to attend a soccer game that afternoon—those cheering on the soccer field would be "secular" Jews; but among *Mizrachim*, going from the synagogue to the soccer game is a common, socially acceptable pattern. This approach has come to be called *masorti* (traditional), as opposed to the two poles of *dati* (religious-Orthodox) and *chiloni* (secular). (The Conservative movement in Israel calls itself Masorti; however, the vast majority of *Mizrachi masorti* Jews are not affiliated with it.)

Culturally, even early on the *Mizrachim* had an important positive impact on the developing state. Their music, dance, food, accent, and holiday customs helped root Israel in its surroundings, largely preventing it from feeling like a European outpost. Middle Eastern–style popular music has become a major industry. Israeli "folk dance" integrates *Mizrachi* dance; in fact, the choreographers who created the folk dances of Israel today studied *Mizrachi* immigrants' dances together with the dances of earlier European arrivals and used them all as raw materials in a conscious effort to build an Israeli culture. During Hanukkah, all Israelis eat the customary *Mizrachi* jelly doughnuts (*sufganiyot*), not Ashkenazic potato pancakes. Standard Israeli Hebrew follows the Sephardic/Mizrachi—not the Ashkenazic—pronunciation. And of course, the Israeli "national foods" are not Ashkenazic bagels and lox, but Middle Eastern classics: falafel, hummus, and shawarma.

In effect, the *Mizrachi* migration forged a new Israeli culture and even a new Israeli Judaism—one that not only is rooted in the European experience that gave rise to Zionism, but is more diverse, inclusive, and universal.[15]

Memory

The memory of the *Mizrachi aliyah* was highly fraught for decades and inescapable. Geographical and class separation were facts of life. Sometimes—as in the demonstrations in Wadi Salib, Haifa in 1959, the Black Panthers' rallies in Jerusalem in 1971, and Uzi Meshullam's protest over the alleged kidnapping of Yemenite babies in 1994—the *Mizrachi* frustration turned violent. For the most part, the struggle for equality and for recognition of past wrongs has become a permanent part of ongoing public discourse in cultural media and the political arena. The immigrants' struggles to survive and integrate, the personal and communal identity conflicts, and the preservation and modernization of *Mizrachi* culture are common themes in Israeli popular literature, theater, film, and music, as well as topics for academic research.

15. The immigration of Ethiopian Jews that began in the early 1980s has been a kind of replay of the *Mizrachi* experience, compounded by an even greater cultural/religious distance from established Israeli society and by the added factor of race. Here, too, the romance of ingathering has collided with the formidable obstacles to absorption and integration. Progress is evident, but huge challenges remain.

An example of a *Mizrachi* custom that has become part of mainstream culture is the Moroccan Maimuna festival. In Morocco, Maimuna is a minor holiday celebrated the day after the end of Passover by exchanging home visits and gifts of special foods—especially *mufletas*, a yeast-dough crepe—with both Jewish and gentile neighbors. Moroccan immigrant community leaders have promoted its observance in Israel as a positive way to preserve their heritage and involve the larger population. Many towns hold publicly sponsored Maimuna festivities, and the home visits of various politicians generally draw considerable media attention.

More recently, many *Mizrachim* have been reconnecting with pride to the *piyut* tradition, bringing this classical element of their culture to the mainstream through local amateur singing groups and the artistry of professional musicians—from rabbis and cantors to pop singers.

TEXT FOR DISCUSSION

Meir Buzaglo, a philosopher, *Mizrachi* activist, and son of the *payetan* Rabbi David Buzaglo, has written and spoken extensively on the *masorti* approach to tradition. What do you see as the long-term risks and benefits of this approach for Jewish continuity?

> The *masorti* [*Mizrachi* traditional Jew] sees himself as one link in the chain that includes the world of his parents. The glue that holds this link in place is not the certainty that his parents hold the best theory, but simply his loyalty to what his parents have transmitted to him. . . . The *masorti* is likely to accept the covenant and the belief in the revelation at Sinai, but not because he rationally accepts his parents' belief. His position vis-à-vis his parents is one of shame, of love, of honor, and of loyalty.
>
> —Meir Buzaglo, *A Language for the Faithful* (Hebrew) (Jerusalem: Keter/ Mandel, 2008), p. 51

FURTHER READING

Bashkin, Orit. *The New Babylonians: A History of Jews in Modern Iraq.* Stanford: Stanford University Press, 2012. An account of the internal and external factors leading to the end of the historic Iraqi Jewish community in the twentieth century.

Chouraqui, Andre. *Between East and West: A History of the Jews of North Africa*. Philadelphia: Jewish Publication Society, 1968. A comprehensive account from ancient times to the 1960s.

Shapira, Anita. *Israel: A History*. Translated by A. Berris. Waltham MA: Brandeis, 2012, pp. 222–47. A leading contemporary historian's account of the mass migration.

Stillman, Norman. *The Jews of Arab Lands: A History and Source Book*. Philadelphia: Jewish Publication Society, 1979, pp. 1–110. A brief historical overview.

Swirski, Shlomo. *Israel: The Oriental Majority*. London: Zed Books, 1989. A survey of the achievements and challenges of *Mizrachi* integration into Israeli society; includes a collection of interviews.

28. Benefits and Costs of Military Power

THE SIX-DAY WAR, 1967 CE

HISTORY

The First Two Decades of Statehood

During the decades leading up to independence, the *Yishuv*, supported by Jews in the West, laid the groundwork for most of the key institutions in the state. However, in 1948 the dress rehearsal ended. The new citizens of the new state had to take full responsibility for their country's fate.

The 1950s and '60s were times of rapid growth, not only in population and economy, but in all areas of culture, agriculture, industry, education, and defense. The challenges were often daunting: nagging violence at the borders; isolation from surrounding nations; having to absorb masses of immigrants into a small country with a small economy; coping with the dissonance between the vision of "milk and honey" and the reality of forbidding deserts and malarial swamps; building a strong democracy from a diverse, often divided population that largely lacked any experience with democracy—and all of this without a constitution and even a clear consensus on what "Jewish statehood" meant.

There were hard times and political crises, military adventures and misadventures, disillusionment and occasional civil unrest. Still, the work in progress made constant progress. The state consolidated its democracy, grew its economy, and defended itself—more than fulfilling the dreams of its pioneers. And despite the fact that most Jews continued to live in the Diaspora, Israel came to serve as a center and a beacon for world Jewry in its language, arts, religion, scholarship, and national pride—and as a living laboratory for the development of Jewish identity and culture.

Buildup, Provocation, Response

Arab rejectionism continued unabated, not only isolating the state (no land access in any direction), but generating an endless series of larger and smaller border incidents and fostering within the Israeli populace a garrison mentality, a consciousness of always having to live by the sword.

The forces maintaining the conflict were complex. Both Western and Communist powers had an interest in keeping the oil-rich Arab nations dependent on their military support. And it was in the interest of Arab leaders like Egypt's Gamal Nasser to keep their people's attention focused on an external enemy rather than on internal issues such as social inequality. Meanwhile, forces in Israel that had opposed partition (see chapter 26) had not yet relinquished hope for a larger territory, including all of Jerusalem and the West Bank of the Jordan; a permanent peace settlement based on the 1949 armistice lines would have dealt a blow to that hope. Also, Israel's leaders, primarily products of twentieth-century Europe, operated from a powerful sense of victimhood, as well as a self-image as representing a "higher" civilization in a harsh and primitive environment where the only *lingua franca* was the language of force.

The ongoing border violence with Egypt escalated into the Sinai Campaign of 1956, when the Israeli army, with British and French air support, rapidly crossed the Sinai Peninsula to seize the Suez Canal (which Egypt had just nationalized). However, the Americans forced a rapid withdrawal and Israel gained nothing—not even the hoped-for downfall of the charismatic nationalist Egyptian president Gamal Abdel Nasser, who was seen as a threat. Perhaps even worse, Israel's alliance with the British and French against Egypt only confirmed Arab perceptions that the Jewish state was a Crusader/colonialist entity.

The borders quieted down until the 1960s. With the 1964 founding of the Palestine Liberation Organization, the Palestinians became an organized factor in the region. Over the next three years, Palestinian guerillas carried out dozens of attacks or attempted attacks from bases in Lebanon, Syria, and Jordan.

Israel and Syria each claimed the right to divert water from the Jordan River and its sources, along the armistice lines. Diversion projects by both sides led to exchanges of fire in 1965–66.

In May 1967, Egypt used the pretext of supporting its ally Syria to move large numbers of troops into the Sinai Peninsula—that is, toward its long border with Israel—and then requested that the UN withdraw its peace-keeping force that had served as a buffer since 1956. The secretary general of the UN, U Thant, complied—without bringing the matter to the General Assembly or the Security Council—and then Egypt announced the closure of the Red Sea shipping passage to Israel's port, Eilat. Israel viewed the blockade of its shipping lane to Africa and Asia as an act of aggression, especially since most of Israel's oil was imported from Iran, via the Red Sea. What Nasser really intended is not known, but its effect was an escalating war fever among the political leadership and the masses in both Israel and the Arab world. For Israel, this was a *casus belli*; for the Arabs, it marked the opening shot in the third and hoped-for final round of the battle to eliminate Israel. Both sides mobilized, diplomatic efforts stalled, and it became clear that the European powers had no interest in intervening. Israelis felt isolated and surrounded, haunted by Holocaust memories.

On the morning of June 5, Israel launched a carefully planned surprise air assault on air bases in Egypt, Syria, and Jordan, effectively neutralizing their air forces. In the ensuing ground combat, the Israelis proved to be much better motivated, organized, informed, and led than their enemies, who agreed to cease-fires just a few days later. Israel not only held off the threat of destruction; the Jewish state pushed the Arab armies back in three directions, conquering the Golan Heights from Syria, the West Bank and East Jerusalem from Jordan, and the Sinai Peninsula from Egypt.

The Israelis were surprised by their success. Indeed, the conquest of the West Bank and East Jerusalem had not been planned or considered before the war, but when Jordan decided to join the Arab war effort, they seized the opportunity. In the course of six days of fighting, Israel lost about eight hundred soldiers, the Arabs around fifteen thousand.

War, Peace, and Turning Points since 1967

The euphoria of Israelis—and Jews around the world—at the Jewish state's deliverance from the threat of its destruction was very powerful. Indeed, many saw the surprising victory—which encompassed the conquest of Judea, Samaria, and the Old City of Jerusalem—as a clear manifestation of divine providence, restoring the biblical borders of the Holy Land.

This euphoria continued for six years, accompanied by a burst of economic growth, an increased standard of living, and feelings of optimism and national pride. The "Jewish emergence from powerlessness" seemed indeed to have been proved and vindicated.

At the same time, this meant the Jewish state would have to face the dilemmas and responsibilities associated with power. Already in the first weeks after the war, the future of the newly occupied territories became a central theme in public discourse and political debate—and it remains so half a century later.

Meanwhile, the post-victory euphoria, empowerment, and pride also morphed into a degree of arrogance that blinded the political leadership to options for peace and the dangers of further war. On Yom Kippur, October 6, 1973, Israel was caught off-guard: Egypt and Syria launched a surprise attack. By the time a cease-fire was signed on October 23, around twenty-seven hundred Israeli and nineteen thousand Arab soldiers had died. Israel's borders remained unchanged, but the country had a more sober evaluation of its leaders, its power, and its place in the region.

The humiliating surprise attack on Yom Kippur and the painful losses incurred in fighting armies that for six years had been the butt of jokes burst the 1967 bubble of Israeli invincibility. While Israel "won" the war, in the sense of not relinquishing territory, the state was forced to admit that its neighboring Arab adversaries had to be taken seriously. The people and their leaders realized that long-term survival by superior force alone was not assured; therefore, diplomatic dialogue would be necessary. Six years later, in 1978, a chastened Israel signed the Camp David peace treaty with Egypt, which required Israel's withdrawal from the Sinai Peninsula, restoring it to Egyptian sovereignty.

The ensuing decades saw a series of military and diplomatic events, including peace treaties with Egypt (1978) and Jordan (1994) and localized armed conflicts in Lebanon (1982 and 2006) and Gaza (2008 and 2014). Whether these have been stages in a process leading to the normalization of Israel's place in the region and clarification of its borders is impossible to say at this juncture. Indeed one effect of this drawn-out uncertainty has been heightened polarization in public discourse, both in Israel and beyond, even to the point of violence. Within the Israeli political arena, as well as among diaspora Jews, there are widely disparate views regarding whether a stable peace is possible and, if so, how Israel can advance it. Both Palestinians and Israelis see themselves as "righteous victims," and each nation has supporters around the world.

It is sometimes hard to identify the truth through the polemical haze. One side's "myths" are the other side's "facts." Meanwhile, larger changes in the region's geopolitical realities—uprisings and armed conflicts within and among surrounding nations (e.g., the Arab Spring) — make it even harder to understand local developments. For example: is Hamas a manifestation of a world conflict between Islam and the West or a local expression of Palestinian resistance to Israeli rule?

Timeline: 1947–2014

1947   The United Nations approves the Partition Plan for Palestine.

1948   Israel declares independence.

1948   El Al, Israel's national airline, makes its first flight.

1949   Armistices with neighboring countries are signed, but border incidents and skirmishes continue.

1951   Israel's Jewish population reaches 1.35 million — more than double the prewar number.

1952   Gamal Abdel Nasser leads the "Free Officers" revolt, overthrowing the Egyptian monarchy and establishing a modernizing, nationalistic regime.

1956   After several years of escalating border raids and reprisals, Israel, in alliance with France and Britain, conquers the Sinai Peninsula (hoping to bring down Nasser), but U.S. and UN pressure force Israel's withdrawal.

1960   Israeli intelligence agents kidnap Adolph Eichmann, a key figure in the Nazi Final Solution, and bring him from Argentina to Israel, where he is tried and executed in 1962.

1963   David Ben-Gurion suddenly resigns the premiership, apparently on account of an internal dispute in his Mapai (Israel Workers) Party.

1964   The Palestine Liberation Organization (PLO) is founded in Jerusalem, with the goal of liberating Israel-controlled Palestine by armed struggle.

1966   Israel dismantles the military government that had authority over state areas with a mostly Palestinian Arab population.

1967   June 5–10: the Six-Day War.

1970   "Black September," when escalating tensions between the PLO and the Jordanian government lead to the PLO's violent expulsion from Jordan.

1973   Yom Kippur War (Israel versus Egypt and Syria).

1974   Gush Emunim (Bloc of the Faithful), an activist movement devoted to Jewish settlement of the West Bank to hasten the messianic restoration, is established.

1977   The *Mahapach*: The socialist Zionists lose control of the government for the first time since 1948. Menachem Begin becomes prime minister.

1977   Egyptian president Anwar Sadat flies to Jerusalem to address the Knesset, becoming the first Arab leader to open the door to peace with Israel.

1978   Begin and Sadat sign a peace treaty, facilitated by U.S. president Jimmy Carter. Israel commits to withdraw from the Sinai Peninsula.

1982   First Lebanon War: Israel drives out PLO forces operating from Lebanon and occupies a "security zone" along the border.

1987   The First Intifada breaks out—uprising of the Palestinians in the territories Israel occupied in 1967.

1987   Hamas (Arabic acronym for "Islamic Resistance Movement") is founded in Gaza, in opposition to the secular nationalist PLO.

1991   First Gulf War: Israel is hit by SCUD missiles from Iraq.

1993   The Oslo Accord, establishing the Palestinian National Authority in parts of the West Bank and in the Gaza Strip, is signed by Yasser Arafat and Yitzchak Rabin, facilitated by U.S. president Bill Clinton.

1994   Israel signs a peace treaty with Jordan.

1995   Prime minister Yitzchak Rabin is assassinated by a nationalist extremist religiously opposed to Israel's withdrawal from the West Bank.

2000   Israeli troops withdraw from the security zone in southern Lebanon.

2000   The Second Intifada breaks out—armed uprisings in the West Bank and Gaza, followed by several years of terror attacks inside Israel.

2000   "The Events of 2000": Palestinian Arab citizens riot within Israel; thirteen are killed by police and army fire.

2002   Israel begins constructing a separation wall along its border with the West Bank.

2003   A Western coalition invades Iraq and overthrows President
       Saddam Hussein.
2005   Israel unilaterally withdraws from the Gaza Strip but maintains
       control of its border and coastline.
2006   Second Lebanon War: The Shiite militia Hezbollah launches
       rocket attacks on sites across the north of the country; Israel
       strikes Hezbollah by air and in ground fighting. There is signifi-
       cant collateral damage in Lebanon; Israel suffers painful losses.
2007   Hamas wins election in the Gaza part of the Palestinian National
       Authority.
2008   Hamas rocket attacks lead to a large-scale Israeli military opera-
       tion in Gaza.
2011   Popular protests escalate into revolutions in Tunisia, Syria,
       Egypt, Libya, and Yemen.
2014   Hamas rocket attacks and kidnappings lead to a large-scale
       Israeli military operation in Gaza.

PRIMARY TEXT

During the summer of 1967, a network of kibbutz intellectuals assembled
groups of demobilized soldiers on various kibbutzim to discuss their war
experiences. These conversations, mostly with reservists in their twenties
who had served in combat units during the Six-Day War, were recorded,
edited, and compiled into the book *The Seventh Day* (in Hebrew *Siach
Lochamim*—"Warriors' Discourse"). The majority of participants were Ashkenazic, left-wing kibbutzniks, heirs of the pioneers, who had been raised
with a consciousness of being part of an elite leadership. While in this sense
their voices were not representative of all Israeli soldiers, it turned out that
the questions they asked were extremely resonant throughout the country.

Soldiers Talk about the Six-Day War: Two Discussions

I

[pp. 106–9] Chanan: I had the lousi-
est feeling at the beginning. I hated
the war, I didn't want that we here
would spill blood for tactical cal-

culations. . . . There was a feeling that the Russians were creating tensions here just to show: you do it in Vietnam—we'll do it here. And I said: We'll fight for our homeland, we will spill blood, but to do this for the sake of intrigues between the USSR and the USA? I didn't believe we'd succeed in changing borders, and if we did—that we'd manage to hold on to them. . . .

Avishai: We won't hold on to them for long.

Chanan: One thing is clear to me: that we won't return to the existing borders, at least in the [Golan] Heights—which is not to say that we won't give up any part of the Heights. . . .

Avishai: I don't have a defined opinion, because I think that to a large extent the opinions of the Arabs in the West Bank will determine. This is not just a handful—they are close to a million residents. I am not a racist, but I know one thing. I read statistics. For every 1,000 inhabitants, the Arabs in Israel have close to 60 births, and the Jews—20. Do a simple calculation and in just one generation. . . . And that's worrisome. . . . So I say, very nice, a binational state. But only if

The colonial period may have been over, but it was clear that much of what happened in the developing world depended on the interests of the Western powers. Ten years earlier Israel had spilled blood to conquer the Sinai as part of this game, only to be forced to relinquish it within weeks.

The strategic significance of the Golan Heights became an emotional issue once Israeli communities and agriculture in the upper Jordan Valley came under shelling from the heights.

The conquest of a large Palestinian population acutely raised the question of how to define a "Jewish state."

we have in it a dominant majority, because otherwise it won't be the state of the Jews. . . .

Amir: The problem is, what's the goal? You can't talk about long-term peace if you continue holding international borders that aren't [legally] yours. . . . In my opinion, long term you won't be able to hold them, and not only won't you be able, but you shouldn't. Today you can hold them only as a means of [bargaining] pressure.

Samuel: I was, happily, in the army six years — outside the kibbutz, and I was cut off from the humanistic education of Hashomer Hatzair. . . . I say in the simplest way: it could be that our friends were killed now by the very people whom we did not kill in Sinai. And the people you did not kill now — will kill us in the next round.

Amir: Shmuel, understand one thing: A man is born and a man dies . . . and also parents die — and when their child grows up he will turn into a soldier, and there will be another round and again he'll be killed, and again you will kill him . . . and if one time you stop this chain, and thus stop killing — then there will be a chance for peace. Otherwise you have no chance, no chance.

Is a Jewish majority necessary? By what means? At what cost?

Within Amir and Shmuel's dialogue are the essential questions haunting the Zionist project since the beginning: Is there any hope that a Jewish state can live in harmony and cooperation with its neighbors? Is the enmity based on historical or cultural realities that can be changed? Or is it embedded in deeper forces that cannot be changed, and can only be controlled by the constant threat—or use—of force?

Shmuel: Peace will now sprout from humane steps. It is clear to me that the Arabs really hate us. . . . There is one sentence that I keep repeating: In war as in war. In your not killing them, you haven't caused them to love you more. It is a fact that there are many stories of [enemy] soldiers who put up their hands, and when we turned our backs, they shot at us, they went and killed just those who refrained from killing them. That's how it is. Regarding the future there are two opposite possibilities: On one hand, wonderful peace with commercial relations and tranquil and secure borders. But there is another option: to hold the borders that promise us security, with a military government in the West Bank. Perhaps this sounds cynical, but it can be done.

Amir: I don't want a twenty-year peace. . . . I don't want twenty years of quiet. I prefer a war in ten years, followed by stable peace, to having a war every ten years with no peace ever.

II

[pp. 266–67] Shai: I have a feeling that if it would guarantee peace, I would relinquish the Old City of Jerusalem. Not Jerusalem as a capital, of course! Or I would at least

Beyond the possibility of peace and the means for attaining it, the Six-Day War conquests opened a deeper question: the religious, messianic significance of the events and places. For many Israelis (and Jews elsewhere), Israel's conquest of the Old City, including the Temple Mount, had messianic meaning. For Shai, a secular kibbutznik, Jerusalem is a nationalistic symbol, but many others heard in the announcement "The Wall is in our hands" the footsteps of the Messiah.

guarantee, in Jerusalem, access for Jews. But this is so complicated and so dependent on the guarantees that there would really be peace. . . . It's a question.

[p. 225] Question: you are not religious. Why is Jerusalem so meaningful?

Shai: First of all it's not the Wall, it's Old Jerusalem. This had no religious expression. So it seems to me. When I try to explain this to myself today, I can't give a precise answer, but it seems to me that Old Jerusalem was always for us a symbol of something unfinished. That it is ours. That this city must be ours. This is our capital city. This is perhaps the symbol of our nineteen-year longing. Jerusalem was like Gush Etzion, a symbol of something that had been taken from us, a symbol of some kind of defeat in the previous war. It is hard for me to know the exact reason, but it is clear to me that it had no religious significance at that moment. . . . I just know that at that moment we were filled with joy.

Gush Etzion was a group of settlements in the West Bank near Jerusalem that was brutally conquered by the Jordanians in 1948 and remained a bitter symbol of the cost of independence.

—Avraham Shapira, ed., *Siach Lochamim* (Tel Aviv: Young Members Group of the Kibbutz Movement, 1967), pp. 106–9, 225, 266–67; used by permission of Avraham Shapira

The Seventh Day rapidly became a best seller (ultimately it would go through several editions and sell 150,000 copies). Published just a few months after the war, when the market was flooded with victory albums, it aroused strong emotions. Discussed in the popular press, in literature, and in film, it would have a lasting impact on public discourse.

To many readers, the soldiers' ambivalence and self-doubts, their questions about sanctity of land and power and violence and Israel's place in the region, constituted evidence of a kind of moral sensitivity, a badge of honor for Israel and the Israeli army. Others, especially as time passed and the military occupation of the West Bank and Gaza continued over a third generation, cynically viewed the soldiers' agonizing as "shooting and crying," mere attempts at self-justification for participating in a war of conquest.

LEGACY
Impact

Since the War of Independence, Israel has experienced many violent conflicts: 1956, 1967, 1973, 1982, 1987, 2000, 2006, 2008, 2014. However, the Six-Day War was unique in the depth and breadth of the changes it wrought in Jewish experience and thought, in both Israel and the Diaspora. In examining the earliest turning points in Jewish history, such as Abraham's call and the Revelation at Sinai, we have little information about "what really happened," but a lot of information about how the memory of events influenced the later course of history. The Six-Day War presents the opposite challenge: we know what happened in the most intimate detail, but we remain too close to the events to be able to draw conclusions about their long-term impact. For example:

- Partition revisited: The debate over the partition of Palestine into two states was reenergized by Israel's conquest of the West Bank and Jerusalem. For twenty years, the world that had essentially created Israel by partitioning Palestine in a UN vote, had gotten used to the 1949 map, and despite Arab opposition, accepted Israel as a "normal" state with clear boundaries. Since 1967, the forces opposing partition have found their voice — be they Palestinians who claim all of Palestine west of the Jordan as their homeland, secular Israelis who believe the 1949 borders are indefensible, or Orthodox Zionists who see Israel's conquest of the West Bank as part of a divine plan. The debate over the ultimate location of Israel's borders has come to dominate Israeli and Jewish communal political discourse, and as the neighboring states have come to accept Israel and even sign peace treaties with the state, the Israeli-Palestinian conflict (especially in the West Bank and Gaza) has only become more constant and acute. The enterprise of settling Jews in the territories occupied in 1967—whether initiated or merely tolerated by the Israeli government—is understood differently by different observers: A negotiating ploy? A way to peg future borders? Execution of a divine plan? A way to prevent partition? Colonialist exploitation? None of the above? This ambiguity is a source of constant political tension.

- The meaning of the state: At the outset, Israel's creation was generally seen as a vindication of Herzl's political Zionism: the nations of the world had decided to admit the Jews as an equal nation, with their own state. While there were messianic tropes in Zionist rhetoric (ingathering of the exiles, redemption), the dominant theme was normalization: "A nation among the nations." But in the wake of the Six-Day War, the messianic interpretation of events became a serious factor in political life. A deeply committed, activist, and influential Israeli minority (represented by the "Jewish Home" party, which received about 7 percent of the vote in the 2015 election, but whose views are shared somewhat by a much larger segment of the population) came to view the events of 1948 and especially 1967—the return to Jerusalem and the biblical heartland of Judea and Samaria (the West Bank)—as evidence that the redemption had begun. For those who hold this view, biblical descriptions of divinely promised borders, a rebuilt Temple in Jerusalem, the subjugation of the Canaanites, and the divine punishment of Israel's enemies serve as practical guides for Israeli policy today. If so, then, for example, negotiations with the Palestinians is pointless, for God has already set the border and rejected their claims. And there is nothing sacred about democracy: it is only a temporary phase, pending the reestablishment of the Davidic monarchy.

- Jerusalem: In the UN Partition Plan of 1947, Jerusalem, as yet undivided, was to have been internationalized within the projected state of Palestine, with access guaranteed to all. During the War of Independence, Israel held on to the western side of the city and a corridor to the coast; the Old City, with its historical and religiously significant sites (e.g., the Temple Mount) remained under Jordanian rule. Israel's conquest of East Jerusalem and its surroundings in 1967 was a very emotional experience for Jews worldwide, as the Temple Mount — considered Judaism's holiest site — which had been inaccessible to Jews since 1948, suddenly and unexpectedly came under Jewish sovereignty. The Western Wall of the Temple Mount immediately became a major national symbol and pilgrimage destination. Since then, Israel has administered the city as a single municipality, but it remains divided into Jewish and Palestinian Arab neighborhoods, with differential distributions of resources, a source of resentment among Arab citizens. The question of whether the city has truly been unified — and whether it should be (amid the backdrop of its division into two separate municipalities from 1948 to 1967) — remains controversial.

The Six-Day War thus initiated major changes in the spiritual and political landscape of the Jewish state and the entire Jewish world, even as its changes to Israel's physical borders remain unrecognized by the nations of the world. Israel has annexed the Golan Heights and East Jerusalem, but not the West Bank; in 2005 it withdrew from Gaza, though it still controls its borders. Israelis are deeply divided over the future of their borders — a division that generates political instability and even paralysis. The resolution of this ideological and territorial controversy, however it comes, will certainly be a "turning point."

Memory

The Six-Day War has been memorialized in music and literature, in elements of the annual Memorial Day for Israel's fallen soldiers, and in monuments around the country. The famous David Rubinger photograph of soldiers arriving at the Western Wall has become part of the national iconography; and popular songwriter Naomi Shemer's celebratory version of the song "Jerusalem of Gold" an unofficial anthem for Jews around the world. "Jerusalem Day," commemorating the conquest of East Jerusalem, has entered the national calendar, with local celebrations and pilgrimages to the city.

To some extent, the trauma of the Yom Kippur War eclipsed the proud memories of the 1967 war in Israeli consciousness. Notably, a Naomi Shemer song—the wistful "Lu Yehi," an adaptation of the Beatles' "Let It Be"—expressed the national spirit at this time as well. Since 1973, Yom Kippur has taken on a whole new layer of meaning within Israel: a day traditionally solely devoted to individual introspection in the context of the religious community has been transformed also into one of collective national soul-searching and remembrance.

Consciousness of the burden of the 1967 victory remains ever-present in Israeli life and culture. There is no day when it does not occupy a place on the front pages, and any attempt to print a map of Israel is ipso facto controversial. Often, too, it seems that the Israel-Palestinian issue absorbs more of the world's attention than larger and more brutal conflicts around the globe. Worldwide, the Jewish generation for whom the victory of 1967 was a kind of antidote to the Holocaust, for whom the narrative was Israel's David against the Arab Goliath, is being replaced by a generation whose historical memory goes back only so far as Palestinian terror attacks and Israeli rule over unhappy Palestinians—and who tend to reassign the David and Goliath roles. The meaning of 1967 and the future of Israel's democracy and borders continues to generate strident conflict among Jews worldwide.

TEXT FOR DISCUSSION

Yeshayahu Leibovitz (1903–94), an Orthodox scientist and prominent public intellectual who opposed entangling nationalism and religion, was one of the first and loudest voices to argue that the 1967 victory posed moral dangers—a controversial platform both then and now. What do you make of his views?

> What happened in June 1967 transformed Israel into a conquering power, into an instrument for the violent domination of another people. This, I fear, may be the ruin of the state of Israel; Jews here may go the route

of the white minority in South Africa. The occupation corroded Israel's social fabric, and it has led to a belief in the utility of military force to solve political problems.

—Yeshayahu Leibovitz, "Liberating Israel from the Occupied Territories," *Journal of Palestine Studies* 15, no. 2 (Winter 1986): 105

FURTHER READING

Gelvin, James. *The Israel-Palestine Conflict: One Hundred Years of War*. Cambridge: Cambridge University Press, 2007. A brief, objective survey, up to 2007.

Hartley, Cathy. *A Survey of Arab-Israeli Relations*. London: Europa, 2004. An encyclopedic survey featuring a large collection of primary sources.

Morris, Benny. *Righteous Victims*. New York: Random House, 1999, pp. 302–443. A detailed history from the Six-Day War through the Yom Kippur War.

Ravitzky, Aviezer. *Messianism, Zionism and Jewish Religious Radicalism*. Chicago: University of Chicago Press, 1996. A classic study of the different manifestations of Zionism's encounter with messianism.

Rubinstein, Amnon. *The Zionist Dream Revisited*. New York: Schocken Books, 1984, pp. 76–126. An examination of the Six-Day War's impact on Israeli life and thought.

Shapira, Anita. *Israel: A History*. Translated by A. Berris. Waltham MA: Brandeis University Press, 2012, pp. 271–354. A leading contemporary historian's account of this period.

Shapira, Avraham, ed. *The Seventh Day: Soldiers' Talk about the Six-Day War*. New York: Scribner's, 1970. English translation of *Siach Lochamim*—reflections by Israeli soldiers immediately after the war.

29. The Feminist Revolution

THE ORDINATION OF WOMEN, 1972 CE

HISTORY

Gender in the Tradition

In the preceding twenty-eight chapters, the 50 percent of the Jewish nation who are of the female gender have gone almost completely unmentioned. This glaring omission can be attributed to two factors:

1. Even being a "people that dwells apart," the Jews have been influenced by their gentile environment in every age. For most of its history, human society has been patriarchal, men wielding the political and economic power. While it is possible to find "points of light," exceptions to this norm in Jewish settings, by and large Jewish life has reflected the male-dominated culture of surrounding societies.
2. Men also oversaw the recording and transmitting of information about history and social norms. Thus, regardless of women's actual roles in life and leadership, the documents we have from and about the past were written by men, about men, and for men. The extent of women's contributions may have been lost or suppressed along the way. The richness of women's premodern religious thought and ritual practice has only begun to be researched in recent decades.

A number of Jewish women are often mentioned to exemplify women's important roles in various periods. However, the list is short, suggesting that these are the exceptions that prove the rule. Here are some frequently cited examples:

- The Matriarchs (Genesis 12–35). Sarah, Rebekah, Rachel, and Leah each played an important role in steering the historical drama of the first three Israelite generations; both Sarah and Rebekah, for example, upended the established patriarchal system by causing the

younger son to be favored over the first-born in carrying the family spiritual inheritance (Genesis 21 and 27, respectively).
- The Hebrew midwives, and then Moses's mother and sister and Pharaoh's daughter, outsmarted Pharaoh's decree to kill all Israelite male babies, thereby saving Moses's life and playing a pivotal role in the redemption story (Exodus 1–2).
- Several prophetesses (as the Bible refers to them) play a leadership role in the biblical narrative. For example, Moses's sister Miriam leads the women in song after the miracle of the Red Sea (Exodus 15:20–21), and Deborah leads the people to victory in a war with the Canaanites (Judges 4).
- Two biblical books are named for their heroines: Esther, who courageously saved her people from genocide; and Ruth, a young Moabite widow whose loyalty to her Israelite mother-in-law led her to throw in her lot with the Israelite people.
- In several talmudic stories, Beruriah shows herself to be wiser in applying the Torah to life than her husband, the renowned scholar Rabbi Meir (e.g., Babylonian Talmud, *Berachot* 10a).
- In the sixteenth century, Gracia Mendes Nasi, a wealthy merchant and communal leader, helped many Conversos flee from Portugal (see chapter 16) and supported Jewish communities in Palestine.

The patriarchal nature of Jewish society also endured in the fabric of *halakhah* and custom. Over the years, various biblical concepts and practices evolved into an elaborate rabbinical framework governing women's place and roles — a framework that itself evolved as the circumstances of Jewish life changed.

One of six orders of the Mishnah/Talmud and several additional tractates (see chapter 12), as well as a vast corpus of later commentary and legislation, specifically addressed the legal framework of women's lives. At different times and places, how this framework was implemented depended on the particular cultural context. For example, the Bible takes polygyny (meaning "multiple wives"; "polygamy" refers to multiple spouses of either gender) for granted and gives men the authority to divorce a wife at will. The Talmud went on to leave polygyny alone but introduced the requirement of a *ketubah* (marriage contract) to provide some protection for women in marriage and divorce. In Muslim countries, where polygyny was standard, Jews continued the practice until modern times. However, in Christian Europe, monogamy was normative, and the first major halakhic authority there, Rabbenu Gershom (eleventh-century Germany— see chapter 14), issued prohibitions against marrying multiple wives and against divorcing a woman without her consent.

Another example: The Bible (Leviticus 15:19–31) describes a menstruating woman as being in a state of "impurity" transmissible by touch and prescribes bathing and a sacrifice for purification. In the halakhic literature the purification process is elaborated in detail, and the prohibition against contact is restricted to the woman's husband; her social and religious life is not otherwise affected. However, in Ashkenaz (but not in other regions), a folk tradition developed, perhaps under the influence of Orthodox Christian traditions, that a menstruating woman may not touch a Torah scroll.

When it came to structuring gender roles in Jewish practice, a key halakhic concept was women's release from the obligation to perform positive, time-determined mitzvot (commandments), such as public prayer—ostensibly because their domestic duties would conflict with such scheduled religious acts. But since religious obligation was seen as a means to holiness, women's exemption was not a benefit, but a relegation to a diminished status. This principle, together with the perception of women as potential stimulants of male lust and even immorality, kept women out of scholarship, leadership, and governance roles and led to valuing women for their modesty and domesticity. Women were not counted in the minyan, the quorum of ten required for public worship. Nor were women allowed to sit together with men in the synagogue; rather, they were required to pray in a separate section, often a screened balcony.

Within this overall patriarchal structure with its clear hierarchical separation between genders, some Jewish laws and practices did recognize women's rights. For example:

- The *ketubah*, the halakhic marriage contract described in the Talmud, served in essence as a required prenuptial agreement and protected the woman from being left without resources in the case of divorce or widowhood. The husband was required to guarantee a sum for his wife's support in such circumstances.

- That contract also specified the woman's right to sexual satisfaction and material support by her husband. If these obligations were not met, she could appeal to the rabbinical court to force her husband to grant a divorce.
- This right to sexual satisfaction, in turn, served as the basis for a halakhic derivation permitting the use of birth control. If a pregnancy might be dangerous, it must be avoided—but the woman's right to sexual satisfaction still stands.
- In *halakhah*, a mother's life overrides the general prohibition against abortion. If the mother's life is in danger, protecting the fetus is no longer the predominant concern—abortion is *obligatory*.

In each of these examples, the rabbis remained loyal to biblical law but added mechanisms to mitigate its harsh treatment of women. The husband was still formally in control, but the wife's wishes and needs—for life, for sustenance, for sexual satisfaction—set limits on this control.

Rabbi Judith Hauptman, a professor of Talmud at the Jewish Theological Seminary, offers a nuanced look at the talmudic approach to women, arguing that it was possible for the rabbis to believe in a patriarchal system and still be moved by concerns for women's rights and welfare, within the limits of their particular historical and cultural context:

The rabbis upheld patriarchy as the preordained mode of social organization, as dictated by the Torah. They thus perpetuated women's second-class, subordinate status. They neither achieved equality for women nor even sought it. But of critical importance, they began to introduce numerous, significant, and occasionally bold corrective measures to ameliorate the lot of women. In some cases, they eliminated abusive behaviors that had developed over time. In others, they broke new ground, granting women benefits that they never had before, even at men's expense. From their own perspective, the rabbis were seeking to close the gap that had developed over time between more enlightened social thinking and women's more subordinate status as defined by the received texts, biblical and rabbinic, without openly opposing such

texts. In almost every key area of law affecting women, the rabbis introduced significant changes for the better. . . . They cannot . . . be called
feminists. More accurately, we can regard them as helpful to women.

— Judith Hauptman, *Rereading the Rabbis: A Woman's Voice* (Boulder CO:
Westview Press, 1998), pp. 4–5

Feminism and Judaism

Over the past century, the rise of a view that calls into question patriarchal structures that have long been taken for granted around the world
could not help but impinge on Jewish consciousness as well. In its wake
the Jewish community now possesses a significant body of literature (Jewish feminist thought and commentary, gender-neutral liturgy, halakhic
innovation), impressive leaders and scholars such as theologians Judith
Plaskow and Rachel Adler and historian Paula Hyman, and innovative
institutions of education such as Yeshivat Maharat in New York (offering
Orthodox ordination to women).

The Reform movement, and later the secular Zionist movement, led
the Jewish people in recognizing women's equality within Judaism, as
they were the least constricted by loyalty to *halakhah* and custom. Nevertheless, even they spent decades struggling with their response to feminism. While the Reform movement had introduced gender-mixed seating
in synagogues as early as the mid-nineteenth century, the Reform seminary, Hebrew Union College–Jewish Institute of Religion, did not ordain
a woman rabbi until 1972, more than a hundred years later. And while the
socialist Zionists may have recruited young men and women to live and
work together while building an egalitarian society, the diaries of women
pioneers in Palestine bemoan their relegation to the kitchen and nursery.

The story of the ordination of women in the Reform movement is a
case study of how ideology could be trumped by culture. The movement's
leadership—rabbinic and lay—agreed in 1922 that their belief in gender
equality dictated women's ordination. However, the general discomfort
with the idea of a woman rabbi was not so easily overcome: It took fifty
years until a woman was ordained (Sally Priesand, by HUC-JIR, in 1972).
It seems that in the revolt against patriarchy, liberal Jewish settings were
influenced by the resistance and ambivalence in the surrounding society,

by political considerations and subconscious obstacles that bore no direct relationship to Jewish tradition per se.

In any case, in the past century, the Jewish world has witnessed momentous change. Outside of Orthodox communities, women and men now function equally in every aspect of Jewish life, as rabbis, scholars, and lay leaders. And within the Orthodox world, too, change has begun. Orthodox feminism is a movement in its own right, and today a growing number of women have Orthodox rabbinical ordination. A few communities have even engaged them as spiritual leaders.

Timeline: 1851–2015

1851   Anshe Emeth Synagogue in Albany, New York, a Reform congregation, becomes the first synagogue with gender-mixed seating.

1875   Disgruntled members challenge the decision of New York's Bnei Jeshurun Synagogue to introduce gender-mixed seating in court. The challenge fails, and a large contingent of members resign.

1893   The Congress of Jewish Women convenes in Chicago. A milestone in the development of Jewish feminism, it leads to the founding of the National Council of Jewish Women, a social and social-action organization.

1909   "Uprising of the Twenty Thousand": a strike by mostly Jewish women workers, led by Jewish women activists, is a turning point in the unionization of garment workers in New York.

1912   Henrietta Szold founds Hadassah, the women's Zionist organization.

1917   Sarah Schenirer founds the first Bais Yaakov school, providing Jewish and general studies for Orthodox girls, in Krakow, Poland; it achieves rabbinical sanction and rapidly expands to a network of schools throughout the world.

1920   Ratification of the Nineteenth Amendment to the U.S. Constitution, guaranteeing universal women's suffrage.

1920   Elections for the *Yishuv*'s first Assembly of Delegates of in Mandatory Palestine. Both men and women are able to vote and serve; however, there are separate polling stations for the Old

Yishuv Orthodox, and their votes are counted double, as they refuse to allow women in their community to vote.

1922   The first bat mitzvah (Jewish coming-of-age ceremony for a girl), arranged by Reconstructionist Judaism founder Rabbi Mordecai Kaplan for his daughter Judith. Up until now, bar mitzvah (literally, "son [obligated by] the commandments") had been limited to boys. The bat mitzvah ceremony rapidly becomes normative in non-Orthodox congregations throughout North America.

1922   The Central Conference of American Rabbis (national organization of Reform rabbis) states its support for women's ordination. However, the Hebrew Union College (Reform rabbinical seminary) votes to continue its men-only admissions policy.

1935   Regina Jonas is privately ordained a rabbi in Berlin, thereby becoming the first ordained woman rabbi. However, she never finds a pulpit position. Later deported to Theresienstadt, she serves as a chaplain to the inmates for two years before being sent to Auschwitz, where she is killed in 1944.

1969   Veteran Labor Party politician Golda Meir becomes the fourth prime minister of Israel, leading the country through the trauma of the Yom Kippur War.

1972   Sally Priesand is ordained as the first Reform woman rabbi at the Hebrew Union College–Jewish Institute of Religion. She embarks on a successful career as a pulpit rabbi.

1974   The Reconstructionist Rabbinical College ordains its first woman graduate, Sandy Sasso.

1985   The Jewish Theological Seminary ordains the first Conservative woman rabbi, Amy Eilberg.

1992   Naama Kelman-Ezrachi becomes the first woman rabbi ordained in Israel, by the Hebrew Union College–Jewish Institute of Religion.

1994   Israel's Supreme Court rules that the rabbinical courts (dealing mainly with matters of marriage and divorce) must allow women to be trained and to practice as "rabbinical court pleaders" (attorneys appearing before the court).

2000   Rabbi Elyse Goldstein edits *The Women's Torah Commentary*, the first feminist commentary on the Torah.

2009   Yeshivat Maharat opens in New York, providing rabbinical training and ordination to Orthodox women (despite opposition from various other Orthodox institutions).

2015   The Orthodox Rabbinical Council of America reaffirms its prohibition against ordaining women as rabbis.

2016   The Ramban Synagogue in Jerusalem hires as assistant rabbi Karnit Feintuch, the first woman rabbi to serve an Orthodox synagogue in Israel.

PRIMARY TEXT

Susannah Heschel, a professor of Jewish studies at Dartmouth College, has written extensively about feminism's impact on Judaism. In this excerpt, she considers the question of women's rabbinical ordination in a significantly broader context than equality of opportunity and authority. Her contribution is one of many examples in which women's ordination opened up creative—even revolutionary—developments in Jewish thought, scholarship, liturgy, and practice.

Susannah Heschel, "Gender and Agency in the Feminist Historiography of Jewish Identity"

Can women be Jews? When the Jewish Theological Seminary, the seat of Conservative Judaism, decided to ordain women as rabbis, it faced a dilemma: all students (until then, all men) were expected to observe Jewish religious law, observing the Sabbath and holidays strictly, praying three times a day, wearing a head covering, and so forth. Should the new women students follow the Jew-

Heschel highlights the feminist "catch" in simple egalitarianism: If granting women equal status to men means requiring them to act like men, is that truly equality? The unspoken assumption is that the Judaism practiced by men is the true, authentic Judaism, to which women have now been allowed to enter. But that assumption is itself non-egalitarian.

ish laws incumbent upon men, but
from which women are exempt?
For example, men are required to
put on phylacteries for weekday
morning prayers, whereas women
are not only exempt, but, according to some authorities, forbidden to wear phylacteries. Men are
expected to wear a head covering (yarmulke), whereas women
are not (though married women,
in Orthodox custom, wear a scarf,
hat, or even a wig). Men wear ritual fringes under their clothes
every day, donning a prayer shawl
with fringes for morning prayer,
whereas women, again, are exempt
or forbidden. The legal niceties
aside, the question goes to the
heart of Jewish identity: if the
new women rabbinic students are
required to follow the laws incumbent upon men, it implies that only
men are real Jews and that pious
Jewish women, who have been
exempt from those laws, are somehow less than fully Jewish. Why
does becoming a rabbi require
both women and men to follow the
role of Jewish religious men, even
when it forces women to violate
the laws regulating women's piety?

For a woman to be a Jew, the rabbinical ruling insinuates, means
becoming a male Jew, and the

Heschel points out that the ordination of women rabbis offers an
opportunity to reexamine the entire
structure of Jewish practice.

According to this line of argument,
the ordination of women should
open up a new discussion about Jewish law, practice, and belief, taking
into account the historical experiences of both genders—and requiring the Jewish people to (finally) stop
taking the patriarchal view of tradition for granted.

question of ordaining women rabbis is really a question of whether
Jewish women can become Jewish men. Why not encourage or at
least permit male rabbis the same
exemptions from religious observance that have defined Jewish
women's piety—allowing men to
become women? At the same time,
if the role of rabbi is to be opened
to women, should not all aspects
of Jewish religious life, especially
those heretofore limited to men,
be opened to women? The gender
inequalities of Judaism that have
been overcome as a consequence
of modernity have brought women
opportunities—such as rabbinical ordination—that were closed
to them for two thousand years.
At the same time, opening men's
privileges to women has reified
Judaism according to the normative rules applied to men, rather
than to women, and discounted the
legal normativity of women's religious practice.

At the same time, the decision to
ordain women rabbis has brought
to light the implication that the
nature of the Jewish, as experienced by Jews, is not fixed and uniform but differs with the genders.
There is no singular "Jewish" but
male and female Jewishnesses. . . .

Through the centuries, even when relegated to a secondary position in Jewish law, and excluded from the male-only rabbinate that devised and interpreted the law, women were able to exert agency by defining their Jewish identity in contradistinction to that of men, sometimes through ambiguous behavior that could be interpreted as devout piety or rebellion against rabbinic strictures. For example, medieval Judaism saw a discussion among rabbis of a new custom that arose during the tenth century among some Jewish women of refraining from synagogue attendance during periods of menstrual and parturient ritual "impurity." Such periods of "impurity," as defined in the Bible and subsequently expanded in rabbinic law, banned sexual intercourse and physical contact between a husband or wife, lest she convey impurity to him. Yet rabbinic law did not require the wife to leave her home nor was she freed of the usual housewifely obligations of cooking and cleaning nor of the obligation to say her prayers (public prayer was never required of women). The custom of staying away from the synagogue during women's periods of impurity has no formal basis in Talmudic law, in other words, and

According to Jewish law, a menstruating woman may not have any contact with her husband until she has been "purified" in a *mikveh* (ritual bath), seven days after the end of her menstruation. This prohibition only applied to physical contact with her husband, and not to any other aspect of her daily life, religious life, or social behavior. Folk tradition added more restrictions that had no basis in law.

yet some Jews came to endorse a prohibition against ritually impure women entering the synagogue. Jewish communities were divided: Sephardim rejected the prohibition, while Ashkenazim endorsed it, at least as custom. According to the rabbinic discussions, it was women who, motivated by piety, thought it proper not to come into the synagogue—or, if they did, not to look directly at a Torah scroll, not to pray or mention the name of God, not to touch a Hebrew book. While the rabbis did not codify that practice as law, they did acknowledge the custom, and they praised the women for their piety.

The historian, however, might ask whether that custom indeed reflects women's piety or perhaps an utterly different motivation. How is women's agency to be defined, and how are her religious motivations to be taken into consideration? Historians of Judaism have no extant written documents by women prior to the early modern period, and in reading male-authored texts about women's actions, we have to read between the lines to understand their motivations. Were all the women who refrained from entering a synagogue during periods of men-

Since only men wrote Jewish historical and legal texts, we have no way to know what women thought in the past. Heschel theorizes that perhaps they were not thinking what the men thought they were thinking. This is plausible. Alternatively, it might be a projection of a modern feminist consciousness onto the minds of women who naturally accepted the assumptions of their patriarchal society.

strual "impurity" motivated by a
piety born of rabbinic Judaism that
imagines menstruation as incompatible with the sanctity of synagogue? Or is it possible that at least
some women engaged in a kind
of "strike," taking a vacation from
synagogue attendance as long as
male-authored laws forbidding
marital intimacy during menstrual
"impurity" were in force? In other
words, if my husband can't touch
me, why should I go to the synagogue and watch his prayer service from behind the curtain of
the women's section, or gaze with
adoration at the Torah scroll that
defines me as "impure"?

—Susannah Heschel, "Gender and Agency in the Feminist Historiography of
Jewish Identity," *Journal of Religion* 84, no. 4 (October 2004): 590–92; used by
permission of the University of Chicago Press

LEGACY

Impact

The feminist revolution has dramatically changed the nature of Jewish
experience. While cultural resistance still exists in the liberal movements
and halakhic strictures impede the rate of change among the Orthodox,
still, from the perspective of gender equality, the Jewish world of today
would be unrecognizable to a visitor from a century ago:

- In the liberal movements, more women than men are being
  ordained as rabbis and cantors.
- Women serve as spiritual leaders within the liberal movements, as
  communal leaders from local to national levels, and as Judaica scholars.

- Women are considerably more Jewishly knowledgeable than their ancestors — some of them fluently reading and chanting from the Torah in congregations throughout the world.
- Many women observe the commandment to wear tallit (prayer shawl) and tefillin (phylacteries) — traditionally a male prerogative/ obligation — during morning weekday worship.
- Feminist Jewish scholarship is a recognized and respected field, both in the Jewish world and in general academia.
- Gender-neutral and non-patriarchal language (such as avoiding male pronouns when referring to God) is standard in the most recent prayer books of the liberal Jewish movements.
- Both women and men participate in a variety of new rituals acknowledging women's participation in Jewish life, such as the *simchat bat* (rejoicing for a daughter) naming ceremony for newborn girls; and placing a "Miriam's cup" of water on the seder table (to commemorate the midrash crediting Moses's sister Miriam with miraculously providing water for the Israelites in the desert).
- Traditional Jewish rituals have been changed or reinterpreted to recognize women's equality and spirituality. In particular, in wedding ceremonies it is now common to modify the traditional wording (which implied the groom's "acquisition" of the bride) to symmetrical, egalitarian language. Immersion in the *mikveh* (ritual bath) often now celebrates the spiritual impact of "living waters" rather than emphasizing women's biologically based impurity and has been adopted to recognize life-cycle events such as divorce, miscarriage, and healing.
- Women's study groups and worship minyans (quorums) have proliferated. Communities of women gather to study and pray together on Rosh Hodesh (the first day of the Hebrew month — traditionally a minor "women's holiday" when women were exempt from work, perhaps based on a perceived parallel between the lunar and menstrual cycles). And on the holiday of Purim, they read the Scroll of Esther, a biblical book in which women are the protagonists.

These changes are affording half of the Jewish people a new world of opportunities and challenges — and all of the Jewish people a new world of ideas and practices. Women as rabbis, cantors, text scholars, and lay leaders have brought innovative modes of interpretation, rituals, and approaches to spirituality that have enriched Jewish intellectual and spiritual life.

This transformation is still a work in progress. Among the challenges are the following:

- While gender equality has been achieved, at least officially, in the liberal movements, the various divisions of Orthodoxy are still struggling to address the conflict between traditional forms of Judaism and the moral claim of equality. In some instances, a backlash against women's equality has led to restricting women's public roles more than ever. In Israel, certain Orthodox communities have begun to insist upon buses with gender-separate seating; others demand women's exclusion from singing at public musical events—issues that as of this writing have not been resolved.
- The "traditional" *Mizrachi* culture in Israel (see chapter 27) values loyalty to traditional norms without reference to formal halakhic authority. Thus, many Israeli Jews who do not view *halakhah* as binding nonetheless believe that patriarchal hierarchy in Jewish practice is inviolable. They do not feel obligated to attend synagogue regularly, but will refuse to enter one where the seating is mixed and a woman officiates.
- The liberal movements have experienced a "feminization" of Jewish institutional life: As women have taken their place within it, many men have lost interest and pulled back from involvement. The same phenomenon has been observed in American Protestant denominations. It is not yet clear what this means and where it is going.

Memory

The encounter between feminism and Judaism is too new for historians to identify rituals and other institutions that preserve the memory of this encounter. A growing body of literature is devoted to Jewish women's creative expressions since the advent of gender equality in Judaism, but it is too soon to memorialize this encounter as a whole or to assess where it is going.

The feminist critique of patriarchy seems to be part of a larger critique of traditional assumptions about identity—gender, religious, ethnic, and racial. Will the demise of patriarchy lead to the demise of ascribed identity in general? And, if so, what will Judaism look like? The ordination of women, it seems, may not be a culmination, but an early marker of a long-term and deeply revolutionary turning point in Jewish life and thought.

TEXT FOR DISCUSSION

Do you believe women's entry into the rabbinate has changed the very nature of the rabbinate, as this text states? If so, how?

> The complexity with which we now understand gender roles — sets of expectations and behaviors that were assumed and taken for granted in previous generations — brings new sophistication to how we understand the role of "rabbi." . . . Evidence suggests that a new rabbi has emerged in the present day, a role that blends, in myriad ways, those voices that we might once have labeled "male" and "female." This is, without a doubt a positive development. In addition to having a more holistic tool set with which to serve congregants and constituents in varied rabbinic roles, today's rabbi is better able to be accepted as his or her authentic self without building the walls, boundaries, or limitations of separation that . . . [have been seen as] the hallmark of rabbinic life. Thankfully, the yoke of symbolic exemplarhood is not one that today's rabbis must bear — at least not by necessity.
>
> — Sara Mason-Barkin, "The Rabbi as Symbolic Exemplar: A Feminist Critique," in *The Sacred Calling: Four Decades of Women in the Rabbinate*, ed. Rebecca Einstein Schorr and Alysa Mendelson Graf (New York: CCAR Press, 2016), pp. 650–51

FURTHER READING

Adler, Rachel. *Engendering Judaism*. Philadelphia: Jewish Publication Society, 1998. A leading feminist scholar who became a Reform rabbi presents her proposal for reenvisioning and renewing Judaism.

Baskin, Judith, ed. *Jewish Women in Historical Perspective*. Detroit: Wayne State University Press, 1991. Scholars' essays on the historical experiences of Jewish women from the Bible to the present.

Goldstein, Elyse, ed. *New Jewish Feminism*. Woodstock VT: Jewish Lights, 2009. A collection of essays by leading thinkers and scholars.

Nadell, Pamela. *Women Who Would Be Rabbis*. Boston: Beacon Press, 1998. A history of nineteenth- and twentieth-century events leading to women's ordination.

Plaskow, Judith. *Standing Again at Sinai: Judaism from a Feminist Perspective*. San Francisco: Harper, 1991. A pioneering feminist critique of and vision for Judaism.

Schorr, Rebecca Einstein, and Alysa Mendelson Graf, eds. *The Sacred Calling: Four Decades of Women in the Rabbinate*. New York: CCAR Press, 2016. An anthology of essays on the various experiences of women rabbis.

30. The Fall of the Iron Curtain

THE LIBERATION OF SOVIET JEWRY, 1989 CE

HISTORY

The Jews in the Soviet Union and Communist Eastern Europe

By the mid-twentieth century, the Jewish community in Russia had seen significant losses. Many thousands of Jews had migrated, primarily to North America but also to South America, Western Europe, and Palestine. Others perished in the Holocaust. Still, when World War II ended, about two million Jews remained, and almost another million had survived in Eastern European countries that became part of the Soviet bloc of nations.

Their liberation in 1989, almost half a century later, after decades of suppression, would rapidly and drastically alter their lives.

From the beginning, Jews had played a disproportionate role in the ideological ferment and political activism leading to the Russian revolution. To many Jews it seemed clear they had everything to gain and nothing to lose by overthrowing the antisemitic, cruel tsarist regime.

In the early twentieth century, the Jewish socialist organization the Bund had more than thirty thousand members; Lenin's Social Democratic (Bolshevik) Party had eight thousand. Even in 1917 the Bundists significantly outnumbered the Bolsheviks. The Jewish revolutionaries were eager subscribers to the socialist ideal of universal, secular humanity and so were happy to leave religion behind.

Despite this enthusiasm and a shared dedication to overthrowing the tsarist regime, the relationship between Jewish activists and the Bolshevik leaders was fraught, particularly over the issues of national identity and rights. Lenin and Stalin accepted the demands of various nationalities such as Ukrainians, Georgians, and Poles to maintain their own identities and socialist parties, envisioning a socialist confederation of nationalities, but they believed the Jews could not claim to be a nationality and hence were to be denied that status. In addition, they interpreted the Jews' clinging to their identity as a bourgeois remnant, not a natural right. This view would become the underpinning of Soviet policy and never change.

Despite this tension, during the 1917 revolutions and the ensuing civil war, the Jews supported the revolution. The Communist rulers encouraged their support by immediately erasing hundreds of tsarist anti-Jewish laws, welcoming Jews into leadership positions, campaigning vocally against antisemitism as a "counterrevolutionary tool," and establishing a government mechanism (the Yevsektsiya—Jewish "section" of the Communist Party) to oversee Jewish communal life. Indeed, at first, the revolution seemed to have fully and finally emancipated the Jews of Russia.

However, the idyll was short-lived. The Yevsektsiya's true purpose quickly became clear: it was not to rebuild Jewish life, but to hasten assimilation. Teaching Hebrew and Jewish religion was forbidden, communal institutions were forced to disband, contact with Jews and Jewish institutions abroad was cut off, and emigration was prohibited. The Jews' hope of emancipation became the Bolsheviks' opportunity for cultural erasure.

Moreover, despite official opposition to antisemitism, the Jews' forced integration into the bureaucracy, factories, and farms from which they had been excluded opened new opportunities for antisemitic sentiments and expressions—and Bolshevik leaders, just like the tsars, exploited these situations for their own purposes. For example, Stalin's various purges disproportionately targeted Jews, who, he said, were disloyal and perpetrators of "economic crimes" such as theft of government property and black-marketeering.

Thus, while on the one hand Jews were free to enter all areas of political and economic life—a great liberation—at the same time the traditions of antisemitism, the Bolshevik rejection of Jewish nationality, and the arbitrary cruelty of the Stalinist dictatorship made their position vulnerable. There were some bitter ironies. Hundreds of thousands of Jews were saved from the Nazis by being forcibly transferred eastward away from the border. The Soviets denied the validity of a Jewish nationality, but the Jews' internal passports designated their nationality as "Jewish," making it next to impossible to escape one's outlawed identity.

Another manifestation of this ambiguous approach to Jewish nationality was the Soviet plan to create an autonomous Jewish region in Birobidzhan, an inhospitable area of Siberia. In 1928 the government unveiled the plan and in the 1930s marketed it, even to the point of offering free private farms. A trickle of Jews moved there, establishing their own cultural institutions. At its peak, in 1948, about thirty thousand Jews lived in Birobidzhan; today, under two thousand remain.

During the Cold War decades (the 1950s through the 1980s) the Jews of the Soviet Union (and Eastern Europe) experienced suppression and stagnation. Assimilation processes that had begun with the revolution did their work over generations; many Jews rejected their Jewish identity and tried to protect their children from it. While some Jews in the periphery (especially in non-Slavic areas such as Georgia and the Caucasus) continued to live some kind of traditional Jewish life "under the radar" and a modest underground Jewish cultural life persisted in the cities, for the great majority of the Jewish community, generations of suppression, propaganda, and isolation led to a general attenuation of Jewish knowledge and commitment and even to alienation from or active opposition to Jewish identity.

Revival and Activism

In the mid-1960s the opposition to Soviet totalitarianism that had been festering for decades began to find open expression in political activism and literature. While the society remained closed, and oppressive measures continued, somehow forces pushing for openness and democracy slowly managed to take root and grow. The reasons for this shift are open to debate: Had the regime become less repressive after Stalin's death, or had the repressive measures lost their effectiveness because of accumulated resentment? Was it ultimately simply impossible to maintain total closure on the passage of ideas across the border? In any case, a number of heavy-handed suppression attempts in the 1960s and '70s—such as the 1966 sentencing of satirical poets Yuli Daniel and Andrei Sinyavsky to seven years of hard labor—created international public relations debacles for the Soviet Union and stimulated increasingly open resistance at home.

This phenomenon found expression in specifically Jewish activism as well. For Soviet Jews, the 1967 Six-Day War was a kind of watershed, when the dissonance between the Soviet government's glorification of the Arab armies (concomitant with diplomatic, economic, and arms support to Egypt and Syria in the run-up to the war) and the decisive Israeli victory was glaringly apparent. The Jews felt great pride in Israel's victory, and those who sought to reclaim their national and/or religious identity experienced their people's triumph as a source of strength. Underground study circles, secret smuggled libraries, even public gatherings on Jewish holidays became features of urban life in the late 1960s.

In 1970, a group of sixteen refuseniks (persons whose application for exit visas had been refused) attempted to hijack a small plane in Leningrad to fly out of the country. Long prison terms—and death sentences to the leaders, Mark Dymshits and Edward Kuznetsov—aroused an international outcry, and the sentences were reduced on appeal.

Jewish organizations abroad and the Israeli government started taking an active interest in fostering this movement and in pressuring the Soviet government to change its policies regarding both Jewish cultural expression and emigration.

Just as Jewish activism was arising in the Soviet Union in the late 1960s and early '70s, three developments in the West created conditions for this activism to find a powerful resonance there:

- Jews had been active in the civil rights movement in the United States, and it had become an article of faith that struggling for justice—by means of public campaigns, demonstrations, and civil disobedience—was a valid way to express Jewish identity.
- The rise of the Black Pride movement in the United States had helped many Jews realize that they could legitimately take public action on behalf of their own ethnic group without jeopardizing their status as loyal citizens.
- The 1967 victory had begun to change Israel's image from an endangered underdog to a powerful, self-reliant state—and, in fact, one newly embroiled in controversy over the disposition of its conquered territories. Thus Israel lost some of its romance as a "cause" for struggle.

North American Jewry was galvanized by a new cause: the liberation of Soviet Jews. The young rebels (e.g., Student Struggle for Soviet Jewry) who, in good 1960s form, first took up the issue, succeeded within a few years in forcing it onto the agenda of the Jewish establishment, where it remained central until the fall of the Iron Curtain in 1989. Educational programs about the plight of Soviet Jews were ubiquitous, as were liturgi-cal expressions, vigils and demonstrations, lobbying the U.S. government to pressure the Soviet government, and secret missions by "tourists" to establish contact and smuggle resources to Russian Jews.

Throughout the 1970s and '80s, much of the West's activism focused on emigration. The phenomenon of the refuseniks had become central: Soviet authorities were employing a variety of methods to torment those applying for an exit visa, among them denial of employment, imprison-ment, and Siberian exile. The prohibition against emigration was not aimed specifically at Jews—no one else was allowed to leave either—but Jews constituted the vast majority of those who wished to emigrate.

A number of refuseniks—Vladimir and Masha Slepak, who lived in limbo for seventeen years; Anatoly (Natan) Sharansky, Ida Nudel, Alexan-der Lerner—became celebrities as public campaigns in the West demanded their liberation. Meanwhile the situation was complicated by the Soviet policy of granting exit visas only to Jews emigrating to Israel, in order to "respect" the emigrants' nationalistic sentiments. However, in many cases the Jews' sentiments were not nationalistic, but simply political/economic, and those who were released preferred to stay in Europe or move on to North America. This generated ambivalence and tension among activ-ists in the West, Israeli institutions, and the emigrants themselves. Israel needed the highly educated immigrant population, and the country's Zion-ist leaders believed that Israel should be the only destination and those opting out were somehow traitors to the cause. Moreover, some activists and emigrants were concerned that violating the terms of Soviet policy would endanger the whole enterprise.

All this activity provided unity and strength to Western Jews (despite sometimes strident disagreement over strategy and control) and offered material and spiritual support to the Jews behind the Iron Curtain who sought to reconnect with their identity. Moreover, diplomatic pressures by Western governments in the wake of Jewish protests and lobbying may have helped push the Soviet Union to raise emigration quotas after 1970—though the risk of refusal and punishment still hung over the heads of exit visa applicants. Between 1968 and 1987, 270,000 Jews emigrated, more than 12 percent of the Jewish population.

After the Fall

After the Soviet Union's democratization and breakup in 1989, the liberation of Soviet Jewry suddenly became irrelevant. While antidemocratic and antisemitic tendencies did not disappear, and in some cases the collapse of totalitarianism unleashed long-suppressed ethnic, nationalistic, and religious demons, the transition nonetheless had two immediate positive impacts:

- Opening the border, leading to mass Jewish emigration to Israel, Western Europe, and North America. Between 1990 and 2006 about 1.6 million of the remaining 2 million Jews emigrated (the numbers are imprecise because of questions regarding "who is a Jew" after decades of intermarriage). Nearly a million arrived in Israel, with the remainder divided between North America and Germany.
- Enabling the Jews who remained in the former Communist states to openly explore, study, and practice Judaism and rebuild their connections with world Jewish life. Jewish institutions throughout the world—the Jewish Agency, various religious movements and philanthropic organizations—became very active, training leaders and providing financial and professional support for local institutions such as synagogues, schools, and camps. Local institutions have since taken root and are gaining in self-confidence. A new wave of Jewish life continues to develop.

Timeline: 1903–96

1903	At the Russian Democratic Party conference in London, Lenin's Bolshevik faction takes over, and the Bund's demands for recognition of Jewish national identity are formally rejected.
1905	Widespread strikes and protests across Russia lead to the establishment of a constitutional monarchy, with guarantees of civil rights and an elected parliament.
1913	Mendel Beilis, a Jewish factory worker in Kiev, is acquitted of a ritual murder charge, in a highly publicized jury trial.
1917	The democratic revolution is followed six months later by the Bolshevik takeover.

1918	The Yevsektsiya, the "Jewish section" of the Communist Party, is established to supervise Jewish life.
1918–20	Civil war rages as the "White" armies seek, unsuccessfully, to overthrow the Bolshevik government; pogroms, mainly in the Ukraine, cause large numbers of Jewish casualties and a significant wave of emigration to the West.
1919	All Jewish communal institutions are abolished.
1928	The Soviet government attempts to create a Jewish autonomous region in Birobidzhan in Siberia.
1929	The government prohibits Sabbath observance.
1930	The government disbands the Yevsektsiya as "no longer necessary."
1952	Thirteen prominent Yiddish poets are executed, culminating the Soviet government's four-year campaign (complete with intimidation, institution closings, and exile) to erase the remnants of Jewish culture.
1953	The "Doctors' Plot": A group of physicians, mostly Jews, are accused of plotting to murder Soviet leaders. Plans are prepared to deport thousands of Jews to Siberia but are never carried out, apparently because of Stalin's death.
1953	Joseph Stalin dies.
1962–63	Hundreds—mostly Jews—throughout the USSR are subjected to show trials for "economic crimes." Dozens are executed.
1964	The Student Struggle for Soviet Jewry is founded in New York.
1966	Yuli Daniel and Andrei Sinyavsky are sentenced to seven years of hard labor for publishing satirical poems abroad. Public protests in both the Soviet Union and the West mark the beginning of a growing wave of open dissent, the "democratic movement."
1967	The Soviet Union actively supports Egypt and Syria in the run-up to the Six-Day War—diplomatically, economically, and with arms supplies.
1970	A group of sixteen refuseniks plot to hijack a plane and fly to Israel but are arrested and tried for treason. The ensuing

world public outcry leads to a loosening of emigration restrictions.

1971   Major North American Jewish organizations found the National Council for Soviet Jewry.

1974   Nobel laureate Alexander Solzhenitsyn is exiled from the Soviet Union for his criticism of the regime.

1975   The signing of the Helsinki Accords, which ostensibly would bind the Soviet Union to uphold civil rights, provides validation and moral support for the Jewish campaign to secure religious, cultural, and emigration rights. (At the same time, the USSR largely ignored them, and emigration rates decreased.)

1979   The USSR invades Afghanistan, the United States imposes sanctions, and the USSR puts the brakes on Jewish emigration; the annual average drops from twenty-five thousand to one thousand.

1986   General Secretary Gorbachev introduces the policy of glasnost, calling for greater openness and transparency in government.

1987   Some 250,000 protesters gather in Washington during General Secretary Gorbachev's visit, demanding that he give Soviet Jews the freedom to emigrate.

1989–90   The Communist governments in Romania, Bulgaria, Poland, Hungary, Czechoslovakia, and East Germany fall.

1989–90   Elections are held in the Soviet Union in the context of a new, democratic constitution.

1990   Emigration of Soviet Jews to Israel jumps from 13,000 in 1989 to 185,000 in 1990.

1991   The Soviet Union is dissolved.

1996   In Israel, Yisrael Ba'aliyah, a Russian immigrants' party headed by former refuseniks Nathan Sharansky and Yuli Edelstein, receives 5.7 percent of the vote, yielding seven Knesset seats.

1996   The Russian Jewish Congress is established, followed by the creation of parallel organizations in other former Soviet republics.

PRIMARY TEXT

In 1960, Elie Wiesel, a journalist, novelist, and public intellectual, published *Night*, a memoir of his Holocaust experiences, which became a best seller and brought Wiesel into the spotlight as an important voice of Holocaust memory and an interpreter of its moral messages. Five years later, he traveled to the Soviet Union. His account of that visit, *The Jews of Silence*, painted an impressive picture of Soviet Jews' often heroic efforts to liberate themselves both spiritually and politically and raised (still relevant) questions about the effects of protest and the evolution of Jewish identity under and after Communism. Moreover, throughout his book, the "prophet of Holocaust memory" also delivered an impassioned call for Western Jews to take action by publicly and privately supporting the Soviet Jews' struggle.

The Jews of Silence became a kind of manifesto for Western activists fighting to liberate Soviet Jews. It implied an obligation of Jewish action today based on a feeling of shame for American Jews' inaction and/or helplessness during the Holocaust. Those who remained silent "bystanders" would be complicit in oppression.

Elie Wiesel, *The Jews of Silence*

How many were there? Ten thousand? Twenty thousand? More. About thirty thousand. The crush was worse than it had been inside the synagogue. They filled the whole street, spilling over into the courtyards, dancing and singing, dancing and singing. They seemed to hover in mid-air, Chagall-like, floating above the mass of shadows and colors below, above time, climbing a Jacob's ladder that reached to the heavens, if not higher.

Despite raids, arrests, and physical intimidation of Jews who openly expressed their identity, the Soviets, surprisingly, allowed annual Simchat Torah celebrations in various cities.

Tomorrow they would descend and scatter, disappear into the innermost parts of Moscow, not to be heard from for another year. But they would return and bring more with them. The line will never break; one who has come will always return.

I moved among them like a sleepwalker, stunned by what I saw and heard, half disbelieving my own senses. I had known they would come, but not in such numbers; I had known they would celebrate, but not that their celebration would be so genuine and so deeply Jewish. . . .

"What does anyone in America or Israel care if my passport is stamped 'Jewish'? It doesn't matter to me, and it doesn't matter to these young people here tonight. So stop protesting about things that don't bother us. We have long since ceased being ashamed of our Jewishness. We can't hide it anyway. Besides, by accepting it we've managed to turn obedience to law into an act of free choice."

The man I was talking to had served as a captain in the Red Army and had been decorated in Berlin. Like his father before him, he

In the Middle Ages, the last day of the fall Sukkot festival (Leviticus 23:39–43) had come to be celebrated as Simchat Torah (rejoicing of the Torah), when the annual cycle of weekly Torah readings restarts. Traditionally it is celebrated by singing and dancing with the Torah scrolls.

was a sworn Communist. But like all the rest, he suffered on account of his Jewishness. Were he Russian he would have long ago been appointed a full professor at the university. He was still holding an instructorship in foreign languages. One day, he said, he decided that as long as they made him feel like a Jew, he might as well act accordingly. It was the only way to beat them at their own game. "Two years ago I came to the synagogue on the night of Simchat Torah. I wanted to see Jews, and I wanted to be with them. I didn't tell my wife, who isn't Jewish, or my sixteen-year-old son. Why should I burden him with problems? There was time enough for that. I came back last year for the second time. The youngsters were singing and dancing, almost like tonight. I found myself suddenly in the middle of a group of youngsters, and my heart stopped . . . I was standing face to face with my son. He said he'd been coming for the past three years, but hadn't dared to tell me." . . .

. . . I said to one of them, "You don't know Hebrew, you never learned Jewish history, you don't fulfill the commandments, and you don't believe in the God of Israel—in what way are you a Jew?"

The Soviets never understood the irony of their policy of trying to erase Jewish identity while preserving it by force in the official nationality designation "Jew" on internal passports.

The story Wiesel tells of a man who says, "It's enough for a Jew to call himself a Jew," is typical of many Soviet Jewish families who underwent (and are undergoing) pendulum swings of identity within and between generations.

He answered, "Apparently you live in a country where Jews can afford the luxury of asking questions. Things are different here. It's enough for a Jew to call himself a Jew. It's enough to fulfill one commandment or to celebrate one Jewish day a year. With us, being Jewish is not a matter of words, but of simple endurance, not of definition but of existence. If my son were to ask me one day what a Jew is, I would tell him that a Jew is one who knows when to ask questions and when to give answers . . . and when to do neither."

[A conversation with three Jews in Kiev:]

All three asked the same questions. Why are the Jews outside so silent? Why aren't they doing something? Don't they know what is happening here? Or don't they want to know? . . . I could not answer their questions. Why is the Jewish world so indifferent to the Jews in Russia? I don't know. I know only that this apathy, from an historical point of view, borders on the criminal. Even if we assume that our protests are useless to change Kremlin policy, they do change the spiritual climate for the Jewish population. They bring Soviet Jews the comforting knowledge of a single

The challenge now facing the Jews of the former Communist countries is: When liberation finally arrives, what becomes of a Jewish identity that has been anchored in repression and the resistance to it? What is the "heritage" of this Judaism?

fact—that the Jewish people have
not forgotten them, that they are
not alone. . . .

I returned from the Soviet Union
disheartened and depressed. But
what torments me most is not the
Jews of silence I met in Russia,
but the silence of the Jews I live
among today.

—Elie Wiesel, *The Jews of Silence: A Personal Report on Soviet Jewry*, trans. Neal
Kozodoy (New York: Signet, 1966), pp. 76, 80–83, 89, 127. © 1966, 2011 by Elie Wiesel; reprinted by permission of Georges Borchardt, Inc., on behalf of the author

---

LEGACY

Impact

Within the former Communist states, Jewish life has undergone a major
revival. Many (though certainly not all) Jews have celebrated the opportunity to live out their identity. Stories abound of young adults rediscovering
the roots their parents had hidden from them and educating themselves in
the traditions of their ancestors. Religious movements, academic research,
cultural expressions, travel to Israel, fractious intra-communal politics—
all the phenomena of modern Jewish life—can now be found in the former Soviet republics as well as the satellite countries of Poland, Lithuania,
Latvia, and Hungary, such as the following:

- More than forty full-time Jewish day schools throughout the region
  and more than one hundred Sunday schools.
- More than one hundred synagogues, across the denominations. As
  of this writing, most are small congregations and do not have rabbis.
  Some local Reform, Conservative, and Orthodox rabbis serve them, as
  do several dozen rabbis sent from the West by the Chabad Hasidim.
- University Jewish studies programs, freestanding and as depart-
  ments in general universities, including programs for training Jew-

ish educators, in large cities such as Moscow, St. Petersburg, Vilna, Warsaw, and Kiev.

- Kosher restaurants in many cities—at least eight in Moscow.
- Limmud FSU festivals: The idea of an annual, pluralistic festival of Jewish learning and culture began with the first Limmud (learning) conference in the United Kingdom in 1980. Since then Limmud festivals have been held around the globe—and since 2006, throughout the former Soviet Union and Eastern Europe, where they draw thousands of participants.

The large immigration from the former Soviet Union is evident in the ubiquity of Russian language and culture in Israel and in American and European urban Russian enclaves. On the whole, the immigrants have been highly educated and upwardly mobile and have largely integrated into the middle class in just one generation. On the other hand, their integration into Jewish communal life has been more complicated, as the traditional Western models of Jewish affiliation and behavior are foreign to most of them. For example, before 1990 it was difficult to find a grocery store selling pork in Israel; in the cities where the Russian immigrants settled, that is no longer so.

Russian immigrants have enriched Israel with knowledge and skills in various cultural fields, especially in classical music, where they have brought high-quality performance and teaching even to peripheral small towns. In 1991 a group of Russian immigrant actors founded the Gesher Theater in Tel Aviv, which is now renowned nationwide for its creative productions of classic and contemporary drama.

Memory

The struggle for the liberation of Soviet Jewry, so central an element in Jewish communal life for two decades, has already become "ancient history" for those who came of age after 1990. The processes of migration, institution building, and identity formation are still very much in progress. This turning point is still turning; it has not yet found concrete expression in Jewish collective memory.

Recent decades have seen a flowering of literature by immigrant writers such as Gary Shteyngart, David Bezmozgis, and Boris Fishman, who tackle the complexities of their experiences in memoirs and fiction.

TEXT FOR DISCUSSION

Fifty years of ideological opposition to the Jewish religion and of government suppression of Jewish culture, together with persecution, left many Russian Jews—including Larisa Bogoraz, a prominent human rights activist in the Soviet Union—with a painfully fragmented identity. If one has neither religion nor nationality, what is the content of Jewish identity?

Who am I? Unfortunately, I do not feel like a Jew. I understand that I have an unquestionable genetic tie with Jewry. . . . A more profound, or more general common bond is lacking . . . community of language, culture, history, tradition. . . . By all these . . . I am Russian . . . and nevertheless, no, I am not Russian. I am a stranger today in this land.

—Larisa Bogoraz, "Do I Feel I Belong to the Jewish People?" in *I am a Jew: Essays on Jewish Identity in the Soviet Union*, ed. Aleksandr Voronel, Viktor Yakhot and Moshe Decter (New York: Academic Committee on Soviet Jewry, 1973), pp. 63–64

FURTHER READING

Baron, Salo. *The Russian Jew under the Tsars and Soviets*. New York: Macmillan, 1976, pp. 156–342. A detailed account from the First World War until 1976.

Feingold, Henry. *"Silent No More": Saving the Jews of Russia, The American Jewish Effort, 1967–1989*. Syracuse: Syracuse University Press, 2006. An analysis of the various players and events in the Western struggle for Soviet Jews.

Friedman, Murray, and Albert Chernin, eds. *A Second Exodus: The American Movement to Free Soviet Jews*. Hanover NH: Brandeis University Press, 1999. A collection of papers on the history of the struggle.

Gitelman, Zvi. *The Jews of Russia and the Soviet Union, 1881 to the Present*. New York: Schocken Books, 1988. A detailed account, right up to the end of Soviet rule.

Hoffman, Charles. *Red Shtetl*. New York: American Jewish Joint Distribution Committee, 2002. An example of how Jewish life in the periphery continued under Communism.

Afterword

When we look back over the flow of Jewish history as mapped in the preceding chapters, several recurring themes raise interesting questions for reflection.

THE NATURE OF JEWISH IDENTITY

The first turning point, Abraham's call by God, linked divine revelation with national existence. At Mount Sinai this was made more explicit and concrete. The Jews were a nation, an ethno-cultural group—yet they were also members of a religion premised on their being in a special relationship with God. This relationship was understood as a covenant that required them to live their private and communal lives according to God-given laws.

Over and over again, in almost every age, tension and outright strife arose over the balance between these two roots of identity, from the debate over establishing a monarchy to the modern divisions over religious reform and Zionism. In my view, these two components have been inseparable, Jewish identity standing on both.

Looking back—and looking forward at a time when the very concept of the boundaries of identity is being challenged—does that assumption hold?

THE CHALLENGE OF KEEPING THE COVENANT VITAL

From Mount Sinai until the present, Jewish intellectual, spiritual, and political thought and discourse have been preoccupied with one central question: How should the Torah, the basis of the covenant, be interpreted and applied to keep it relevant and authoritative in its contemporary environment? There has never been a time when the Jews were not exposed to powerful forces threatening to undermine their loyalty to the covenant—temptation or force. Deciding when to resist and when to compromise has always been on the agenda, as has the question of who has the authority to decide.

What changes might be acceptable? What changes are unthinkable? What are the limits of interpretation? And how much diversity can be tolerated without making "Jewish identity" meaningless?

CATASTROPHE, HOPE, AND FAITH

A number of the turning points are associated with catastrophes: conquest and exile, expulsions and massacres. In each case, some Jews understood their suffering as evidence of the falseness or failure of the covenant and so abandoned their Jewish attachment. However, in each case—even the Holocaust—the overwhelming response was to seek a reconciliation between the pull of despair/disillusionment and the need/desire to continue to believe and belong. Out of that seeking we have witnessed a vast and rich outpouring of creative expression, from works of mystical thought to liturgical poetry to systematic theologies to song.

What is the secret of this eternal "nevertheless and in spite of everything"?

READING THE MAP OF HISTORY

Already with the destruction of the First Temple, the ideology of sin-punishment-repentance-redemption had become central in Jewish belief. Thus, the assumption that history has a direction, and ultimate national redemption is a certainty, took on a central role in Jewish consciousness. However, waiting patiently was sometimes unbearable. In every age there have been those who thought they could read the map of history and know just where they stood. King Cyrus, Jesus of Nazareth, Bar Kokhba, Sabbatai Zevi, Enlightenment, America, socialism, Zionism—these are all examples of individuals or movements associated with the fulfillment of messianic expectations.

It seems, however, that there is no GPS for the map of history. Nor is it possible to know the long-term meaning of the present moment. Is this limit on our knowledge a stimulus of hope or a cause for despair? How do we live with it?

THE PACE OF CHANGE

In this book, the frequency of turning points increased significantly in the past few centuries. Why might this be so? Could it be simply an artifact? We know a lot more about recent centuries than we do about earlier eras—perhaps there were equally or even more important turning points in the more distant past, of which we are ignorant. Moreover, any historian's identification of turning points (including mine) is colored by his or her own biases; perhaps I've placed disproportionate emphasis on developments that to other eyes may look less significant. Or, perhaps this skewed distribution is a function of the fact that there are a lot more Jews, scattered in a lot more places, in the modern period compared to previous times. Also, the rate of change in human society at large has accelerated significantly in the modern period, so it makes sense that Jewish history would reflect this dynamism.

Today, Judaism faces new challenges in an ever-changing world in which the drive for unlimited freedom clashes with forces seeking to uphold traditional authorities. How will the Jewish nation—and the Jewish religion—evolve and adapt to all this? What new forms, new beliefs, new understandings, new communities will take root and flourish?

To be continued . . .

Bibliography

Each chapter contains suggestions for further reading on the specific historical period under consideration. This bibliography includes general histories, covering longer spans, that can be consulted for additional background or different perspectives on any period. These volumes have not been cited in the individual chapters.

Ben-Sasson, Haim Hillel, ed. *A History of the Jewish People*. Cambridge MA: Harvard, 1976. A thousand pages, divided into six chronological sections, each written by a leading historian of the period.

Biale, David., ed. *Cultures of the Jews: A New History*. New York: Schocken Books, 2002. A collection of scholarly essays on Jewish cultures, organized chronologically, from the Bible to the present.

Johnson, Paul. *A History of the Jews*. London: Weidenfeld and Nicolson, 1978. A comprehensive survey from Abraham to the present by a Catholic journalist—a unique contemporaneous attempt to understand Jewish history as an "outsider."

Mansoor, Manahem. *Jewish History and Thought: An Introduction*. Hoboken NJ: Ktav, 1991. A compact chronological survey of Jewish thinkers, writers, and ideas, in outline form.

Martin, Bernard, and Daniel Jeremy Silver. *A History of Judaism*. New York: Basic Books, 1974. A two-volume survey, with a focus on the development of thought and belief.

Meyer, Michael A. *Ideas of Jewish History*. New York: Behrman House, 1974. An anthology of different approaches to Jewish historiography through the ages.

Potok, Chaim. *Wanderings: Chaim Potok's History of the Jews*. New York: Knopf, 1978. A survey of Jewish history, with emphasis on the premodern periods.

Roth, Cecil. *A History of the Jews: From Earliest Times through the Six Day War*. New York: Schocken Books, 1970. A survey, through the Six-Day War.

Schama, Simon. *The Story of the Jews: Finding the Words, 1000 BCE–1492 CE*. London: Bodley Head, 2013. A noted art historian's off-the-beaten-track account through 1492.

Schwartz, Barry L. *Judaism's Great Debates*. Philadelphia: Jewish Publication Society, 2012. Brief accounts of formative controversies, including debates relevant to this book (chapters 1, 10, 16, 18, 20, 22, and 29).

Trepp, Leo. *Eternal Faith, Eternal People*. Englewood Cliffs NJ: Prentice-Hall, 1962. A survey to the mid-twentieth century, emphasizing the development of thought and belief.

Index

Geiger, Abraham, 257

gender. *See* feminist revolution; women

Germany: in middle ages, 171; Napoleonic Kingdom of Westphalia, 255; Nazis and Nazism, 325, 326–28, 331, 363, 410; Palestine, German Jewish migration to, 341–42; post-Holocaust revival of Jewish life in, 337; Reform movement in, 255–56, 257, 259, 260, 266, 276; Versailles, Conference and Treaty of, 325, 326–27; Weimar Republic (1919-1933), 327, 331; World War I, 315, 325. *See also* Holocaust; Prussia

Gershom, Rabbenu, 168, 394

Gershom ben Yehuda, 171

Gideon, 41, 48–49

Ginsberg, Asher. *See* Ahad Ha'am

glasnost, 416

Gobineau, Arthur de, 330

God: and the Babylonian Exile, 73–87; and Bar Kokhba revolt, 126–27; and the Bible, xviii–xix; calling Abraham, 1–11; calling Moses, 14; and biblical covenants, 26–27; Covenant with David, 56–58; and Exodus from Egypt, 13–24; in cultural Zionism, 299; and fall of Israel, 61–71; in Holocaust, 336–37; and Jewish Identity, 425; as king 49, 56; Maimonides on, 162–63; in mysticism, 183; names for, xxi; and prophets, 57, 63–64, 86, 88–89, 153; Sanctification of God's name (*Kiddush hashem*), 175; and the Sinai Covenant, 27, 29–36. *See also* Abraham, God's call to; Babylonian Exile; Bar Kokhba revolt; covenant; Exodus from Egypt; northern kingdom of Israel, fall of; Sinai, revelation and covenant

Goldlstein, Elyse, 399

Golden Calf incident, 28, 29, 107

Goliath, 59

Gorbachev, Mikhail, 416

Gordon, A. D., 318

Gordon, Yehuda Leib, 301–2

Great Depression, 325

Great Revolt, 113–14, 115

Greek immigration to Middle East, 98–99

Green, Arthur, 237

Gruen, David (David Ben-Gurion), 293, 315, 347, 350, 357, 358, 380

Gulf War, 381

Gush Eminim, 380

Guttmann, Jacob, 165–66

Gypsies (Roma), Nazi persecution of, 328

Hadassah, 273, 397

Hadassah Medical Organization, 349

Hadrian, 127, 128, 130, 131, 133, 136, 138

Haganah, 344, 349

halakhah (the way/Oral Law): Ashkenazic Jewry, rise of, 168, 170–71; development after destruction of Second Temple, 121, 122; emancipation and, 242, 243; "Epistle of Rav Sherira Gaon" on, 146–49; Hasidism and, 237; Iberian Jewry and, 182–83; in North Africa and Middle East, 364, 365; Polish Jewry and, 210, 221; as Rabbinic literature, 141–42, 144 (*See also* Mishnah); Rabbis, emergence of, 110, 122; Reform movement and, 255, 256, 257, 259, 262, 265, 266; Samaritans and, 70; semi-autonomous Jewish communities in Western Europe and, 240; Sinai event and, 32–33, 266; Zionism and, 284, 286

Nathan, 56, 57, 63

National Council for Soviet Jewry, 416

National Council of Jewish Women, 397

nationalism and nationality, 296–97; Jewish nationalism (See Zionist movement); Jewishness as nationality, 283, 284, 289–90, 292; modern nation-state, rise of, 241, 244, 248, 250; race, national identity defined through, 326, 357; religious and national identities, emancipation's effort to reconcile, 243, 245–50; Soviet Jewry and, 410–11; xenophobic nationalism and racial antisemitism, development and rise of, 281, 282–83, 325–26, 330–31

Nazis and Nazism, 325, 326–28, 331, 363, 410

Nehemiah, 88, 89, 90, 94, 95

Neo-orthodoxy, 259

Nero, 119

Netherlands, Jewish community in, 207, 255, 329

"the New Jew," 299–300, 312, 334

Ninth of Ave, 84, 124, 207

Nordau, Max, 111, 301

North African and Middle Eastern Jews, 361–75; cultural influence of, 373–74; growth of Diaspora community (ca. 1000 CE), 82, 123, 146; Iberian Diaspora and, 196, 199, 207, 362–63, 366; Islam, forced conversion to, 179; in Maghreb, 362–63; masorti (traditional) Judaism of, 372–73; mass aliyah (1949-64), 178, 365–66, 371–74; piyut tradition of, 369–70, 371, 374; under Roman rule, 123; social and political position in modern Israel, 371–73. See also Babylonia; specific countries

North America. See American Jewish community

northern kingdom of Israel, fall of, 61–72; biblical and post-biblical interpretation of, 68, 70–71

Nudel, Ida, 413

Nuremberg Laws, 327, 331

Operation Ezra and Nehemiah, 367

Operation Magic Carpet/Wings of Eagles, 367

Operation Moses, 368

Oral Law. See halakhah

Orthodox Judaism: America, migration to, 277; cultural Zionism and, 300; feminism and, 397; Modern Orthodox movement, 265; Neo-orthodoxy, 259; in North Africa, 364, 365; Palestine, Jewish settlers in, 311, 313; Reform Judaism and, 259; ultra- orthodox, 238 (See also Hasidism); Zionist movement and, 284, 285–86, 287

Oslo Accords, 381

Ottoman Empire, 196

Oz, Kobi, 371

Pagis, Dan, 339

Pale of Settlement in Russia, 221

Palestine, Jewish settlement in, 310–24; aliyah, defined, 310; Arab-Jewish tensions, 317, 343–44, 345–46; Balfour, Lord, and Balfour Declaration, 285, 344, 352; British Mandate, 288, 316, 317, 341–46, 348–49, 360; Chovevei Tziyyon colonists, 282, 287, 301, 312–13; Fifth Aliyah (1929–39), 318, 341–42; First Aliyah (1882–1900), 287, 312–13, 314, 315, 316, 322, 372; Fourth Aliyah (1924-29), 317, 341;